John Stuart

Extracts from the Council Register of the Burgh of Aberdeen

John Stuart

Extracts from the Council Register of the Burgh of Aberdeen

ISBN/EAN: 9783337301361

Printed in Europe, USA, Canada, Australia, Japan

Cover: Foto ©ninafisch / pixelio.de

More available books at **www.hansebooks.com**

EXTRACTS

FROM THE

COUNCIL REGISTER

OF THE

BURGH OF ABERDEEN.

1625-1642.

EDINBURGH:
PRINTED FOR THE SCOTTISH BURGH RECORDS SOCIETY
MDCCCLXXI.

AND M'CABE, PRINTER, COWGATE STREET, EDINBURGH.

TABLE OF CONTENTS.

	PAGE
THE EDITOR'S PREFACE,	vii
CONTENTS,	xiii
EXTRACTS FROM THE COUNCIL REGISTER OF THE BURGH OF ABERDEEN,	1
INDEX	295

PREFACE.

THE RECORDS of the BURGH of ABERDEEN are fuller and more complete than those of any other of our Scottish towns, while they commence at a far earlier period.

A fragment of the Burgh Court Records is dated in 1317, and from the year 1397 the series is all but complete to the present time.

Selections from these have been printed for the Spalding Club, in two volumes, which come down to the end of the reign of James VI. In these the Burgh is exhibited in many different aspects, as in its internal government, its relations with other communities, and with the surrounding feudal barons— in its religious and educational institutions, its sports and pageants—its regulations about trade—and in its attitude of unbounded hospitality to guests of all ranks. They furnish many picturesque illustrations of the manners and condition of every class, and of the results of the great ecclesiastical changes of the sixteenth century.

The selections in the volume now printed for the Burgh Record Society, embrace the period from the accession of Charles I. to the end of the year 1642.

We may see from these how tenaciously the citizens still clung to many old customs, and how persistent were the attempts of their rulers to improve them, by enforced religious observances, among which were daily catechisings in Church. These were to be attended by all persons, including masters and mistresses of families, under pecuniary penalties (p. 49). Morning and evening prayers were daily read in the Greyfriar Kirk, but attendance on these does not appear to have been compulsory (p. 62).

At the beginning of the volume several entries occur regulating the wapinschawings and musters then in fashion, which represent the volunteer system of the present day. The feelings of national insecurity which were recently so strong among ourselves, are depicted in a statement submitted to the magistrates by one of the citizens, of the "combustioun, bruttes and rumores of warres, and forane preparatiounes throchout Christendome," although his apt use of that wyse saying of King Solomon, *Felix illa civitas quae tempore pacis providet bellum*, might not have occurred so readily to a remonstrant of the present day.

PREFACE.   ix

We may see also in the arrangements for bealfires, in case of invasion, the substitute for the telegraphs of our time (17), and the anxious provisions for a supply of pure water for the burgh, "frome one spring near the toun," furnish curious matter of comparison with the demands of modern times, which, in the case of Aberdeen, could only be met by the introduction to the town of the waters of the Dee (p. 55).

Several entries illustrate the connection which subsisted between the civic rulers and the schools of the burgh, and others give evidence of the regard in which they held such learned teachers as the grammarian Wedderburne, who was master of the Grammar School (pp. 26, 35, 50, 99).

There is a grotesqueness (continued from earlier times) in their forms of public rejoicing,—as in the "Solemnitie to be usit for the Queenes happie and comfortable delyuerie of a sone." By order of the magistrates, the town was to be warned "be sound of trumpet at the mercat croce . . . to assemble thamselflis this efternoone in thair paroche kirk, and thair to give most humble and hartie thankis to God for hir Majesties happie delyuerie of a sone; and efter ending of sermone, ordaines bonefyires to be put on throw all the streittes of the toune, the haill bellis to ring, the croce to be deckit and hung, a taffill to be coverit thairat, twa peice of wyne, ane quhyit and the uther clairat, to be run thairat, and given to all that pleasses call for the same, the sugar and spyce to be brocht thither in great abundance, a number of glasses to be cassin, the tounes haill great ordinance to be shott, and all the youthes of the toune to tak thair muskattis and accompanye thair magistrattis throw the streittes of the toun in singing psalmes and praising God; thairefter to pas the tyme in shuitting thair muskattis all the nicht ower at thair plesour, and all godlie merriness and pastyme usit that may expres the joy and gladnes of the hartis of the people" (p. 28).

The day on which the king "did resaive the crown of this his ancient kingdome of Scotland at Halirudehous," was appointed to be observed with like solemnities (p. 60).

Many earlier ordinances against the use of plaids by women had been fulminated; but still the "incivil forme of behauiour" was maintained by "many women of this burghe of gude qualitie, wha resortis both to kirk and mercat with thair plaidis about thair heidis." Intimation was ordered to be made from the pulpits, that in case of their persisting in this custom, "not onlie sall thair plaidis be shamfullie markit with a tar stick to thair disgrace, but lyikwayis confiscat and takin frome thame" (p. 59).

Many acts of kindness from the magistrates to the clergymen of the burgh are recorded in the earlier volumes. Thus, in 1560, Mr Adam Heriot, the first minister of the new religion, was presented with "ane garment and haill stand of claythis;" and on the departure of Dr William Forbes, one of the city clergy, to fill a pastoral charge in Edinburgh in 1622, he got a parting banquet, while his wife was presented with " wyne, sugar, and tobacco." In a few years Dr Forbes returned to Aberdeen, and in 1633 he was " written for be the archbishope to teache befoir the Kingis Majestie," when his travelling charges were defrayed by his patrons. Shortly afterwards he was nominated to fill the newly established See of Edinburgh ; and on his finally leaving Aberdeen, he received a grand entertainment, the magistrates giving him a convoy to the Crabstane, and pledging him in a parting cup of *Bon accord*. They also sent commissioners to Edinburgh to represent the burgh, and to " congratulate the bishop's consecration " (p. 63).

Other entries in the present volume will be found to illustrate the views of the period on the subject of trade, royal interferences with burgh elections, and the disorders of the " licht horsemen " of the name of Gordon, while others are valuable for their notices of public men, such as George Jamesone, the celebrated painter ; but the greater number relate to the town's share in the political troubles of the day, beginning with its refusal to subscribe the Covenant, followed up by the miseries, sieges, quarterings, and exactions, which ensued. On two occasions did the Marquis of Montrose take possession of Aberdeen, with the view of compelling the adherence of the citizens to the Covenant ; and a third time he besieged the town with the view of punishing its inhabitants for their support of the principles which he had compelled them to adopt.

Such notices bring home to us more vividly than any general description, the conflicts and miseries of the time; while they are mixed with others, which show how, amid these public broils, the details of domestic and civic life were acted out. On these, however, it is unnecessary to enlarge, as the table of contents, prefixed to the volume, will direct the reader to them in detail. It only remains that I should record my obligations to Mr John Grant Leslie, Sheriff-Clerk Depute of Aberdeenshire, for undertaking the task of collating doubtful passages in the manuscript with the original Record.

JOHN STUART.

EDINBURGH, *October* 1871.

TABLE OF CONTENTS.

			PAGE
1625,	Nov.	31. Statute anent the keping of the sermones,	1
	Dec.	28. The Townes vapinschaw,	2
1626,	Jan.	18. Ane capitane chosin to train vp the inhabitares of the toun in militarie discipline,	3
	Mar.	15. Ane watche appoynted,	4
		22. Ordinance to the Deane of Gild,	5
		The nichtbouris of the toun ordanit to furneis thame selffes with sufficient armour,	5
	June	14. Commissioun for buying of armour,	6
	July	5. Ordinance to Andro Meldroune,	6
	Aug.	9. Licence granted to some nichtbouris to inclose a pairt of St Katherines Hill,	7
		29. Anent the tumultis maid be Macky his souldiours,	8
	Oct.	11. Act aganes superfluous banqueting.	9
		18. Johne Urrey chosin Dreill Maister,	10
1627,	Jan.	3. The Townes bakhous in the College to be repared,	11
	April	4. Persons nominatt to be commanderes at the Wapinshaw vnder the Magistrattis,	11
		11. The Townes Wapinschaw,	12
		25. Answer to the Toun of Edinburghis missive,	12
	May	9. Visitouris of the Schooles,	14
		16. V^c. merkis mortifeit to ane doctour in the grammer schoole,	15
	Aug.	14. Anent the arryving of Spanyeardis in Zetland,	16
		22. Two fyre bittis to be erected be the toun,	17
	Oct.	10. All doggis within the toun to be slayne,	18
1628,	Feb.	13. Wedderburne, Howatt,	19
	July	23. Fraser chosin ane of the doctouris of the grammer schoole,	20
	Nov.	26. Statute anent the demolisheing of choppis,	21
	Dec.	17. Commissioun for apprehending Jesuittis seminarie and mess preistis, and excommunicat Papists	22
1629,	Feb.	18. Ordinance for bigging of the Tolbuith steipill,	24
	April	1. Twa silver coupis giuen be Inglis for serving at the communioun tabillis,	24

TABLE OF CONTENTS.

				PAGE
1629,	April	8.	The ... of grammer schuill dischairget fra... tacking of ...	25
	July	17.	Ma... ... Huntar. Anent the yron wark of th... Tolbuith steiple,	25
	Sept.	22.	Coun... Wedderburne,	26
	Oct.	28.	Vi...tor... appointit for the schooles,	26
1630.	April	13.	Sch... ... be usit at the buriall of the La... ... Drum,	26
	May	26.	Ordo... ... bi... a loft in th... auld ki... for the College,	27
			Ord... ... to the maister of kirk wark for payment of the ... stipend,	27
	June	4.	Sol... ... to be u... at for the Queenes delyveri... of a yong sone,	28
		9.	Anent apprehending of witches,	29
	July	14.	Anent th... ... grammer of Mr Alex Hume,	29
		28.	Chalmer ... electit d'etour of the grammar ... scode in place of Fraser,	30
	Oct.	21.	The Gold... chirm... answer and duly se conce... the bushe fishcing,	31
	Dec.	1.	Ordinance to the thes... er in favour of Wedderburne,	32
			XI lib of fee granted to Mail... for rewling the tounes clokes,	32
1631,	Mar.	9.	Ordinance of Counc... ll in tanouris of the Bedall of the Townes hospitale,	33
		30.	Ordinance to the Thesaurer in favours of Wedderburne,	35
	May	4.	Ordinance against ... ladies repairing to lyik walkis,	35
	June	22.	Anent the plac... ... re of the Lirk of Futtie,	36
	Sept.	11.	Ordinance to the Thesaurer,	36
		14.	A Byla... given be Henry to the hospitall,	37
	Oct.	5.	Statute anent the leg... of the mercattis,	37
			Ratification... of the auld statutes,	37
		12.	Ordin... ... be... ing of a... loons,	38
			Statute anent del... m...	38
	Nov.	2.	Ordinance to the Thesaurer,	39
	Dec.	21.	Ordinance to the Deane of Gild,	39
			Ordinance on taxeres of Melnill,	39
1632,	Jan.	25.	Ordinance to be maister of kirk wark,	39
	Feb.	8.	Ordinance for ringing of bells at nyne houris at evin, and fyue houri... in the morning,	40
			Cont... between the Towne of Aberdein and Mr Robert Douny, Bibbel... ...	40
		29.	Ordinance in tan... mis of the Lirk sacristar,	45
	April	11.	Ordinance to the M... of kirk wark,	46
	June	13.	Ordinance aganis foir loiris and choppis,	47
			Anent the admitting of burgesses,	47
			Ordinance to the deane of gild concerning elwandis and measouris,	48
		20.	Anent the daylie catecheising,	48
	Aug.	15.	Conpeires swome anent the birning of salmound,	49
			Anent the lying of fir and peites,	49

TABLE OF CONTENTS.

				PAGE
1632	Sept.	12.	Anent the erecting of fontanes,	50
			Anent Wedderburnes new grammer,	50
		19.	The tounes consent anent the erecting of fontanes,	51
			Willox appointit keepeir of the clok and ringar of the common bell,	51
			Support grantit be the counsall to the craftis hospitall,	52
	Oct.	3.	Ordinance anent the repairing of the calsies of Month Coveye,	53
		17.	Ordinance anent the begynning of the fleshe, meill, and malt mercattis,	54
	Nov.	7.	Ordinance to the Deane of Gild,	54
1633	Jan.	9.	Ratificatioune of the act maid anent superfluous banquetting,	54
		23.	Dischairge be the Counsall to Jamesone,	55
	Feb.	20.	Act of his Maiesties Privie Counsell anent the fontanes,	55
	May	15.	Act discharging wemen to wear playdis about thair heddis,	58
		29.	Licence grantit to the principall and regentis of the Kingis Colledge,	59
	June	4.	Grant for printing a poesie,	59
		4.	Ordinance to the Thessaurar,	60
		19.	Ordinance to the Thessaurar,	60
			Solemnitie of the Kingis Maiesties coronatioune,	60
	Aug.	14.	A wapinschaw indicted,	61
			Anent glassing the wyndoes of the Grayfrier kirk,	61
	Oct.	2.	Ordinance to the Mr of kirk wark,	62
	Nov.	20.	The doctouris of the grammer schoole ar to obey the maisters directioun in thair doctrine and discipline,	63
	Dec.	4.	Doctor Forbes' expenses to Edin. to be paid,	63
		11.	Anent chambers to be built for students in the College,	63
1634	Feb.	12.	Lord Keythe; Irwingis contra Meldrum,	64
	Mar.	12.	Ordinance anent burgesses for making of thair residences,	66
		26.	Ratificatioun of the act againis mastishe and cur doggis,	66
	April	2.	Ordinance anent the casting of the prayer bell,	67
	Aug.	6.	Support to the Colledge of auld Aberdeine,	67
		13.	Act of Lordis of Privie Counsall for support of the people of Cathnes and Orkney in this calamitous tyme of darth and famine,	67
	Oct.	20.	Comissionars nominat to deal with Doctor Johne Forbes to accept uponn him the function of the ministrie within this burghe,	69
	Nov.	19.	A hearse given be Mr Thos. Gray to the new kirk,	69
	Dec.	17.	Anent the charge gewin to the toun for rysing in armes againes the licht horsemen,	70
1635	Jan.	14.	The Kingis Maiesties letter presentit to the counsell,	70
	Feb.	11.	Ordinance to the Mr of kirkwark,	72
	Mar.	26.	Missive from his Maiestie,	73
	April	8.	Ordinance to the dean of gild anent the Bishopis buriall,	74

TABLE OF CONTENTS.

				PAGE
1635,	May	13.	Licence grantit to Jamesonne,	74
	June	3.	Colectors and Ross cho in commissionaris anent the Bishop of Aberdine's transplantatiounc, .	76
			Anent our nightboures summonlit for comcall of tacmeyis,	77
			Statute anent the playding packed in the tounes packhous,	77
			Taxt Roll of the burrowis, .	78
	Aug.	9.	Licience for ane Frensche schoole,	80
	Sept.	23.	Deserting of the ordinar dyett off election,	80
	Oct.	7.	Charge for macking election of the new councell and magistrattis, &c.	83
	Nov.	4.	Ordinance aganis the carying of blind howattis on the streittis,	88
			Money collected for the ministeris of the Palatinate to be lent for the use of the minister at Futtie,	88
		18.	Anent a lodging for the Bishop,	89
1636,	Feb.	5.	Decreit Lordis of Privie Councell anent the election of the magistratti and councell for this yeir, &c.,	89
		24.	Andro Melville admittit maister of the musick schoole,	96
	Mar.	16.	Anderson appoynted to tak order with layeris of fuilzie on the streittis,	97
			Straquhyne, Straiconn, dischargit of keping schooles,	98
	April	27.	Ane edict to be served for ane doctour to the grammer school,	98
	June	29.	Boyd admittit ane of the doctoaris of the grammer schoole,	98
	July	20.	Gratitude to Wedderburne,	99
	Oct.	5.	Ane watche appoynted,	99
			Theasurer, Brastoun, s,	100
			The craftis concent to be text with the brethrene of gild for tua thousand reallis to by a tenement for ane correction hous,	100
	Nov.	9.	Ane piller to be erected at Petmoddan,	102
	Dec.	14.	Ane loft to be biggit in the Grayfere kirk for the magistrattis and councell,	102
			Report of Commissioner sent to a meeting of the burrowes,	102
		21.	Ratification of the act aganes superfluous banqueting,	105
1637,	Feb.	1.	Discharge Lumysden of his commission anent the licht horsemen,	105
		8.	Contract betwixt the toun and the compartinaris of the wark of the correction hous,	106
		22.	Act aganes forestalleris of the timber mercat,	112
	Mar.	15.	Anent the chappell of Futtie,	113
	April	12.	Charge for removing of middingis aff the streittis and commoun passages about the toun,	115
	June	14.	Lummisden, his discharge of his commission,	115
		21.	Mortimer chosin commissionar anent the licht horsemen,	116
			Coats to be given to the officiares,	117
	July	26.	Tapstaris of drinck, marineris,	117

TABLE OF CONTENTS.

			PAGE
1637,	Aug.	19. Report of commissionar anent the licht horsemen,	118
		Discharge to the toun of thair fyne for the licht horsemen,	119
	Sept.	13. A voluntarie contribution to be vplifted for helping to ransom some inhabitants of the toun of Air from their captivitie with the Turkis,	120
		Iniunction to the sacristar anent the furneshing off candill to the kirk,	121
1638,	Jan.	3. Anent the doctoris of the grammer schoole,	122
		Statute anent lyke wakes,	123
		31. Contribution to the captives of the burgh of Air,	123
	Mar.	21. The lecture of the mathematics to be in a four yeires course,	124
	April	11. Acquittance toun of Air on the ressett of our contribution for releiff of thair captives,	124
		25. Missive from his Maiestie,	124
	May	16. Anent the sale of wyne, aill, or bier,	125
		23. Deacones of craftes conviet for convocating thair craftis in armes,	125
	July	4. A heid of steine wark for livering and loadning ships,	127
		16. The conncellis refusall as of befoir to subscrywe the covenant,	128
		24. Anent the escaping of Alexr. Keyth out of ward,	130
		Sleick, officier committit to waird,	131
		25. Commissioun to be procured for searching and apprehending of Alexr. Keyth,	131
	Aug.	8. A wapinschaw indicted,	132
		15. The baillies appoynted to mak chois of capitanes and commanders at the wapinschaw,	133
		A missive frome his sacred Maiestie,	133
		Missive frome the Marquis of Hammiltoune,	134
	Sept.	26. A missive from his Majestie,	134
	Oct.	5. Exhibition be the Marquis of Huntly of his Maiesties declaration anent the annulling of the service book,	136
		8. Discharging of the trayned band,	137
		The tounes consent to subscrywe the Confession of Faith and generall band appoynted be his Maiestie to be subscrywed be all his lieges,	137
		10. Statute anent the keping of sermones,	139
		31. The haill inhabitants of the toun, fensibill persones, to be trayned vp in militarie exercise,	140
	Nov.	5. Petition anent the directing of ane commissioner to the Generall Assembly,	141
		7. Anent the Generall Assemblie,	143
1639,	Jan.	2. Leslie chosin commissionar anent Alexr. Keyth,	144
		5. Anent the actiones intentit aganes the magistrats be the creditoris of Alexr. Keyth,	144

TABLE OF CONTENTS.

			PAGE
1639,	Jan.	16. Overtures proponit to the brethrene of gild and craftis for defence of the toun,	145
		26. Chusing of conncell of warr, capitanes, and vnder officieris,	147
	Mar.	4. Conncell, Gordoun,	148
		The toun to be fortifeit,	149
		15. Consent brethrene of gild and craftismen to fortifie the toun, and to by muskats and pickis,	149
		16. The deane of gild and thesaurar ordanit to giwe thair band to the Marquis of Huntly for the muskattis and pickis,	150
		20. Anent the tounes evidentis and registeris,	151
		Kirk moneyes to be lent to the toun,	151
		Commissionares direct to the nobilitie of the covenant,	151
		Thesaurar, deane of gild,	152
		25. Commissionares direct of new agane to the nobilitie,	152
		28. The Erle of Montrois answer to oure commissiouaris propositiones,	153
		The townes capitanes qnytted thair charge,	154
		Entrie of the first armie,	154
	April	2. Charge gewin be the nobilitie to the toun,	155
		3. The toun chargit to subscrywe the covenant,	156
		9. A new charge gewin be the nobilitie to the toun, with thair answer thairto,	156
		10. The townes subscription of the covenant,	157
		15. Hay, Farquhar, Moreson, appoynted be the nobilitie to go commissionares to Edinburgh,	157
		Protestatioun Willeame Erskyne for himselff, and in name of the auld covenanters,	158
		17. Compt of Andro Burnet, thesaurar, his debursementis to capitanes and others of the armie,	159
		20. Moir chosin commissionar to meitt at Monymusk,	159
		The townes consent to send fourscoir men to Monymusk,	160
		A watche appoynted,	160
	May	6. Thesaurar, Farquhar,	160
		A letter frome the taibles to send the fourt man to the Bound rod,	161
		10. The tounes answer to the nobilities letter,	161
		13. The townes refusall to lend thair cannon,	163
		The tounes answer to the letter direct to thame from the Lord Fraser and Maister of Forbes,	164
		16. The townes answer to the Laird of Banff and his associattis anent thair demand of frie quarteris to thair soiouris,	164
		27. Ten thousand merkis imposit vpoun the toun for the Generall and remanent nobilitie of the present armie,	166
		28. The toun disarmed,	167

TABLE OF CONTENTS.

			PAGE
1639, May	29.	A note vpoun the payment be the toun of ten thousand merkis imposed vpon thame be the nobilitie, . . .	168
		The townes tuelff peice of cannon, with pulder and ball mellit with be the Erle of Montrois, ...	169
June	7.	The townes answer to the remonstrance made to thame be thair foure commissionares that wer send to Edinburgh be appoyntment of the nobillmen, . . .	169
	10.	The townes testimonie and approbation gewin to Mr Alex. Jaffray, thair prowest, of his dutifull and gude careage in his office, ...	171
	14.	The townes disassenting that thair commissionares re-enter in ward, or that the fynes imposed vpoun thame and some other nichtbouris be payed, ...	172
		The toune chargit to marche in armes with the Lord Aboyne,	173
		The watche appoynted, ...	173
	17.	The Lord Aboyne, his demand of the toun for intertenement of his armie, and the townes answer, . . .	174
	26.	The toune to be convenit, and his Maiesties letter to be intimat to thame, ...	175
		Charge for restoring of plundered goods, . .	176
		Ordinance to the Theasurar, ...	176
	28.	The Kings Maiesties letter manifesting the peace, . .	176
		The tounes consent to contribute for fricing of thair magistrattis of the sevin thowsand merkis gewin to the nobillmen at the intacking of the Brig of Dee, . . .	178
		Gray and Chalmer chosin commissionares to go to his Maiestie at Bervick, ...	178
July	2.	A letter of the Erll Marshallis intimat to the toun, .	179
	11.	The townes answer to the demand made to thame for imposing a taxatioun for payment of a pairt of the quartering moneyes,	180
	17.	Anent the entrie of tenentis to tempill landis and abbottis landis,	180
	24.	Discharge be Wedderburne and Paull, of thair quartering moneyis,	181
	31.	Thesaurar, Farquhar, ...	181
		The conncellis obleisment of thame and thair successoures to releive the present prowest, baillies, deane of gild, and thesaurar, of the moneyis gewin to the nobillmen, .	182
		A missive to be direct to the toun of Edinburgh for excusing our absence from the Generall Assemblie, . .	182
		Blakhall to be presewit for selling of bear and malt at Newcastle,	183
Aug.	7.	Forbes chosin commissionar to the Generall Assemblie, .	183
	7.	Discharge be Gray and Chalmer of thair commissioun to his Maiestie, ...	184
	14.	Jaffray chosin commissionar to the Parliament, . .	186

TABLE OF CONTENTS.

			PAGE
1639, Sept.	4.	Ordenance to the deane of gild and thesaurar,	187
	11.	Ordinance to the deane of gild,	187
		Debts contracted be the toune in the late trubles,	187
Oct.	11.	Act discharging the holding of any kynd of mercat on the Sabbath day,	189
	23.	Anent the timber mercat,	189
		A bell to be rung for convening and disolving of the schoolles at thair ordinarie houres,	190
Nov.	20.	Anent keiping of sermones,	190
		Anent keiping of the streittis clene,	191
		Hyrers of horses,	191
		Ratification of sundry acts,	192
	27.	Moreson appoynted to tak ane accompt off muskattis and pickis,	192
Dec.	19.	Letter from the nobillmen at south for intertencing of some commanderis till the spring,	193
		Suspension to be raised of the charge gewin to the toun for payment of the armes receawed be thame frome the Marquis of Huntly,	195
1640, Jan.	1.	Jaffray chosin commissionar to Edinburgh,	196
	8.	Anent the ressett of strangeris, and no houssis to be sett to excommvnicat papistis,	196
	10.	Suspension to be raised of the charges for the Marquis of Huntlyes armour,	196
	15.	Psalms to be sung daily at evening as well as morning service,	198
	29.	Jaffray, his discharge of his commissioun,	198
		Legacie, Mr Robert Johnstoun to the toun of Aberdeine,	199
Feb.	5.	Anent the Generall Band of Releiff,	200
		Instructiones anent the Band of Releiff,	200
		The Generall Band,	203
	11.	The toun convenit,	206
	14.	The townes answer anent the subscryving of the Generall Band of Releiff, and other particulares demandit of thame,	206
	18.	Imprecations against the covenanters,	207
	19.	Act anent Rob. calseymacker,	208
Mar.	11.	Deane of Gild appoynted to advance vje merkis to Lieutenant Colonell Forbes,	208
April	8.	Jaffray chosin commissionar to a meitting of the nobilitie and estates at Edinburgh,	209
	9.	Chusing of taxtares for stenting the toun for payment of thair tent partis conforme to the Generall Band,	209
	15.	1000 merkis advanceit to Lieutenant Colonell Forbes,	211
		Isobel Blak to be joggit,	212
	22.	Licence gewin to Rob anent the bigging of the steppis of his stair,	212

TABLE OF CONTENTS.   xxi

			PAGE
1640, May	5.	Helen Mearns convict,	213
	6.	Jaffrayes discharge of his commissioun,	214
		Instructiones for commanderis and soiouris,	214
		Ordinance anent Johne Leith of Harthill,	217
	12.	Straquhyn convict of dinging Beith,	218
		Patersones convict,	218
	27.	Commissionar chosin to the Parliament,	219
		Precept from the committe anent silver and goldsmith wark,	221
		Charge to the toune to meitt the Erle Marshall at the Brig of Dee in armes,	222
	29.	The toun convenit for subscryving the articles presented to thame be the Earle Marshall and Generall Maior Munro,	222
June	10.	Warrandis from Generall Maior Monro anent the souldiouris of his regiment,	225
	17.	Lumnisdane chosin commissionar to the Generall Conventioun of Burrowes,	227
		The Grayfreir Kirk to be repared for the Generall Assemblie,	227
July	8.	Dimissioun Wedderburne of his office of maister of the grammer schoole	227
	15.	Chalmer admittit maister of the grammer schoole,	228
		Contract betwixt the toun and Mr Thomas Chalmer, maister of thair grammer schoole,	229
		Pension to Wedderburne,	231
	22.	Leslie and Jaffray chosin commissionares to Generall Assemblie,	232
		A guard at the Assemblie,	232
		Lumisdanes discharge of his commission at the Convention of Burrowes,	233
		Charge that nane of the inhabitantis remowe out of the toune,	233
		Letteris to be direct to the moderatoris of Presbyteries for sending in vivares for the Generall Assemblie,	234
Aug.	3.	The prayers to be red in the Grayfrier Kirk,	235
		Mr Andro Cant chosin ane of the Townes Ministers,	235
	12.	Jaffray chosin commissionar to the Committee of Estate,	236
		A company of soiouris to be levied to the Erll Marshall for the publict service of the cuntrie,	236
	19.	These that removed out of the toun when the Tounes Company wes tacking wp to be depryvit of thair fredome,	238
		Warrant to Mr Robert Farquhar for the moneyes advancit be him for shoes and hardin to Monroes soiouris and for fourtie dayes lone to the Townes Company,	238
Sept.	9.	Hay, Aidy, chossin commissionares to Invernes,	239
	11.	Christen Brow convict,	240
	23.	Names of the provost, baillies, and counceill,	240

TABLE OF CONTENTS.

			PAGE
1640,	Sept.	23. A nightly watche appointed,	241
	Oct.	3. Searche to be maid for runawayes,	241
		7. Dr Wm. Guild chosen to be Principal of the King's College,	242
		14. The bell of the grammer schoole lent to Doctor Guild,	243
		22. The toun and the Lord Sinclare, anent the quartering of his soiours,	243
		23. George Ross conviet,	244
		28. Moir chosin commissionar to the Committie of Estate,	245
	Nov.	11. Patrick Leslie chosin commissionar to the Parliament and to a meitting of the burrowis,	246
		12. Act of the committee of estates of Parliament anent the pryces of schooes, boottes, hyddis, and tanning of leather,	248
	Dec.	2. Patrick Stewart depryved of his place in the Gild Bretherenes Hospitall,	251
		16. Yoole vacance dischairgit,	252
		23. Leslye his discharge of his commission at the Parliament and meitting of the burrowis,	252
1641,	Jan.	6. Inimetions to the kirk sacristar,	253
	Feb.	17. Act aganes abstracteris of thair cornes from the tounes mylnes,	255
	Mar.	17. Hay and his servantis pickiemen at the tounes mylnes conviet,	255
		Ordinance of counsell aganes servantis gewares of any more nor the dew multure and knaveeship for grinding of thair maisteris malt, and aganes pickiemen exacteris of more nor thair due,	256
		19. Vulgine and Bellie conviet,	256
		25. Election of Mr George Gilespie minister,	257
		31. Mr Andro Cant resavit as ane of the ministers,	257
	April	7. Deane of Gild, calsiemacker,	258
		28. Ratification of the Act maid anent the entrie of tenentis to Tempill Landis and Abbottis Landis,	258
	May	4. Sherar and Burnett conviet,	259
		7. The touns ratificatioun of the Act of counsell maid aganes persewers of actions befoir inferiour judges,	259
		19. Act for dimoleshing the fauld biggit in the Linkis,	260
		Restraint of careing sand from Heidinishill,	260
		26. Statute anent the wool mercat,	260
	June	14. Act anent transporting of passengeris out of the cuntrie,	261
		15. Mariorie Jack conviet,	261
		Andersone and Makie conviet of usurping the rights of gild burgessis,	262
		16. Moresom admittet ane of the doctouris of the grammer schoole,	262
		23. James Peir conviet of assaulting Crombie,	263
	July	6. Fraser conviet of injuring Bessie Forbes,	264
		Watsone conviet of dinging over Margaret Andro,	264

TABLE OF CONTENTS. xxiii

				PAGE
1641,	July	6.	Robert Massie convict for putting hands on Wm. Gordon,	264
		7.	Act discharging some abuses at Buriallis,	265
		9.	Lord Sinclare and the toun anent the billeting of his soiours,	265
		10.	Intimatioun anent the soiours,	266
		12.	The tounes consent to quarter the Lord Sinclares soiouris for tuentie dayes,	256
	Aug.	3.	Walker convict of injuring his master,	267
			James Alexander, convict,	267
		11.	Band Farquhar to the nichtbouris for quartering the Lord Sinclares regiment,	268
		25.	Commissioun to the provest to petition his majestie for some particulares in regaird of oure townes losses,	269
	Sept.	6.	Alex. Cuming, convict,	269
		17.	Anent two booths in the Round Table,	270
			Peter Crombie, convict,	271
	Oct.	6.	Anent the buriallis in the kirkyard,	272
		25.	The old barrowes and pheasses to be comprysed and lent to the maisteris of the correction hous,	272
	Nov.	20.	Smith and Kemp, convict,	272
		30.	Duncan convict,	273
			Gordon convict,	273
	Dec.	11.	Sara Fowler convict,	273
		15.	Thrie dayes play grantit to the scholares at the beginning of ilk quarter,	274
		22.	Patent, Robert, Duke of Lennox to the toun, of the office of admiralitie within thair boundis,	274
1642,	Jan.	5.	Act anent the tounes mortclothes,	276
	Feb.	11.	Act for removing of the court de guard,	277
		16.	Commission to Farquhar,	278
			Lumnisdane his discharge of his commission,	278
			The lectures and morning prayeris to be in the auld kirk,	279
	Mar.	16.	Act aganes bannares and swearares,	279
		30.	Thesaurar appoynted collector of the pryces of muskattis and piekis,	281
			The pheissis lent to the masters of the correctioun hous,	282
	April	6.	Act againes prenteissis and wtheris sitting in daskis within the kirkis of this burghe,	282
			Ordinance to the maister of the kirk wark,	283
			Bonaccord coup gewin to the vse of the kirk,	283
		13.	Anent the patronage of the kirk Sanct Nicolas,	283
			Act for ane taxatioun,	284
		22.	Elspet Meldrume convict,	285
	May	4.	Protestation Leslie,	285
		11.	Licence to Dickson to vse his tred of macking gouff ballis,	286

TABLE OF CONTENTS.

			PAGE
1642,	May	27. David Philp convict,	286
		30. Bellie and Wilson convict,	287
		Aydie convict,	287
	June	8. Mure convict,	287
		15. Lady Rothiemay hir mortification of ane thousand pundis for maintenance of ane maistres of schoole to bring vp young wemen,	288
	July	26. Donaldson convict,	290
	Aug.	12. Andro Mowat convict,	291
		16. Smith, Hoode, and Rany convict,	291
	Sept.	19. Philp and Fraser convict,	291
		30. Wm. Walker skipper oblist not to transport persons to forane countries,	292
	Oct.	5. Thesaurar collector of the muskat money,	292
		19. Ordinance to bursars in the colledge,	293
	Nov.	23. An aid for repair of the colledge,	293
		A weeklie lesson in Hebrew to be in the colledge,	293
	Dec.	14. Swan admitet doctor of grammar school,	294
		21. Act contra yoole day,	294
		Moreson to set caution,	294

ERRATUM—Page 279 margin - For 1812 read 1642.

EXTRACTS

FROM THE

RECORDS OF THE BURGH OF ABERDEEN.

31 November 1625.

THE quhilk day the provest, baillies, and counsall, considering that the Lord's day is greatlie prophained and brockin within this burght, be ane great many of the inhabitantes thereoff, in that some of thame uses gainging and playing in the linkes and walking about the feildes, some of thame passes to tavernes and ailhousses, and utheres remaines wilfullie at home within thair housses in tyme of sermon on the Sabboth day, als weill befoir as efter noone, to the great dishonour of God and scandall of the Gospell; for remeid quhairof it is statute and ordanit that quhatsumener inhabitant within this burght shall be noted and fund giltie heirefter in braking of the Lordis day be gaming or playing, walking about the feildes, passing to tavernes or ailhousses, or be wilfull remaining in thair housses in tym of sermon on the Sabboth day, ather befoir or efter noone, that thay sall pay the payne and unlaw of twentie shillinges *toties quoties* to the

31 Nov. 1625.

Statute anent the keping of the sermones.

EXTRACTS FROM THE [1625.

31 Nov.
1625.
—
Statute anent the keping of the sermones

Collectour of Kirk Session for help and releiff of the poore; And in caice of refusall or inhabilitie of any persone offending in the premisses to pay the penaltie foirsaid presentlie upoun thair apprehensioun or convictioun, efter lawfull tryall, to be punished in thair bodies be imprissonment, or efter sic uther maner as the magistrates shall injoyne, conforme to the tenor of his Majesties Actes of Parliament maid thairanent.

28 Dec.
1625.
—
The Townes vapinschaw.

28 *December* 1625.

The quhilk day for obedience to the generall proclamationn and charge giuen in to all his Majesties lieges, fensibill persones, alsweill to burgh as land within this kingdome, for giweing thair mustures and wapinschawing, this twentie aucht of December instant, the provest and baillies of this burgh causet convein be the tounes commoun drummer, all the inhabitantes of the toun, alsweill frie as unfrie, fensibill persones, at the mercat croce, in thair best armour, and thairfra merchet efter thair magistrates to the Linkes, quhair the rolles of the haill four quarteres of the toun were callet, and notice takin of the armes careit be euerie man; and thaireftir the toune being ranckct and put under commandement, the muscateres be thame selfes, the pickmen be thame selfes, and these that careit two handet swordis being ranket about the tounes three ensengzeis, thay merchet all in ordour and rank in that pairt of the tounes linkes quhair the toune heirtofore hes euer beine in vse to mak thair mustures, to wit, in the principall pairt of the linkes betwixt the first hole and the Quenis hole, and haveing merchet thair a certaine space, they than returned in order to the towne, and haueing marched diuerse and sundrie tymes in the Castleget round about both the croces, wer then dismissed be command of the magistrates; and it is to be remembered that there mustered this day   muskateres, and als many with pickes, speares, and crosboltes, and some sexteen with two handet swordis. Quhairof the Conncell thinkes meitt that thair shall be giuen up to the Lordis of his Maiestie's Privie Counsall.

18 *January* 1626.

The said day anent the petitioun giuen in to the prouest, baillies, and counccll be George Johnstoun, younger, burges of this burgh, for him selff, and in name and behalff of such nichtbores and comburgesses of the toun as does assist and concur with him in the busines followeing, be the quhilk petitioun the said George humblie desyres thair wisdomes wald be pleased to tak to thair serious consideratioun that wyse saying of King Solomon, *Felix illa ciuitas quæ tempore pacis prouidet bellum*, and the rather becaus albeit we haue long injoyed, and do yit still be the mercie of God injoy ane happie pace; yit the winnersall combustioun, bruttes and rumores of warres, and foran preparationnes throchout Christendome, should waken ws out of our securitie, and stir ws wp to be wpon our gaird, and to prepair for the storme efter so long ane calme, that we may be in reddines alsweile for persewte as defens as his Maiesties seruice, and our awin particular necesseteis and occasiones shall present: The most graue and ancient of this citie ar sensible of our waiknes at the present, ather to defend or offend our enemeis, if it sould fall out (quhilk God forbid) that we war assaulted at unwarse be ane meir handfull: In such ane caice of necessitie it becomes all loyall and trew hearted subjectes, alswell in regard of thair alledgeance and bund deutie to their king and countrie, as for thair awin guid and saiftie, to be prepairing thame selffes with conuenient armour, both offensive and defensive, as lykwayes to be training wp and exerceising thame selffes quhow to handle thair armes: And since ane great many of the nichtbores and inhabitantes of the toune ar willing to contribute of thair proper means for furnishing ane competent yeirlie pensioun to any qualefeit gentilman who hes borne charge at armes in the Low Countrie, that will tak wpon him to train wp in militarie discipline the nichtbores of the toune efter the ordour vseit in the Low Countreis, they humblie desyre the Counccelles approbatioun thairto, and to mak choose of the persone quhome they think most fitting for the imployment, and they sall at thair awen charge, promyd and contribute to gratifie him

[margin: 18 Jan. 1626. Ane capitane chosin to train vp the nichtboures of the toun in militarie discipline.]

18 Jan.
1626.
———
Ane capitane chosin to train vp the nichtboures of the toun in militarie discipline.

for his paines as at mair lenth was contenit in the said petitioun; quhilk being red and considderit in Counccll, and the new and auld counsallers hauing deliberatly adnysed and consulted thairwpoun, they allow of the motioun as being both necessar and proflitable for the furtherance of his Maiesties seruice, and for the guid and benefeit of the toun, and giues thair approbatioun and consent thairvnto; lykas for that effect they instantlie maid chooss and nominatioun of Capitane Arthure Forbes, quho is ane gentilman, that hes borne charge in the Low Countreis, and is accompted the most qualifeit and fitt for the busines of any in thir pairtes; upon conditioun alvayes that the petitioner and his associattes satisfie him for his paines at thair awin proper charges, be ane voluntarie contributioun, to be collected amongst the nichtbours of the toun, such as they sall be pleased voluntarlie to condissend to, and no vther wayes, and with speciall conditioun also, that the said Capitane Arthure Forbes shall haue no power to caus the nichtboures of the toune, or any of thame, lift armes in any peice of seruice whatsoeuer, without the express warrand and directioun of the prouest, baillies, and councell of this burgh for the tyme haid and obtenit thairto; lykas wpoun thair warrand and directioun he shall be obleist to lead the nichtboures of the toune both in pace and war, and to pas wpon seruice sa oft as he shall be comandit be the magistrates and councell for the tyme, and no wther wayes. And the employment of the said Capitan Arthure in the seruice aboue specifeit to indure for the space of three yeires efter the dait heiroff allanerlie, and no longer.

15 March
1626.
———
Ane watche appoynted.

15 March 1626.

The samen day the prouest, baillies, and councell being informed that the tounes of Edinburght and Leyht, and wther burrowes in the south pairtes of this realme, hes ane nightlie watche be reasone of the iminent dainger whairin this haill kingdome standes of invasioune be forane enemeis, to witt, the King of Spain and his confederates: Thairfoir thinkes it meit and expedient that thair shall be also ane watche keipet in this burght, and for that effect appointes that twelff persones shall watche everie nicht, thairof sex at the Blokhous, and uther sex at the Castelhill, and gif any persone shall be absent from the watche, being lawfullie warnit thairto, without ane lawfull excuise, to incur the unlaw of . . . to be payed to the tounes use unforgiven. As lykwayes ordaines all the inhabitantes of this burght, alsweill frie as unfrie sensible persones, to be charget be the drum passand throw the haill streits of the toune, to prepair and furnishe thame selffes with sufficient armour, alsweill offensive as defensive, within . . . dayes nixt efter the dait heirof, as lykwayes to convein and assemble thame selffes in armes at the mercat croce of this burght als oft as any warning shall be maid to thame for that effect be the drum or be the common bell, be nicht or be day, and to follow thair magistrates as they sall be directed to any peice of seruice that shall occur, under the pain of death.

15 March 1626. — Ane watche appoynted.

22 March 1626.

The samen day the conncell ordaines Mr Mathow Lumysden, deane of gild, to deburse the soume of ane hundreth merks money to be send south with the prouest for buying taffetie to be ane hand signyie, and for buying ane droum, and for doing sic uther of the tounes effaires as is given to the prouest in commissioun uponn compt to be giuen be him at his returne, that in caice he be super-expendit he may be reimbursed: Quhilk soume sall be allowed to the said deane of gild in the comptes.

22 March 1626. Ordinance to the Deane of Gild.

The said day the prouest, baillies, and conncell, appointes and ordaines that all the inhabitantes of this burght, fensibill persones, shall furneis thameselffes with sufficient armour, some with pickes and corslettes, and utheres with muskates and bendrolles, as thay sall be commandit and injoyned be the magistrates, betwixt the dait heirof and the twentie four-day of Junii nixt, to come under the paine of

The nicht-boures of the toun ordanit to furneis thame selffes with sufficient armour.

6   EXTRACTS FROM THE   [1626.

22 March 1626.
—
The nichtboures of the toun ordanit to furnis thame selffes with sufficient armour.

fourtie pundis, to be payed be ilk persone contraveinand being solvend; and in cace of thair inhabilitie to pay the unlaw, to be depryved of thair fredome being friemen; and being unfrie, to be wardet at the pleasour of the magistrates till thay gine obedience and furnish thameselffes with sufficient armour, and this act to be intimatt be the drum throw the haill streittes of the toune that naine pretend ignorance thairof.

14 June 1626.
—
Commissioun for buying of armour.

14 *June* 1626.

The samen day the proue st, baillies, and councell, in respect of the skearsitie of armour in this burght, ordaines commissioun to be giuen to Gilbert Hervie eldar, who is presentlie bown, God willing, to Flanderes, to by thair for the tounes vse,—Two hundreth muskattis, and three hundreth pickes with pulder, and uther furnitour requisite; and thairwith ordaines the haile inhabitantes within this burgh, fensible persones to be charget be the drum throuch the haill streittis of the toune, to prepair thame selffes with pickes, corslettes, muskattes, pulder, and leid, in all convenient dilligence againe the nixt Wapinschaw, and to send to Flanders for that effect with the present occasioun of the ship of this burgh callet the Sampsone, presentlie bown thair, vnder the paine of fourtie pund money, to be payed be ilk persone that shall not be sufficientlie armed at the nixt Wapinschaw, as also be euerie ane quha shall not declair be his aith that the armes he beares belonges to him selff as his awin proper gudes.

5 July 1626.

5 *July* 1626.

The quhilk day the prouest, baillies, and councell, ordeanet Andro Meldrome, collector of the tounes impost and shoar silver, to build and set up in all convenient diligence a beakin, without the heid of the Bulwark, about that pairt whair ane beakin stuid of auld; and

1626.] RECORDS OF THE BURGH OF ABERDEEN. 7

the expensses to be deburst thairupoun thay ordain to be allowed to him in his comptes. *5 July 1626.*

9 August 1626.

The quhilk day anent the petitioun geivin in to the provost, baillies, and conncell, be Alexander Jaffray, Andro Meldrome, Robert Cruikshank, and Thomas Cargile, for thame selffes and in name of thair nichtboures, the remanent proprietares of the yardis mercheand to Sanct Catharines hill, mackand mentioun that quhair that pairt of the said hill betwixt the auld chappell and the lard Forbes yaird, is maid ane filthie vennell, whairthrow the nichtboures cannot have commodious access to the said hill, desyrand thairfoir licence to big ane laich dyk or reaveling of tymber about the pairt foirsaid, for preserveing and keiping the same clein in tyme coming, from sic filth and pollutioun, promising gif it pleis their wisdomes to grant the said licience, that they shall plant the boundis with trees, and mak it a comoun walking place to these quha shall contribute thairto; in respect the bigging of the said dyik, and inclosing of the boundis, will nowayes be preiudiciale to the auld passages wset and wount to and fra the said hill, as at moir leuth wes contenit in the said petitioun: Quhilk being red in conncell, and thay conveining vpoun the boundis, and haweing sichted and consideret the same, thay find the boundes to belong in propertie to the toune as a pairt of the said hill: Neuertheles in respect the same is filthilie abuset as ane vennall, and is altogidder vnproffitable and serves to the toune for no wse at the present, the provost, baillies, and conncell grants licience and libertie to the petitioneres, vpoun conditioun alwayes as is vndirwrittin, to big a dyick or raveling of tymber, betwixt the chappell wall and the lard Forbes back dyke of his yaird, and to inclose the saides boundes, and grantes libertie to euerie nichtbour that contributes to the building thairof, to have ane key for thair awin vse, with this alvayes conditioun, lykas it is

Licience granted to some nichtboures to inclose a pairt of St Katherines Hill.

9 August 1626.

Licence granted to some nichtboures to inclose a pairt of St Katherines Hill.

heirby speciallie declaired, that it shall be lesome to the prouest, baillies, and councell of this burgh for the tyme, to dimolishe the said tymber dyk, and to appropriat and apply the said haill boundis to the commoun benefeit of the toun for sic vse as they shall think the same most suting for the tyme, as being the tounes propertie belonging to them in commoun, but preuidice alwayes to the proprietares of the yairdes mercheand to the said hill, of thair passages thairto vset and wount, conform to thair infeftments grantet to thame thairupoun.

29 August 1626.

Anent the tumultis maid be Macky his souldiours.

The samen day the prouest, baillies, and councell, considdering the many dissordouris, tumultes, and commotiounes maid within this burght be the souldeouris now present within the samen, levied be Colonell Macky and his capitaines for his Majesties service in the pairtes of Germanie, and how that some of the nichtbouris of the toune hes bein in great dainger for not haveing armes reddie upoun thame the tyme of the saids tumultes: Thairfoir and to the effect the nichtboures may be upon thair gaird whan any sic tumultes shall fall out heirefter, and for the better repressing thairoff: Ordaines the haill inhabitantes of this burght fensible persones, to wear thair swordis about thame at all occasiounes whan thay walk on the streattes so long as the saides souldioures remaines within the toune: As lykwayes ordaines both mercheandis and craftsmen to hawe long wapins in thair boothes to the effect they may be moir reddie to assist the magistrates for repressing such insolencies in tyme cumming, and in cace any fensible persone inhabitant within the toune shall be fund walking on the streittes, and not haweing his suord about him dureing the space aboue mentioned, the persone contraveining shall incur the unlaw of fywe merkes *toties quoties* to be payed to the Deane of Gild for the commoun benefeit of the toune. Lykas it is ordanit if any such tumultes shall fall out, that the nichtboures of the toune, how sone notice sall be giwine to thame, shall assemble thame selffis and repair to thair magistrates, and accompany thame for taking ordour with all such persones as shall be moweres and raiseres of the saides tumultes, and ordaines intimatioun to be maid heiroff be the drum throu the haill streites of the towne, that nain pretend ignorance of the premisses.

29 August 1626.
——
Anent the tumultis maid be Macky his souldiours.

11 October 1626.

The quhilk day the prouest, baillies, and councell, considdering that albeit the abuse of superfluous and costlie banqueting laitlie within these few yeires cropin in within this burgh at the baptizeing of young childrene, wes expreslie prohibite and forbidden be speciall act and ordinance, set doun againes the same be the councell of this burgh for the tyme, upoun the auchtein day of Februar 1624 yeires; neuertheles they find the said abuse yit still to continew in a heich degrie, to the offence of God, the hurt of honest men's estates, and to the sclander of the toune: And searcheing out the causses of the grouth and continewance of the said abuse, thay find the principall and cheiff caus thairoff to be the impunitie and owersicht granted to the brackeres of the said act in tyme bygain, flor remeid quhairoff, and for repressing and abolisheing of such abuse heirefter, it is statut and ordanit that no inhabitant within this burght, of quhatsoever rank, qualitie, or degrie thay be off, shall at any tyme heirefter invite anie ma persones to be gossopes or cumberes at the baptizeing of thair childrene, bot four gossopes and four cumberes at the most; and that thair shall be bot sex wemen at the most invited or employed to convey the chyld to and fra the kirk, nather yit shall thair be any mair persones invited to any denner, supper, or afternoones drink at a baptime, or yit any other tyme dureing the haill space of the womanes chyldbed, or at the wpseat, bot sex men and sex wemen at the most: And withall ordaines that naine presume to have at any such tyme any kynd of suggoures, droiges, or confectiounes brocht from forane cuntreis, nather yit any kynd of vennesoune, wyld meat or baiken mait, under the pain of fourtie pundis

11 October 1626.
——
Act aganes superfluous Banqueting.

11 October
1626.
—
Act aganes
super-
fluous
Banqueting.

money to be exacted preceislie but favour, of ilk persone contraveinand in any of the pointes abone prohibited, *toties quoties*, to be payed to the deane of gild of this burgh, and applyed to the tounes publict use and benefeit: And forder, becaus the sin and vyce of excessive and extraordinarie drinking is become too frequent now adayes, both to burgh and land, to the dishonour of God, and abuse of his gude creatoures, quhilk pairtlie proceidis in that many disordourlie people gewin to riot and intemperancie, ar sufferit and forborne not onlie to drink wancht and scoall at thair pleasour, at all publict meitinges whair thay happin to be present, bot also to urge and compell thair nichtboures in companie with thame to doe the lyk, or than presentlie to move a quarrell and doun looke at thame for thair refuisall, ffor repressing of the quhilk abuse heirefter within this burgh, it is statute and ordanit, that no inhabitant within the samen whosoever, shall presume in any tyme cuming, at quhatsumenir meiting, publict or privat, to compell or urge any of thair nichtboures sitting at table with thame, to drink or scoall any quantitie of wyn, aill, or beir, farder nor thay sall be pleased to drink, under the lyk pain of fourtie pundis, to be exacted of the contraveinar and urger, without favour *toties quoties*, and payed to the commoun benefeit and use of the toune, as said is, and the contraveinares to be tryed alsweill be thair aith as be witnesses: And ordaines this act to be publictlie intimat out of pulpet the nixt Sabboth, in both the kirkis of this burgh, that nain pretend ignorance thairoff.

18 October
1626.
—
Johne
Urrie
chosin
Dreill
Maister.

18 *October* 1626.

The samen day the provest, baillies, new and auld counsallis, being convenit in the councell hous, nominates and chuises Johne Urrie to be generall dreill maister, to teich and instruct the nichtboures and inhabitantes of this burgh, to handill thair armes in place of Capitane Arthure Forbes, who wes nominat of befoir to that use, bot now is employed in his majestie's service, under Collonell Mackye, in the pairtes of Germanie:

And this employment of the said Johne Vrrie to indure till Witsonday
nixt to come, whome the counsall ordaines to be satisfied for his paines,
be voluntarie contributioun of the nichtboures that receaves the benefeit,
or be sic wther forme as shall be thocht most expedient be the councell,
and siclyk the councell thinkes meit, that thair shall be sex nominat out
of everie quarter to be dreill maisteres under the said Johne Vrrie, for the
greater furtherance and expeditioun of the work.

18 October
1626.

Johne
Vrrie
chosin
Dreill
Maister.

3 January 1627.

The quhilk day the prouest, baillies, and councell ordaines the
tounes bakhous within the College of this burgh, to be repaired upoun
the tounes commoun chairges in all convenient diligence, and maid a
comodious duelling hous to Mr Willeam Forbes, doctor in divinitie, ane of
the tounes ordinar ministeres, to serve him for ane duelling hous so long
as he remaines actuall minister within this burgh; lykas the said bakhous
is ordainit to remain ane commoun hous belonging to the toun for serveing
ane of thair awin ministeres for his duelling in all tyme cumming, or for
sic uther publict use as the councell of this burgh for the tyme shall
appoint the samen, and George Andersone, maister of Kirk Wark, is
ordanit to deburse sic as shall be requisite for perfyting of the said wark
as he shall be directed be the magistrates or maister of wark to be appointed for the wark forsaid, quhilkis debursementes shall be allowed to
him in his comptes.

3 January
1627.

The
Tounes
bakhous in
the College
to be re-
paired.

4 April 1627.

The said day the prouest, baillies, and councell nominattes and
appointes Johne Vrrie, Mr Mathow Lummysden, Thomas Cargill,
Alexander Chalmer, Patrick Leslie, George Moriesoun, Thomas Melnill,
Androw Meldrome, Andro Birnie, Thomas Gairdyn, tailyeour, Hew Anderson, goldsmyth, to be commanderes vnder the magistrates at the tounes

4 April
1627.

Persons
nominatt
to be com-
manderes
at the
Wapin-
shaw vnder
the Magi-
strattis.

4 April 1627.

Persons nominatt to be commanderes at the Wapinshaw vnder the Magestrattis.

wapinshaw appoynted to hauld the allevint day of Apryll instant, viz., the said Johne Vrrie to be principall commander vnder the magistrate, and the remanent persones aboue named to command vnder thame as serjeandes, and to carie partizens to that effect: And ordaines intimatioun to be maid be the drum, that nain presume, nor tak vpoun thame to command at the said wapinshaw, or to carie a partizan vnder the paine of fourtie pundis money, to be payed be ilk persone contraveining to the deane of gild for the behowe of the toune, and that nain presume to carie armes befoir thame, except the magestrates under the pain foirsaid.

11 April 1627.

The Townes Wapinschaw.

11 April 1627.

The quilk day for obedience of the generall proclamatioun and charge gewin to all his Maiesties liege sensibill persones als weill to burgh as land within this kingdome for gewing thair mustures and wapinschawing, the prouest and baillies causet convein be the townes common drummeres all the inhabitants of the toun, sensible persones als weill frie as vnfrie, in the tounes commoun linkes, in that pairt thairof quhair the toune ewer heirtofoir hes bein in vse to mak thair mustures, to witt, betwixt the first hoill and the Quenis hoill, and thair causet call the rolles of the haill four quarteres of the towne, and tak notice of the armes cariet be euerie man, and thairefter, thay being ranket and put in commaundement, it wes fund that thair wes twa hundreth muskateres and ane hundreth pickmen by and attour the commanderes that gawe thair mustures.

25 April 1627.

Answer to the Toun of Edinburghis missive.

25 April 1627.

The said day anent the missive direct from the towne of Edinburgh to the prouest, baillies, and counceill of this burgh, for keiping a meiting of the burrowes appoynted to hauld at Edinburgh the first day of May nixt to come, concerning certane particular effeares mentioned in the said missive quhairof the tenour followes. "Rycht honorabill and loveing freindis and nichtboures: the calamitie of the tyme makes ws resent the daylie hurt sustenit, especiallie be the bodie of our estate of the burrowes, the intercourse of tred (the cheif friend of our common weill) being contracted be occasioun of foran ennemyes, and that litle occasioun left, we can hardlie enjoy it without sein daiuger, and our home effeares does not a litle pinshe us, so that both at home and abroad our effeares requyres some spedie course to be taken: our shippes are taken daylie be the Dunkirkeres, our sea-fairing men detenit in bondage, the penall statutes are licklie to be put to executioun, notwithstanding of these letteres we haue purchest in the contrar be our commissioner, and euerie man hes his eye thairwpon, that by our loss that way they may profficitt thame selffes, and that which is left to the burrowes, which is thair commoun landis given thame for publict vses, sustentatioun of thair ministrie, scooles, and hospitales, the teicheres quhairof ar liklie to be drawen under the compas of this commissioun, so that quhar we look wpon the generall conditioun of our estait, we cannot but be compairtineres of your greiff, and lest the delay of such courses as micht in some manner releiff you of these sores micht be imputed to ws, we ar earnestlie to entreat you, as ane feilling member of the estait, to tak the foirsaid greivances to your earnest consideratioune, and to send your commissioneres sufficientlie instructed for meiting and conveining at this burgh the first of May nixt, with continuatioun of dayes, with the remanent commissioneres, with ample commissioun to doe in the premisses, and all other thinges concerning your estait, as thay shall think most meit and expedient for the weill both of the countrie in generall, and the estait, quhairof you ar memberes in particular: recommending to your cair that you send such as are sufficientlie experienced in such effeares weill instructed with your best advyse in the foirsaid effeares: so hoipeing the wechtines of these particulares shall be ane sufficient motive to stir wp your myndis to avaick from the slumber of negligence in this perrellous tyme, and attending thir commissionares the said day as you tender the weill of the estait,

25 April 1627.
Answer to the Toun of Edinburghis missive.

25 April 1627.
—
Answer to the Toun of Edinburghis missive.

we comitt you to God, and restis your loveing freindis and nychtbouris, the prouest and baillies of Edinburgh, subseryveand be Mr Alexander Guthrie, our clerk, at our command. Sic subscribitur, A. Guthrie. Edinburgh, 18 Aprilis 1627." Quhairwith the prouest, baillies, and counsall adnysing, they find it not expedient that any commissioner be sent at the present for keiping of the said dyet, both becaus of the shortnes of the tyme, the missive not being delyuered vnto thame till this morning, as lyckvayes in respect of the approtcheing of the Generall Couventioun of Burrowes at Air in July next, whair the baill burrowes ar to be present be thair commissioneres, and at the whilk tyme the fittest occasioun will be offered for advysing and resolving vpon the best course to be takin in all the saidis particulares mentioned in the said missive; and, in the meintyme, ordaines a letter to be direct to the prouest and baillies of Edinburgh, bearand our adnyse, and excuseing our absence from the meitting.

9 May 1627.
—
Visitouris of the Schoolles.

9 May 1627.

The quhilk day the prouest, baillies, and councell nominates and appointes Thomas Collinsoun, Robert Johnstoun, Mr Alexander Jaffray, and Mr Wedast Lowsoun, to assist and concur with Doctour Forbes, Doctour Dun, Doctour Johnstoun, eldar and younger, and Mr Robert Barroun, in the visitationn of all the schooles in this burgh, alsweill the grammer scoole, as the Musick and English scooles, and to tak notice of the forme of doctrine and discipline in all the saides scooles, and how the maisteres and scolleris observes the lawes and injunctiounes set doun, and to be set doun to that effect, and whairin they find any of the maisteres of the saides schooles deficient ather in doctrine or discipline, that they report the same to the councell of this burgh, with thair adnyse how all defectes and abuses shall be repaired, to the intent that the magistrates and councell may accordinglie give ordour for reformatioun, conforme to ane act formerlie set doun to this same effect vpon the tent day of Junuar last bypast: Lykas it is appointed that the lawes of all the schooles shall be imprinted and publictlie affixt in everie scole, that nather maister nor scoller pretend ignorance thairoff.

9 May 1627.

Visitouris of the Schoolles.

16 *May* 1627.

16 May 1627.

V^e merkis mortifeit to ane doctour in the grammer schoole.

The said day the prouest, baillies, and councell underwritten, thay ar to say Paull Menzies, prouest; Mr Dauid Rutherfuird, alderman; Gilbert Cullan, Mr Johne Mortimer, Mr Thomas Johnstoun, Johne Hay, baillies; Thomas Colinsoun, Robert Johnstoun, Henrie Forbes, George Riccard, Robert Alexander, Thomas Cargill, Dauid Adye, George Morisoun, Androw Meldrum, Andro Biruye, Thomas Robertsoun, cordiner, and William Ord, wricht, being convenit in the councelhous, the said Paull Menzeis, prouest, exhibit and delyuered reallie befoir thame in reddie down tauld money on the counsall tabile the somme of fyve hundreth merkes vsuall money of this realme: Quhilk somme ane nichtbour of this burgh (who obscuires his name), out of his zeall to the godlie and wertuous educatioune of the youth in the grammer scoole of this burgh, hes frielie gewin and mortified to be employed on bank be the prouest, baillies, and councell of this burgh for the tyme, to the vss efter following—viz., he destinattes and appoyntes the annualrent of the said fyve hundreth merkes to be gewin and bestowed yeirlie in all tyme cumming, to the doctour of the grammer schoole of this burghe as ane help to his prouisioun, prouyding the said doctour be chosen and placed be the prouest, baillies, and councell of this burgh for the tyme: Quhilk somme of fyve hundreth merkes wes instantlie delyuered to Robert Alexander, present thesaurer of this burgh, who grantes the receipt thairof, to be waired and employed to the vse forsaid and no utherwayes, and to be furtheummand to that effect perpetuallie in all tyme cumming, whairwpoun the said Paull Mengzeis askit act and instrumentes.

11 *August* 1627.

14 August 1627.
Anent the arryving of Spanye-ardis in Zetland.

The quhilk day the new and auld counccelles being convenit in the councell hous, upoun certan knouledge and aduertesment gevin to thame of the arryvall of fourtene Spanish shippes of warr in Zetland upoun the sext day of August instant, whair great numberes of sojoures are landet furth of the saides shippes, and waisting thes ylls with all crewalty, so that the inhabitantes so many as can have occasioun of shipping ar fleeing with thair wyffes and childrene for saiftie of thair lywes, in respect quhairof the saides prouest, baillies, and councell findes it expedient that all gude meanes be used lying in thair possibilitie that may resist these crewall enemyes in cace of thair cuming in thir boundes, referring the succes to the gude pleasour and prouidence of God, whome we besoik to direct all to his glorie, and to the comfort and saif gaird of this toune and countrie: And first of all be reasoun the cuming of the said naival concernes this haill kingdome, it is thocht meit that aduertesment be gevin thairof be a lettre from the prouest and baillies to the Lordis of his majesties most honourabill Privie councell, and thay petitioned to give spedie and tymous ordour for resisting the farder invasioun and incursioun of the said commoun enemye: As lykwayes it is thocht meit that lettres shall be direct to the Erle of Erroll, the Lord Forbes, and to the most speciall barrones of this shirrefdome, giveing notice to thame of the certantie of the landing of the said enemye in Zetland, and with all craveing thair ayd and assistance in cace of any assault of the said enemye, quhilk God forbid.

Item it is thoucht expedient that thair shall be a musture and wapinshaw of the haill inhabitantes of this burght fensible persones on Thursday nixt, the sextein of this instant, and thay to be chairget this day to that effect be the drum; ilk persone absent, or that shall not be sufficientlie armed, under the paine of fourtie pundis.

Item it is thoucht necessar that thair shall be a nichtlie watche of tuelff persones to begin this nicht, and that eurie man watche in proper persone, as he shall be charget under the pain of ten pundis, to be payed be ilk persone absent to the deane of gild unforgewin, and the watche to begin at Futtie quarter.

14 August 1627.
Anent the arryving of Spanyeardis in Zetland.

Item thair shall be four capitanes chosin, with leiutenentes, hand signeies, and serjandis, to comand the toune as the magistrates shall give thame direction, and to instruct the nichtboures to handle thair armes, and the saidis capitanes to be chosen be the provest, baillies, and councell.

Item that euerie nichtbour prouyd himselff with pulder and bullet.

Item that the mercheandes quha hes pulder to sell, be delt with be the magistrates to sell the same to ther nichtboures at a reasonable raitt, and novayes sufferit to exact exorbitant pryces be reasone of the present necessitie.

Item that euerie nichtbour of the toun shall promeis be his great aith, not to leave the toune in cace of invasioun be the enemye, bot to abyd still within the samen, and to follow thair magistrates and commanderes as occasioun shall offer, at thair best endevoires, for defence of thair lyives, thair wyffes, bairnes, and estates, so long as the magistrates keipes the toune.

Item that all keipares of ines, staibleres, and uthers inhabitantes quhasoeuer that receaues or ludges any straingeres, aduerteis the baillie of the quarter quhan any strainger hapnes to ludge with thame, or quhan any horses of strangeres ar stabled with any of the staibleres, under the pain of tuentie pundis, to be payed to the deane of gild be ilk persone failyeand heirin being *soluendo*: And in cace of thair inhabilitie to pay the wnlaw, to be banished the toune.

22 August 1627.

22 August 1627.
Two fyre bittis to be erected be the toun.

The quhilk day Mr Thomas Johnstoun, baillie Alexander Jaffray, and Mr Alexander Jaffray, and David Adye, ar appointed be the councell to go to the Hill of Brymmound, within the friedome of this burgh, and thair to mark and designe the most commodious pairt for setting up of ane fyir bitt to give notice to the countrie pople of the approtcheing of forau

22 August 1627.
Tuo fyre bittis to be erected be the toun.

enemeis, as lykwayes to considder quhat pairt about the toune is most fitting for ane uther fyir bitt, and best ansuerable and most conspicuous to give show and warning to the keipar of the fyir bitt on the said Hill of Brymmound, and ordaines the foirnamed persones to report thair diligence to the councell, that accordinglie ordour may be geivin for up-putting of the saidis fyir bittes; as also for interteaning and keiping tham upoun the tounes charges so long as necessitie shall requyr the same. Conforme to the quhilk directioun the saids commissioneres went to the said Hill of Brymmound, and thair designed and marked the most conspicuous pairt for up-putting ane fyir bitt thairupoun, and causit gadder and erect ane great cairne of stanes thairat, quhilkes thay causit to be buildet, prepaired, and maid fit for receaveing of the said fyir bitt; and siclyk thay declaired that the east gavill of the Chappell on the Castel hill is the most convenient pairt about the toune for setting up the first fyir bitt, and will give the best and cleirest demonstratioun to the wther fyir bitt on the said Hill of Brymmound. Quhilk report and aduyse being considderet be the councell, thay allow thairof and ordaines the same to be put in executioun accordinglie with all convenient diligence possible.

10 October 1627.
All doggis within the toun to be slayne.

10 *October* 1627.

The said day the prouest, baillies, and councell being credeblie informed that thair is great harme and skaith sustenit in the countrie, and in the auld toun, by the byitting of wod doggis; thairfoir thocht it expedient that all doggis, both litle and meikle, within this toune, shall be all slayne; and heirfoir ordaines intimatioun to be maid be the drwm throu the haill streittes of the toune, that all these that hes doggis caus fell thame within fourtie aucht houres efter the chairge, wnder the pain of twentie pundis, to be payed be ilk persoun contraveining, but favour, by and attour that the tua scurgeres ar appointed to fell all doggis that thay find on the streittes, but any blame or harme to be susteined be thame thairthrou.

13 *February* 1628.

The quhilk day anent the petitioun geuin in to the prouest, baillies, and counsall be Mr David Wedderburne, maister of the grammer scoole of this burghe, makand mentioun that, for the weill and benefite of his scollares, he had agreit with Andro Howat to instruct and learne thame to wreit, and to schaw thame some principles of arithmetik euerie day betwixt ten and tuelff in the foirnoone, conforme to the band geuin be the said Andro to that effect; quhairof he thocht gude to acquant thair worships of the conneall, and to crave thair approbatioun and consent thairto; quhilk band being opinlie red in counsall, thay allow thairof as being a mein to further the bairnes in the grammer scoole in thair wreiting, and thairfor ordaines the said band to be registrat in the tounes bookes, *ad futuram rei memoriam*, of the quhilk the tenour followes: "I, Andro Howat, burges of Aberdene, bindis and oblesses me be thir presentes to Mr David Wedderburne, maister of the grammer schoole of Aberdene, to teache the scollares of the said grammer schoole betwixt ten and tuelff houres, in wreiting and arithmetik, according to the said maister, his directioun, promiseing in the mein tyme, with Godis grace, to liue without scandall, imploying all possible diligence for the weill of the said scoole, as also faithfulnes to the maister and his doctoures whatsoeuer, in all pointes of deutie, and in speciallie to be rewled and governed in euerie point be the said maister, that concerneth, or shall concerne, my calling in that schoole. As for the reward, I will refer it to the discretioun of the parentes, and withall promiseth to serue the said maister David, the foir noone tyme dureing the tyme of his being maister in that scoole. Thir thinges I promes be the grace of God, vnder the pain of infamie, the yeir of God j^m sex hundreth tuentie aucht yeires, the sext day of Februar, befoir thir witnessis Alexander Gray and George Andersoun. *Sic subscribitur*, A. Howat, with my hand. George Andersoun, witnes; Alexander Gray, witness."

23 July 1628.

Fraser chosin ane of the doctouris of the grammer schoole.

23 *July* 1628.

The same day the provest, baillies, and councell considering that grammer scooles ar the seminaries both of kirk and policie, most necessar it is that thair be painful maisteres and instructeres planted in euerie scoole for the godlie and vertuous educatioun and teaching of the youth in pietie, gude letteris, and gude maneres; and with all considering that thair being onlie ane doctour in the grammer scoole of this burgh, vnder Mr David Wedderburne, present maister thairof, thay two ar not habill be thame selffis allane to discharge such exact ductie in teaching and instructing the youth in the said scoole as the exigence of that service requyres, and harwith haveand respect that a nichtbour of the toun (who obscuires his name) out of his zeale to the floorisheing of the said grammer scoole, hes gavin in to the councell of this burgh the somme of fyve hundreth merkis money, quhilk he hes mortified for euer, to be laid on bank, and the annuel rent thairof to be employed *pro tanto* as ane help for maintenance of ane vther doctour, to attend and instruct the youth in the said grammer schoole, thairfoir the saidis provest, baillies, and councell, findis it uerie expedient that thair shall be ane vther doctour conjoyned to be a fellow laborar with the maister and present doctour of the said scoole, for the better and more exact instruction and education of the youth being thairin for the tyme; and for this effect thay have maid nominatioun and election of Mr Alexander Fraser, sone to vmquhill Adame Fraser of Finzeauch, as ane young man qualefied for the chairge, and recommendit to thame be the principall of the college, and be the said Mr David Wedderburne; and for his painis and service thay give and grant, and be thir presentes gives and grantes to the said Mr Alexander, yeirlie, and ilk yeir during the will and plesour of the councell of this burgh allanerly, the somme of ane hundreth pundis money to be payed to him as follows, viz.,—ane hundreth merkis to be payed to him be the deane of gild of this burgh out of the accidentes of the deanrie of gild, and fiftie merkis be the tounis thesaurar as the annuel rent of the saidis fyve hundreth merkes, mortified as said is to that vse, to be payed at two vsuall termes of the yeir, Witsonday and Martimes in winter, be equal portiones, the first termes payment therof beginand at Martimes next to come, in this instant yeir of God, j^m six hundreth tuentie and aucht yeires; with the speciall condition that the said Mr Alexander tak no kynd of scolladge from any of the bairnes being within the said scoole, but that he content himself with the said stipend of ane hundreth pundis allanerlie, during the councellis pleasour, and that in full satisfactioun of all he can crave for his service in the said scoole during his abode within the same; and the said Mr Alexander being personallie present, acceptit the said charge in and vpon him, with the condition foirsaid, and gave his aith *de fideli administratione*.

23 July 1628.

Fraser chosin ane of the doctouris of the grammer schoole.

26 November 1628.

The quhilk day the provest, baillies, and counsell considering that the wark of repairing of the commoun calsies of this burghe is alredye begun, and that the said wark is greatlie hinderit be a number of choppis biggit and extendit on the kingis calsie outwith the gutter; and withall haveand respect that choppis aucht not to be tollerat, as being a deformitie to the kingis hie streites, and a diminesheing of the same; thairfoir statutes and ordaines quhair any choppis ar or salbe fund biggit in haill or in pairt outwith the commoun gutter, vpoun any pairt of the kingis hie street, that the samen salbe taken in againe within the gutter, sa that samekill of any chop as is outwith the gutter salbe takin doune and dimolishit, and na choppis to be biggit outwith the gutter in any tyme comeing, but prejudise to dimolishe the haill choppis quhair thair is any decreit or ordinance of counsall standand for that effect, and sic uther choppis as the awnares of houssis hes not warrand of counsall to big the same, and ordaines intimatioun to be maid heirof be the hand bell throw the haill streitis of the toun, chairgeing all nichtbouris and inhabitantes that hes choppis, or any pairt thairof outwith the commoun gutter, to tak

26 Nov. 1628.

Statute anent the demolisheing of choppis.

26 Nov.
1628.
Statute anent the demolisheing of choppis.

17 Dec.
1628.
Commissioun for apprehending Jesuittis seminarie and mess preistis, and excommunicat Papists.

doune and dimolishe the same, and to draw thame within the gutter, that the samen may be current and have passage, and that the calsies may be biggit and repairit in a compleit and ordorlie forme.

17 *December* 1628.

The said day, in presens of the proueest, baillies, and counsall, compeirit Mr Williame Guild, minister of the kirk of King Eduard, and Mr Alexander Ross, minister at the kirk of Inshe, commissionares, direct be the bishop and ministris of the diocie of Aberdeine to the lordis of his Majesties most honourabell Privie Counsall, anent the papistis in this diocie, and gave in and exhibite befoir the saidis proueest, baillies, and counsall, ane commissioun given be the saidis lordis for searching, seiking, taking, and apprehending of all Jesuittes, seminarie and mess preistis, and excommunicat papistis: Quhilk commissioun the proueest, baillies, and counsall ordaines to be registrat in the tounes bookes, *ad futuram rei memoriam*, quherof the tenor followes: "*Apud Halieruddhous, secundo die mensis Decembris anno domini millesimo sexcentesimo vigesimo octavo*, Forsameikill as the Lordis of Secret Counsall ar informed be the Commissionares frome the presbitries of Aberdeine and Murray, that thair is a very great and continewing grouth of poprie within the diocies of Aberdeine and Murray, and that thair insolencies, presumptionne, and pryd is come to that height that they dar opinlie avow thair professioun, to the offence of God and disgraice of his Maiesties governament; they have thair ordinarie conventicles and meitingis in sindrie pairtis of the cuntrie for the exerceise of thair fals religioun, and now at last sundrie Jesuites and seminarie preistis haveand come frome beyond sea to this kingdome, they have tane the boldnes to resort to the burghe of Aberdeine quher they have poysoned dyverss of the inhabitantis thairof with thair hereticall opinionees, and hes corrupted thame in thair obedience and alleageance, keiping thair meitingis within the said burghe upoun the Sondayes befoir noone in tyme of devyne service; quhair they and utheris popishlie affected within the said burghe hes the exerceise of thair religioun, and in all thair publict meitingis they vaunt of thair numberis credite and freyndship, disdaining and contemning the ordouris and censures of the kirk, and gives great occasioun of offence and scandall to the kirk and to the trew religioun presentlie professit within the kingdome: For remeid quhairof in tyme comeing the Lordis of Secret Consall hes given and grantit, and be the tenor heirof gives and grantis full powar and commissioun, expres bidding and chairge, to Patrik, Bishop of Aberdeine, and to the prouest, baillies, and ministeris of Aberdeine within thair awin boundis, and within the boundis of the auld toune of Aberdeine, conjunctlie and seuerallie, to pas, searche, seik, and tak all and sindrie Jesuittis, seminarye and mess preistis, and excommunicat papistis lyand at the horne, hauting, frequenting, and repairing within the said burghe of Aberdene and auld toune thairof, and to committ thame to ward within the tolbuthe of Aberdeine, and to deteane thame thairin upoun thair awin expensses, ay and quhill thay resaive directioun frome the saidis Lordis concerning thame, with power lykwayis to the saidis bishop, prouest, baillies, and ministeris to try and informe thame selflis, quhen, quher, and be whome thir unlauchfull conventicles and meitingis ar keipit and holdin within the said burght of Aberdeine and auld toune thairof; and accordinglie to searche, seik, tak, and apprehend all sic persones who keipis the said unlauchfull conventicles and meitingis, and the awnares and maisteris of housses quhair they ar keipit, and to committ and deteane thame in ward in maner foirsaid: And for the better executioun of this commissioun, with powar to thame to convocat the inhabitantes of the said burght and auld toun sa oft as neid beis in armes, and to mak oppin durris and use his Majesties keyis, and to dorse and performe all and ewerie uther thing quhilk may tend to the executioun of this commissioun, firme and stabill have and and for to haulde, all and quhatsumeuir thingis salbe laufullie done thairin; chairgeing and commanding heirby all and sindrie the inhabitantis within the said burght, and utheris his Majesties subicctis whome it may concerne to renerence, acknawledge, and obey, concur, fortilie, and assist the saidis

17 Dec. 1628.

Commissioun for apprehending Jesuittis seminaire and mess preistis, and excommunicat Papists.

17 Dec.
1628.
———
Commis-
sioun for
appre-
hending
Jesuittis
seminarie,
and mess
preistis,
and
excom-
municat
Papists.

commissionares conunetlie and seuerallie in all thingis tending to the executioun of this commissioun; and for this effect to put thameselffes in
armes and battens, and awate uponne the saidis commissionares. . . .
Chairgeing and commanding lykwayes the said Bishop of Aberdeine,
pronest, baillies, and ministeris thairof, that they and curie ane of thame
have a speciall cair and regaird to caus diligent attendence be given that
naine of thir Jesuittis, seminarie and mess priestis, nor na excommunicat
and rebellious traffecqueing papistis be sufferit to hawe resset or beild
within the said burght or auld tonne thairof, and that na unlauchfull con-
venticle nor meiting be keipit within the said bonndis . . . and suffer
not thair toune to be infectit nor sclanderit with the just imputatioun of
suche crymes.

18 Feb.
1629.
———
Ordinance
for bigg-
ing of
the Tol-
buith
steipill.

18 *February* 1629.

The samen day the pronest, baillies, and counsall thinkis it expedient
that the pricket of the Tolbuith steipill salbe biggit and perfyted in all
convenient diligence; and that aikin tymber salbe provydit and bocht to
that effect quhairevir the same maybe had, and ordaines the tounes
thesaurer to furneis moneyes for bying of the said tymber, quhilk salbe
allowit to him in his comptis.

1 April
1629.
———
Twa siluer
coupis
giuen be
Inglis for
serving at
the com-
munioun
tabillis.

1 *April* 1629.

The quhilk day in presens of the pronest, baillies, and counsell,
convenit in the counsellhous, compeirit Paull Inglis, merchand burges of
Aberdeine, and gave in and presentit unto thame twa siluer coupis of
tuantie ane vnces weyght, quhilk he frelie gives and dedecattis to St Nicolas
paroche kirk of this burghe for serveing at the Lordis tabill the tyme of
the ministratioun of the holy communioun in all tyme comeing: Quhilkis
two couppis the saidis pronest, baillies, and counsall accepted, render-
ing thankis to the giver for his religious and charatibill dispositioun in

giveng thairof for the use forsaid, and promising to mak the same furth command to that effect; lyke as instantlie they causit grave the said Paull Inglis name thairupoune, in memorie that he wes the giver thairof to the kirkis vse, and delyuerit the same to George Andersone, maister of kirk wark, to be keipit be him to the vse abov specificit allanerlie, wha grantis the ressett thairof, and promeissis to be comptabill, and mak the same furtheunand accordinglie.

marginal: 1 April 1629. Twa siluer coupis giuen be Inglis for serving at the communioun tabillis.

8 *April* 1629.

The prouest, baillies, and counsall, upoun certaine gude respectis and consideratiounes moveing thame, dischairges the maister of the grammer schoole of this burgh in giveing his scholares leive to the bent, or in exacting any bent silver frome thame in tyme comeing, be resone of the inconvenientis that fallis out frequentlie be the occasioun forsaid.

marginal: 8 April 1629. The maister of grammer schuill dischairget frome tacking of bent silver.

17 *July* 1629.

The said day, in presence of Paull Menzeis of Kyndmondye, prouest, and Patrick Leslie, baillie, compeired William Huntar, smith, frieman of the said burgh, and actit and oblegit him to work the yron work for the pryckit of the Tolbuith of this burghe, sufficientlie to the contentment of the magistrates and uther honest men comitted to the owersieing of the said wark, ay and quhill the wark be compleitlie endit and perfyted: For performance of the quhilk yron work of the said pryckit, to the contentment of the said magistrates, the said William fand James Mathewsone as cautioner for him, and to pay and delyuer to the said magistrates of the said burghe for the tyme the soume of ane hundreth pundes Scottes money, in caice he failzie if he doe in the contrar, and that by and attour the working of the said wark in maner forsaid; for quhaes travelles, and paines to be tane be the said William in the said bussines, the saidis magistrates of the said burghe obleissis thame and thair successouris to

marginal: 17 July 1629. Magistrates, Huntar. Anent the yron wark of the Tolbuith steiple.

17 July
1629.
—
Magistrates.
Huntair.
Anent the
yron wark
of the
Tolbuith
steiple.

pay to the said William, four merkes Scottes money for ilk steane of wrocht yron work of the sufficiencie forsaid, and the said William actit him to releiff his cautioner of the premisses, and of all that may follow thairon.

22 Sep.
1629.
—
Councell.
Wedderburne.

22 *September* 1629.

The said day the proueet, baillies, and conncell for dyuerse gude respectis and consideratiounes moveing thame, agries to give tuantie merkis quarterlie to Mr David Wedderburne, maister of the grammer schole, of augmentatioun to his stipend, of fourscoir pundis, to be payit to him be the tounes thesaurar during the counccllis plesour and his gude deserveing allanerlie, the first quarteris payment begynnand at hallowmes nixt.

28 Oct.
1629.
—
Visitouris
appointit
for the
schooles.

28 *October* 1629.

The samen day Mr Thomas Colinsone, Mr Alex. Jaffray, Thomas Nicolsone, Andro Meldrum, baillies; Mr Robert Farquhar, deane of gild, and Willeame Forbes, ar chosin visitouris of the schooles of this burghe till Michaelmes nexttocum, quha being present, acceptit the said chairge in and wponn thame, and promist to do thair diligence thairin, and to report the same to the counsall.

13 April
1630.
—
Solemnitie
to be usit
at the
buriall of
the Laird
of Drum.

13 *April* 1630.

The quhilk day the prouest, baillies, and counsall, understanding that Alexander Iruing of Drum, is to be buriet in Sanct Nicolas kirk of this burghe, the xxii. day of Apryll instant, to the quhilk buriall they ar earnestlie invitit be the present Laird of Drum, his sone: Thairfoir, and in consideratioune of the long continueit freyndschip betuixt this toune and the hous of Drum, as lyikwayis in regard that the said Alexander hes left in legacie ten thousand pundis to be mortifiet for mantenance of poore scholares to be brocht up in the grammer schole and college of this burghe, togidder with sex hundreth merkis to the edifice of our kirk, and four hundreth merkis to the tounes hospitall, the counsall findis it expedient that the toune sall honor the buriall of the said Laird of Drum efter the best forme they can; and for this effect it is appointit that the baillies ewerie ane within thair awin quarter, sall inroll sa mony of the inhabitantis for caryeing of pickis and muskattis to accompanye thair magistrattis at the said buriall, lykeas they appoint the tounes great ordinance to be all shott in significatioune of the tounes love and respect caried to the defunct and hous of Drum.

15 April 1630.
Solemnitie to be usit at the buriall of the Laird of Drum.

26 May 1630.

The samen day the provest, baillies, and counsall, thay ar to say Paull Mengzeis of Kynmundie, provest, Thomas Colinsone, Mr Alex. Jaffray, Thomas Nicolsone, Andro Meldrum, baillies; Mr Dauid Rutherfuird, Gilbert Mengzeis of Petfoddellis, Thomas Crombye of Kemnay, Mr Robert Farquhar, deane of gild, Robert Skeyne, thesaurer, John Leslie, Andro Howysonne, and Alexander Duff, findis it expedient that thair be a loft biggit in the south yle of the auld kirk, and at the south end of the said yle, abone the tailzeouris dask, for the principall, regentis, and studentis in the college of this burghe, in respect they find that pairt to be most commodious for heiring, and most convenient for the college, the entrie quhairof they ordane to be biggit outwith the kirk anent the pairt forsaid, and appointis Mr Robert Farquhar, deane of gild, and George Andersone, maister of kirkwark, to be maisteris of wark to the bigging of the said loft, and the expenssis and chairges in bigging thairof to be payit with the kirk moneyis, and quhat salbe debursit thairon, ordanes the same to be allowit in the kirk comptis.

26 May 1630.
Ordinance for bigging a loft in the auld kirk for the College.

Eodem die.

The samen day the provest, baillies, and counsell, considering that the sacristar and keipar of the paroche kirk of this burgh hes beine in vse in tymes bygane to resaive payment of his fie of fourtie punndis from the

Eodem die.
Ordinance to the maister of kirk wark for payment of the sacristares stipend.

Eodem die.
Ordinance to the maister of kirk wark for payment of the sacristares stipend.

collectour to the kirk sessioune out of the moneyis destinat for the poore, whilk they find nocht agrieable with resone that the poore sould be anyway defraudit of thair dew, and thairfoir sould be payit be the maister of kirk wark out of the kirk moneyis, lykeas for that effect they ordane George Andersone, present maister of kirk wark, to pay to Thomas Cowye, secraster, fourtie pundis money for his fie, of the Martimes and Witsonday termes last bypast, and siclyke ordanes the maister of kirk wark and his successouris to pay the said fourtie pundis yeirlie in tyme comeing to the said Thomas and his successouris, sacristares, and keipares of the kirk for the tyme, at Witsondey and Mertimes in wynter, be equall portiounes, whilk salbe allowit to him in his comptis.

4 June 1630.
Solemnitie to be usit for the Queenes delyverie of a yong sone.

4 *June* 1630.

The said day the provest, baillies, and counsall having this morning received a letter frome the Lordis of his Majesties most honourabell Privie Councell, mackand mentioune that they have laitlie resauit advertcisment of the Queenes Majestie hir most happie and comfortable delyverie of a sone, to the exceiding great blissing of this natioune, for the which, as it becometh gude subiectis to expres thair joy in most solemne maner, so they thocht gude to adverteis this burghe thairof, to the intent they may give ordour and directionne for using a solemnitie within the same, in suche ample and full maner as at any tyme heirtofoir they hawe beine accustumed, as at mair lenth wes conteinit in the said letter, daitit at Halieruidhous, the secund day of Junii instant, qubilk being red in counsall, they all gave praise to God for suche joyfull newis, and ordainit the samen to be presentlie published and divulgat to all the inhabitantis of this burghe, that they may give praise to God for these gude tydingis; and for this effect ordaines the toune to be warnit be sound of trumpet at the mercat croce, and be the drum passand throw the haill streittes of the toune, to assemble thameselffis this efternoone in thair pariohe kirk, and thair to give most humble and hartie thankis to God for hir Majesties happie delyuerie of a sone; and efter ending of sermone, ordaines bonefyires to be put on throw all the streittes of the toune, the haill bellis to ring, the croce to be deckit and hung, a taiffill to be coverit thairat, twa peice of wyne, ane quhyit and the uther clairat, to be run thairat, and given to all that pleasses call for the same, the sugar and spyce to be brocht thither in great abundance, a number of glasses to be cassin, the tounes haill great ordinance to be shott, and all the youthes of the toune to tak thair muskattis and accompanye thair magistrattis throw the streittes of the toune in singing psalmes and praising God; thairefter to pas the tyme in shuitting thair muskattis all the nicht ower at thair plesour, and all godlie merriness and pastyme usit that may expres the joy and gladnes of the hartis of the people: And ordaines the deane of gild and thesaurer to furnishe the pulder, wyne, suggar, and glasses to the crowd forsaid, as is above devysit, and the expensses to be debursit thairon the counsall ordaines to be allowit to thame in thair comptis.

4 June 1630.
Solemnitie to be usit for the Queenes delyuerie of a yong sone.

9 *June* 1630.

The samen day the prouest, baillies, and counsall thinkis it expedient that ane commissioun be procured frome the Lordis of his Majesties most honourabell Privie Counsell to the Shireff of Aberdeine and his deputes, prouest, and baillies of Aberdeine, for apprehending of all these wemen that wer given up and delaited be Marioun Hardie, as witches, and ordaines the said Marioun Hardie's depositioun thairanent to be drawin up, and to be subscrivit be the Bishop of Aberdeine, and be the magistrattis and ministeris of this burghe, for the better procuiring of the said commissioun, and the deane of gild to deburse the chairges thairon, quhilk salbe allowit in his comptis.

9 June 1630.
Anent apprehending of witches.

14 *July* 1630.

The said day the prouest, baillies, and counsall ordaines the somme of fourtie pundis to be given to Mr Dauid Wedderburne, maister of the

14 July 1630.
Anent the new grammer of Mr Alex. Hume.

14 July
1630.
——
Anent the
new gram-
mer of Mr
Alex.
Hume.

Grammer schole, for making his chairges to Edinburgh, being chairgeit to compeir befor the Lordis of Privie Counsall, anent the new grammer set out be Mr Alexander Hume, quhilk somne they ordaine to be peyit to the said Mr Dauid, be Robert Skeine, thesaurer, and the same to be allowit to him in his comptis.

28 July
1630.
——
Chalmer
admittit
doctour
of the
grammer
schoole in
place of
Fraser.

28 July 1630.

The said day the prouest, baillies, and councell considering that Mr Alex. Fraser, ane of the doctouris of the grammer schole of this burghe, hes demittet the place in thair handis, be resone of his resolutioun to employ his studies elsquhair, and that Mr Thomas Chalmer, sone to vmquhill Mr Thomas Chalmer, burges of the said burghe, a tounes bairne, is a meit and qualefiet youthe fitt for supplie of the said roume, thairfoir they have nominat and electit, and be thir presentes nominatis and electis the said Mr Thomas Chalmer to be ane of the doctouris of the said grammer schoole in place of the said Mr Alexander Fraser, and for his paynes and travellis they give and grant to the said Mr Thomas, yearlie, and ilk yeir during the will and plesour of the counsall allanerlie, the soume of ane hundreth pundis of stipend, to be payit to him as followes, viz.,—the soume of ane hundreth merkis be the deane of gild out of the accidentis of the deanrie of gild, and fyftie merkis be the tounes thesaurar for the annual rent of fyve hundreth merkis mortifiet be a nichtbour of the toune, as a supplie of the provisioun appointit for the second doctour of the said schole; and that at twa vsuall termes of the yeir, Witsunday, and Martimes in winter, be equall portiones, the first termes payment thairof begynand at Martimes nixt, j^m vi^c and threttie yeiris instant, with this speciall conditioune, that the said Mr Thomas tak no kynd of scolladge from any bairnes within the said schole, but that he content him selff with the said stipend of ane hundreth pundis during the counsallis plesour allanerlie, in satisfactioune of all that he can crave for his service in the said schole, sa lang as he abydes within the samen; and the said Mr Thomas being personallie present, acceptit the said chairge in and upoun him, with the conditioun forsaid.

28 July 1630.

21 *October* 1630.

Chalmer admittit doctour of the grammer schoole in place of Fraser.

The quhilk day the haill gild brethrein of this burghe being warnit to this day be the hand bell, and conveinand for the maist pairt within the Tolbuith, it wes exponit to thame be Robert Alexander, deane of gild, that the toune of Edinburghe had latlie directit missive to this burghe, desyrand ane commissioner to meit with the burrowes at Edinburghe, upoun the tuantie aucht day of October instant, tutcheing the plantatioun of a bushe fisheing, vrgeit be the kingis maiestie, lykeas conforme thairto the counsall had alreadie nominat Maister Vedast Lowsone, commissionar for this burghe, for keiping of the said Conventionne; and becaus the mater of the said fisheing concernis the said gild brethreine in particular, and that the said toune of Edinburghe had directit heir certain articles and overtures to be advyseit and answerit to be the said commissionar, at the said meiting the said deane of gild causit the samen articles to be publictlie red in presens of the said gild brethrein, whilkis articles and answeris maid thairto ar heirin insert as followes, viz.,—First, gif our associatioun with England be expedient. It wes refuisit. Item, gif the Englishe, obeying the lawes of the countrie, may be sufferit to plant in ane pairt of the Yles: it wes refuisit vnto the tyme thair be ane vnioun, becaus the burrowes will undertak the fisheing be thame selflis, and it is onlie proper to thame be thair liberties.

21 Oct. 1630.

The Gild brethrenis answer and adryse concerning the bushe fisheing.

Item, the burrowis vndertaking the fisheing, gif it be expedient that the nobilitie and gentrie be admittet to stok with thame: answerit, that they will be content to admitt thair stoking, with conditioun that thay have not libertie to import any commodities from forrane cuntries, except so muche as may serve for the furniture of thair awin houssis allanerlie.

Item, gif thay salbe admittit, how far thair stok salbe adventurit in exporting and importing, and wpoun quhat conditioun thay salbe admittet, and gif thay salbe refuisit, gif the burrowes will undertak it allane?

21 Oct.
1630.
—
The Gild brethrenis answer and adryse concerning the Bushe fisheing.

And if the burrowes condiscend to vndertak it, in quhat maner, if as thay vse it presantlie be burgessis at thair pleasour, or in ane companye? For answer, the gild brethreine agries that the burrowes vndertak the fisheing be thame selfis allane, provyding it be done be the burgessis of everie burghe at thair plesure, and nawayes to be done be companyes.

1 *December* 1630.

1 Dec.
1630.
Ordinance to the thesaurer in favour of Wedderburne.

The said day the proue st, baillies, and counsell haveand consideratioun that the new grammer laitlie reformed be Mr David Wedderburne, maister of the grammer schuile of this burghe, can nather be printit nor publishit for the vse of yong scholares, whome the same concernis, vnto the tyme the same resaive approbatioune from the Lordis of Counsall: thairfoir they have thocht meit and expedient that the said Mr David address himself with the said wark to Edinburgh, in all convenient diligence for procuring the saidis Lordis thair approbatioun thairto, and ordaines the somme of ane hundreth pundis money to be delaursit to him be the tounes thesaurer for making of his expenssis in the said erand.

1 *December* 1630.

1 Dec.
1630.
XI lib of fie granted to Mailing for rowling the tounes clokes.

The counsall grantis fourtie pundis of fee yeirlie to Robert Mailing, for his paynes in rowling of the tounes thrie clokes to witt, the kirk clok, Gray Frier clok, kirk and Tollmith clokes, and ordaines the tounes thesaurer to answer him of tuantie merkis, and the Mr of kirk wark of fourtie merkis yeirlie, in compleit payment of the said soume during his service, at tua vsuall termes in the yeir, Witsonday and Martimes in wynter, be equall portiounes, begynnand the first termes payment at Martimes last, and so furth yeirlie thairefter, ay and quhill he be dischargit be the counsall.

9 *March* 1631.

Ordinance of Counsall in favouris of the Bedallis of the Townes hospitale.

The said day the provost, baillies, new and auld conncellis, haveand consideratioune that the hospitall of this burghe, quhilk wes fundit of auld in the yeares of God 1459, be vmquhill Mr John Clatt, channon of Aberdeine, who in his tyme fundit the hous quhilk is the hospitall, togidder with ane annuall rent of four pundis money out of Mondynes, within the Schyrreffdome of Kincardyn, and some Ruiddis in the toun of Kintoir, for mantenance of ane cheplane to serve in the said hospitall, is now of laite, within these thrie yeiris bygane, not onlie repaired and enlarged in the edifice thairof, both in lenth and hight, and maid meikill more commodious and casefull for Bedallis then it wes abefoir; bot lyekwayis thair is mortifiet and given thairwnto be the liberalitie and cheritie of gild burgessis of this burgh, dyverse sommes of money, quhilk now be the cairful owersicht and manageing of the magistrattis and conncell of this burghe for the tyme, is incressed and come to suche grouthe, that the annuall rent thairof will intertaine some fyve or sex honest decayed brethrein of gild of this burghe, in meait and clothcing eftir a decent and comelie forme; and since, praised be God, the rent of the mortifiet moneyis to the said hospitall is growin to suche perfectionne be the liberalitie and charitie of merchandis, gild burgessis of this burghe, thay find that nane sould injoy that benefite, nor be admittit, nor plaiced in the said hospitall, except onlie decayit brethren of gild of this burghe; as lyekwayes they find that these quha ar alredye admittit, and suche as salbe admittit in the said hospitall heirefter, sould have competent provisioun and allowance for thair honest intertainement in meait and clothing in all tyme comeing, that thay be not burdinable nor chairgeabill to any; and for this effect, haveand convenit dyverse of the gild brethrein of this burghe, wha had friclie given and mortifiet of thair meanes to the said hospitall, eftir mature deliberatioune and advysement, the saidis new and auld conncellis be advyse foirsaid, appointis, ordanes, and allowes to everie bedall within the said

9 March 1631.

Ordinance of Counsall in favouris of the Bedallis of the Tounes hospitale.

hospitall alredie admittit, and that sallhappin to be admittit within the samen heirefter be the magistrattis and councell of this burghe for the tyme, the soume of ane hundreth pundis Scottis money yeirlie, for thair maintenance and provisioun, to be payit to everie ane of thame monthlie, out of the rediest of the rentis of the said hospitall be the maister thairof for the tyme, extending ilk month to the soume of aucht pundis sex schillingis aucht pennyes, the first monethis peyment begynand wpon the first day of Apryill nixt to cum, and so furth to be payit proportionallie ilk moneth in all tyme comeing; as lyikwayis by and attour thair ordinar allowance forsaid for thair alimentar chairges, the saidis new and auld counsallis appoints and ordanes that thair salbe gownes, sarkis, hoise, and shoes furneist to everie ane of the saidis bedallis as thair necessitie sall requyre, be the sicht and directioun of the counsall of this burghe for the tyme: And in lyik maner, thay declair and ordane that the cullour of thair gownes and habitt salbe sad tannis in all tyme comeing: And appoints and ordanes twa hundreth towns loadis of peites to be yeirlie given and laid in to thame be the maister of the said hospitall for the tyme: Lykeas thay appoint Paull Inglis, present maister of hospital, to give and furnishe to thame sex plaites, sex trinsheouris, twa broteclothes, sex servioles, twa pottes, twa pannes, ane speit, ane pair of rax, ane cruik and tanges, and ane laiddill: As also to furnishe and give gownes and clothes to the thrie present bedallis alredie enterit in the said hospitall—To witt, James Leslie, Willeame Thomesone, and Robert Stewart, all gild burgessis of this burghe, of sad tannis, Inglis cloth or Scoths clothe, as he may most commodiouslie have the same, and quhat the said maister of hospitall debursis thairwpoune, is ordanit to be allowit to him in his comptis: With speciall alwayes conditioun and provisioun, that the saidis bedallis and thair successoris wha sallhappin to be plaiced and admittit within the said hospitall at any tyme heirefter, salbe all singill persones wanting wyiffes, and that thay keep thair ordinarie dyet at bed and buird within the samen hospitall, and onnawayes be fund vaiging on the streites, nor drinking in ailhousses nor tavernes, nather yet passing out of the towne to landward or elsquhair, without licience of the magistrattis of the said burghe for the tyme had and obtenit thairto: And lyikwayes, that everie morning and evening thay convene alltogidder in thair oratour, and have thair ordinar publict prayeris for the King, the Kirk, the Toune of Aberdeine, and all thair benefactouris, efter reiding of ane chaptour in the Bybill ilk morning and evening: And that they, and euerie ane of thame be present at the sermones and prayeris appointit for thame: And keip and observe the injunctiones foirsaidis, and all other injunctiounes to be set downe to thame heirefter, be the councell of this burghe for the tyme, vnder the paine of deprivatioune.

9 March 1631.
Ordinance of Counsall in fauouris of the Bedallis of the Tounes hospitale.

30 *March* 1631.

The quhilk day the prouest, baillies, and conncell gives and grantis to Mr David Wedderburne, maister of thair grammer schole, the somme of ane hundreth merkis money to help to defray the greit chairges quhairin he hes bein drawin be his long attendance in Edinburgh, Sanctandrews, and Glasgow, in the purches and obteining of the conncel and clergies of this kingdome, thair approbatioun and allowance to his new reformed grammer, to be payit to him be Alex. Stewart, thesaurer, quhilk somme they ordane to be allowit to the said thesaurer in his comptis.

30 March 1631.
Ordinance to the Thesaurer in favoris of Wedderburne.

4 *May* 1631.

The said day it is statute and ordainit be resone of the great insolencie of scholares at nicht-walkis, some attending thair parentis, and wtheris the maister of the musick scholl, in a greater number then may sufficientlie serve at sic occasiounes; that na scholar within this burghe salbe sufferit to repair to any lyik or nicht walk in tyme comeing, except onlie four scholares of the musik schole, whan the maister himsellf is desyrit: And ordaines intimatioun heirof to be maid to Patrick Dauidsone, maister of the said musick schole, to the effect he pretend no ignorance,

4 May 1631.
Ordinance againis scholares repairing to lyik walkis.

4 May 1631.
Ordinance againis scholares repairing to lyik walkis

with certificatioun gif he contraveine this present ordinance, to be dischargit frome any lyikwalk heireftir himselff.

22 June 1631.

22 June 1631.
Anent the plantatioune of the kirk of Futtie.

The said day in presens of the provost, baillies, and councell, compeirit Mr Robert Barone, ane of the ordinar ministeris of this burghe, and declairit that certain weill affected nichtbouris of the toune had grantit to a voluntarie contributionne of fyve thousand and four hundreth merkis, Scottis money, or thairabout, whilk wes devysit be thame to be mortifiet and employit on annuallrent in all tyme comeing, for provisioun of ane minister to the kirk of Futtie, desyrand thairfoir that thair wisdomes wald be pleased to tak the necessitie of that plantatioune to thair serious consideratioune, and to deliberat in dew tyme anent the finding out of a qualifiet persone to fill the roume, sieing the moneyis grantit ar to be payit at Martimes nixt; whairanent the saids provost, baillies, and councell advysing, and being cairfull (in respect of the said mortificatioun, and necessitie of the poore people of Futtie, whome that mater doeth chieflie concerne) to have the roume plantit with all convenient diligence, thairfoir they thocht meit and expedient to deall with Mr Alexander Ross, minister at Inshe, a tounes bairne, for undertaking of the chairge of the ministrie at the said kirk of Futtie; and for that effect instantlie nominat Mr Vedast Lowsone, baillie, to deall with the said Mr Alexander thairanent, in the tounes name, and to report his diligence to the counsall this day aucht dayis.

11 Sept. 1631.
Ordinance to the Thesaurer.

11 *September* 1631.

The councell ordaines the thesaurer to pay to George Andersone twentie-fyve pundis ane sh., debursit be him on the wark of the tolbuith steipell, whilk salbe allowit to the said thesaurer in the comptis.

14th *September* 1631.

The said day in presens of the proueist, baillies, and counsall, compeirit personallie Gilbert Hervye, elder, and gave in ane great bybill to serve for the use of the beddallis in all tyme comeing; Lykeas the same wes instantlie delyuerit to Paull Inglis, maister of St Thomas Hospitall to that effect; and the said Paull ordainit to caus chengzie the same to the Latrone of the Oratorie of the said hospitall.

A Bybill given be Henry to the hospitall.

5 *October* 1631.

Item, it is statute and ordanit that thair salbe no kynd of fleshe or vivares bocht or sauld on the mercat day, or any mercat or arles given thairwpon in tyme comeing, till aucht houris in the morning at the soonest, neither sall it be lesum to any flesher, frie or unfrie, to cutt and carve thair beiff and muttone on the shulderis and flankis as vsuallie hes beine heirtofoir, nor yit to spuilzie the caireages of beiff or muttone in the craig, spar rib, or any wther pairt quhatsumeuer, under the payne of fourtie shillingis, to be exacted of the contraveinar for the first fault, and confiscatioun of the beiff and muttoun so spuilziet or carved, for the second fault, to the vse of the tounes hospitall; and that na mercat be maid on meill and malt befoir tuelff houris in the day at soonest, according to the auld statutes maid thairanent of befoir.

Statute anent the begining of the mercattis.

Eodem die.

Item, the proueist, baillies, and counsall ratifies and approves the statutes and ordinances maid be thair predecessouris, magistrattis, and counsall of this burghe, againis blasphemares of Goddis holie name, prophaneris and brakeris of the Lordis Sabbothe, with the statutes maid againis cowperis, websteris, cordoneris, and purchessares of suspensiounes and advocatiounes againis the magistrattis and counsall of the

Eodem die. Ratificatioune of the auld statutes.

Eodem die.
Ratification of the auld statutes.

same burghe: ressettaris of strangeris and settaris of houssis to thame without licience of the magistrattis, and anent the keiping of the loche and burne from filthe and polutionne; againis keiparos and gaddereris of middingis on the commoun streites; againis all abstracteris of cornes from the tounes commoun mylnes: anent officiares for wearing daylie thair suirdis and halbertis, and all and sindrie wther actis, constitutiounes, and ordinances quhatsumever maid be thair predicessouris for observeing gude rewle and ordour within this burghe, to be keipit and observit be the nichtbouris and inhabitantis of the samen efter the forme and tenour thairof in all poyntis, vnder the paines conteinit in the saidis actis to be wpliftit of the contraveinares, but favour.

12 October 1631.
Ordinance for bigging of a fleshous.

12 October 1631.

The said day the prouest, baillies, and counsall thinkes it meit and expedient for the case of the fleshouris, friemen of this burghe, and advancement of the tounes commoun gude, that a fleshous salbe biggit in all convenient deligence, at the back of the tounes new hous, on the north syid of the castell gett, and nominatis George Moresone, deane of gild, maister of wark to the bigging therof, wha is ordainit to provyd materiallis therto, and the expenssis to be debursit be him thairwpon, to be allowit to the said deane of gild in his comptis.

Eodem die.
Statute againis fleshouris.

Eodem die.

The samen day the prouest, baillies, and counsall hes statute and ordanit, that na fleshour within this burghe, shall slay ony nolt, sheip, nor wther gudes, nor bestiall, wpoun the kingis hie streites, nor without housses, in tyme comeing, vnder the payne of fourtie shillingis, to be peyit be the contraveinar to the deane of gild, *toties quoties*, as they sal happin to failzie thairin.

2 November 1631.

The said day the proucst, baillies, and counsall ordanes Johnne Leslie, thesaurar, to deburse to Mr James Rait, minister at Marickirk, the soume of ane hundreth merkis Scottis money quhilk wes grantit to him abefoir be act of counsall of the dait, the sex day of November 1627, of help to the bigging of the brig of Luther, and reparatioun of the north-watter brig, be resine the wark is neir perfytit alredy.

2 Nov. 1631.
Ordinance to the Thesaurer.

21 December 1631.

The proucst, baillies, and counsall ordanes George Moresoun, deane of gild, to visite the vaultis of the wardhous, and to caus help, and repair thame in all convenient diligence, the expenssis quhairof salbe allowit to the said deane of gild in his comptis.

21 Dec. 1631.
Ordinance to the Deane of Gild.

21 December 1631.

The said day the counccll, considdering the great paynes takin be Robert Melvill in rewling of the tounes three clokis, towitt the kirk, gray frier, and tollmith clockis, grantis to him tuantic merkis of augmentatioun to his ordinarie stipend of fourtie lib, mackand now in all fourscoir merkis money, thairof feftie merkis to be payit to him be the maister of kirkwark for the twa kirk clokis, and tuantic pundis be the tounes thesaurer for the tollmith clok yeirlie, at Witsonday and Martimes in winter, be equall portiounes, the first termes peyment begynnand at Martimes last bypast.

21 Dec. 1631.
Ordinance in favores, of Melvill.

25 January 1632.

The said day the proucst, baillies, and counsall ordanis Mr Vedast Lowsone, maister of kirkwark, to putt wp commodious scittis and shelflis

25 Jan. 1632.
Ordinance to the maister of kirk wark.

25 Jan. 1632.

Ordinance to the maister of kirk wark.

in the Colledge Librarie for the vse of the bookes and studentis thairin; and appointes the haill bookes within the kirk librarie to be transportit to the said librarie within the Colledge, thairin to remaine in all tyme comeing: And for this effect the saidis bookes to be put in inventar and catalogue, and delyverit accordinglie to the bibliothecar be the said Mr Vedast Lowsone, and quhat expenssis he debursis in putting wp of the saidis seattis and shelflis, the counsall ordanis to be allowit to him in his comptis.

8 February 1632.

Ordinance for ringing of bellis at nyne houris at evin, and fyne houris in the morning.

8 *February* 1632.

The said day the provest, baillies, and counsall ordanis the tounes twa drummeris to go throw the haill streites of this burghe togidder daylie, heirefter at four houris in the morning, and aught houris at nicht; and Johne Pollak, as the yonger man, is ordanit to pas to Andro Inglis hous at all occasiounes for keiping the saidis dyetis: Lykeas they appoint ane of the great bellis in the kirk steipill, with the commoun bell, and the bell of the gray frier kirk, to be rung euerie day in tyme comeing, the spaice of halff ane hour, at fyve houris in the morning, and nyne houris at ewin.

Eodem die.

Contract betwixt the Towne of Aberdein and Mr Robert Donny, Bibliothecar.

Eodem die.

The quhilk day the provest, baillies, and counsall admittis and receaves Mr Robert Donnye, bibliothecar of the tounis librarie within the colledge of this burgh, during all the dayis of his lyiftym, wpoun the conditiounes specifiet in the contract underwritten, past betwixt the counsall and him thairanent : Quhilk contract, be mutuall consent of both the pairties, is ordanit to be registrat in the tounes bookes *ad futuram rei memoriam*, and to the effect executioun may be direct thairin, as neid beis in maner specifiet thairintill, off the quhilk contract the tennour followes:—" At Aberdeine, the aucht day of Februar, the yeir of God, j^m

sex hundreth threttie twa yeiris, It is appointit and agriet betwixt the *Eodem die.*
richt honorabill Paull Mengzies of Kynmundie, provest of the burghe of Contract
Aberdeine, Thomas Colinsone, Mr Alexander Jaffray, Andro Meldrum, betwixt
George Johnstoun, baillies of the said burgh, George Moresone, dean of the Towne
gild, and Johne Leslie, thesaurar of the same burghe, for thame selfflis, be of Aberdeine and
vertew of thair generall offices, and in name and behalff of the councell Mr Robert
and communitie of the said burghe on the ane pairt, and Mr Robert Douny,
Dounye, sone lawfull to vmquhill Williame Dounye in Banchorie, on the Bibliothecar.
wther pairt, in forme, substance, and effect efter following—that is to
say, Forsameikill as vmquhill Thomas Reid, Esquire, Secretar for the
Latine tongue to our late Soverane, King James of blessed memorie, for
the love he caryed to the said toune of Aberdeine, and wishing the new
colledge and scholes thairof sould florishe, be his letter will and testament, left in legacie to the said toune of Aberdeine his whole librarie of
bookes, quhilkis bookes he ordanit to be put in the bibliothek of the said
new colledge, thairin to remaine in all tyme comeing: And withall the
said vmquhill Thomas, haveand consideratioun that ane bibliothecar wes
requyrit in suche a citie, wha sould be comptabill for the saidis bookes to
the consall and clergie of the said toune and colledge, according to the
catalogues of his resset, and that thair could be nane had without a
meanes quhairby to leive, thairfoir he left in legacie the somme of sex
thousand merkis Scottis money, as a patrimonie be the quhilk the bibliothecar of the said bibliothek micht leive, whilk somme he ordanit to be
imployit wpoun annuallrent be the provest, baillies, and counsall of the
said burgh of Aberdeine, with advyse of Mr Robert and Mr Adame Reidis,
his brether german, ay and while the annuallrent thairof sould accress
with the stok to suche proportionne as the samen micht by so meikle
gude land lyand within the said burghe or schirrefdome of Aberdeine, as
sould pay yeirlie of siluer rent the somme of sex hundreth merkis money
foirsaid, whilk somme of sex hundreth merkis as the yeirlie rent and
dewtie of the said land, be destinat, mortifeit, and appointit to be given
for mantenance of a bibliothecar and keipar of the said bibliothek in all

Eodem die.
Contract betwixt the Towne of Aberdein and Mr Robert Donny, Bibliothecar.

aiges to come; lykeas he nominat and designit the said Mr Robert Donnye, his sister sone, to the said office, and to the rent and benefite thairof induring his lyftyme, whome he appointit to hold the doore of the said bibliothek opin and patent four dayis in the weik, to the effect the schollares and clergie of the said burghe of Aberdeine micht haue the vse of the saidis bookes within the samen; lykeas also he nominat and appointit the prouest, baillies, and counsall of the said burghe of Aberdeine for the tyme, as haueing the cair and chairge of the manageing of the saidis moneyis, and wairing of the samen wpon the bying of land, to be perpetuall patrones of the said bibliothecar, and to haue the full power of his nominatioun and admissioun in all tyme comeing, as the said vmquhill Thomas, his letterwill and testament, daited at London, the nynteine day of May, the yeir of God, j^m sex hundreth tuantie-four yeris, at lenth proportis, conforme quhairwnto the prouest, baillies, and counsall of the said burghe for the tyme, receaved from the executouris of the said vmquhill Thomas Reid, his whole librarie of bookes, according to the catalogue thairof, quhilkis were all impute be thame in the librarie of the said colledge, and ar yet all extant within the samen, in als gude caice as they wer the tyme of thair ressett and intromissioun thairwith; lykeas also they resaived frome the saidis executouris at the feast of Martimes, in the yeir of God j^m sex hundreth tuantie-fyve yeiris, the soume of thrie thousand four hundreth thretteine pundis twa shillinges wsuall Scottis money, in satisfactionne of the said legasie of sex thowsand merkis, becaus the remanent thairof wes exhausted, pairtlie for quote and confirmatioune, and pairtlie evicted frome the saidis executoris, sen the deceas of the said vmquhill Thomas, for vnknowin debtis not conteinit in his testament: Quhilk soume of thrie thowsand four hundreth thretteinn pundis twa shillingis, be the cairfull manageing of the prouest, baillies, and counsall of the said burgh for the tyme, hes accressed with the annuallrentis thairof, sen the tyme foirsaid of the said tonne of Aberdeine thair intromissioun with the samen, to the soume of sex thousand pundis money foirsaid, whairwith they entend, God willing, how sone thay can

find convenient occasioune, to by so muche land as will extend to sex
hundreth merkis money in yeirlie rent, or sex chalderis of victuall, to be a
constant provisioun and stipend to the said bibliothecar in all tyme comeing, for implement of the will of the defunct; and, in the mid tyme, till
the said occasioune of bying some peice of land may be had, and to the
intent that the saidis schollares and clergie of the said toune and colledge
be not longer frustrat of the wse and benefite of the saidis buikis, the
saidis provest, baillies, and counsall hes admittit and resauit, and be
thir presentis admittis and resaives the said Mr Robert Dounye bibliothecar of the said librarie during all the dayis of his lyiftyme, wha presentlie hes acceptit, and be thir presentis acceptis the said chairge and
office in and wpoun him, wpoun the conditiounes underwrittin—that is to
say, the said Mr Robert grantis him to have resaved the day and dait
heirof from the saidis provest, baillies, and counsall, the haill buikis within
the said librarie, whilkis apperteinit to the said vmquhill Thomas Reid,
Esquyer, with the haill bookes left to the said colledge be vmquhill Mr
Duncan Liddell, doctor in phisick, togidder also with all wther buikis
within the said librarie, giuen thairwnto be quhatsumener persone or persones at any tyme bygaine, conforme to the severale catalogues thairof
subscryveit be the said Mr Robert; lykeas the said Mr Robert bindis
and obleissis him, his airis, executouris, assignayis, and successouris
quhatsumener, to keip the saidis haill bookis, and to mak thame extant
and furthcummand within the said librarie, with all wther bookis that
happinis to be given and put within the said librarie thairefter, during
the said Mr Robert hes lyiftyme, conforme to the catalogues maid and to
be maid thairwponne; and lyikwayes the said Mr Robert, conforme to
the will of the fundater, sall hold the doore of the librarie patent and
opin four dayes of the week the whole yeir, alsweill in tyme of vacance as
at other tymes, to witt, Monday, Wedinsday, Freday, and Saturday,
euerie ane of these dayes in sommer, frome sevin houris till allevin afoirnoone, and frome twa till five in the eftirnoone; and in the winter tyme,
frome nyne till twelff in the afoirnoone, and frome twa till four houris in

Eodem die.

Contract
betwixt
the Towne
of Aber-
dein and
Mr Robert
Douny,
Bibliothe-
car.

Eodem die.
Contract
betwixt
the Towne
of Aber-
dein and
Mr Robert
Donny,
Bibliothe-
car.

the efternoone: and siclyik he sall admitt no schollar to be ane ordinar student within the said librarie without ane subserynet warrand from the magistrattis and counsall of Aberdeine, and these wha salbe depute be thame: whilkis students at thair entrie to the said librarie, sall give thair aithes that they sall not tak out ane book furth thairof, nather sall they blot any book, nor tear the leaves of ane book, nor fold the leaff of ane book, quhairin gif they contraveine, they sall pay the triple of the pryce of the book: whilk warrand for admissioun of the saidis studentis to the said librarie, the said Mr Robert sall keip and registrat the whole names of the saidis studentis in ane paper booke, according to the tyme and warrand: Item, he sall not len furth ane book to any man, of quhat estate or degrie so ever he be: Item, he sall mak tables and indices of the haill buikis within the said librarie, *ordine alphabetico*, of everie science be thame selffis, for the commodious wse of the saidis schollares: Item, he sall keip the saidis bookis frie from dust and corruptioun, and sall haue a fyre for that effect as necessitie requyres: Item, he sall subiect himsellf to all these conditionnes, and quhatsumeuer els salbe thocht fitting be the counsall of Aberdeine for the tyme, to be set doun heirefter for the weill of the saidis studentis, buikis, and bibliothek; for the quhilkis caussis the saidis prouest, baillies, and counsall, bindis and obleissis thame and thair successoris, prouest, baillies, and couneall of the said burghe in tyme comeing, to thankfullie content, pey and delyver to the said Mr Robert Dounye yeirlie, and ilk yeire during all the dayis of his lyftyme, the soume of sex hundreth merkis money foirsaid, at twa wsuall termes in the yeir, Witsonday and Martimes in winter, be equall portionnes, the first termes peyment thairof begynnand at the feast of Witsonday nixttocum, in the yier of God, j^m vi^c threttie twa yeiris, and so furthe termlie thairefter, induring his lyftyme: Provyding allwayis that how sone it sall happin, the prouest, baillies, and counecll of the said burgh, to by so muche land as will extend in yeirlie rent to sex hundreth merkis, or sex chalderis victuall, for the vse of the said bibliothecar, the said Mr Robert, sall accept the rent of the said land fra thame furth, and manageing thairof himselff in full satisfactioune of his said stipend of sex hundreth merkis in all tyme thairefter, during the spaice foirsaid, all fraud and gyill secludit; and for the mair securitie, baith the saidis pairties ar content, and consentis that thir presentis be insert and registrat in the buikis of Conncell and Sessioun, or tounes buikis of Aberdeine, to hawe the strenth of ane confessit act and judiciall decreit, that letteris and executoriellis of horning be ane singill chairge of sex dayis, and all wther executoriellis necessar, the ane but prejudice of the wther, may be direct thairon in forme as effeiris. And to that effect constitutes thair lawfull procuratouris, *promittendo de rato* be thir presentis, written be Walter Guthrie, writtar in Aberdeine, and subseryveit be the saidis pairties, dey, moneth, yeir, and plaice foirsaidis, befoir thir witnessis, Sir Thomas Burnet of Leyis, knicht baronet; Mr Robert Reid, minister at Banchorie; Mr Patrik Dun, docter of phisick; Mr Vedast Lowson, lait baillie, burges of Aberdeine; and Johne Ingrahame, clerk depute thairof. *Sic subscribitur*, P. Menzeis, prouest; Thomas Colinsone, baillie; Mr Alexander Jaffray, baillie; A. Meldrum, baillie; George Johnstoune, baillie. Mr Ro. Donnye, Sir Thomas Burnet, witnes; Patrik Dun, witnes; Mr Vedast Lowsone, witnes; Mr Robert Reid, witnes; Jo. Ingrahame, witnes.

Eodem die.
Contract betwixt the Towne of Aberdein and Mr Robert Donny, Bibliothecar.

29 *Februarye* 1632.

The said day the prouest, baillies, and counsall haveand consideratioun, that the stipend allotit to Thomas Cowye, sacristar, is but verie meane, and scairce habill to interteane him honestlie, sieing he wantis the benefite of baptismes that he had abefoir, and quhilk is now bestowit on Alexander Gray, reidar, as a forder help to him: Thairfoir they have thocht gude, statut and ordainit, that the severall penalties eftermentionat, salbe upliftit and resaived be the said Cowye, to his awin behowe, as a supplie and help to his provisioun, frome all and quhatsumevir persones within this burghe wha sal happin to be convict heireftir in any of the particulares following, viz.:—Of ilk persone convict of fornicatioun,

29 Feb. 1632.
Ordinance in fauouris of the kirk sacristar.

EXTRACTS FROM THE [1632.

29 Feb. 1632.

Ordinance in fauouris of the kirk sacristar.

threttein s. iiiid.; frome ilk adulterar, fourtie shillingis; frome ilk persone convict of sclander befoir the session, sex shillingis; and frome ilk persone accuisand ane wther of sclander wnjustlie, sex shillingis; frome ilk persone convict of brak of the Sabboth day, four shillingis; frome ilk persone warnit to compeir befoir the sessioun, and not compeirand, *toties quoties*, thretteine s. four d.; frome ilk persone convict of scolding and blaspheming of Goddis name, four shillingis; frome ilk persone that gives wp thair banes for marriage, and performes not the same accordinglie, tuelff shillingis; for proclamationne of banes and mariage of all and quhatsumeuir persones within the kirk of this burghe heirefter, fra ilk pairtie, tuelff shillingis; frome ilk persone convict for resset of banishit persones, tuelff shillingis; frome ilk persone convict for setting of housses to strangeris without licience of the magistrattis, and being delaitted be the said Thomas, thretteine s. iiiid.; fra ilk persone warnit to the examinationnes and not compeirand, sex shillingis; fra ilk fornicatour failzeand to mak thair repentence at the day appointit be the sessioun, thretteine s. iiiid.; for the buriall of ilk persone in the kirk, tuelff shillingis, and in the kirkyard, sex shillingis, and this, by and attour the fourtie pundis of stipend to be payit yeirlie to the said Thomas Cowy, during his service, be the maister of kirk wark; and, for the letter obteaning peyment of the saidis penalties, and putting of this present act to execution, the saidis prouest, baillies, and counsall, ordainis the tounes officiares and serjiandis to concur with and assist the said Thomas in poynding and destreingzeand thairfoir, as they salbe requyrit.

11 April 1632.

Ordinance to the M.^r of kirk wark.

11 *April* 1632.

The said day the prouest, baillies, and counsall appoints Mr Vedast Lowsone, maister of kirk wark, to tak out the tounes kirk bell callit the Laurence, furth of Williame Walkeris barque, whairin the said bell wes shippit to hawe beine transportit to Midleburghe, thair to hawe beine cassin of newe be resone of a rift thairin; and that becaus belles, and all metall of that kynd ar forbidden gudes exceptit furth of the peace betwixt the kingis of Britane and Spayn, and so is lyable to the danger of Dunkirkeris, to be takin as lanfull pryse, and to endanger lyikwayes the haill gudes and merchandise in the said burgh.

11 April 1632.
Ordinance to the M^r of kirk wark.

13 *June* 1632.

The samen day the provest, baillies, and counsall votes and concludes all in ane voce, that quhan any stair or chop within this burghe salhappin to fall or decay hereftir, it sall nawayis be lesume to the heretour of the landis to quhom any sic stair or chop belongis, to big wp or repair the same of new againe, becaus the kingis hie streitis is greatlie nidderit and wrongit thairby.

13 June 1632.
Ordinance againis foirstairis and choppis.

13 *June* 1632.

The samen day the provest, baillies, and counsall, advysedlie considering the great hurt susteanit be the toune be the admitting of dyverse and sindrie persones burgessis of this burghe gratis, but payment of any compositioun, wha not onlie makis benefite thairby thameselffis, but lyikwayes procures by thair admissioun alsa great libertie and freedome to thair children, as uther nichtbouris of the toune, wha hath gevin dew satisfactioun and payment for thair burgesship, for remeid quhairof thay have all in ane voce statute and ordanit, and be thir presentis statutes and ordanes that the sones and dochteris of all burgessis of this burgh, alsweill gild brethren as craftisman, wha sall happin to be admittit heirefter gratis, salhave na benefite nor fredome be thair fatheris burgesship, nather befoir nor efter his deceas, but be payment of compositioun thairfoir, at the modificatioun of the provest, baillies, and counsall for the tyme. Persones of counsall present, Paull Menzeis, provest, &c.

13 June 1632.
Anent the admitting of burgesse.

13 June 1632.

13 June 1632.

Ordinance to the deane of gild concerning elwandis and measouris.

The samen day the provest, baillies, and counsall ordanis George Moresoun, deane of gild, to visite and consider the haill weychtis and measouris quhilk Thomas Clerk, takisman of the tounes weyhous and toll customes, hes in his custodie and keiping, and the samen being fund sufficient, to stampt thame with the tounis stampt, that na uther weychts nor mesouris be vsit be him during his takis, bot sic as ar stampit as said is. And siclyke that the said deane of gild caus stamp the haill merchandis elvandis, and wechtis of this burghe betwixt and the fyfteine day of Julii nixt, and to caus intimat to thame be the drum, that na elne nor weycht, unstampit with the tounes stampt be vsit be any of thame, nather within nor without the toune, in thair buithes, commoun faires, nor utherwayes in tyme comeing, vndir the paine of ten pundis, to be peyit be the contraveniar, *toties quoties*, incais of failzie, to the deane of gild of the said burghe for the tyme, and imployit on the commoun warkis and effairis of the toune, whilk intinationn wes instantlie maid be the drum passand throw the haill streites of the toune, to the effect nane sould pretend ignorance.

20 June 1632.

Anent the daylie catecheising.

For samickill as catecheising, whilk is a most effectuall meanes for instructing of Christanes in the groundis of thair religioun, haith not bein so cairfullie exerceisit within this congregatioun these many yeiris bygane, as the necessitie of such a busienes doeth requyre, whairthrow ignorance hath so muche prevaillit amongst ws, and the present ministeris of this burghe tackand the mater to thair serious consideratioun, thay be advyse of the magistrattis and counsell have resolued upoun a constant course for supplie of that defect in tyme comeing, and have appointit for that effect the exercise of the catecheising to be performed be Goddis assistance everie day of the weik heireftir, except Setterday allanerlie, within the parochie kirkis of this burghe, both in the sommer and wynter seasones, from twa houris till four houris in the afternoone; Thairfoir it is statute and ordanit that all and quhatsumevir persones within this burgh alsweill maisteris and mistressis of families as haue bairnes and servandis capabill of instructioun sall repair to thair paroche kirkis at all occasiounes as they salbe warnit be the kirk officer, thair to be catecheisit and instructit in the materis of thair faith and Christiane religioune; and the persone absent being maister or mistres of a familie, to pay tuantie schillingis of vnlaw, and ilk bairne and servant sex schillingis aucht pennyes of vnlaw, *toties quoties*, to the collectour of the kirk sessioune, for the vse of the poore, and the maisteris of ilk familie to be comptabill for thair bairnes and servandis to the effect forsaid: And ordanis intimatioun heirof to be maid out of pulpitt in both the kirkis of this burghe, that nane pretend ignorance.

margin: 20 June 1632.
Anent the daylie catecheising.

15 *August* 1632.

margin: 15 Aug. 1632.

The samen day Alexander Chalmer, Robert Irwing, Johne Mylne, Wm. Andersone, Johne Maleis, and Cornelius Calder, cowpares, compeirand all personallie in presens of the counsall, gave thair corporall and solemne aithes, that thay sall not put thair burne on any salmound to be packit be thame in tyme comeing, but onlie on sufficient fishe, full reid and sweit, and nather ar gillit nor sour fishe, wnder the pain of deprivatioun.

margin: Compares suorne anent the birning of salmound.

Eodem die.

margin: Eodem die.

The said day the magistrattis and counsall wndirstanding that the act and ordinance maid and set doune wpon the tuantie thrie day off August 1626, restraining the nichtbouris of the toune to pas beyond the Bowbrig Wollmanhill, and outwith the Gallowgett port, to by any fir comeing to this burgh to be sauld, and dischairgeing the bringeris of fir to the towne frome affmaking of thair leadis, hes not being put to dew executioun, bot that the same is daylie contraveinit both be the nichtbouris and bringeris of fyr to the toune to sell, notwithstanding of the certificatioun

margin: Anent the bying of fir and peites.

Eodem die.
Anent the lying of fir and peites.

conteinit in the said act: Thairfoir they ordaine the forsaid act and ordinance to be intimat be the drum throw the haill streitis of the toune of new againe, that nane pretend ignorance, with this additioun, that the bringeris of peites to the toune to be sauld in tyme comeing, and nichtbouris of the toune lying of peites at any of the pairties befoir prohibite, sal incur the pain and unlawes conteinit in the said former act, towitt, vnder the payne of fyve merkis to be payit to the deane of gild be ilk nichtbour contraveinand the premisses, and confiscatioune of all sic fyr and peittis as salbe maid owergaine eftir thair comeing to the toune to be sauld.

12 Sept. 1632.
Anent the erecting of fontanes.

12 September 1632.

The prouest, baillies, and counsall considering the great necessitie quhairin the nichtbouris of the toune standis throw want of poore and cleane watter to serve thair houssis, and that the most pairt of the watter quhairwith they ar presentlie servit, comeing onlie frome the loche is filthillie defyillit and corruptit, not onlie be gutteris daylie rynning in the burne, but also be litsteris, and the washing of clothes, and abwssing of the watter in sindrie partis, with wther sortis of uncleannes: And being most cairfull to provyd a remeid for serveing of the toune with pure watter, and in a more easie maner, have all in ane voce thocht meit and expedient that fontanes salbe erectit for that effect with all convenient diligence: And becaus the same must be done at the tounes commoun chairges, they ordaine the haill nichtbouris and inhabitantis of this burgh to be warnit be the drum to compeir in the Tolbuithe on Freday nixt, the fourteine day of September instant, to give thair advyse thairanent, and thair consent to be craveit to stent the toune be taxatioune for peyment of the necessar chairges to be bestowit on the said wark.

12 Sept. 1632.
Anent Wedderburnes new grammer.

12 September 1632.

The samen day the prouest, baillies, and counsall, givis and grantis to Mr Dauid Wedderburne, maister of the grammer schole of this burghe, the somme of tua hundreth merkis Scottis money, for printing of the new grammer laitlie set out be him be resone of his dedicatioun of the same to the magistrattis and counsall, whilk somme they ordaine to be payit to the said Mr Dauid be George Moresone, deane of gild, and the same to be allowit to the said deane of gild in his comptis.

12 Sept. 1632. — Anent Wedderburnes new grammer.

19 September 1632.

19 Sept. 1632.

The said day the haill toune, both brethren of gild and craftismen, being conveinit in the tolbuith for giveing answer to the overture proponit unto thame abefoir, anent the erecting of fontanes within this burgh, for serveing the toune with pure and cleane watter in a more easie and commodious maner nor in tymes past, wer all in ane voce content, and consentit that fontanes sould be erectit within the said burgh in all convenient diligence to the effect foirsaid, and the gild brethren wer content for thair pairt to be stentit be taxatioun for defraying of the chairges to be bestowit thairwpoun, lykeas Thomas Gairdyn, tailyeour and deacone, conveinar of the haill craftis of this burgh, for himselff and in name of the saidis craftis promeist the somme of ane thowsand merkis Scottis money to the help and furtherance of the said wark, to be payit pairt and pairt lykas the same proceedis, provyding thay be frie of the said taxatioun; and the saidis fontanes being erectit, they wer content to contribute and be stentit with the rest of the nichtbouris of the toun to the mantenance and upholding of the samen in all tymes thairefter.

The toune consent anent the erecting of fontanes.

19 September 1632.

19 Sept. 1632.

The prouest, baillies, and counsall nominatis and appointis Alex. Willox, wricht, to be keipar and rewlar of the tounes commoun clokis, towitt, the tolbuith clok, the clok of the hie kirk and colledge kirk, as lyikwayes to ring the tounes commoun bell in the tolbuith steipill at fyue

Willox appointit keeper of the clok and ringar of the common bell.

19 Sept.
1632.
———
Willox appointit keepeir of the clock and ringar of the common bell.

houris in the morneing, and nyne houris at evin, and ilk Wedinsday to the counsall at aucht houris in the morning, for the spaice of ane yeir nixt efter the dait heirof; and grantis to the said Alex. for his service and fie during the said spaice, the somme of ane hundreth merkis Scottis money, to be payit to him quarterlie be the maister of kirk wark and tounes thessaurar, viz.: be the said Mr of kirk wark, fourtie merkis, and be the thessaurar fourtie pundis money, begynnand the first quarteris payment wpon the first day of October nixt; lykeas the said Alexander being personallie present, acceptit the said chairge, in and wpoun him, and promeist to do ane honest dewtie thairin.

19 Sept. 1632.
———
Support grantit be the counsall to the craftis hospitall.

19 *September* 1632.

The said day, anent the supplicatioun given in to the provest, baillies, and counsall be Thomas Gairdyn, tailyeour, deacone conveinar of the haill craftis of this burghe, for himselff and in name and behalff of the remanent deacones and brethren of the saidis craftis, mackand mentioun that thay had causit build and repair the Trinitie Freiris Place of this burghe, quhilk Mr Williame Guild, ane of the tounes ordinar ministeris, hed laitlie conqueist and mortifiet to be ane hospitall for decayit craftismen within the samen, wpoun the bigging quherof they had bestowit the best pairt of the moneyes quhilk they had to the foir in thair commoun boxes, sua that thair stok and rent for the present wilbe but verye meane; and seing that poore decayit craftismen hes no place in the gild brethrenes hospitall, and the nichtbouris of the craftis are most willing to contribute to the wark according to thair power, wherbe thair brethren may be suppliet, and the toune and sessioune easit of a burdeine: Thairfoir thay humblie desyrit thair wisdome of the counsall to put to thair helping hand to the furtherance of the wark: And in regaird that thay ar memberis of this commoun wealth, to grant unto thame thair cheretabill help and support thairunto, for the quhilk thay sould endevore to approve thameselffis thankfull and both reddie and fordward in any thing concerning the gude and weill of the toune according to thair power, as in the said supplicatioun, at lenth wes content; quhairanent the saidis provest, baillies, and counsall, advysing, and considdering the necessitie and gudnes of the wark, they gaue and grant, and be thair presentis gives and grantis to the deacones and maisteris of the craftis of this burgh, the compositioun of ane gild burges sic as they sall present to the counsall (except the gild wyne silner), whilk wilbe twa hundreth merkis yeirlie, and ilk yeir for the spaice of fyve yeiris nixt eftir the dait heirof, to be imployit on profite, and furth comand be thame in all tyme comeing, to the behoue of the decayit craftismen wha salhappin to be admittit in the said hospitall as bedallis thairof; with conditioun alwayes, that the deacones, maisteris, and friemen of the saidis craftis and thair successoris carie and behave thame-selffis dewtifullie in all thingis to the counsall, whiche shall tend to the commoun weill and benefite of the toune, and bear burdyne thairin with the gild brethren thairof, according to thair power. And at the expyring of the saidis fyve yeiris, that they mak just compt and rekning to the counsall of the wairing of the saidis moneyes, quhilk salbe acquired be the saidis compositiounes, togidder with the yeirlie annualrent that sall accress thairwpoun. Persones of counsall present, Paull Mengzeis of Kin-mundie, provest; Thomas Collinsone, Mr Alexander Jaffray, Andro Mel-drum, George Johnstoun, baillies; Mr Vedast Lowsone, Patrik Leslie, George Morisone, John Leslie, Mr William Moir, Johne Lowsone, Mr Robert Skeyn, Alexander Ramsay, Thomas Mowat, George Meldrum, James Cryistie, tailyeour, and William Ord, wrieht.

19 Sept. 1632.

Support granted be the counsall to the craftis hospitall.

3 October 1632.

The counsall ordanis letteris to be direct be the magistrattis to the lairdis of Arbuthnot, Drum, Leyis, Muchall, Elsick, and vther barones and gentlemen in the Mearnes, to meit at the calsies of Month Cowye, on Monday nixt, the aucht day of October instant, for sichting of the saidis calsies, and to considder what will repair the same, to the effect report thairof may be maid to the lordis of Privie Counsall.

3 Oct. 1632.

Ordinance anent the repairing of the calsies of Month Cowye.

17 Oct. 1632.

Ordinance anent the begynning of the fleshe, meill, and malt mercattis.

17 October 1632.

The said day the prouest, baillies, and counsall ordainis intimatioun to be maid be the hand bell throw the haill streites of the towne, that na fleshe be bocht nor sauld till the same present the mercat, and that na mercat be maid thairof till aucht houris in the morning ilk Seterday, wndir the panis of ten pundis money, to be peyit be the contraveinar to the deane of gild, *toties quoties*; and that na mercat be maid of meill till allevin houris, and of malt till tuelff houris ilk mercat day, wndir the lyik panis and vnlaw; and the baillies, with the constables, *per vices*, to attend that na abuse be committit anent the premisses.

7 Nov. 1632.

Ordinance to the deane of gild.

7 November 1632.

The magistrattis and councell appointis Mr Mathew Lumisden, deane of gild, to caus weir twa hundreth frankis wpoun furnisheing of confectiounes for his Maiesties comeing into this his ancient kingdom of Scotland, whilk sounic salbe allowit to the said deane of gild in his comptis.

9 Jan. 1633.

Ratificatioune of the act maid anent superfluous banqueting.

9 January 1633.

The said day the prouest, baillies, and counsall ratifies and approves the act and ordinance maid be the prouest, baillies, and counsall of this burghe for the tyme, wpoun the ellevint day of October 1626 yeirs, againis wachting, and scoalling, and superfluous banqueting at baptismes; and ordaines the same to be put to dew executioun againis the transgressouris thairof in tyme comeing, vnder the paynes thairin conteinit; with this additioun, that nane be fund danceing throw the toune at marrage feastis, nor yit any persounes invytit or desyrit to nichtwalkis heireftir, bot a few number of the narrest nichthouris of the defunct, vnder the lyck paynes, and that the maister of musick school bring with him onlie four schollares to everie lyikwalk quhuerunto he is desyrit himselff, for eschewing of perturbatioun; and ordaines intimatioun of the said act to be maid out of pulpitt of new againe in both the kirkis of this burghe, on sonday nixt eftir sermone, to the effect nane pretend ignorance.

9 Jan. 1633. Ratificatioun of the act maidanent superfluous banqueting.

23 *January* 1633.

The said day in presence of the prouest, baillies, and councell, compeirit George Jamesone, painter, burgess of Aberdeine, ar. and executer to umquhill Williame Jamesone, writtar in Edinburghe, his brother germane, and exponit and declairit, that the said umquhill Williame, befoir his deceas, left his haill mathimaticall instrumentis and bookes in legacie to the toune for the use of the professor of mathimatiques within the colledge of the said burghe, and studentis in that professioun present and to come: And conforme thairto the said George delyuerit instantlie the saidis haill instrumentis and bookes, at the directioun of the magistrattis and counsall, to Mr Williame Johnstoun, doctour in phisik, and present professor of mathimaticques within the said colledge, be ane speciall inventar writtin and subscryveit be the said Mr Williame on the end of the catalogue of umquhill secretarie Reidis librarie.

23 Jan. 1633. Dischairge be the counsall to Jamesen.

20 *February* 1633.

At Halyruidhous, the sewent day of Februarie, the yeire of God, j^m sex hundreth and threttie three yeires, anent the supplicatioun presentit to the Lordis of Secret Counsell, be the proeust, baillies, and counsall of the burghe of Aberdeine, making mentioun that where they hawing takin to thair consideratioun the great necessitie quhairin thair toune stoode throw want of pure and cleane watter, and how that the watter whairwith the said toune was served, came frome ane litle loche at the syde of the toune, whilk is so filthilie defyled and corrupted, not onlie be gutteris daylie running in the loche, but also by the letstaris who wash all their cloathes in the said loch, and by the nighbouris of the

20 Feb. 1633. Act of his Maiesties Privie Counsell anent the fontanes.

20 Feb.
1633.

Act of his
Majesties
Privie
Counsell
anent the
fontanes.

tounne who wash all thair cloathes there, and suche of the nightboures as dwell ewest to the loche, thay cast all thair filth and excrementis in the same, so as the watter comeing therefra to the said tounne is so corrupted and vnsavourie in the taste, and of suche ane greene and vncomelie cullour, as nather the nighboures of the tounne, nor strangeris repairing thairto, can make anie vse of the said watter: And the supplicantes being carefull in imitatioun of other pairtes, and in speciall of the nighbour countrie, where great care is tane for preserwing of thair watter, to prowyde a remeid for the serveing and furnishing of thair tounne with pure and cleane watter, they concluded and find it meit and expedient, with vniforme voice, that ane draught sould be drawin frome ane spring within ane mylne of thair tounne, by the quhilk the watter sould be drawin frome that spring to the said tounne, and that some fountanes sould be erected in the most convenient pairtes of the said tounne for that effeck: And becaus this work could not be brought to perfection, but vpoun the commoune charges of the said tounne, they thairfoir warned the haill nighboures of thair said tounne be towik of drum, to conveene with thame vpoun the fourteine day of September last, for giveing of thair advice anent this worthie and commendable worke, and thair consent to ane taxatioun to be imposed vpoun the said tounne for that effect: And according to the appoyntment, the haill communitie of the tounne, both gild brether and craftismen, haveing conveened in the tolbuith of Aberdeine, vpoun the nynteine day of September last, and the overtour and propositioun foresaid, and the expediencie and necessitie thairof, for furnishing and serving of the said tounne with pure and cleane watter, and the erecting of fountanes to that effect being intimat and schawn vnto thame, the haill bodie of the said tounne, all in ane voyce, agreed vpoun the expediencie and necessitie of the said work, and the erecting of fountanes to that effect: And all the gild brether consented to be stented for defraying of the chairges of that work, and wheras the deacoun conveener of the craftes his consent to the stenting wes craved for himselff, and in name of the remanent craftis of the tounne, he for himselff, and in name of the haill bodie of the craftis, acknowledging the necessitie of the bringing of the watter, and erecting of the fountanes to that effect, consented to contribute, and to be stented with the rest of the nighbouures of the tounne toward the maintenance and vphaulding of the watter draught and fontanes to be erected as said is; bot thay made scruple to be stented in any soumes of money for bringing of the worke to perfection, bot offered ane certane somme of money to that effect, prowyding that thay wer frie of taxatioun: And vpon this litle difference betwixt the craftes and gild brether, this important work tending so far to the weill of the said tounne, and preserving of the health alsweill of strangeris repairing thairto as of the proper inhabitantes of the same, is lyke to be frustrat, to the disgrase of the said tounne, and to the heavie grief of the honest and weill disposed citizens thairof: And the gild brether, vpon whome the most pairt of the burdeine of this work will ly, refuises in anie case to be stented, vnlesse the commoun and observed custome in materis of this kynd be observed, and that the haill inhabitantis of this burghe, alsweill gild brether as craftis be stented, wherin they respect not so muche the payment of the somme, whilk thay will freelie and willinglie vnderly, as the preparatiue whilk the refuissale of the craftis may produce in matteris of this kynd heirafter: And whereas this oppositioun and contradictioun made be the craftes being dewlie considderit, is ane mater of no moment, and aucht not to be respected in so important a caus as this, seing thair pairt of anie stent to be imposed wpoun the said burghe will onelie extend to the sewint pairt, being sett and collected at the greatest rigour, and the portioun of the gild brether will extend to sewin parts of aucht, and the stent to be imposed wpoun the craftes being considderit, with thair offer, there will not pas three hundreth pundes in difference betweene thair offer and the stent, quhilk is a mater of no moment, and not worthie to be respected in suche a commoun caus so neerlie importing the weall and credite of the said tounne: humblie desyiring, thairfore, the saidis Lordis that the saidis supplicantis may hawe commissioun and warrand be act of counsall in maner, and to the effect

20 Feb. 1633.

Act of his Majesties Privie Counsell anent the fontanes.

20 Feb.
1633.

Act of his Maiesties Privie Counsell anent the fountanes.

vnderwrittin, lykas at mair length is conteuit in the said supplicatioun: Quhilk being read, heard, and considderit be the saidis Lordis, and they being thairwith, and with the two actes of counsall of the said burghe off Aberdeine, conteinyng the proceedinges in this mater weill and throghlie advised, and finding this wark neerlie to concerne the weill and credite of the said toune: Thairfore the saidis Lordes hes giwin and grantit, and be thir presentes giwis and grauntes warrand and commissioun to the saidis proucst, baillies, and counsall of Aberdeine, to sett doune ane certaine soume of money toward the forderance and advancement of the worke foirsaid, to be payed be the haill nighboures and inhabitantes of the said burgh, and to nominat and appoint certane stenteris to stent thair saidis nighboures; and the said stent being set doune, ordanis letteris to be direct, charging the personnes stented to mak payment of that soume, that thay and ilk ane of thame salbe stented vnto, to the collectouris to be nominat and appoynted to that effect be the saidis proucst, baillies, and counsall of Aberdeine, within three dayes nixt after the charge, vnder the paine of rebellioun, and putting of thame to the horne: And if thay failzie thairin, the said space being bypast, to denunce this disobeyeris, rebellis, and put thame to the horne, and to escheit, and gif neid beis, to poynd and distrenzie: with power lykewayes to the saidis proucst, baillies, and counsell of Aberdeine, if neid beis, to committ to waird suche of the personnes stented, as refuise to mak payment of thair stent to the saidis collectonrs as said is, to remaine thairin wpoun thair awin expenssis till thay mak payment of thair said stent. *Extractum de libris actorum secreti consilii S. D. N. Regis, per me Jacobum Prymrois, clericum eiusdem, sub meis signo et subscriptione manualibus. Sic subscribitur, Jacobus Prymrois.*

15 May 1633.

Act discharging wemen to wear playdis about thair heiddis.

15 May 1633.

The said day the proucst, baillies, and counccll, considering the incivill forme of behaviour vsit be a great many wemen in this burghe, of gude qualitie, wha resortis both to kirk and mercat with thair plaidis about thair

heidis, and be thair example the meaner sort of wemen wsis the same
forme of incivilitie, quhilk gives offence to strangeris to speik reprotche-
fullie of all wemen generallie of this toune: for remeid quhairof, it is
statute and ordanit, that na wemen within this burghe, of quhatsumeuer
rank, qualitie, or degrie thay be of, preswme, or tak wpoun hand to resort
to kirk or mercat with thair plaidis about thair heidis in tyme comeing,
with certificatioun to these that salhappin to failzie and contraveine this
present ordinance, not onlie sall thair plaidis be shamfullie markit with a
tar stik to thair disgrace, bot lyikwayis confiscat and takin frome thame
be the officeris in quhat pairt soeuir thay be fund haveand thair plaidis
about thair heidis; and ordainis intimatioun to be maid out of pulpit in
bothe the kirkis of this burghe, on Sonday nixt, that nane pretend
ignorance, and to the effect executioun may follow thairon fra thane
furth.

15 May 1633.
——
Act dis-
charging
wemen
to wear
playdis
about thair
heiddis.

29 May 1633.

The said day the prouest, baillies, and counsall gives and grantis
libertie and licence to the principall and regentis of Kingis College of
Aberdeine, to crave ane voluntarie contributioun of the inhabitantis of
this burghe to help to the reparatioun of the steipill of the said colledge
laitlie dimolishit and brokin doune be tempest and storme of weather.

29 May 1633.
——
Licence
grantit
to ye prin-
cipall and
regentis of
the Kingis
Colledge.

4 June 1633.

The prouest, baillies, and counsall grantis twa hundreth merkis
money to Williame Merser, musician, for defraying of the chairges bestowit
be him in printing of a poesie whilk he hed laitlie composit and dedicat to
the toune. . . .

4 June 1633.
——
Grant for
printing a
poesie.

4 June 1633.

Ordinance to the Thessaurar.

4 *June* 1633.

The prouest, baillies, and counsall being informed that Mr Williame Forbes and Mr Robert Baron, doctouris in divinitie, and twa of the ordinar ministeris of this burghe, is writin for be the Archbishop of Sanct Androus, to teache befoir the kingis majestie at Edinburghe, hes thairfoir ordainit the tounes thessaurar to debourse to ilk ane of thame the soume of ane hundreth merkis money, for making of thair chairges to Edinburgh, to the effect foirsaid.

19 June 1633.

Ordinance to the Thessaurar.

19 *June* 1633.

The said day the baillies and counsall ordainis Charles Keilo, thessaurar, to deburse the soume of ane hundreth and allevin pundis money to Eduard Raban, printer, for printing of ane buik dedicat be Doctour Barron to the counsall, and alse for printing of same poiesies writtin be Mr Daniel Wedderburn and Mr George Robertsone, wpoun the kingis maiesties comeing to this his ancient kingdome, and salbe allowit to the said thessaurar in his comptis.

Eodem die.

Solemnitie of the Kingis Maiesties coronatioune.

Eodem die.

The samen day the baillies and counsall being trewlie certifiet that yisternicht, the auchteine day of Junij instant, our most dread and gratious soverane Charles, be the grace of God king of Great Britane, France, and Ireland, Defender of the Faithe, did resaive the croun of this his ancient kingdome of Scotland at Halirudehous: Thairfoir thay ordainit the same to be signifiet to the haill toune, and publict sermone to be maid in the kirk, that the people may resort thairto, and giue thankis to God for so glad tyidingis; the haill bellis to be rung; baill fyres to be set on be everie man befoir his awin house; the croce to be hung with tapestrie; twa punsheounes of wyne, with the spyeerie in great, to be brocht and spent thairat; the tuelff peice off ordinance on the Castellhill to be shot, and the nichtbonres of the toune, eftir sermone, to accompanye thair magistrattis, expressing the melodie of thair hartis, in praising and singing of psalmes, and thaireftir the youthes and wther weill affected persones, to spend the rest of the day in schooting of muskattis and burning of poulder: And ordaines Mr Matho Lumisden, deane of gild, to provyd the wyne and spycerie, to the effect foirsaid; and what he deburssis thairwpoune, salbe allowit to him in his comptis.

Eodem die.

Solemnitie of the Kingis Maiesties coronatioune.

14 August 1633.

The samen day the proueast, baillies, and counsall, thinkis it meit and expedient that thair salbe a publict wapinshaw of all the inhabitantis of this burghe, fensible persones, wpoun Wadinysday nixt, the tuantie ane day of August instant, quhilk thay ordaine to be intimat be the drum throw the haill streites of the toune, chargeing all fensible persones, both frie and wnfrie, to prepair thame selffis, and be in redynes to giue thair musture and wapinshaw in the linkes of this burghe the day foirsaid, in thair best armour, to witt, with pikes, corslettis, and muskattis, wnder the payne of fourtie pundis, to be payit be ilk persone absent.

14 August 1633.

A wapinschaw indicted.

14 August 1633.

The said day the new and auld counsallis being conveinit in the tounes counsal hous, and haveand consideratioun that Doctor Williame Guild, ane of the ministeris of this burght, hes this day voluntarlie wndertakin, for the glorie of God and for the publict gude and benefite of the inhabitantis of this burghe, frielie on his awin chairges and expensses, to glass all the wyndoes of the Grayfrier kirk of this burghe, with sic convenient diligence as he possiblie can, except the southeast gavill windo of

14 August 1633.

Anent glassing the wyndoes of the Grayfrier kirk.

14 August 1633.
Anent glassing the wyndoes of the Grayfrier kirk.

the said kirk, whilk is all glassit be Alexander Stewart, merchand, wpon his proper chairgis: whilk kirk, for mony yeiris heirtofoir, throw laik of glass wyndoes, hes lyen waist without ony divyne worship or exercise thairin, houbeit the same be a pleasant and magnifick edifice lyand in the hart of the toune, verie commodious and easefull for the whole inhabitantis, and could not hitherto (eftir many essayes) be gotin performed: Thairfoir, and to the effect the chairges, whiche the said Doctor Williame Guild now bestowis, be not in vaine; and that the said kirk whilk wes buildit and dedicat to Goddis worship and service, sould not stand waist as formarlie it hes done, the saidis new and auld conncellis, all in ane voce, hes evir heireftir appointit the morning and evining prayeris, both sommer and wynter, to be daylie red be the townes reidar in the said Grayfrier kirk, as being the most commodious kirk for that use, howsone the wyndoes thairof salbe glassed, and hes appointit some commodious daskis and seatis to be erected and set up for the ease of the nichtbouris and inhabitantis of the toun thairin.

2 October 1633.
Ordinance to the Mr of kirk wark.

2 October 1633.

The samen day the new and auld counsallis and deacones of craftis of this burghe convenit at the electioun, ordainis the great bell of the kirk lyand on the shoir to be send to Flanderis, in James Farquhares barque, callit "The Mackrell," whairof Patrik Findlay is maister undir God, and thair to be cassin of new againe of the same proportioun as the said bell is for the present, be the cair and owersicht of Walter Robertsone, merchand: and Mr Thomas Gray, Mr of kirk wark, is appointit to agrie with the skipper for the fraucht, as also to satisfie the whole chairgis in casting the same of new againe, whilk salbe allowit to the said Mr Thomas in his comptis.

20 November 1633.

The said day the provest, baillies, and counsall, finds and declaires that Mr Thomas Chalmer, secund doctour of the grammer schole of this burghe, is, and sould be lyable to the maisteris admonitioun as the wther doctour, and obey his directioun both in doctrine and discipline, and in all wther thingis concerning the weill and florisheing of that schole as salbe preserveit unto him, and thairfor wes ordanit sua to conforme himself in tyme comeing, whilk the said Mr Thomas personallie present promeist to do and performe.

The doctouris of the grammer schoole ar to obey the maisters directiouns in thar doctrine and discipline.

4 December 1633.

The said day the provest, baillies, and counsall nominatis and appointis Andro Meldrum, baillie, and Maister William Moir, commissionares, to pas south with Doctor Williame Forbes, ane of the ordinar ministeris of this burghe, wha is laitlie callit heirfra to be Bishop of Edinburghe, and to congratulat his consecratioun in the tounes name; and ordainis Robert Skeyne, thessaurar, to deburse the somme of four hundreth merkis Scottis money, to the saidis commissioneris to acompt, for macking of the said Doctor Williame, and his whole companyes chairges in thair southgoing till he be in Edinburghe.

Doctor Forbes' expenses to Edin. to be paid.

11 December 1633.

The quhilk day in presens of the provest, baillies, and counsall of the burghe of Aberdeine, compeirit Maister Patrik Dun, principall of the colledge of the said burghe, and exponit and declairit to thame that for scairstie of chamberis and want of beddis to serve the haill studentis within the said colledge, sindrie of the schollares wes forceit to ly in the toun housses, quhair they wer buirdit to the great hinderance of thair studies; and sieing that Doctor Williame Forbes, ane of the ordinar ministeris of this burgh, quha hed his duelling in the backhous of the

Anent chambers to be built for students in the College.

11 Dec. 1633. — Anent chambers to be built for students in the College.	said colledge, is callit to be Bishop of Edinburgh, and to remove thither shortlie, he thairfoir earnestlie intreatit thair wisdomes of the counsall that they wald be pleasit to grant him entrie to the said backhous, to the effect he may caus big wp chamberis and beddis thairin for the ease of the schollares in tyme comeing: Quhairanent the saidis prouest, baillies, and counsall advysing, thay find the petitionares desyre most reasonable, and thairfoir gives and grantis libertie and licience to him to enter presentlie to the said backhous, and to big wp chamberis and beddis within the samen, for the weill and ease of the studentis within the said colledge in all tyme heirefter, provyding allwayis that the said principall and regentis of the said colledge, nor thair successouris, claime nor pretend na richt to the Grayfrier kirk of the said burghe in tyme comeing, but as neid beis, that they remuve the samen in the tounes fauouris. Lykeas it is heirby declairit be the saidis prouest, baillies, and counsall, and als be the said Mr Patrik Dun, that the said Grayfrier kirk is and sall be allwayis exceptit furth and fra the dispositioun and mortificatioun maid be the toun to the maisteris and memberis of the said colledge, of the Grayfrier's plaice and yard thairof, and that the samen kirk wes, is, and salbe speciallie and particularlie reserveit to the toune as ane of thair awin kirkis, to be wsit be thame for Goddis worship and service in all tyme comeing. . .

12 *February* 1634.

12 Feb. 1634. — Lord Keythe, Irwingis, contra Meldrum.	The quhilk day anent the complaint giuen in to the prouest, baillies, and counsall of the burghe of Aberdeine, be Willeame Lord Keythe, Sir Alexander Irwing of Drum, knicht, Robert Irwing of Fedderet, and Marioun Douglas, relict of vmquhile, Alexander Irwing of Drum againes Androw Meldrum, baillie, burges of Aberdein, mackand mentioun that quhair vmquhile Sir Robert Keythe of Benholme, knicht, grandvncle to me, the said Willeame Lord Keythe, and the said vmquhile Alexander Irwing of Drum, father to the saidis Sir Alexander and Robert Irwings, and husband to the said Marioun, men in thair tymes notourlie knawin be thair gude

careage to this ancient and worthie toune in all dewtie and loyall freyndschip, as become affectionat freyndis of thair plaice, being callit to thair rest, wer honorablie interred within the paroche kirk of the said burghe at thair awin earnest desyre, to crowne the zeall quhilk thay caried in thair lyftym to the said toune, and haveand thair lyen now be the spaice of certane yeires, the said Andro Meldrum haveand his wyiff laitlie depairtit within this burghe, he be himselff at the least wtheris in his name, contraire all Christiane pietie or regaird to the bodie of these honorable defunct persones, quhilk aught not onlie to hawe beine spairit, bot honored, and quhais corps not being as yit putrifiet and consumed to dust, hes diggit vp thair graves, castin vp and removeit thair bodies, brokin thair kistis, and hes vsit suche wther inhumane outrages wpoun these honorabill corps as become no gude Christiane ather to hawe performeit or beine accessorie vnto, as wes notourlie knawin to thair wisdomes of the counsall, to whome the said compleinares had tane thair first recourse for redress, desyirand thairfor thair wisdomes of the counsall to have consideratioun of the premisses, and to tak sic ordour thairanent as may assuage thair greiff conceavid for the same, and may incite the saidis complainares, heirefter to intertene that loyall freyndschip quhilk befoir many ages hes beine bred and euer since continewit betwixt the toun and thair predicessouris, whilk they did earnestlie desyre be the said petitioun, as in the said complaint subscryveit with thair handis at length is conteanit. *Sic subscribitur*, Wm Keith, Sir A. Irwing, Robert Irwine." The saidis compleinares compeirand personallie in presens of the saidis proust, baillies, and counsall, and the said Andro Meldrum being also personallie present, and the said complaint at lenth red in thair audience, the said Andro Meldrum declairit be vertew of his solemne oath that what wes done in the said mater wes by his knowledge and consent, nather gaue he any ordour nor desyrit his said vmquhill spous to be buriet in the grave quhair she now lyes, and thairfoir protestit he be frie of any damage, hurt, or prejudice, that the toun or kirk salhappin to susteane thairby in thair right and priviledges to that pairt of the said kirk in tyme comeing; in respect of the quhilk

12 Feb. 1631.

Lord Keythe, Irwingis, contra Meldrum.

12 Feb. 1634.

Lord Keythe, Irwingis, contra Meldrum.

complaint and declarationn foirsaid, the prouest, baillies, and counsall, for setling of the busines, ordaines Mr Alexander Jaffray, baillie, Mr Patrik Dwn, Patrik Leslie, and Mr Thomas Gray, four of thair number, to tak notice, and try all thairanent, and the premisses being fund of veritie to tak sic ordour thairwith as they sall think expedient. Persones of counsall present, Sir Paull Mengzeis of Kynmundie, knicht, Prouest Gilbert Mengzeis of Petfoddellis, Mr Alexander Jaffray, Johne Hay, Thomas Nicolson, baillies; Mr Patrik Dwn, Patrik Leslie, Mr Thomas Gray, Johne Leslie, Robert Skeyne, Mr Willeame Moir, Robert Smith, James Robertson, Thomas Mowat, Paull Colinson, James Crystie, tailyeour, and Willeame Ord, wricht.

12 March 1634.

Ordinance anent burgesses for making of thair residence.

12 *March* 1634.

The said day it is statute and ordainit be the prouest, baillies, and counsall, that all burgessis and friemen of this burgh, alsweill alredie admittit as to be admittit heireftir, sall mak thair actuall residence, and remaining within the same burghe in tyme comeing, according to the actis of thair admissioun, and wther actis and ordinances maid and sett doun aganis burgessis for making of thair residence, and that thay sall nawayis duell nor keip opin buithes in the countrie at na tyme heireftir, vnder the paine of deprevatioun, *ipso facto*; and ordaines the deane of gild and his successoris to put this present ordinance to dew executioun in all poyntis.

26 March 1634.

Ratificatioun of the act aganis mastishe and cur doggis.

26 *March* 1634.

The samen day the prouest, baillies, and counsall, ratifies and approves the act and ordinance maid and set doune by thair predicessouris, prouest, baillies, and counsall of the said burghe for the tyme, with consent of the haill toune, wponne the fourteine day of February 1623 yeiris, aganis the haveares and keipares of mastishe and cur doggis within the same burghe in tyme comeing; and ordainis the said ordinance to be intimat throw the haill toune be the drum, to the effect nane pretend ignorance, and that all sic mastishe and cur doggis be removeit and put away within fourtie aucht houris, vnder the payne of fourtie pundis of vnlaw, to be payit be all persones to the deane of gild.

26 March 1634.
Ratificatioun of the act againis mastishe and cur doggis.

2 *April* 1634.

The samen day the pronest, baillies, and counsall ordains ane letter to be drawin wp in the tounes name, and subscryveit be the magistrattis, and send to Midleburghe to Herman de Pitt, merchand thair, for casting the prayer bell of new againe, conforme to the commissioun alredie send to him with the said bell, and quhat chairgis salbe debursit wpon the casting or transporting bak of the said bell, the saids pronest, baillies, and counsall ordainis the same to be advanceit and payit be Mr Thomas Gray, Mr of kirkwark, whilk salbe allowit to the said Mr Thomas in his comptis.

2 April 1634.
Ordinance anent the casting of the prayer bell.

6 *August* 1634.

The pronest, baillies, and counsall grantis the somme of four hundreth merkis to the maisteris and regentis of the Colledge of auld Aberdeine, for thair help to repair the steippill of the said Colledge, whilk wes brokin doune wpoun the   day of Februar 1633 yeris, be extreme tempest and storm of weather, to be debursit be the deane of gild, and the same is ordanit to be allowit to him in his comptis.

6 August 1634.
Support to the Colledge of auld Aberdeine.

13 *August* 1634.

Followis the tenour of ane act and ordinance of Secret Counsall, grantit be the Lordis thairof, in favouris of the necessitous people of Cathnes and Orknay, wha ar in great distres and miserie throw famine, whilk the saidis Lordis hes recommendit to the cheretabile help and supplie of all the inhabitantis within the schirreffdome of Aberdeine.

"At Edinburghe, the nyntein day of Junij, the yeire of God j^{m} sex

13 August 1634.
Act of Lordis of Privie Counsall for support of the people of Cathnes and Orkney in this calamitous tyme of darth and famine.

15 August 1634.

Act of Lordis of Privie Counsall for support of the people of Caithnes and Orkney in this calamitous tyme of darth and famine.

hundreth threttie four yeiris, anent the supplicatioun presented to the Lordis of Secret Counsall be Johne, Bischope of Caithnes and Bischop of Orknay, makand mentioun that quhair the pitiefull and deplorable estait of the people within the counties of Caithnes and Orkney, of whome greate numberis by famyn hawe miserablie perished this yeire, hath mowed the saidis supplicantis, out of thair bound dewtie and Christian commiseratioun of thair calamitie, to present to the saidis Lordis the desolatioun quhilk, in these bounds, is lyk to fall out if some present course be not taine for preventing of the samen; for this last harvest befoir the cornes wer fullie ryped and cutt doun, such tempestuous and bitter weather blew frome the ocean vpoun theise pairtes, that the cornis wer some blasted as thay never filled, and what semed to be filled did nowayes answer to the peoples expectatioun, the boll of aittis in many pairtes not gewing ane peck of meale; and whair thair did appeare to be ane chalder of beir, the same did not rander the fourt pairt to the seid quhairby the third rig lyeth vnsown, and in many pairtis the halff is not sowin, quhilk hes caused so greate dearth and famyne in these partis that multitudes dee in opine feildis, and thair is nane to burrie thame, bot whair the minister gois furth with his man to burrie thame wher they ar found, the ground yeildis thame no cornis, and the sea affoordis thame no fisches as formarlie it wount to do, the picture of death is seene in the faces of manie, some dewore the sea waire, some eat dogs, some steall foullis, of nyne of a familie, sewin at once died; the husband and the wyfe expyring at an tyme, manie ar redacted to that extremitie that thay ar forced to steale, and thairefter ar executed, and some hawe desperatlie rune to the sea and drowned thameselffes; so great is the famen, that the people of mean estate hawe nothing, and theise of great rank hawe nothing that thay can spair, humblie desyring thairfoir the saidis Lordis, that thay may hawe thair letteris of recommendatioun in fawouris of thais poore people in maner and to the effect vnderwrettin, lykas at mair length is contenit in the said supplicatioun, quhilk being hard, red, and considderit by the saidis Lordis, and thay finding the desyre

thairof resonabile, thairfore the saidis Lordis hes recommendit, and be 13 August 1634.
the tennour heiroff recommends the pitiefull and deplorable estait of the
poore people in the countrie of Orkney and Zetland to the charitable Act of Lordis of Privie
consideratioun of the Lordis of his Maiesties Privie Counsell, the sena- Counsall for support
touris and memberis of the College of Justice, the prouest, baillies, coun- of the people of
sall, and communitie of Edinburgh, and to all otheris weill disposed Chris- Caithnes and Ork-
tians, to burghe and land within this kingdome; and siclyik, the saidis ney in this calamitous
Lordis recommendis the pitiefull and deplorabile estait of the inhabitantis tyme of
within the boundis of Caithnes to the charitable consideratioun of all the darth and famine.
inhabitantis to the brughe and land within the schirrefldome of Aberdeine,
and to the prouest and baillies thairof, and to the borrowis, prouestis,
baillies, counsellouris, and inhabitantis benorth the samen, requesting
thame, and ewerie ane of thame, to extend suche proportioun of thair
Christian charitie and benevolence towardes the releiff and supplie of the
necessiteis and deplorabill estait of thais poore people, as the nature of
the caus requyres. *Extractum de libris actorum."*

20 October 1634.

The said day the prouest, baillies, and counsall gives and grantis 20 Oct. 1634.
thair speciall powar, commissioun, and warrand to Patrik Leslie, prouest, Commis- sioneris
Mr Thomas Gray, Mr Matho Lummisden, and Mr Robert Farquhar, nominat to deal with
baillies, and Mr Patrik Dun, principall of the Colledge of this burghe, to Doctor Johne
deall with Mr Johne Forbes, doctour and professour of divinitie in the Forbes to accept
Kingis Colledge of Aberdeine, to accept wpoun him the chairge and func- upoun him the functioun of ane of the ministeris of the said burgh, in plaice of umquhill tion of the ministrie
Williame, Bishop of Edinburghe. within this burghe.

19 November 1634.

The samen day Mr Thomas Gray, baillie, gave in ane great brasin 19 Nov. 1634.
hearse for decoratioune of the kirk of this burghe, whilk wes ordanit to A hearse given be
be hung wp in the south yle of the new kirk, for serveing of the kirkis Mr Thos. Gray
wse in all tyme comeing. to the new kirk.

17 December 1634.

17 Dec. 1634.
Anent the charge gewin to the toun for rysing in armes againes the licht horsemen.

The said day the prouest, baillies, and counsall being chairgit, be vertew of our Soverane Lordis letteris, to ryse in armes, assist and concur with Thomas Crombie of Kemnay, shireff of Aberdeine, and the noblemen, barones, and wtheris within the said schireffdome, wha have receavit the lyke charge, to pas, follow, and persew Adame Gordon, brother to Johne Gordonne of Park, ——— Gordon, yonger of Invermarkie, Williame Gordone, son to ——— Gordone of Gellachie, Johne Gordone, son to the gudeman of Achannachie, Nathaniell Gordonne, son to the gudeman of Ardlogie, Alex. Leith, brother to the gudeman of Harthill, Robert Gordon, brother to the Laird of Gight, Johne Gordone in Rothiemay, William Ross in Ballivet, ——— Makgillivoriche, servitour to the laird of Park, and all wther brokin men being in thair companye, quhairevir thay may be apprehendit within the boundis of the schirrefdome foirsaid, and to exhibite and present thameselffes to justice, to vnderly thair deserveit punishement for thair abuse and contempt of his Maiesties authoritie and lawis, in braking furth vpoun the laird of Frendraucht his grvnd, spoyling and laying of the same waist, all in ane voce thocht it meit and expedient to adheir to the exemptioun grantit be our late deceassit soverane, King James the Sext, of blessed memorie, to the toune and haill inhabitantis thairof, exeming thame frome all such raidis.

14 January 1635.

14 Jan. 1635.
The Kingis Maiesties letter presentit to the counsell.

The quhilk day in presens of the prouest, baillies, and counsall of the burghe of Aberdeine, conveinit in the tounes counsalhous, compeirit Mr Patrik Chalmer, syreff-clerk of Aberdeine, and declairit that in absence of Thomas Cromby, syreff principall of Aberdeine, for the present at Edinburgh, he delyuerit yesterday, the xiiith day of Januar instant, to Gilbert Colinsone, baillie, his Maiesties missive direct to the baillies and counsall of this burghe; and as he then requyrit the said baillie to conveine the remanent baillies and counsall, and to opin the said missive, and to give redie and due obedience to the desyre thairof; so now the said Mr Patrik of new againe, in name of the said syreff to whome the delyuerie of the said missive, and report of the obedience thairwnto wes committit be his Maiestie, requyrit the whole baillies and counsall presentlie assemblit, to opin, read, and considder the said missive, and to give dew obedience to his Maiesties royall plesour thairin conteanit; quhilk missive being presentit with all dew reverence, in presence of the said prouest, baillies, and counsall, was opinit and publictlie red in thair audience, whairof the tenour followis:—

The Kingis Maiesties letter presentit to the counsell.

"To our trustie and weelbeloued the baillies and councell of our cittie of Aberden.

Charles R. Trustie and weelbeloued, we greet yow weel, whereas we ar informit of some seditious convocatiounes practised amongst yow, comeing as we heir especiallie frome the electioun yow have latelie made of one Patrik Leslie for your prouest, whom we wer informit to have wrongit your trust in his careage at our late parliament, and thairfoir to hawe deserved no suche chairge, and in regaird we hawe alwayes formerlie found yow forward for our service, and accordinglie have dispensed our favour to yow in quhat micht concern your liberties and priviledges, now being cairfull of that which may concerne our service and the peace and weell of that our citie in redressing of the abuses past, and preventing the lyke inconvenient, it is our pleasour for that effect that yow remove the said Patrik Leslie frome being your prouest, and in his place we wish yow to mak choice of Sir Paull Mengzes, who wes formerlie in that chairge; so not doubting of the performance of this our plesour, we bid yow fareweell frome our court at Whithall, the 10th of December 1634." Eftir publict reading of the quhilk missive and all respective consideratioune takin of the tenour and contentis thairof, the saidis prouest, baillies, and councell all in ane voce, with all submissive dewtie and obedience, humblie acknowledgit thameselflis bund to the speedie and reall performance of his Maiesties royall plesour thairin conteanit;

14 Jan.
1635.
The Kingis
Maiesties
letter presentit to
the counsell.

lykeas the said Patrik Leslie, present prouest, for himselff and his awin interest, humblie acquiesced in his Maiesties plesour signified concerning him be the said missive, and instantlie conforme thairto, dimittit and laid donne the said office of prouestrie at his Maiesties feit, to the effect choice may be maid of the said Sir Paull Mengzeis to be prouest in his sted, according to the warrand and desyre of the said missive, whairwpoun command was given to the baillies to conveine presentlie the late counsall of this burghe, the yeir immediatlie bygaine, with the haill deacones of craftis, and thay that have vote with the present counsall in the electioun of the prouest and remanent magistrattis of this burghe; and accordinglie the said auld counccll, in the yeir immediatlie bypast, with the sex deacones of craftis being fullie conveinit in the said counsallhous, and his Maiesties missive aboue writtin being againe publictlie red in thair audience, the saidis new and auld counsallis, and haill deacones of craftis, being seuerallie demandit be the said Gilbert Colinson, baillie, whome they wald chuise to be prouest in place of the said Patrik Leslie, who had voluntarlie dimittit his office of prouestrie as said is, thay all in ane voce, with all submissive respeck and obedience acknowledgeit thame selffis band not onlie to the redie and present performance of his Maiesties royall plesour signified be the said missive, bot lyikwayis to everie wther thing lying in thair possibilities that may concerne his Maiesties service; lykeas instantlie be thair wniforme voyces they elected and choosed the said Sir Paul Mengzeis to be prouest of this burghe till Michaelmes nixt to cum, in place of the said Patrik Leslie; and the said Sir Paull being personallie present, acceptit the said office of prouestrie in and wpoun him, and gave his aith for faithfull administratioun thairin.

11 Feb.
1635.
Ordinance
to the Mr
of kirkwark.

11 *February* 1635.

The quhilk day the prouest, baillies, and counsall, haveand red and considerit the compt of Walter Robertson, dean of gild of this burghe, of his debursementis at his late being in Flanders on the casting of the great bell of Sanct Nicolas paroche kirk of the same burghe, callit the "Laurence," and stoking thairof, and for francht outward and hameward, and wther chairges requisete in that busines, quhilk wes cassin and stocked of new againe in Midleburghe, in anno 1634, being send thair for that effect he warrand of the magistrats and counsall for the tyme, he resone of a great rift in the same, quhairthrow the said bell wes wnprofitabill, and could not serve for publict vse, they find that the said Walter hes debursit and advancet of his awin proper moneyis on the casting and stoking of the said bell, and for the outward and hameward francht and vther charges in that busines, the somme of tuelff hundreth fourscoir fourtein pundis sevinteine schillingis Scottis money, comptand onlie dolour for dolour; and thairfoir they ordaine Robert Johnstoune, maister of kirkwark, to refound and pey back againe the lyik somme to the said Walter Robertsonne of the rediest of the kirk moneyis in his handis, quhilk salbe allowit to the said Mr of kirkwark in his comptis.

11 Feb. 1635.
Ordinance to the Mr of kirkwark.

26 March 1635.

The quhilk day the provest baillies, and counsall haveand this day receaved a grations and favourable missive frome the kingis most excellent maiestie, thay ordaine the same to be registrat in thair counsall booke *ad futuram rei memoriam*, whairof the tenour followis, "To our trustie and weelbeloved the provest, baillies, and counsall of our citie of Aberdein."
"Charles R.,
Trustie and weelbeloved, we greet your weell, Vnderstanding of your willing and redie obedience to our letter in removeing of your late provest, and accepting Sir Paull Mengzeis, knicht, in that chairge, we doe thairin acknowledge your gude affectioun to our service, and giue yow hartie thankis for the same, assureing you that heirefter wee wilbe spairing to giue any suche furder ordour vnles thair be some speciall occasioun moveing ws thairunto: As for your signature sent wnto ws for ratifieing your liberties, we have at this tyme returnit the same to our advocat to be conferred

26 Mar. 1635.
Missive from his Maiestie.

26 Mar. 1635.

Missive from his Majestie.

with the last ratificatioune of our late royall father, and yff nothing be materiallie disconforme, or yff any thingis be added by yow of new whairbe we nor nane of our gude subiectis ar prejudgeit that he forthwith caus exped the same wnder our cachet and seallis, vtherwayis to returne it dirated by him vnto ws, that it may pas oure signature heir, and be returned back for that purpose; we bid you farewell, frome our Court at Whythall the tuelff day of February 1635.

8 April 1635.

Ordinance to the dean of gild anent the Bishopis buriall.

8 April 1635.

The quhilk day the prouest, baillies, and counsall, ordainis the tounes haill tuelff peice of ordinance to be shot the morne at the buriall of vmquhill Patrik, late Bishop of Aberdeine, in testimonie of thair affectioun and deserveit respect to him, thairof thrie peise to be shot at the lifting of the corps out of the cheppell on the Castelhill, and the wther nyne to be shot howsone the buriall passis by the tounes merche at the Spitillhill, and thairifter the said haill ordinance to be chairgit and shot of new againe at the interring of the corps, and the haill bellis to be tollit during that ilk tyme; lyke as they appoint Walter Robertsone, deane of gild, to caus mont and mak in redines the said ordinance to the effect foirsaid, and what he debursses thairwpoun salbe allowit to him in his comptis.

13 May 1635.

Licence grantit to Jamesoune.

13 May 1635.

The quhilk day the prouest, baillies, and counsall of the burght of Abirdeine wnderwrittin, thay ar to say, Sir Paull Mengzeis of Kynmondy, knight, prouest, Gilbert Collisoun, Maister Thomas Gray, Maister Mathow Lumysden, Maister Robert Farquhar, baillies; Walter Robertsoun, deane of gild; Robert Cruikschank, thesaurar; Robert Johnstoun, Thomas Mortymer, George Mengzeis, Robert Alexander, Daniel Aidye, Alexander Burnett, Thomas Paip, Paull Mengzeis, Hew Andersoun, goldsmith, and George Pyper, wricht, being conveinit in the tounes counsallhouse aneut the peti-

tioun gewin in to thame be George Jamesoun, indweller in the said
burght, makand mentioun, that for sameikle as a greate pairt of the playfeild belongeing to the toune whair comedies were wont to be actit of
auld besyde the well of Spa, is spoilled, broekin, and cariet away be speat
and inundation of watter, and is lyabill to the same danger, and inconvenient heireftir, so that unles some course be taikin to withstand suche
speattis and invndationnes, the whole playfeild, within a short space of
tyme will alluiterlie decay, and serwe for no wse; and the said George
tacking notice of the tounes prejudice heirin, and withall havand consideratioun how this little plott of ground may be vsefull to the toune
heirefter, out of his naturall affectioun to this his native citie, he is content
wpon his awin chairges, not onlie to mak some fortificatioun to withstand
the violence of speattis in tyme coming, bot lykewayes to mak some
policie and planting within and about the said playfeild for the publict
vse and benefitt of the toune, wherof he hes takin occasioun be this his
petitioun to acquaint thair wisdomes of the counsall, humblie desyiring for
this effect, that ther wisdomes will be pleased to grant him frie libertie,
licence, and tolerance to mak sic building, policie, and planting within
and about the said plott of ground, as he sall think most fitting and convenient, both to withstand the violence of the watter fra doinge forder
harme thairwnto, and to the effect the same may redound to the publict
wse and benefitt of the toune: onlie this muche he desyiris for his trawellis,
cost, and expenssis to be bestowit on this work, that he may hawe
a lease of this plott of ground and the wse thairof to his awin behowe
during his lyftyme allanerlie, and eftir his deceas, he is content that the
magistrattis and counsell of this burght for the tyme intromett thairwith,
and apply the same in all tyme thaireftir in the publict wse and benefitt
of the toune as they sall find most convenient, without any recompense
to be sought be him, his aires, executoris, assignayes, or successoris, for
any chairges that he sallhappin to bestow thairwpoun, as at mair length
wes contenit in the said petitioun: quhilk being red, hard, and considderit
be the saids proueast, baillies, and counsall, and thay thairwith being ryplie

13 May
1635.
—
Licence
grantit to
Jame-
soune.

13 May
1635.

Licence
grantit to
Jame-
soune.

advysed, thay find the desyir thairof to be most reasonable as being a motioun tending to the publict gude and benefitt of the toune, acknowledging thairby the petitionar to expres himselff as a weall affected citizen towards the furtherance and increse of policie in this his native toune; and thairfoir be thir presentis thay giwe, grant, and sett to the said George Jamesonn a lease and tack of the said plott of ground callit the Playfeild during all the dayes of his lyftyme allanerlie, his entrie thairto to be and begin the day and date heirof, with full power, libertie, and priniledge to him to build and mack sic policie and planting in and about the said plott of ground in all pairts, and throughout the haill bounds and limites thairof as he sall think most convenient, payand thairfoir yeirelie during his lyftyme to the thesaurar of the said burght for the tyme in name of the toune, thrie shillings foure penneis vsuall Scottes money at the feist of Witsonday yeirlie, if the same be asked allanerlie, for all vther maill or dewtie that may be requyred thairfore during the space forsaid, with this alwayes conditioun and prowisioune, that immediatlie eftir the deceis of the said George, the magistrattis and counsall of the said burght for the tyme, in name of the toune, or thair thesaurar in thair name, sall hawe full and frie power to mell and intromett with the said Playfeild, haill policie, building, and planting within and about the same *brevi manu*, without any proces of law or declaratour, and to apply the same to the publict vse and benefitt of the haill toune in all tyme thaireftir, without any recompense to be gewine be the toune to the aires or executors of the said George, for any cost or charges he sall happin to mak and debourse in planting and building thairvpoun, quhairunto the said George Jameson consentit, and agriet and accepted of his lywerent tak abone writtin wpoun the conditioun foirsaid.

3 June 1635.

The samen day the provest, baillies, and counsall being crediblie informet that ane reverend fader in God, Adame, Bishop of Dumblane, is to be transplantit frome his former chairge in that bishoprick, and to be resaneit and admittit Bishop of Aberdeine wpon Sonday, the second day of August nixttocum at Halierudehous: Thairfoir thay think meit and expedient to direct commissionares frome this burghe for attending of the said dyet, and to congratulat the said reverend father his transplantationne and new admissioun in the tounes name, and thairwith to mak his convoye hameward to this burghe wpoun the tounes chairges, for the quhilk effect they instantlie nominat Gilbert Colinsone, baillie, and Mr Alexander Ross, doctor in divinitie, ane of the tounes ordinar ministeris as commissionares for thame, and ordaines Robert Cruikschank, thesaurar, to debursc the somme of four hundreth merkis to the saidis commissionares to ane compt for making of the said reverend father and thair awin chairges, whilk somme salbe allowit to the said thesaurar in his comptis, of the quhilk somme the said Gilbert Colinsone, baillie, delyuerit bak to the thesaurar the somme of   at his returne frome Edinburgh, in respect the said reuerend father wes not redie to come north till the beginning of September nixt.

3 June 1635. Colinsone and Ross chosin commissionaris anent the Bishop of Aberdeine transplantationne.

3 June 1635.

The provest, baillies, and counsall appointis a not to be guien to Mr Robert Petrie, thair agent, of the names of the nichtbouris of the toune quha ar chairgit for conceallit moneyis at the instance of the Earle of Kennowle; and Mr James Baird, advocat, to be employit as the tounes procuratour, to compeir befoir the Lordis of Sessioun for defence of the said actioun, and informatioun to be send to him for that effect.

3 June 1635. Anent our nichtboures summondit for conceallid moneyis.

3 June 1635.

3 June 1635.
Statute anent the playding packed in the tounes packhous.

The samen day the prouest, baillies, and counsall hes statute and ordanit, and be thir presentis statutes and ordaines that ilk pack and fardell of playding, whilk sallhappin to be packed heirefter in the tounes commoun packhous, haveing lyen in the said packhous twa nichtis efter paking, sall pay nichtlie fra thane furth, ay and quhill the same be transportit and removeit out of the said hous, the dewtie following to the tounes tennent and takisman thairof—viz., aucht pennyes for ilk pack, and four pennyes for ilk fardell, and the nichtboures of the toune to be frie of the said bygaine dewtie befoir the dait heirof.

3 June 1635.
Taxt Roll of the burrowis.

3 June 1635.

The Generall Taxt Roll of the whole burrowis of this kingdome, maid and set doune at ane particular conventioun, haldin at Edinburghe in October 1635, be the commissionares thair convenit and appointit for that effect, bearand ilk burghes pairt of the somme of ane hundreth pundis of all taxationnes, ordanit to continew for the spaise of thrie yeares and longer during the burrowes plesour :—

Edinburghe,	28 lib., 15ss.
Perth,	5 lib., 10ss.
Dundie,	9 lib., 6ss., 8d.
Aberdeine,	8 lib.
Stirling,	1 lib., 16ss.
Glasgow,	5 lib., 10ss.
Sanctandrous,	3 lib.
Dysart,	1 lib., 10ss.
Linlithgow,	1 lib., 10ss.
Aire,	2 lib., 1ss., 4d.
Hadingtoun,	1 lib., 16ss.

Kirkaldie,	2 lib., 6ss., 8d.	3 June 1635.
Montrose,	2 lib., 13ss., 4d.	Taxt Roll of the burrowis.
Coupar,	1 lib., 4ss.	
Anstruther Easter,	1 lib., 11ss.	
Drumfreis,	2 lib., 4ss.	
Innernes,	2 lib.	
Brechin,	1 lib.	
Irwine,	1 lib., 3ss.	
Elgine,	1 lib.	
Jedburghe,	0 lib., 18ss.	
Kirkudbrighe,	1 lib.	
Vigtoun,	0 lib., 15ss.	
Petinweyme,	0 lib., 15ss.	
Dumfermline,	0 lib., 12ss.	
Dumbartane,	0 lib., 12ss.	
Reinfrew,	0 lib., 10ss.	
Lanrik,	0 lib., 16ss.	
Abirbrothok,	0 lib., 10ss.	
Bruntyland,	0 lib., 16ss., 8d.	
Peibles,	0 lib., 10ss.	
Carraill,	1 lib., 4ss.	
Kinghorne,	0 lib., 11ss., 8d.	
Tayne,	0 lib., 12ss.	
Selkirk,	0 lib., 10ss.	
Anstruther Waster,	0 lib., 6ss., 8d.	
Culros,	0 lib., 12ss.	
Dunbar,	0 lib., 12ss.	
Bamff,	0 lib., 8ss.	
Whythorne,	0 lib., 5ss.	
Forfar,	0 lib., 6ss., 8d.	
Rothesay,	0 lib., 5ss.	
Forress,	0 lib., 6ss.	

3 June 1635. Taxt Roll of the burrowis	Ruthglein,	0 lib.,	5ss.
	North Bervick,	0 lib.,	4ss.
	Cullen,	0 lib.,	4ss.
	Narne,	0 lib.,	4ss.
	Lawder,	0 lib.,	5ss.
	Innerkeithing.	0 lib.,	10ss.
	Kelranye,	0 lib.,	3ss., 4d.
	Annan, .	0 lib.,	3ss., 4d.
	Sanchar,	0 lib.,	3ss., 4d.
	Lochmaban,	0 lib.,	3ss., 4d.
	New Galloway.	0 lib.,	1ss.

9 August 1635.

Licience for ane Frensche schoole.

9 August 1635.

The counsall grantis licience to Alexander Rolland to teache ane Frensche schoole within this burghe for teacheing of the youth, sic as sall pleas to come wnto him, and for that effect to put wp ane brod or signe befoir his schoole doore, to give notice of the said licience to all wha ar desyrous to learne the Frensche tongue.

23 Sept. 1635.

Deserting of the ordinar dyett off election.

23 September 1635.

Apud Aberden vigesimo tertio die mensis Septembris anno domini millesimo Sexcentesimo Trigesimo quinto.

The quhilk day the proust, baillies and councell of the burghe of Aberdene, eftir following, Thay ar to say Sir Paull Mengzeis of Kynmundie, knicht, proust, Gilbert Colinson, Mr Thomas Gray, Mr Matho Lumisden, and Mr Robert Farquhar, baillies, Walter Robertson, deane of gild, Robert Cruikshank, thesaurar, Robert Johnstoune, Dauid Aidye, Alexander Burnet, Thomas Mortimer, Thomas Paip, George Mengzeis, Paul Menzes, Hew Andersone, goldsmith, and George Peyper, wricht, nane being absent but Gilbert Menzes of Petfoddellis, Patrick Leslie, and Robert Alexander, being

convenit in the counsalhous of the said burghe as wpoun the ordinar day
of thair electioun, in a peaceable and quyet maner, for electing and chusing
of the new counsall and magistrattis of the same burghe for the yeir to come,
to witt, whill Wedinsday immediatlie preceiding Michaelmes, in the yeir
of God MVI^c threttie sex yeiris, according to the decreit pronunceit be our
late soverane Lord King James, of blissed memorie, in the moneth of
December 1592, anent the electioun of the counsall, provest, baillies, deane
of gild, thesaurar, and other officemen of the said burghe in all tyme
thaireftir, compeirit in the midtyme in presens of the saidis provest,
baillies, and counsall, ane reverend father in God, Adame, Bishope of
Aberdeine, ane of the lordis of his maiesties most honourabill privie
counsall, and Thomas Crombye, shireff principall of Aberdeine, whome the
said reverend father desyrit to be eye witnes, and to bear testimonie of
his proceidings in the present busines; and befoir any thing proceidit in
the said electioune, the said reverend father affirmet both be publict
and privat discourse oft and dyvers tymes had be him with the magistrattis and most pairt of the counsall, that thair is ane notor and evident
divisioun sensiblie seine amongst thame, anent the electioun of thair magistrattis and counsall, to the apparant danger of the commounwealth; for
preventing quhairof the said reverend father desyrit the counsall presentlie
conveinit, with wniforme consent to continew the present dyet of thair
electioun, till sic tyme as he may acquant his maiestie and lordis of secret
counsall thairwith, that ordor may be given be thame for setling of the
present divisioun and of all factious plottis amongst thame heireftir, quhilk
continuatioun of the dyet, the said reverend father declairit sould be
but brak or prejudice of the tounes liberties; lyke as accordinglie he
craveit the voces of the counsall presentlie conveinit if they wald consent
to the said continewatioun: And eftir they wer all voceit be his lordship
thairupoun, sevin of thame, to witt, Sir Paull Mengzeis, provest, Gilbert
Colinsone, Mr Thomas Gray, baillies; Walter Robertsone, deane of gild;
Robert Johnstonne, George Menzeis, and Paull Mengzeis, consentit at the
said reverend father's desyre to the continuatioun of the present dyet of

23 Sept. 1635.

Deserting of the ordinar dyett of election.

23 Sept.
1635.
—
Deserting
of the
ordinar
dyett of
election.

the electioun and nyane of thame, viz: Mr Matho Lummisden, Mr Robert
Farquhar, baillies; Robert Cruikshank, thesaurar; Daniel Aidye, Alexr.
Burnet, Thomas Mortimer, Thomas Paip, Hew Anderson, and George
Pyiper, disassentit to any continuatioun of the present dyet of thair electioun, bot that the same sould go on this day, according to the decreit
foirsaid given be our said late soverane lord King James of happie
memorie, and anniversarie custume continuallie observeit sensyne, sieing
they wer heir assemblit in peaceable maner for that effect. And the said
reverend father be resone of the diversitie of the saidis voyces and of the
distractioun and divisioun he sies amongst the present magistrattis and
counsall, out of his auctoritie as ane of the lordis of his maiesties privie
counsall, in his maiesties name requyrit thame to dissolue and desert
the present meiting, and to continew all proceiding in the said electioun,
till he acquant his maiestie and lordis of privie counsall thairwith and
that thair plesure and commandiment be reportit bak againe to thame
thairanent, and in the midtyme willit and commandit the present magistrattis, counsall, and officemen, to continew in thair severall stationnes,
and in keiping and exerceing everie ane his awin place and office during
the said space, as they will be ansuerable to his maistie, declairing that
this continuatioun sould be but brak of thair liberties: Quhilk command
given be the said reverend father in his maiesties name, the saidis proueist
baillies, and counsall instantlie obeyit, and conforme thairto, brak wp and
dissoluet thair present meiting; and the persones disassentares aboue
named tuke instrumentis that they wer willing and redie for thair pairtis
to proceid to the said electioun in peaceable and calme maner conforme to
the foirsaid decreit given be our said late soverane King James of blissed
memorie, protesting that they be frie from exerceing of any office, or sitting as counsallours frome this tyme furth in respect they wer chosin
thairto onlie for ane yeir, whilk expyris this present day, and that quhatsumeuir detriment the toune sall susteane in thair liberties or vtherwayis
be deserting of this present dyet, that the same be not impute to thame,
bot that they be frie and blameles thairof, be resone of thair willingnes

and rediences to proceid presentlie to the said electioun, according to the foirsaid decreit and consuetude inviolablie heirtofoir observeit sen the giving thairof, lykeas the foirnamed persones consentares aboue named, protestit in the contrair, in respect of thair consent given to the foirsaid continuatioun at the desyre of the said reverend father, for the guide and peace of the commoun weall; and the said reverend father, as abefoir requyrit and desyrit the present magistrattis and counsall to continew in thair seurall places and government of the toune, ay and quhill his maiesties plesour or warrand frome the lordis of secret counsall be direct to the toun thairanent, as they wilbe ansuerable to his maiestie at thair heighest chairge and perrell.

23 Sept. 1635.
Deserting of the ordinar dyett of election.

7 October 1635.

Apud Aberden, septimo die mensis Octoberis, anno domini millesimo sexcentesimo trigesimo quinto.

The quhilk day in presence of the provest, baillies, and counsell of the burghe of Aberdeine conveinit in thair councellhous for making electioun of the new counsell and magistrattis of the said burghe for the yeire to come, for obedience to the chairge eftirspecifeit, gewin to thame for that effect, and for preservatioun of the tounes liberties, compeirred Richard Foullartoune, and declairit that ane noble and potent erle, Johne, erle of Traquair, lord thesaurar depute of this kingdome, had directit to him oure souerraine lordis letteris, gewin be delyweranee of the lordis of his maiesties most honourable privie counsall, for chairging the provest, baillies, and counsall of the said burghe, and otheris hawing woce in thair electioun, to proceid this day to the electioun of thair new counsell and magistrattis for the yeir to come, in respect that the ordinar dyet of thair electioun wpoun considerable respects wes continewit; lykeas the said Richard declaired that conform to the warrant of the saids letteris he had causit Robert Merser, messinger, charge particularlie the provest, baillies, and counsall of this burghe to that effect, quilkis letteris the said Richard

7 October 1635.
Charge for macking election of the new councell and magistrattis, &c.

7 October 1635.

Election of the new councell.

gawe in and producit befoir the said provest, baillies, and counsell as the warrand and ground of thair meitting for making of the said electioun, off the quhilkis letteris the tennour followes,—" Charles be the grace of God, King of Greate Britaine, France, and Ireland, defendar of the faith, to oure loiuttis, Robert Merser, messingeris, our schirreffis in that pairt coniunctlie and seuerallie, speciallie constitute, greitting, Forsamcikill as the lordis of oure priuie counsell ar informed that of late there hes beine some contestatioun within oure burghe of Aberdeine amongs the nighboures and inhabitantis thairof aneut the electioune of the magistrattis and counsall of oure said burghe; quhilk contestatioune is yit fostered and interteanied within the same burghe, for preventing whairof, and for the better preserwatioun of the liberties of oure said burghe anent the electioun of thair magistrattis and counsall, the ordiner dyet whairof hes beine wpoun some considerable respectis continewed, Oure will is heirfoir, and we charge you straitlie, and commands that incontinent thir oure letteris sene, ye pas and in oure name and auctoritie, command and charge the prouest, baillies, counsell, and otheris, hawing vote in the electioun of the magistrattis of oure said burghe, to proceid in a calme and peaceable maner to thair said electioun, upoun Wedinsday nixt, the sewint day of October. . . . Gewin under our signet at Edinburgh, the penult day of September, and of oure reigne the elleuint yeire 1635." Eftir the productioun and reiding of the quhilkis letteris, and incalling of the name of God by publict prayer according to the accustumed maner, the saidis prouest, baillies, and counsell proceidit to thair electioun in maner following. . . . Sir Paull Mengzeis, prouest and moderator for the tyme, finding Patrik Leslie to be present, whome his maiestie wpoun just occasion of offence removed the yeire bygaine frome the office of prouestrie, causit publictlie reid in counsall his maiesties letter direct to that effect; as lykewayes causit reid the letter direct to the prouest, baillies, and counsall of this burghe latelie in September last be my Lord Archbishope of Sainct Androus, primat and Lord High Chancellar of this kingdome, whairby his lordship, for the caussis mentioned in the said letter, willed and requyred thame in his maiesties name that they suld not make chuse of the said Patrik Leslie to be thair prouest, nor yit suffer him to haue woyce in thair counsall, and thairfor the said Sir Paull Mengzeis, prouest, in his maiesties name and auctoritie, requyred and commandit the said Patrik Leslie to remowe frome this present electioun . . . And the said Patrik Leslie declared that he hawing obeyit his maiesties letter in remowing from the office of prouestrie, quhilk buir no remowinge of him frome being a counsellour, he wes this day come for obedience to the chairge of secret counsall, gewin to him to elect the new councell and magistrattis. . . . And hawing got the letis from the handis of Mr Robert Farquhar, baillie, to woyce as a counsellour and begun to wote, the said Sir Paull, Gilbert Meingzeis of Petfoddellis, Gilbert Colinsoun, baillie, and Robert Johnstoun, impedit and interrupted the said Patrik from any forder woyceing. . . . and siclyk the said Patrik allegit that the most pairt of the counsall approwes and consentis to his proceiding and voceing in the said electioun, and the said Sir Paull protestit againes the said Patrik Leslie for impeding and hindering of the said electioun, and keiping wp of the lites contrair to the command of the saids letteris as he allegit. And the said Patrik protestit in the contrair, in respect he wes willing to giwe his woyce and the lites from him when he had endit, quhilk the foirnamed persones wald not permitt, in respect thay ar commandit be my Lord Chancellares letter not to suffer him to hawe any voce; and becaus the said Patrik Leslie keipit up the lites that wer drawin up for chusing of the new counsell be the space of thrie or foure houres or thairby, and wald not giwe thame out of his hands till he sould sett to his nottes and woyce to the samen, the prouest causit draw up the samen litt ower againe on ane other paper, and desyrit the counsall present to give their woyces for chuseing of the counsall; lykas, accordinglie, the said Gilbert Collisoun, Maister Thomas Gray, baillies; Gilbert Mengzeis, Robert Johnstoun, Walter Robertsoun, Robert Alexander, George Mengzeis, and Paull Mengzeis, gawe thair woyces of new againe and markit the said paper; and Mr Mathew Lummysden and Mr Robert Farquhar, baillies, refused to mack any new electioun in respect thay hawe gewine thair woyces alredie to the lites

7 October 1635.

Election of the new councell.

7 October 1635.
Election of the new councell.

first drawin wp and presentit; lykeas also Thomas Mortimer, Robert Cruikshank, Daniel Aedye, Alexander Burnett, Thomas Paip, Hew Andersoun, and George Pyper, refused to nott or give thair woyces to any litt except that quhilk wes first drawin up and markit be the said Gilbert Mengzeis and the foure baillies, quhilk wes gewin be Mr Robert Farquhar, baillie, to Patrik Leslie to be woyeed be him, whome the prouest, Gilbert Mengzeis, and Gilbert Collisoun, wiolentlie, as thay allegit, impedit be following him frome place to place in the counsalhous, and drawing of the said Patriks hand and the pen frome the paper; and the said Patrik Leslie desyrit the clerk to come and sie him mark the saids lites, conforme as he hes done to the rest of the hous, whairwnto the clerk answered he wes content swa to do if the prouest, baillies, and counsall wold command him to that effect; and the said Patrik desyred a woice of the hous whither or no the clerk suld attend his marking of the lites, quhilk the prouest as moderator, the said Gilbert Mengzeis and Gilbert Collisoun wald not suffer to go to woting, be reasone of my Lord Chancellares warrant to the contrair; and the said Patrik taking the new lites in his hands, and begynning to nott the same eftir he had gewin his note thairto, the prouest tuke the new lite out of his hand. . . . and immediatlie thaireftir the said Patrike Leslie went out of the counsalhous and returned bak againe within a short space with the said first lites in his hand, notted, and woyeed be him in presence of Robert Merser, messinger, and nottar, as he declared and presented the same to the saids Thomas Mortimer, Robert Cruikshank, and remanent persones, his adherentis aboue named, for putting thair nottes and woyces thairto, desyring the clerk to attend thair marking, notting, and woyeing of that litt as he had done abefoir. Bot the said Sir Paull Mengzeis, prouest, &c. . . . commandit him to the contrair, becaus the said Patrik Leslie had alterit the forme of the electioun be carieing the lites furth of the counsallhous, and putting his notes and markes thairunto in ane uther hous privatlie be himselff allane, and presenting the same markit be him as said is . . . Lykas the said Sir Paull requyrit the saids Maister Matho Lummysden, Maister Robert Farquhar, baillies, Robert Cruikshank, Thomas Mortimer, Alexander

Burnet, Dauid Aedye, Thomas Paip, Hew Andersonn, and George Pyper, to proceid in the said electioun, as thay who hes woce thairin, and to nott thair wyoces wpoun the said second lite, whairunto the remanent of the counsall wha had power to wote had alredie woted. . . . Quhilk thay all refuised to do, and wald wote to no lites except that quhilk the said Patrik Leslie, the said Gilbert Mengzeis, and the foure baillies, had alredie notted. . . . Lykas the said Patrik gewing the first lite to thame furth of his said markis. . . . thay all went on and sett to thair noites and voyces to the samen desyiring the clerk to number thair nottes and woyces, quhilk the said pronest. . . . inhibite the clerk to do, be resone of the blotting of the said lite. . . . And the saids Patrik Leslie, Mr Mathew Lummysdene, Mr Robert Farquhar, Robert Cruikshank, Thomas Mortimer, Alexander Burnet, Dauid Aedye, Thomas Paip, Hew Andersonn, and George Pyper, be resone of the said contramand gewin to the clerk to number thair woyces, went avay all of thame togidder abruptlie furth of the counsalhous, and left and deserted the said electioun for thair pairtis. In respect whairof the said Sir Paul Mengzeis. . . . protestit against thame and ewerie ane of thame for thair wilful contempt of the said chairge, and that thay be ansuerable to his maiestie and lords of privie counsall for the same; and the said Mr Mathew Lummysden . . . and remanent persones. . . . protested in the contrair. . . . And than the said Sir Paull Mengzeis, pronest, and sic uthers of the magistrattis and counsall as remaned with him, to witt, Gilbert Colinsoun, Maister Thomas Gray, baillies, Gilbert Mengzeis, Robert Johnstoun, Walter Robertsoun, deane of gild, Robert Alexander, George Mengzeis, and Paul Mengzeis, for obedience to the chairge of the saids letters, and for preserwatioun of the tounes liberties proceidit to the electioun of the said new counsall. . . . and . . . thay electit, nominat, and choosit thir personnes eftir following, viz., Gilbert Cullen, Thomas Collisoun, Johne Hay, George Johnstoun, yor, Willeame Forbes, yor, George Moresonn, Thomas Nicolsoun, Paull Collisoun, George Cullen, Robert Smyth, Paull Inglis, James Robertsoune, Willeame Patrie, James Chrystie, tailyeour, and Robert Forbes Baxter, to be of the new counsall of this

7 October 1635.
Election of the new counceell.

7 October 1635.
Election of the new councell.

burghe for the yeire to come. . . . to the quhilk new counsall swa electit. . . . thir foure personis of the auld counsall. . . . to witt, Sir Paull Mengzeis, Gilbert Mengzeis, Robert Johnstoune, Mr Thomas Gray, wer electit and chosin to be lykewayes counsellours. . . . Thay proceidit to the electioun of the magistrattes and uther officemen of the burghe for the yeir to come. . . . and . . . thay electit and chusit ane honorable man, Robert Johnstoun, to be prouest. . . . and . . . thay electit and chusit Johne Hay, George Johnstoun, youngar, Willeame Forbes, younger, and George Moresoun, to be baillies. . . . . . . thay electit and chusit Paull Colinsoun to be deane of gild. . . . and thay electit and chusit Robert Smyth to be thesaurar.

4 Nov. 1635.
Ordinance aganis the carying of blind bowattis on the streittis.

4 November 1635.

The samen day the prouest, baillies, and counsall expresslie discharges and inhibites any blind bowattis to be cariet throw the toune heirafter, ather be schollares or wtheris quhatsumevir, wnder the payne of braking of the saidis bowattis and warding of the cariers thairof, and ordanis intimatioun heirof to be maid be the drwm, that nane pretend ignorance; and siclyke the saidis prouest, baillies, and counsall statutes and ordaines that na maner of persone be fund vagand on the streites efter ten houris at nicht, wnder the payne of warding, and to be wtherwayis punishit at the descretioun of the magistrattis, according to thair demerites.

4 Nov. 1635.
Money collected for the ministers of the Palatinate to be lent for the use of the minister at Futtie.

4 November 1635.

The said day the prouest, baillies, and counsall ordainis the moneyis in Andro Burnetis handis, collectit for the distrest ministeris of the Palatinat to be upliftit be . . . and employit on profite for the wse and behove of ane of the tounes ministeris, serving the cure at the kirk of Futtie; lykeas now as then, and then as now, they destinat and appoint the said soume to the use foirsaid in all tyme comeing.

18 November 1635.

The samen day the provest, baillies, and counsall being crediblie informed that the right reverend father in God, Adame, Bishop of Aberdeine, is to repair to this his diocie shortlie for making of his residence thairin with his familie and servandis, and considering that he cannot be commodiouslie easit within his awin pallace in auld Aberdeine for the present, thairfoir they appoint Robert Smith, thesaurer, to tak and provyd ane comodious lodgeing within this burghe for the said bishopis use till Witsonday nixt wpoun the tounes chairges, and to have the same redie and prepairit againis his heir comeing.

Anent a lodging for the Bishop.

Apud Aberden quinto die mensis Februarii, anno domini millesimo sexcentesimo trigesimo sexto.

5 Feb. 1636.

The quhilk day, in presence of Robert Johnstoun, provest, Paull Collisoun, deane of gild, Paull Inglis, James Robertson, James Crystie, tailyeour, and Robert Forbes, baxter, foure of the present counsellouris of the burghe of Aberdeine, conveinit in the tounes counsalhous, compeirit Mr Mathew Lummysden, burges of the said burghe, and produceit ane decreit of the lordis of his majesties most honorable privie counsell, of the date the tuentie sext day of Januar last bypast. . . . quhairoff the tennour followes:—"At Edinburghe, the tuentie sext day of Januar, the yeire of God M sex hundreth and threttie sex yeires, anent oure soveraine lords letteris direct makand mention, fforsameikle as his majestie is informed that the provest and others, officers of the burghe of Aberdeine, hes beine chosin this yeere contrare to the approved custome of that burghe used at all preceiding tymes, wherin his majestie being unwilling that anie innovatioun be made, or any factious or unlawful way be used, quhilk may procure and foster distractioun in the said toune; and anent the chairge giwen to Robert Jonston, present prowest, Sir Paull Mengzeis, late prowest of the said burghe, George Jonstoun, Johne Hay, George

Decreit Lordis of Privie Counsell anent the election of the magistrattis and counsell for this yeir, &c.

5 Feb.
1636.
———
Decreit
Lordis of
Privie
Councell
anent the
election of
the magi-
strattis and
councell
for this
yeir, &c.

Moreson, and Willeame Forbes, present baillies of the said burghe, Gilbert Colisone, Mr Thomas Gray, Mr Mathew Lummysden, and Mr Robert Farquhar, late baillies of the said burghe, Gilbert Mengzeis of Pitfoddells, Walter Robertson, merchant, Robert Alshonnar, George Mengzeis, Paull Mengzeis, yonger, who wes counsellers of the said burghe this last yeir, and Walter Robertson, clerk of the said burghe, to hawe compeirit befoir the saids lords in maner following, to witt, the present provest and baillies, and those who were in office this last yeere bygaine, to have compeired be thame selffis, or be twa of their number for either syde; and the persons forsaids who were counsellers of the said burghe this last yeere bygaine, and the said Walter Roberson, clerk, to have compeirit personallie before the saids lords at a certaine day bygaine, and the said Walter Robertson to have brought and exhibite with him the acts of the electioun of the present provest, baillies, and counsell of the said burghe, with the haill acts, minuts, instruments, and protestationnes tane in the said electioun, and the lytis of both the saids pairties at the electioun, to have bene seene and considderit be the saids lords; and if it sould be fund that the said electioun hes not beene made according to the usuall and accustomed maner observit in the said burghe, that than and in that cais to have heard and seene thame decernit to nominat for this yeere maister Alexander Jaffray to be thair provest; and thair officers, who this last yeere had the chairge to be continewed; and the persons forsaids who wer counsellers of the said burghe this last yeir, to have ausuerit upoun thair behaviour and cariage in the said electioun, and for thair proceiding thairin aganis the ancient custome of the said burghe; and thay and all the personis forsaids to have compeirit in maner forsaid, wnder the paine of rebellioun and putting of thame to the horne, with certificatioun to thame if thay failzied, letteris sould be direct *simpliciter* to hawe put thame thairto; lykeas at more length is conteaned in the saids letteris, executiouns and indorsatiouns thairof, quhilks being callit, and the saids Sir Paull Mengzeis, George Johnstoune, Gilbert Mengzeis of Pitfoddells, Walter Robertsone, merchant, Robert Alshonner, George Mengzeis, and

Paull Mengzeis, yonger, Mr Robert Farquhar, Gilbert Colisone, Mr Mathew Lummisden, and Walter Robertsone, toune clerk, compeirand all personallie; and the said Robert Johnstoun being excused be ane testimoniall, testifieing his infirmities and inabilitie to travell; and the saids George Johnstoune and George Moresone compeirand in name of the saids Johne Hay and Willeame Forbes, and the said Mr Thomas Gray being excused in respect of his absence furth of the cuntrie afore the charge foirsaid given to him for his compeirance, the said Walter Robertsone, clerk, for obedience and satisfactioun of the chairge foirsaid, given unto him, producit and exhibite befoir the saids lords the process of the electioun of the present provest, baillies, and counsell of the said burghe, with the acts, minuts, instrumentis, protestationnes, and lyts made and tane in the said electioun; quhilk proces, acts, instrumentis, lytis, and protestationnes being red, hard, and considderit be the saids lords, and thay being thairwith and withall that wes proponed, producit, and alledgit be either pairtie in this mater weele advysed, the lords of secreit counsell findis and declaris that the said electioun hes not beene made in that faire and peaceable maner quhilk became dewtifull and goode subjectis to have done in a mater of this kynde, quhilk hes occasioned and fosters some factions and hearts-burning among the neichbouris of the said burghe, to the disturbance of the publict peace and tranquillitie of the same, and thairfore the saids lords, according to his majesties missive letter, written and directed to thame, hes nominat, made, and electit . . . the said Mr Alexander Jaffray to be provest of the said burghe for this present yeere, to witt, till the ordinar tyme of electioun about Michaelmes nixt; and lykewayes hes continowit and continowis that same space the baillies, deane of gild, thesaurar, and counsellers of the said burgh, being trafficqueing merchants and actuall inhabitants within the same burghe, and suche as ar of anie other conditioun or qualitie, that they be removed and others chosin in thair place, in thair severall charges, places, and offices whairin they servit this last yeere bygaine, to witt, afore Michaelmes last, ordaining and commanding thame as thay will be answerable

5 Feb. 1636.
—
Decreit Lordis of Privie Counsell anent the election of the magistrattis and counsell for this yeir, &c.

5 Feb.
1636.

Decreit Lordis of Privie Conncell anent the election of the magistratis and conncell for this yeir, &c

upone the dewtie of thair chairge to accept the said charge in and upon thame, and to continew in the administratioun and discharge thairof till the tyme foirsaid, commanding heirby the haille inhabitantis of the said burghe to reverence, acknowledge, and obey the magestratis now nominat, electcd, and continewed be the saids lordis in all and everie thing tending to the furtherance and advancement of thair place and chairge, and good of the said burghe, as thay and everie ane of thame will ansuer wpoun the contrare at thair perrell, commanding also the persons who sall have vote in the said electioun, heireftir to make thair electioun in a faire and peaceable maner, according to the ancient custome of the said burghe, so that his majestic be not farther trublit thairwith ; and the saids lordis declaris that thir presentis salbe without prejudice of the liberties of the said burgh heirefter, and quherwnto this decreit and ordinance sall mak no derogatioun. *Extractum de libris actorum secreti consilii S. D. N. regis per me Jacobum Primerose, clericum euisdem sub meis signo et subscriptione manualibus. Sic subscribitur Jacobus Prymrois.*" Efter production and publict reiding of the quhilk decreit, the said Maister Mathew Lummysden intimat the samen to the saids Robert Johnstoune, Paull Colisone, Paull Inglis, James Robertsoun, James Crystie, and Robert Forbes, requiring thame to give obedience thairwnto, be removing thameselfflis frome thair places and offices whairin thay haue serwit fra Michaelmes last, and be giving way to the pronest, baillies, deane of gild, thesaurar, and counsellouris, electit in thair rowmes be the decreit abonewrittin. . . For obedience to the quhilk decreit, intimatioun, and requisitioun . . . the said Robert Johnstoun, Paull Collisoun, Paull Inglis, James Robertsoun, James Crystie, and Robert Forbes, for thame selffis and thair awin interest, with all dew respect instantlie removed thameselfflis furth of the counsalhous in peace and calme maner, and gave way to the pronest, baillies, deane of gild, thesaurar, and conncellouris electit in thair rowmes be the said decreit . . . and siclyik wpoun the tent day of the said moneth of Februar, the yeir of God foirsaid, compeirit within the tounes counselhous, Alexander Gariauche, messinger, and producit oure soueraine lords letteris, given

and direct be the saids lords of privie counsell . . . be wertew
whairof the said Alexander Gariauche, in oure soweraine lords name and
auctoritie, chairgit the said Mr Alexander Jaffray to conveine within the
counsellhous of the said burghe, within tuentie four houres efter the charge,
under the paine of horning, and there to accept wpoun him the office of
prouestrie of this burghe till the electioun at Michaelmes nixt, and to give
his aith for faithfull administratioun thairin, and siclyk chargit Gilbert
Collison and Mr Mathew Lummysden, twa of the baillies of the said burghe
the yeire bygaine; the other two baillies, to witt Mr Thomas Gray and
Mr Robert Farquhar being absent out of the tonne, the ane at his woyage
in France, the other in Edinburghe; and in lyik maner chairgit Sir Paull
Mengzeis, Robert Johnstoun, Patrik Leslie, Walter Robertsoun, merchant,
Thomas Mortimer, Robert Alexander, Dauid Adye, George Mengzeis,
Thomas Paip, Paull Mengzeis, Hew Andersone, goldsmith, and George
Pyper, wricht, to accept the office of counsellouris in and wpoun thame,
and thairwith such other particular offices as thay did bear and exerce
the yeire bygaine. . . . and to giwe thair aithes for faithfull administratioun of the samen . . . conforme to the tenour of the saids letters in all poyntis whairof the tennour followes: "Charles . . . For-
sameikle as the lords of oure privie counsaill, wpoun dyvers good respectis
and consideratiounis importing the peace and quietnes of oure burghe of
Aberdeine, and setling the government thairof this present yeere, hawe
made choise of Maister Alexander Jaffray to be prouest of oure said
burghe for this present yeere, and hawe continewed the baillies, deane of
gild, thesaurar, and counsell, who served the last yeere, to supplie the
same place and charge this yeere, Oure will is . . . that . .
you . . . charge the present prouest, baillies, deane of gild, thesaurar, and the remanent personis who wer wpoun the counsell of oure
said burghe this last yeere bygain, to conveine in the counsellhous of
oure said burghe within tuentie foure houres nixt efter thay be chairgit
be yow thairto, and theire to accept the saids offices *respectiue* wpoun
thame. . wnder the paine of rebellioun and putting of thame to

5 Feb.
1636.
—
Decreit
Lordis of
Privie
Councell
anent the
election of
the magi-
strattis and
counsell
for this
yeir, &c.

5 Feb.
1636.

Decreit Lordis of Privie Councell anent the election of the magistrattis and councell for this yeir, &c.

oure horne . . . Given under our signet at Edinburghe, the tuentie sext day of Januar, and of oure reigne the ellevint yeire M sex hundreth threttie sex." For obedience to the chairge of the whilkis letteris and decreit foirsaid. . . . compeirit personallie within the said counselhous the said Maister Alexander Jaffray, and declared and protest publictlie in presence of the counsell. . . . that he wes nowayes accessorie to the procureing of any suche warrant frome his majestie to the saids lords of privie councell for making nominatioun or electioun of him to the said office of prouestrie, neither wes he desyrous of suche a burdine, newirtheles humblie acquiescing in his majesties royall pleasure . . . the said Maister Alexander Jaffray acceptit of the said office of prouestrie of this burghe in and wpoun him till the ordinar tyme of electioun at Michaelmes nixt . . . and lyikwayes compeirit the saids Gilbert Collisoun and Maister Mathew Lummysden . . . and . . . acceptit the said office of baillierie . . . Siclyik the said Walter Robertsoun, merchant . . . acceptit the office of deanrie of gild . . . And in lyk maner the saids Sir Paull Mengzeis, Robert Johnstoun, Thomas Mortimer, Robert Alexander, Dauid Aedye, George Mengzeis, Thomas Paip, Paull Mengzeis, Hew Andersone, and George Pyper . . . acceptit the office of counsellouris . . . Moirouer, the saids prouest, baillies, and counsall, tacking to thair considderatioun whereas be the saids lords decreit . . . it is speciallie declared that the baillies, deane of gild, thesaurar, and counsellouris of the said burghe . . . shuld be continewit . . . thay being alwayes trafficqueing merchants and actuall inhabitantis within the said burghe . . . and in respect Gilbert Mengzeis of Pitfoddells, who was a counsalour last yeire, is nowayes a merchant trafficquer, bot is the kingis barone, and hes bene commissionar chosin for the barounes of the shirreffdome of Aberdeine to parliament and conventioun of estates, it wes . . . fand . . . for the most pairt that the said laird of Pitfoddells falls within the compass of the said exceptioun . . . lykas they declare him not to be a counsalour . . . thairefter compeired the said Patrik Leslie, who was chairgit as being a counsallour the yeere bygaine . . . and producit ane act of the saids lords of secreit counsell, whairby thay hawe exemit him to be a counsallour for this present yeire for the caussis conteinit in the said act whairoff the tennour followes,— "At Edinburgh, the twentie eight day of Januar, the yeire of God M sex hundreth and threttie sex yeires, Anent the supplicatioun presented to the lords of secret counsall be Patrik Leslie, merchant, burges of Aberdeine, makand mentioun that whair he hes had no litle caus of greif and displeasour this long tyme bygaine for his majesties offence tane aganes him wpoun occasioun of his behaviour at the late parliament, and he cannot express how farre this grief oppresses and vexes him both in the spirit and persone; and for reparatioune thairof, he will studie in all tyme comeing to the wttermost of his endevouris to approve himselff a most duetiefull and obedient subject to his majestie; and wheiras he is upoun the counsall of the burghe of Aberdeine for this present yeire, he fears that this sall breed some new matter of offence to his majestie and the saids lords, and thairfoir his humble petitioun to the saids lords wes, that he might be fred and exonered of this chairge . . . Quhilk being . . . considdered be the saids lords . . . the lordis of secrett counsall ordaines . . . the provest and baillies of the said burgh of Aberdeine to provyde and foresie that the provest, baillies, and counsell of the said burghe subsist of nyneteine personnes, and that the said Patrik Leslie be nane of that number." . . . Efter the reiding of the quhilk act . . . thay electit ane uther counsallour in his place in maner following, to witt, the sute roll of the haill brethren of gild of the said burghe being red, thair wes nominat furth thairof certaine gild brethren to be ane lite for chuising a counsellour in place of the said Patrik Leslie . . . and furth of the said lite, Mr Willeam More wes electit and chosin to be a counsellour in his roume during the said space . . .

5 Feb. 1636.

Decreit Lordis of Privie Councell anent the election of the magistrattis and counsell for this yeir, &c.

24 *February* 1636.

24 Feb. 1636.

Andro Melville admittit maister of the musick schoole.

The quhilk day anent the petitioun gewin in to the prouest, baillies, and counsell be Andro Meluill, burges of this burghe, makand mentioun that forsameikill as in the moneth of October last, he gave in his petitioun to the counsell then for the tyme, desyiring to be admittit maister of the musick schoole of this burghe, now vacand be deceas of vmquhill Patrik Dauidsone, last maister thairof, in regaird of the said Andro his long serwice as doctor of the said schoole vnder the said Patrik, be the space of these eighteine yeires bygaine, and of the councellis promeis made to him two yeires since, that he shud be preferred to that place if he outleiwed the said Patrik: to the quhilk former petitioun the counsell continuvet thair answer till thair farder advysement, and in the meane tyme appoyntit the said Androw to continew in attending the said schoole, and in the vptaking of the haill benefitt thairof to his awin vse; and now, becaus the said schoole and the youth thairin cannot be convenientlie taught nor disciplined without the help of a doctor, and that he cannot enter in conditiounes with any for that effect till first he know the councellis pleasure if thay will admitt him maister, he thairfoir humblie supplicat the saids prouest, baillies, and counsell that thay wauld be pleased to grant him admissioun to the said office of maister of thair musick schoole, and to the stipend and casualities belonging thairto *ad vitam vel ad culpam;* as for his qualificatioun for the place thair wisdomes hes had pruiff thairof for a long tyme, be his continewall teichinge of the youth in musick these eighteine yeires past, and as for his diligence, lyff, and conversatioun, thair wisdomes ar witnesses also thairwnto, whairanent he submittis himself to thair awin censure, as at more length wes contenit in the said petitioun: quhilk being red, hard, and considderit be the saids prouest, baillies, and counsell, and thay being thairwith weill advysit, and withall havand consideratioun that the said Andro Meluill hes gewin sufficient pruiff of his qualificatioun in the airt of musick, and of his paynfulnes and diligence in attending on the said schoole continewallie sen his first entrie thairin be the space of these eighteine yeiris bypast, as lykewayes be reasone of his guide lyff and conversatioun, and of his bypast careage without scandall or repruiff, the saids provest, baillies, and counsall, all in ane voyce, without oppositioun or contradictioun, hes admittit and receaved, and be thir presentis admittis and receaves the said Andro Meluill to be maister of the musick schoole of this burghe, for instructing of the youth in the airt of musick, singing, and playing, *ad vitam vel ad culpam*: quhilk fault, if any sal be committit heirefter be the said Andro worthie of deprivatioun, salbe tryed be the provest, baillies, and counsall of the said burghe for the tyme, as onlie judges thairto; and gewis and grauntis to the said Andro the samen yeirlie stipend out of the tounes commoun guide, and the lyke salarie and scholage of his scholares quhilk wes due and in vse to be payed to the said vmquhill Patrik Dauidsone, the said Andro finding a qualifeit doctor vnder him to teache his scholares and to attend with him on the schoole, and siclyk he and his doctor taking wp the psalme in bothe the kirkis of this burghe, bothe at preiching and prayeris morning and evening, Sabbath day and weik dayes; and the said Andro compeiring personallie in counsell, acceptit the said office in and wpoun him with the burdine, conditiounes, and for the stipend and salarie aboue specifeit, and gave his aith for his diligence and faithfull administratioun thairin.

24 Feb. 1636. Andro Melville admittit maister of the musick schoole.

16 *March* 1636.

The samen day the counsall appoyntis Hew Anderson to tak ordour with these that layes fuilzie on the kinge his streit, in the Gallogett and vnder the stairis thairof, and to confiscatt all that salbe fund lying thairon any longer space then tuentie foure houres.

16 March 1636. Anderson appoynted to tak order with layeris of fuilzie on the streittis.

16 *March* 1636.

Straquhyne, Straitton, dischargit of keping of schoolles.

The said day the prouest, baillies, and counsall vnderstanding that Mariorie Straquhyne, and   , her daughter, and also Margaret Straitton, hes at thair awin hands, without licence craved or obteinit of the tounes counsell, taken wp English schoolles within this burghe, and teaches thair schollares to reid, thairby prejudging the maisteris of the English schoolles who ar authorized and admittit be the counsall; thairfore dischairges the foirnamed persones, and ilk ane of thame, fra keiping or haulding of any schoolles within this burghe for teaching the bairnes to reid, efter the Ruid day nixt to come; and inence they keip any schoolles thairefter, that the same be for learning of bairnes to sew and wywe pearling allanerlie, and no farder, and that be licence and warrand of the tounes counsell, had and obteinit to that effect, and no wtherwayes.

27 *April* 1636.

Ane edict to be serveit for ane doctour to the grammer schoole.

The samen day the prouest, baillies, and counsell ordanes ane publict edict to be serveit on Sonday nixt at both the kirk doores of this burghe, and at the colledge yett, inviting all yong schollares wha ar litt to teache grammer, and ar desyrous to be admittit ane of the doctouris of the grammer school of this burgh in place of Mr Thomas Chalmer, last doctor thairof, to compeir within the sessioun of the same burghe, wpoun the tuantie nynt day of Junij nixt to come, at twa houres efter noone, to wndirly tryall of thair learning, gude lyff and conversatioun, to the effect the best and most qualifiet, efter tryall and examination, may be admittit to the said vacant rowme in place of the said Mr Thomas Chalmer.

29 *June* 1636.

Boyd admittit ane of the doctouris of the grammer schoole.

The said day anent the edict serveit to this day for filling wp of the place of Maister Thomas Chalmer, ane of the doctors of the grammer schooll of this burghe, now vacant in the tounes handis be his dimissioun, compeirit within the kirk sessioun hous Maister James Boyd, lawfull sone to Archibald Boyd, burges of the said burghe, and offert himsellff reddie and willing to wnderly tryall and examinatioun for the said plaice, wha being examined and tryit in his literature, gude lyff and conversatioun, wes fund meit and qualifeit for the place.

<small>29 June 1636. Boyd admittit ane of the doctouris of the grammer schoole.</small>

20 July 1636.

The same day the prouest, baillies, and counsell ordaines Walter Robertsoun, dean of gild, to deburse feftie pundis money to Maister Dauid Wedderburne, maister of the grammer schoole, for his paynes in drawing wp of new vocables for the weill and benefite of the young schollares within the said grammer schooll, whilk somme salbe allowit to the said dean of gild in his comptis.

<small>20 July 1636. Gratitude to Wedderburne.</small>

5 October 1636.

The quhilk day the prouest, baillies, and counsell being crediblie informed that the plague of pestilence incressis at Londoun, Newcastell, and dyveris other tounes in England, as lykewayes in Holland, and in Elsingoore in Denmark, and that sindrie of our nightbouris of this burghe ar for the present absent out of the cuntrie in some of these pairtis; in consideratioun whairof, and of the danger that may ensew, alsweill be oure awin nightbouris, as be strangeris repairing to the port and herbrie of this burghe, the saids prouest, baillies, and counncell, appointis a watche of twellf personis to be keipit both day and night at the blockhous, and sic other pairtis as the magistrattis sall think expedient for watching the herbrie, and taking just notice and tryell of all shippis cuminge within the same frome forane cuntries; and for this effect ordains the drum to be send throw the toune, chairging all nightboures and inhabitantis of this burghe, that sallhappin to be warnit be the tounes officiares for keiping of

<small>5 October 1636. Ane watche appoynted.</small>

5 October 1636.
Ane watche appoynted.

watche, that thay keip the same in propper persone, vnder the paine of tuentie pundis of wnlaw, to be preceislie exactit of ilk absent, *toties quoties*, but favour, to be payed to the deane of gild for the publict vse and benefitt of the toune.

5 October 1636.
Theasurer, Brastounes.

5 October 1636.

The samen day the prouest, baillies, and counsall grantis tuelff rix dolouris to Robert and Nicholas Brastounes, Inglishmen, to mak thair chairges in cumming to this toune fra Edinburghe, and remaining heir be the space of fyiftein dayes, and returning frome this bak againe to Edinburghe, being broght hither for advysing with thame anent the erecting of ane correctioun hous, to be payed to thame be George Meldrum, thesaurer, quhilk salbe allowit to him in his compts.

12 Oct. 1636.
The craftis consent to be taxt with the brethrene of gild for two thousand merkis to by a tenement for ane correction hous.

12 October 1636.

The said day Williame Andersoun, goldsmith, deacone of the hammermen, and George Pyper, deacone of the wrightes and conpares, compeirand in presens of the prouest, baillies, and councell, reported and declaired, in name of the haill craftis of this burghe, as havand speciall warrand and directioun frome thame, that they ar content to contribute with the brethreine of gild for the soume of two thousand merkis, Scottis money, for helping to by a commodious tenement of land in this burghe, to be a correctioun hous for the wark of macking of braidcloath, vpoune the conditiounes efter following, and no wtherwayes, viz.:—

In the first, That thair granting to the erecting of the said hous be nowayes prejudiciall nor hurtfull to the craftis, liberties, and commoun decreit betwixt the brethrein of gild and the craftis of this burghe.

Secundlie, That the same be nowayes prejudiciall to the saids craftis in bying of woll within this burghe on the mercat dayes, befoir Witsonday or eftir the same, conforme to the said decreit.

Thirdlie, The said craftismen consentis to be stentit for thair pairtis with the rest of the inhabitantis of the toune, for the said tua thousand merkis, for this present yeire allanerlie, for lying of the said hous, and disassentis to any farder taxatioun heireftir for that caus.

Fourthlie, That the craftis salbe acceptit to putt in thair talent to the said hous, according to thair habilities, with the brethrein of gild, and to receawe proffitt and commoditie thairfoir, according to the proportioun of the moneyes to be gewin in be thame.

Fyiftlie, Incais the said hous decay, and that thair be no employment thairin, in that cais the saids craftis to receane lak againe frome the awnares of the said hous sic taxatioun and impositioun as thay happin to be stentit to for bying of the said hous.

Sextlie, That the workmen in the said hous by no yarne to mak in claith, and that thay tack in no yarne to be wowin in the said correction hous, except sa meikle as salbe wrought and spun within the same allanerlie, and no more.

To the quhilkis haill conditiounes and articles the prouest, baillies, and counccll agreit and condiscendit, with this limitatioun and restrictioun, that whairas in the fourt article, the saids craftismen desyres that thay be acceptit to put in thair talent to the said hous according to thair habilities, with the brethreine of gild, and that thay receave benefitt accordinglie, quhilk is granted to the saids craftismen, prowyding that thay contract presentlie with the merchantis undertakeris of the said work, and giue in and advance presentlie thair pairt of the moneyes requisite for accomplishment and perfyting of the same, according to the proportioun of thair vndertaking, wtherwayes refuisses any benefitt to thame for the space of ten yeires to come; quhilk being intimat to Thomas Robertson, deacone conveinar, and George Pyper, wricht, and thay tackand to advyse thairvpoun with the craftis, thay efter advysement with thame, reported and declaired to the magistrattis that for the present nane of the craftis were disposed to lay in or advance any moneyes to the said work for ten yeires to come.

12 Oct. 1636.
The craftis consent to be taxt with the brethrene of gild for tua thousand merkis to by a tenement for ane correction hous.

9 *November* 1636.

9 Nov. 1636.
Ane piller to be erected at Petmedden.

The samen day the provest, baillies, and counsall, ordaines Andro Burnett, maister of the mortifiet moneyis, to caus build and erect with all convenient diligence, ane piramid or pillar vpoun the landis of Petmedden, givin and mortifiet be vmquhill Doctor Liddell, for mantenance of sex bursares in the college of this burghe, and that according to the draught and modall alredie drawin be advyse of Doctor Willeame Johnstoun and Mr Wm. Moir to that effect, and to agrie be thair advyse, and be advyse of Johne Liddell, with ane meson for bigging thairoff, and what he deburses thairwpoun to be allowit to him in his comptis.

14 *December* 1636.

14 Dec. 1636.
Ane loft to be biggit in the Grayfreir kirk for the magistrattis and counsell.

The samen day Mr Willeame Moir, maister of kirkwark, wes ordainit to big and erect in most decent and comelie forme, ane loft within the yle of the Grayfrier kirk of this burghe, befoir the pulpett, for the use of the provest, baillies, and counsall. . .

14 *December* 1636.

14 Dec. 1636.
Report of Commissioner sent to a meeting of the burrowes.

The said day, in presens of the provest, baillies, and counsall, compeirit personallie Thomas Mortimer, baillie, commissionar direct frome this burghe to ane particular meiting of the burrowes at Edinburghe, wpoun the fyfteine day of November last bypast, and made report of the burrowes proceidinges in suche materis as wes handlit at the said meiting, and producit the extract of the actis thairoff, and also of thair dealling with my Lord Highe Thesurar and remanent lordis of privie counsall, anent the matter of the custumes intendit to be hightit, and doune calling of the dollouris, and withall, the said commissionar declairit that he haveing gottin certaine knowledge (at his beinge in Edinburgh the tyme foirsaid), that thair was a letter purchest frome his majesties handis for annulling of the last electioun of the magistrattis and counsell of this burghe, which did tend greatlie to the owerthrow of our ancient priviledges, &c. by supplicating of the saids lords, and trew relatioun of the calme and peaceable proceedinges of the said electioun, procurit frome their lordships ane missive direct to his sacred majestie, testifieing the same; off the quhilk missive he brought with him the just copie under the subscriptioun manuall of James Prymroise, clerk of privie counsall, to the effect the same may be registrat in the tounes bookes, and made extant to the posteritie, *ad futuram rei memoriam*, quhilk being red in presence of the saids prouest, baillies, and counsall, thay fand that the said Thomas hes dewlie acquyttit and dischairgit himsellf in the said commissioun, and all in ane voce ratifiet and allowit his proceidingis in the premisses, and ordanit George Meldrum, thesaurar, to debuirse to the said Thomas the somme of   for defraying of his super expenssis at the said meiting, with the somme of   debursit be him for extract of the saidis actis of burrowes, and wponn sindrie wther the tounes effaires in Edinburgh; lykeas thay ordanit the copie of the letter foirsaid to be insertit in the Counsall Register of this burghe, to the effect aboue specifiet, quhairof the tennour followes:—

14 Dec. 1636.
Report of Commissioner sent to a meeting of the burrowes.

Most Sacred Soueraine.

There was a petitioun givin in to youre maiesties counsall, the last counsall day, in name of the prouest and baillies of Aberdeine, compleaning vpoun some sinister informatiouns made to your maiestie, that the former dissensions and distractiounes there, did yit continue, quhairby your maiestie wes moued to direct a warrand vnder your royall hand, to the bishops of Aberdeine and Ross, and either of thame, to take notice of thir distractiounes, and accordinglie to provide for settling the peace of that burghe; this petitioun being at length heard, and we finding oure sellfs verrie farre interest and wronged, that the sinceritie of oure honest and vpwright endeavouris in the prosecutioun and following out of that bussienes according to your Maiesties royall directioun sould be brought in questioun, be privat persones abusing your maieteis sacred cares to thair onne corrupt endis, we did recommend to the B. of Ros to call for the

14 Dec.
1636.
——
Report of Commissioner sent to a meeting of the burrowes.

warrand frome, on Thomas Cargill (in whois handis the same wes), and to exhibit it befoir ws, and the said Thomas having delivered this warrand to the said bischope, he produced it in counsell, scalled and closed, and at oure desyre openned the same: which being red be oure clerk in counsall, the informatioun wes fund be the whole table to be abusive, without ground or warrand of truth, and that as your maiesties sacred cares wer abused therein, so this bussienes being formerlie by your maiestie remitted vnto ws, and we having accordinglie settled the same for the good of your maiesties service and peace of that toune, we find ouresellfis so muche touched in oure obedience and diligence in discharge of your maiesties former commandementis so muche wronged be this informatioun, that we hawe preswmed, in justificatioun of oure owne procedours, to testifie the trueth, that there occurred nothing at the counsall table thir many yeires bygaine wherein we took so great paines as in this, and having spent a nomber of dayes thairwpoun in end, we brought it to a goode and paceabill conclusioun, and since that time they have lived in that Christiane harmonie and dewtifull obedience which becometh good and faithfull subjectis; and at the last electioun of thair magistrattis for this subsequent yeare, there was suche ane vnanime consent in that action, as the lyke hath not beene seene in that toune, and amongs the whole personis who had voice in the election, there is but ane who differed frome the rest in the choise of thair proueist, which is not vsuall in suche actiones: This being the trewe state of the bussienes, we ar bold to represent the same to your maiesties royall consideratioun, humblie beseiking your maiestie to approue of what we hawe formerlie done heirin, and to take suche course for punishing suche informeris, and barring suche groundless and vniust informationnes, as in the deepnes of your maiesties royall judgment sall be thought most fitting; and so praying God to blisse your maiestie with a long and happie reigne, we rest your maiesties most humble and obedient subjectis and servantis. *Subscribitur.* Sant Andrewes, Traquair, Glasgow, Hadintoun, Winton, Southesk, Da. Edenburgh, Jo. B. of Moray, Jo. Rossen, Val. Brechinensis, Ja. Carmichaell, Sir Thomas Hop, Jo. Hamiltoune. *Vera copia. Sic subcribitur,* G. Prymrois."

21 December 1636.

The samen day the proucst, baillies, and counsall ratifies and approwis the act and ordinance made be thair predicessoures wpoun the allewint day of October 1626, againes superfluous banquetting at baptismes, and ordaines the said act to stand in force, and to be putt to executionn in all pointes againes the contravenares thairof in tyme coming, and to be intimat of new againe out of pulpitt for that effect, in both the kirkis of this burghe on Sonday nixt, that nane pretend ignorance thairof.

Ratification of the act aganes superfluous banqueting.

1 February 1637.

The quhilk day in presence of the proucst, baillies, and councell, compeired Maister Mathew Lumysden, commissionar direct frome this burghe to the lordis of his maiesties privie counsell, for presenting vnto thame this tounes diligence in searching of the licht horsemen, and after he had at length declaired his haill proceedingis in that busiones, and how the saids lordis of privie counsell had continewit the mater till the first councell day of Junij nixt to come, the said commissionar producit a nott of the said continewatioun extract furth of the bookes of secrett counsell, and withall he made report of his diligence in all other particulares contenit in his commissioun, and in speciall he produceit ane acquittance vpoun the payment of this burghes fourt and last termes taxationn, payable to the Lords of Sessioun, quhilk is ordanit to be registrat *ad futuram rei memoriam*. And furder, the said commissioner declairit that be his debursmentis in some of the tounes commoun effaires, he was super expendit in nyne dollouris, whairof he is ordanit to be refoundit be George Meldrum, thesaurar, and the same to be allowit to him in his comptis; and the proucst, baillies, and counsell havinge hard and considderit the diligence vsit be the said commissioner in his said commissioun, thay fand that he dewlie acquyttit and dischairgit himselff thairin, and thairfoir allowit of the samen in all pointes.

Discharge Lumysden of his commission anent the licht horsemen.

8 Feb.
1636.

Contract betwixt the toun and the compartinaris of the wark of the correction hous.

20 Jan.
1611.

This day, at command of the counsall, the prin^{ll} contract betwixt the counsell and the M^{rs} of the correctioun hous wes delyverit to Mr Rt. Farquhar, baillie. " Robert Frqnhar "

8 February 1637.

The quhilk day, in presens of the provest and baillies of the burghe of Aberdeine, convenit in the tounes counselhous, compeirit personallie the pairties contracteries in the contract underwrittin, subscrywit with thair hands, made anent the erecting of ane correction hous within the said burghe, and consentit to the registratioun of the said contract in the counsell register of the said burghe, thairin to remaine *ad futuram rei memoriam*; and to the effect executioun may be direct thairon as neidbeis, at the instance of ather of the pairties in maner specifiet thairintill, to the quhilk the saids provest and baillies interponit thair authoritie, and ordanit the said contract to be registrat in the saids bookis to the effect foirsaid, whairof the tennour followes—"At Aberdeine the aucht day of Februar, the yeir of God j^m sex hundreth threttie savin yeares, it is appointed, contracted, finallie endit, and agriet betwixt Maister Alexander Jaffray, provest of Aberdeine, Johne Hay, Andro Meldrum, Thomas Mortimer, and John Leslie, baillies of the said burghe; George Rickard, deane of gild, and George Meldrum, thesaurar of the said burghe for thameselfis, invertew of thair offices, and tackand the burdine on thame for the councell and communitie thairof on the ane pairt, and the said John Leslie, Maister Robert Farquhar, George Moresoun, Mr Thomas Gray, Walter Cochrane, Williame Scott, Alex. Farquhar, and Adame Gordon, burgesses of Aberdeine, for thameselfis, and in name and behaff of suche wther persones thair compartineris as salbe pleasit with thame to be wndertakeris of the work wnderwrittin and takand the burdine for thame, and also for the maisteris of the said wark on the wther pairt in forme and effect following, that is so say, forsameikill as it is thocht necessar and expedient be the haill nichtbouris and inhabitantis of the said burghe, alsweill burgesses of gild as craftismen, being convenit within the Tolbnith in twa seuerall courtis wponn the sewint and twelff dayes *respectiue* of October last by-past, that ane correctioun hous salbe erected within the same burghe, and the tred of making of bredcloath, carseyis, seyis, and wther manufactoris settled thairin, for advancing of wertew and suppressing of vyce amongst the comonues: And seing the erecting, furnishing, and manteining of the said hous with toolis, instrumentis, wooll, and wther furniture, to sett and keip the maisteris servandis and prisoneris at wark, will draw to great chairges and expensses whilk the toune is not habill to wndergo wpoun the commoun chairge, being alredie burdinit with great debt; thairfore the saidis provest, baillies, counsall, and communitie, have voluntarlie grantit ane taxatioun of twa thousand markis Scottes money to be payed to the persones, wndertakeris aboue named, and thair compartineris, admittit or to be admittit to that societie, as ane help and supplie to thaim for erecting and furnishing of the said wark, quhilk somm of twa thousand merkis the saidis provest, baillies, and counsall, for thameselfis, and takand the burdine on thame for the communitie of the said burghe, binds and obleissis thame to pay and delywer to the saidis persones wndertakeris betwixt the date heirof and the fyfteine day of March nixt to come, but longer delay, and giwes full libertie, power and commissioun to the saidis wndertakeris to erect the said correctioun hous with all convenient diligence, and to plenishe the samen with workeris and weaueris of bred-clothe, carseyis, seyis, freiss, and all wther clothes, stuflis, and wther manufactories that ar made, hawe bein, or salbe made within Sainct Paullis Wark in Edinburghe, vnto the quhilk hous, and to the maisteris and workeris to be planted thairin, the saidis provest, baillies, and counsall, giwes full fredome and libertie to vse and exerce the said tred in maner abone writtin during thair remaining within the samen allenarley, with this expres conditioun, that it sall nawayes be lesome to the maisteris of the said hous nor thair seruantis to resaiwe yairne nor wark from any persone whatsumevir to be wrought within the samen for wages, but onlie to the merchandis, erectoris, and furnisheris of the hous, to be wrought to thair behowe, nather sall it be lesome to the said maisteris and workeris to cutt or sell any clothe but in haill peisses, at least twelff elnes in length, and that onlie to the erectoris and furnisheris of the said wark, and be thair permissioun to merchandis, burgesses of the said burghe,

8 Feb. 1636.

Contract betwixt the toun and the compartinaris of the wark of the correction hous.

8 Feb.
1637.
Contract
betwixt
the toun
and the
comparti-
neris of
the wark
of the
correction
hous.

for the whilk somme of twa thousand merkis to be payed as said is, and for the causses aboue specefeit, the saidis John Leslie, Maister Robert Farquhar, Mr Thomas Gray, George Moresoun, Walter Cochrane, Williame Scott, Alexander Farquhar, and Adame Gordoun, persones wndertakeris foirsaids, faithfullie bindis and obleisses thame, thair aires and executoris, with all convenient diligence efter the resett of the said money, to erect and furnish ane correction hous to the said toune of Aberdein, and to hawe the samen clair and redie, plenished with ane maister and workmen, and furnished with toolles and instruments necessar, and wooll to be wrought, within sex monethis space nixt efter the payment to thame of the said somme, with ane sufficient prisone whairin the maister of the said correction hous sallbe obleist to resawe fra the magistrattis of the said burghe all vagabonds, strong and sturdie beggares, idle and maisterles persones strong in bodie and habill to work, servants disobedient to maisteris, children disobedient to parentis, lend leivars, pyikers, commoun scoldis, and wncorrigible harlottis, not amending be the discipline of the kirk, as they sallbe pleased to send thairwnto, vpoun whome the said maister sall vse suche discipline and correctioun as is vsed in the correctioun hous of Edinburghe, or in any wther correctioun hous elsquhair, or as the saids magistrattis sall appoint him to inflict wpoun the saids prisoneris, and to keip thame close in prisone, and not suffer thame go abroad, and to hald thame at contineuwall wark till thay be releassit be warrand from the saids magistrattis, and to giwe the saids persones such competent dyet as thay sall deserve be appoyntment of the saids magistrattis, and to do all wther dewtie to thame that the maister of the correctioun hous of Edinburghe is obleist to do to the prisoneris send to him be the magistrattis of that toune, and to suffer nane of thame to be relived with meat, drink, or clothing, or any wther thing be any freind or wther means, bot be the maister of the hous, except be speciall warrand from the saids magistrattis, and to hawe and keip ane habill man to attend the saids prisoneris, and hald thame at wark, and to caus ane of his servands everie Sabboth day reid prayeris wnto thame: With speciall alvayes promisioun that the saids prisoneris sall not exceid the number of ten persones to be at on tyme in the said hous, as alse that the said maister be nawayes obleisit to resawe within the hous naturall fooles, bedleims, lunatick, creppill, impotent, decrepit, deaff, dumb, or infectionat persones, bot onlie such as salbe sound in bodie, healthfull, corrigible, and habill to wirk, not wnder the aige of tuelff years, nor aboue the aige of sixtei: For interteaning of the quhilkis prisoneris not exceiding the number of ten personis at on tyme as said is, the said prouest, baillies, and counsall, bindis and obleissis thame and thair successoures, magistrattis and counsall of the said burghe, to caus the collector of the kirk sessioun thairof to pay yeirelie and ilk yeire to the maister of the said hous the soume of twa hundreth and fourtie pundis vsuall Scottes money, be fower equall portiones, to witt thriescoir pundis money foirsaid, ilk quarter during the space of ten yeires begynnand, the first quarteris payment immediatlie efter the said hous beis erected and plinished, with ane maister, servantis, and meterialls for working; and if any generall seiknes or infectioun sallhappin to come amongst the prisoneris in the said hous, the said maister salbe obleist wpoun his awin chairges to interteane the seik for the space of twa dayes, if the number of the seik personis exceid not foure persones at on tyme, and if the seik personis exceid the number of foure at on tyme, than the saids magistrattis to be obleigit to take ordor for thair mantenance or release; lykeas the persones wndertakeris abonenamed, obleissis thame that the maister of the said hous the first yeire of his entrie thairwnto, sall resaive from the saids magistrattis ane prenteis, and ane wther prenteis ilk twa yeares thaireftir, during the said space of ten yeares, and that frielie without any prenteis fie to be givin with thame, quhilkis prenteisses being within the age of fourteine yeires, and aboue the aige of tuelff yeares, salbe obleigit to serue in the said correctioun hous for the space of nyne yeires as prenteis, and ane yeire thaireftir for wages, and being aboue the age of flourteine yeiris, salbe obleigit to serue in the said hous for the space of sewin yeires as prenteis, and twa yeires thaireftir for

8 Feb. 1637.

Contract betwixt the toun and the compartineris of the wark of the correction house.

8 Feb.
1637.
———
Contract
betwixt
the toun
and the
compartineris of
the wark
of the
correction
house.

competent wages, whilkis prenteisses the said maister salbe obleigit to intertcane in meat and clonthes during thair prentiship as becometh thame, and faithfullie and trewlie to instruct thame in all pointis of the craft of bredeloath making, and wther cloath and stuffs wrocht in the said hous, whilk the maiester can do himselff, and to conceall na poynt thairoff fra thame; lyikas the saidis prenteisses and ewrie ane of thame salbe obleigit straitlie, befoir thay resawe thair libertie, within thrie yeires thaireftir to pay tuentie pundis money foirsaid to the correctioun hous for making ane stock to help to manteane it. Off the quhilkis soumes swa to be resaived from the prenteisses to be send to the said hous be the magistrattis allanerlie at the tyme foirsaid, the saidis wndertakeris obleisis thame to mak just compt, reckning, and payment to the pronest, baillies, and counsall of the said burghe at the tyme of the wpgiveing of the said wark, to be employit be thame fra thanefurth wpoun the commoune effairis of the toune. For the quhilkis causses the saids prenteisses to be resauned in all tyme cuming frome the saids magistrattis, and lykewayes all wther prenteisses to be admittit within the said hous, sall resawe the lyke benefit at thair admissioun to be friemen of thair awin treddis as any wther prenteis to a frie craftisman within the toune. And forder, the maister of the said hous salbe obleigit to resawe from the saidis magistrattis all personis quha ar sound in bodie and healthfull, wha willinglie will be content to kaird and spin wooll not exceiding the number of ten personis at one tyme to be within the said hous, wnto the quhilkis persones the said maister salbe obleigit to furnish wooll, kairdis, and wheillis for kairding and spynning sa meikill as thay salbe habill to wirk, and to pay to the saids persones for kairding and spynning of ewery stane weycht of wool, comptand tuentie thrie pund weight of spun yarne for ane stane, fourtie schillings money foirsaid, and so proportionallie for ewrie pund weicht, or als much more as is or salbe payit in the correctioun hons of Edinburghe for the lyke weicht and wirk; and lyikwayee, the maister of the said hous salbe obleist to keip ane register book quhairin to insert the entrie and releassing of ilk prisoner, and the proceedingis of those who salbe appointit owersieris of the said hous and prisoneris for goode order keiping: lyikas the saids persones wndertakeris bindis and oblessis thame and thair foirsaidis to caus the maister of the said hous condiscend and agrie to all the foirsaid conditiounes, and to be oblist to the saids prouest, baillies, and counsall for performance thairof; and siclyik thay bind and obleiss thame and thair foirsaids to manteane the said hous for the vse befoir mentioned, for making of bredcloath thairin, and for ane correctioun hous to the said toune of Aberdein, wpoun the conditiounes abonewrittin for all the dayes, space, yeires, and termes of ten yeires nixt eftir the erecting of the samen; and failzeing thairof, to pay the said somme of twa thousand merkis to the saids proucst, baillies, and counsall, for the publie vse and benefit of the toune. Lastlie, it is agriet betwixt the saids pairties, that if eftir the expyring of the first sewin yeires of the ten yeires befoir speccifeit, the prouest, baillies, and counsall of the said burghe for the tyme think it not expedient longer to vse the said hous as ane hous of correctioun, nor thaireftir to burden the maister thairof with resawing frome thame of any more prisoneris within the samen, and does release all those who sall happin to be imprisoned in the said hous for the tyme, frathancefurth the saids magistrattis and counsell sall be frie frome payment of the said somme of twa hundreth and fourtie pundis, whilk thay ar obleist to give yeirlie be foure seurall portiounes in the yeire to the said maister for intertenement of the saids prisoneris; and the said maister to be frie frathancefurth frome resawing any more prisoneris or prenteisses from the saids magistrattis. Lyikas the saidis persones wndertakeris (in cais of withhalding of the said somme of twa hundreth and fourtie pundis) salbe frie frome refunding of the said somme of twa thousand merkis, albeit the wark decay eftir the expyring of the said sewin yeares befoir mentionat, it beinge alvayes in the will and optioun of the saids proucst, baillies, and counsell to continew in payment of the said twa hundrethe and fourtie pundis yearlie till the expyring of the whole ten yeires befoir speccifeit, or to dischairge the same at the end of the first sewin yeires as said is. In the quhilkis caisses the

8 Feb. 1637.

Contract betwixt the toun and the compartineris of the wark of the correction hous.

8 Feb.
1637.
———
Contract
betwixt
the toun
and the
comparti-
neris of
the wark
of the
correction
hous.

saids pairties to stand bund and obleist ilk ane for thair awine pairtes to wtheris, in maner abouewrittin, all fraud and gyill secludit; and for the mair securitie, baith the saids pairties are content, and consentis that thir presentis be registrat in the bookes of counsell or burrow court bookes of Aberdeine, to hawe the strength of ane confest act and judiciall decreit, to the effect letteris of horning wpoun ane singill chairge of ten dayes, and all wther executorialls necessar, the ane but preuidice of the wther may be direct thairon in forme as effeiris, and to that effect constitutes conjunctlie and seuerallie thair lauchfull procuratoris *promittendo de rato* be thir presentis, writtin be Johne Ingrahame, clerk-depute of the said burghe, and subscryvit be baith the saids pairties, day, moneth, yeire, and place foirsaids, befoir their witnesses—Walter Robertsoun, commoun clerk of the said burghe, Mr George Robertsoun, Walter Guthrie, nottaries public; and the said Johne Ingrahame. *Sic subscribitur*. Al. Jaffray, prouest; J. Hay, baillie; A. Meldrum, baillie; T. Mortimer, baillie; Johne Leslie, baillie and wndertakers; George Rickard, deane of gild; George Meldrum, thesaurer; Robert Johnstoun, Patrick Dune, Thomas Gray, counsellors and wndertakeris; Thomas Robertsoun, Williame Ord, aboue named, with my hand at the pen led be the conottares under subscryvand, becaus I cannot wreitt.

22 Feb.
1637.
———
Act agaues
forstalleris
of the
timber
mercat.

22 *February* 1637.

The said day, in respect of the abuse latelie croppin in within the timber mercat of this burghe, in that dyvers and sindrie personis, alsweill extraneares as inhabitantis within this burghe, regrattis and foirstallis the said timber mercat, and byis barkis, timber, and timber wark furth thairof, to be sauld againe be thame befoir the same ly and remaine in the mercatt place till the ordinar houre, to witt, till Saturneday at twelff houres in the day, to the great hurt and prejudice of his maiesties lieges, both to burghe and land: Thairfoir it is statute and ordainit be the prouest, baillies, and counsall, that whosoewir sall by any bark, timber or timber wark in the

mercat of this burghe to be sauld againe (except onlie vpoun Saturday — 22 Feb. 1637.
after tuelff houres in the day), that the contraveinar sall incur the vnlaw
of ten pundis, *toties quoties*, to be payed to the deane of gild, to be vpliftit — Act aganes forstalleris of the timber mercat.
preceislie but fauour, alsweill from extranearis duellin in landart, as frome
the inhabitantis of this burghe whatsumewir contraveining the premisses.

15 *March* 1637.

15 March 1637.

The quhilk day, whereas vpoun occasioun of the late vacancie at the — Anent the chappell of Futtie.
Sanct Clementis chappell in Futtie, by transportatioun of Doctor Alexander
Ross, who latelie served the cure thairat, to the particular service of the
toune of Aberdeine and ministrie thairof, it wes thought gude that thair
shuld be ane cleir evidence and demonstration to all posteritie, of the end
and full extent of the mortificatioun of suche moneyis and arable land as
wer mortefeit for the said service of Futtie, that the same might remaine
efter the death of the mortefearis, *ad perpetuam rei memoriam*, for avoiding
all scrupule, dout, question, or danger that might heireftir ensue; thairfore the prouest, baillies, and councell of the said burghe, patrones of the
said chappell and of the saids mortificationes, does heirby declair that the
saids moneyes and land wer nowayes mortifiet for erecting and planting
a new minister within the said burghe of Aberdeine, or for suppleing any
chairge quhatsumeuir, aither of doctrine or discipline within the same,
bot onlie for serving the cure at the said chappell of Futtie, be preaching,
catecheising, and owerseing cairfullie the maneris of the poore people,
inhabitantis within the said toune of Futtie, and redressing abuses amongs
thame, with the concurrance of the saids magistrattis of Aberdeine, and
vsing all other pastorall functiouns incumbent to a preachour of God's
word, and in respect that, besyd the ordinar catecheising befoir the communioun in the said burghe of Aberdeine, the pastours thairof hes ane
extraordinar catecheising, eache of thame ones in the weik throughout the
whole yeire, it is thought meit for the better furtherance of the said extraordinar catecheising, that he who sall serve at the said chairge of Futtie,

15 March 1637.
Anent the chappell of Futtie.

shall concur with the tounes ministeris in this extraordinar wark anes in the weik, in catecheising that quarter of the toune quhilk is called Futie quarter, with this expres provisioun and declaration, that the said concurrence shall give no ground to him nor to any otheris succeiding him in the said chairge of Futtie, to be repute any wayes minister of Aberdeine, or to clame any thing quhilk the said title or reputing may import, nather yit to clame any wther benefitt, augmentatioun of stipend, or vther commoditie whatsumewer more nor the proffitt and annualrent of the moneyes and land mortefieit, and to be mortefieit, for the said chairge of Futtie may afford; in testimonie whairof thir presentis are subscrywit be the saids provest, baillies, and councell, in presence of Doctor Robert Barrone, Doctor William Guild, Doctor James Sibbald, and Doctor Alexander Ross, present ministers of the said burghe, and of Mr Willeame Robertsoun, now serving the cure at the said chappell of Futtie, as witnesses required to the premisses, and testefeing the same to be of treuth and veritie, who also, in testimonie thairof, hawe subscrywit thir presentes with thair hands, day moneth yeir and place foirsaids.

Mr R. Barroune, minister and professor in Aberdene, of divinity.
W. Guild, minister at Aberdene.
Mr Ja. Sibbald, minister at Aberdene.
Mr Willeame Robertsone.
Thomas Robertsone, counsaller.

A. Jaffray, provest.
J. Hay, baillie.
A. Meldrum, baillie.
F. Mortimer, baillie.
Johne Leslie, baillie.
Mr F. Gray.
George Richart, dene of gill.
George Melldrume.
Mr Wm. Moir, Mr of the kirkvork.
Walter Cochrane.
Patrick Dune.
Andro Burnet, elder.
Patrik Dowie.
Mr Johne Moir.

12 April 1637.

12 April 1637.

Charge for removing of middlingis aff the streittis and commoun passages about the toun.

The same day the prouest, baillies, and counsell ordanes intimatioun to be made be the drum throw the haill streittis of the toune, charging all and sindrie persones that hes laid any middingis or fuilzie within this burghe, on the publict streittis, and about the portis, as lyikwayes at the Bowbrig, and on the kingis commoun yett, betwixt the same and the Justice mylnes, at the Woman hill, the Gallowgeit port, and betwixt the same and the Seikhous, the Justice port, Castell Hill, and at the tounes commoun buttis on the north syid thairof, and at the timber laires on the southsyid of the Castell Hill, and on whatsumener wther pairt within or aboute this burghe, that thay remowe and tak away all the saids middingis within ten dayes nixt eftir the chairge, vnder the paine of ten pundis money, to be payed be ilk persone contraveining, to the deane of gild for the publict vse of the toune, to be exactit but favour, *toties quoties*, quhilk intimatioun and chairge wes accordinglie gewin be the tounes commoun drummer to the effect nane shuld pretend ignorance thairof.

14 June 1637.

14 June 1637.

Lumnisden, his discharge of his commission.

The quhilk day, in presence of the prowest, baillies, and counsall, compeired Mr Mathew Lumysdane, commissioner direct frome this burghe, for keiping the   day of Junij instant, befoir the Lordis of his Maiesties Privie Counsall at Edinburghe, anent the matter of the licht horsmen; and after he had declaired his haill proceidinges in that busienes, and how earnest he was with the saidis Lordis for procuring thair dischairge of the tounes fyne anent the said licht horsmen; in end the said matter wes continewit to the fourt day of July nixt to come, quhilk day this burghe is appoyntit to be present be thair commissionar, and to produce sic forder diligence as thay wold vse in the premisses; and, forder, the said commissioner declaired that he had resawed frome my Lord Highe Thesaurar, of this kingdome ane letter direct frome his

14 June 1637.
Lammisden, his discharge of his commission.

Maiestie to the proueist, baillies, and counsall of this burghe, anent oure tounes ministeris, quhilk letter the said commissioner exhibite in counsall, and the same beinge opinit and red, was ordanit to be registrat in the tounes counsall book, quhairoff the tennour followes:—

"To oure trustie and weillbeloued the proueist, baillies, and counsell of oure burghe of Aberdeine, Charles R.,

Trustie and weillbeloued, we greit yow weill, hawing takin into our consideratioun the meannes of your ministeris present prouision and stipends, and that inrespect of the eminencie of thair charge, it is requisite yow hawe able and qualifeit men for discharge of the function of the ministerie, it is oure pleasure that yow lykwayes tak the same into your consideratioun, by provyding thame with suche competencie of augmentatioun as may be answerable to the dischairge of such a publict place, and that either by stenting of the houssis and inhabitantis within that burghe (as wes latelie done by Act of Parliament for oure citie of Edinburghe) or wtherwayes, as yow shall think may best effectuat that end, whairin expecting to heir of your diligence, which we will accompt as gude service, we bid yow fair weill frome our Court at St James, 13 May 1637."

21 June 1637.
Mortimer chosin commissionar anent the licht horsemen.

21 June 1637.

The quhilk day the proueist, baillies, new and auld counccellis of the burghe of Aberdeine eftirnamed, thay ar to say Mr Alexander Jaffray, proueist, &c., Johne Hay, Thomas Mortimer, &c., beinge convenit in the tounes counsellhous, electit, nominat, and chusit Thomas Mortimer, baillie, commissionar for this burghe, to keip the fourt of July nixt befoir the Lordis of his Maiesties most honorable Privie Counsall, anent the mater of the licht horsmen, and for productioun of oure tounes diligence thairin, and to supplicat the saidis Lordis inrespect of our diligence, that our toun be frie of any fyne, and in lykmaner gewis commissioun and warrand to the said Thomas Mortimer to represent to the Lordis Highe Chancellar and Thesaurar, and remanent Lordis of Privie Counsell, our just reasones quhy thay sould not give any farder augmentatioun of stipends to oure ministeris, and to petitioun thair Lordships that they wilbe pleased to mak remonstrance to his Maiestie thairof, and all wther thingis to do for obviating suche augmentatiounes, conforme to the instructiounes gewin to the said Thomas for that effect; and, farder, gewis power to the said Thomas to deall with his Maiesties High Thesaurer for passing oure tounes signature, as also to deall with his Maiesties advocat for docking the same, and to compone and agrie for getting the same signed by his Maiesties hand and past throw the seallis, and with power also to the said Thomas to deburse in all thir particulares as he finds to be requisite for effectuating the same to oure tounes behowe, and to lift moneyes as neid beis for that effect, promitting to hauld firme and stabill whatsumewer the said Thomas shall do in the premisses, and ordaines threttie dollouris to be debursit to the said commissioner for macking his chairges in the said commissioun to ane compt, to be payed to him be George Meldrum, thesaurer, quhilk salbe allowit in his comptis.

21 June 1637.
Mortimer chosin commissionar anent the licht horsemen.

21 June 1637.

The samen day ordaines the tounes sex officiares to gett new coittis of reid Inglis cloath for the generall conventioun of burrowes appoynted to hauld at this burghe, the fourt of July nixt, and ordaines George Rickard, deane of gild, to by the said cloth, and to caus mak and furnishe the same as apperteines. . . .

21 June 1637.
Coats to be given to the officiares.

26 July 1637.

The said day it is statute and ordanit that if any tapster fiust aill, bier, or wther drink to mariner or soiour, not being solvende, the not payment sall nowayes frustrat the skipper or merchand of the marineris service, nor hinder thame frome the sea, being bound to thair voyage.

26 July 1637.
Tapstaris of drinck marineris.

19 Aug. 1637.

Report of commissionar anent the licht horsemen.

16 August 1637.

The quhilk day, in presence of the provest, baillies, and counsall, compeirit personallie Thomas Mortimer, baillie, commissionar chosin for this burghe, to keip the fourt of July last befoir the Lords of his Maiesties most honorable Privie Counsall, anent the mater of the licht horsemen, and for produceing of the tounes forder diligence thairin, and to supplicat the saids Lords inrespect of the said diligence, that the tonne be frie of any fyne; as also to represent to the Lords Heighe Chancellar and Thesaurar, and remanent Lordis of Privie Counsell, the tounes just resones quhy they sould not give any forder augmentatioun of stipend to thair ministeris, and to petitioun thair Lordships that thay wald be pleasit to mak remonstrance to his sacred Maiestie thairof; and efter the said Thomas had declairit his haill proceedingis anent the premisses, he produceit ane act of the saids Lords of Secret Counsall dischairging the tonne of the fyne of fywe thowsand merkis, whairin thay wer adjudgeit abefoir, for thair alledgit neglect of diligence in the executioun of thair office aganes the lawles and brokin men of the name of Gordone, and wtheris of the licht horsemen; and lyikwayes produceit ane extract of the actis of the late generall conventioun of burrowes, haldin at this burghe in July last, togidder with the tounes eque wpoun the payment of thair burrow mailles in exchequer, and the eque of Petmedden, for the termes of Martimes and Witsonday last bypast: lykeas also the said Thomas produceit ane copie of the remonstrances, answeris, and replyes given in be him and Doctor Ross befoir the saids Lords Chancellar and Thesaurar anent the augmentatioun craveit be the ministeris of thair stipends, whilk being red in presence of the saidis provest, baillies, and counsall, and withall the said Thomas having maid report how far he had proceedit in the mater of oure tounes signature: They find that the said Thomas Mortimer, commissionar foirsaid, hes done ane verie fathfull and exact diligence in all the particulares aboue mentionat, and wtheris committit to his charge, and thairfoir exoneris and dischairges him of the said commission, *simpliciter*, and forenir: lykeas they ordaine the said act of discharge of the fyne aboue specifeit, to be insert in the tounes bookes *ad futuram rei memoriam*, off the quhilk act the tennour followes:—

"At Edinburghe, the fourth day of July, the yeir of God, j^m sex hundreth and threttie sewine yeires, anent the terme assigned be the lords of privie counsall to the prouest and baillies of the burghe of Aberdeine, to haue compeired personallie befoir the lordis of privie counsall this present day, and to haue giwen in a report of thair more exact diligence done be thame in the executioun of thair offices aganes the lawles and brokin men of the name of Gordoun, be whome the peace of the cuntrie wes disquieted and trubled, as at more length is conteaned in the principall letteris raised heirwpoun, quhilkis being called this present day, and the saidis prouest and baillies of Aberdeine compeirand be Thomas Mortimer, baillie, thair commissionar, and the saids lords haveing at length hard and considerit the report of thair diligence in the executioun of thair offices aganis the said brokin men, and the saids lords remembring and considering that the fynes imposed wpoun the said burghe of Aberdeine was rather to stirre thame vp to a farder diligence then to punish thame for anye alledgit bygaine neglect of thair duetie, whairwpoun no probatioun wes deducit, nor nothing verefied and provin aganes thame, and finding the diligence now reported be thame to be satisfactorie and sufficient, and that thay haue answerit the dewtie incumbent to thair charge, thairfore the saids lords hes remitted and discharged, and be the tennour of this present act remitts and dischairges unto thame the fyne formerlie decerned aganis thame of fyve thousand merkis, and declaires the prouest, baillies, counsall, and whole communitie and inhabitantis of the burghe of Aberdeine to be fred, exonered, and releived thairof for ewir. *Extractum de libris actorum secreti consilii, S. D. N. Regis per me Jacobum Primroise clericum eiusdem, sub meis signo et subscriptione manualibus. Sic subscribatur.* Jacobus Prymrois.

19 Aug.
1637.

Report of commissionar anent the licht horsemen. Discharge to the toun of thair fyne for the licht horsemen.

13 September 1637.

13 Sept. 1637.

A voluntarie contributioun to be vplifted for helping to ransom some inhabitants of the toun of Air from thair captivitie with the Turkis.

The quhilk day in presens of the prouest, baillies, new and auld councellis, compeirit Johne Kennedy, baillie of the burghe of Air, and producit ane act extract furth of the buikes of his Maiesties Secrett Counsall, mackand mentioun that thair ar fyfteine persones skipperis and marineris inhabitantis of the said burghe of Air, latelie takin prisoneris be the Turkis, and careit be thame to Salie and Argiers in Barbarie, quhair thay are deteined in most miserable slauerie, bondage, and captivitie till they be redeemed be ane great ransom, and thairfoir the lords of privie counsell hes recommendit the saids poore captives to the Christian and charitable consideratioun and compassioun of all estates of persones, both to burghe and land within this kingdome, requesting and desyring all noblemen, prelatts, barrones, and gentilemen, sessiounes of kirkis, presbitries, prouestis, and baillies of burrowes, and all wther his Maiesties subjectis of quhatsumewir rank, qualitie, or conditioun thay be, both to burghe and land, to extend suche proportioun of their benevolence and charitable supplie towards the releiff of thair afflicted brethrein as thay sall think expedient, and to delywer the same to Robert Gordoun, Johne Knicht, and the said Johne Kennedy, baillies of Air, and George Meason, clerk, or any of thame, who ar appoyntit be the saids lords to be resaneris and ingadderares of this charitable and voluntar contribution, as the said act, dated at Edinburghe the twentie ane day of Aprill last bypast at more length proportis, and conforme thairto, the said Johne Kennedy humblie petitioned the saids prouest, baillies, and counsall, that thay wald commiserat the distrest estate of thir poore captives, and accordinglie bestow thair charitable contributioun wpoun thame in sic measour as they sould think most convenient; lykas at the late conventioun of burrowes, hauldin at this burghe in July last, the said Robert Gordoun being than commissionar for the said burghe of Air, crawed this burghes contributioun to the effect foirsaid, whairanent the saidis prouest, baillies, new and auld, councellis, advysing and having a Christian compassion and fellow feilling of such a pitiefull calamitie that hes befallen the Christian brethrein and nightboures be thair detentioun in sic miserable captivitie and bondage vnder the barbarous Turkes, thairfoir hawe voluntarlie condescendit and agreit to give a voluntarie contribution for the vse foirsaid, to be wplifted and collected amongst the inhabitantis of this burghe in maner following, that is to say, thay appoynt the ministeris of this burghe to acquaint the people out of pulpett in both the kirkes on Sonday nixt with the lamentable estate of the poore captives, and thairwith to exhort all the inhabitantis of this burghe of all rankes to extend thair charitable help towardes the releiff of the saids captives, and for this effect appointes the foure baillies to stand at the kirk durres, twa at euerie dur, on Sonday nixt following the said intimatioun, for collecting of the said contribution, and the baillies to caus wreitt the names of all those that contributes, that thairby notice may be takin of the absentis, and thair charitable contribution craved also to the saidis captives.

13 Sep. 1637.

A voluntaire contribution vplifted for helping to ransom some inhabitantis of the toun of Air from thair captivitie with the Turkis.

13 *September* 1637.

The samen day the proucst, baillies, and counccll hes sett donne and injoyned the order following to be keipit and observit be Thomas Coywe, sacristar, in furnishing of the kirk with candill in the winter season, betwixt Halowmes and Candilmes in tyme coming, viz: at morning and evening prayeris, the said Thomas is injoyned to putt tuo lightis in everie ane of the thrie hearssis hinging in the bodie of the kirk, to be lichted a litill befoir the prayer bell begin to ring; wpoun preiching dayes, he is appoynted to putt in the hearse, forganes the pulpit, foure lichts, and these to be lichted at the ringing of the second bell. In the south syd of the kirk he is appoyntit to hawe tuo lichtis in the tuo hearssis, ane in everie hearse; and in the north syd of the kirk als mony, and ane licht directlie vnder the bellis in the croce kirk. Item everie day at fywe houres in the morning he is appointed to licht tuo lightis in the bodie of the kirk, thairin to continew quhill day licht; and other tuo lightis in the evening, to con-

13 Sept. 1637.

Inionction to the sacristar anent the furnessing off candill to the kirk.

EXTRACTS FROM THE [1638.

13 Sep. 1637.
Intimetion to the sacristar anent the furneshing off candill to the kirk.

tinew efter the prayeris till sewin houres at night, and all thir lightis to be fair lightis, to witt, to be at least tuelff pennie candill, for furneshing of the quhilkis lightis in tyme coming, the councell assignis to the said Thomas the dewtie of the haliedayes fische, extending yeirelie to the somme of fourtie four pundis sex schillingis eight pennies; and be thir presentes gewis him power to exact and wplift the said dwetie fra the possessouris and occupiares of the salmond fishings of the Raick, Midchyngill, pott, and fuirds on the watter of Dee, according to the auld vse and wont, viz., for ilk halffnett of fourteine halffnettis of the Raick, tuentie thrie schillingis four penneis, for ilk halffnett of tuelff halfnettis of the Midchyngill, sexteine schillingis eight penneis, for ilk halffnett of tuelff halffnettis of the pott, thretteine schillingis foure penneis, and for ilk halffnett of tuentie halffnettis of the fuirdis, ten schillinges, and with powar to the said Thomas Cowye to giwe acquittances and dischairges thairon to the occupeares of the said fishinges; and as neid beis, to call, charge, and persew thairfoir, and all thingis to do for wplifting of the said dewtie, quhilk necessarlie is requyred to be done thairanent, promitting to hald firme and stabill: the entrie of the said Thomas to the wplifting of the said yeirlie dewtie be vertew of this present act, is declared to be and begin for the fishing nixt to come, of the cropt and yeire of God j^m sex hundreth threttie aucht yeires, and so furth yeirelie thairefter, dureing the will and pleasour of the proueist, baillies, and counsell of this burghe for the tyme, allanerlie.

3 Jan. 1638.
Anent the doctoris of the grammer schoole.

3 January 1638.

The said day, the proueist, baillies, and counsell ordaines the somme of ane hundreth pundis payed yeirlie be the toune to ane of the doctoris of thair grammer schoole, and the salarie and schollage payed be the schollares to the other doctor of the said schoole, to be equallie devydit betwixt the said twa doctouris in all tyme comeinge, in respect of thair equall burdine and paines, and this divisioun to begin at the first change of any of the present doctouris.

3 *January* 1638.

The quhilk day, the proueost, baillies, and counsell, considering that in tymes past thair hes beine great abuses committit within this burghe at lykewalkis both in convocating multitudes of people frome all pairtis of the toune, and in superfluouslie spending of deseart and confectiounes at sic tymes, which breidis great disordour and confusioun, thairfoir and for eschewing of the lyik abusses heireftir, thay have statute and ordanit, and be thir presentis statutes and ordaines, that none be invited or desyrit to a lyik walk within the burghe at na tyme heireftir, except onlie tuelff honest men of the ewest freynds and neirest nichtbonres of the deceassit persone, and the magistrattis nawayes to be invited at any sic occasiounes as being in office, vnles thay be of the qualitie foirsaid, and siclyik that na confectiounes nor deseart be presented at lyik walkis within this burghe in tyme coming, of what conditioun soener the deceassit persone be, vnder the paine of fourtie pnnds, to be exactit of ilk contraveinar, *toties quoties*, but favour, and payed to the deane of gild for the publict benefitt of the toune, quhilk act wes intimat to the haill toune convenit in thair heid court, vpoun the nynt day of Januar instant.

Statute anent lyke wakes.

31 *January* 1638.

The quhilk day, the proueost, baillies, and councell ordaines the somme of ane thowsand merkis contribute be the nichtbonres of this burghe for the distressit captives of the burghe of Air, to be delyuered with all diligence, vpoun thair band to restoir the same, incais it be not employit accordinglie within tuo yeires eftir the date of thair band.

Contribution to the captives of the burgh of Air.

21 March 1638.

21 March 1638.

The lecture of the mathematics to be in a four yeires course.

The said day, Doctour Williame Johnstoun, professour of mathematicques within the colledge of this burghe, compeirand in presens of the provest, baillies, and counsell, wes earnestlie intreatit and desyrit be thame to contryve his ordinar lecture of the mathematicques in a foure yeires course, to the effect the studentis and heirares may hawe the commoun benefite at the change of everie course as in other professionnes; to the quhilk desyre the said Doctour Williame Johnstoun most willinglie condiscendit and agriet and promeist so to do, albeit to his gryter paines, as being most profitable for the schollares and studentis of mathematicques.

11 April 1638.

11 April 1638.

Acquittance toun of Air on the ressett of our contribution for releiff of thair captives.

The same day, Robert Cruikshank producit ane acquittance gewin be the toune of Air on the recept of ane thowsand merkis contribute be this toune towardes the relieff of thair nichtboures, captives in Argires, conteining the said toune of Airis band for reporting a certificat that the saids moneyes ar employit to that vse, and that within twa yeiris eftir the date of the said band, quhilk is dated at Air the fyfteine of Februar 1638, vnder the paine of refounding back againe the said thowsand merkis.

25 April 1638.

25 April 1638.

Missive from his Maiestie.

The said day, the provest, baillies, and counsell haveand resauit ane missive letter direct to thame frome oure soverane lord, the kingis most excellent Maiestie, thay ordane the same to be registrat in the counsall register of this burghe, *ad futuram rei memoriam*, quhairof the tenour followes: To oure trustie and weilbeloned the provest, baillies, and counsell of Aberdeine and ministrie thairof—

"Charles R., Trustie and weilbeloned, we greit you weel, hawing vnderstood frome the reverend father in God, the Bishop of Aberdeine, of the testimonie giwen by you at this tyme of your affection to our service, which is the more considerable in regaird of the neglect of otheris, wee giwe you hearty thankis for the same, willing yow to continue as yow hawe begune, and be assured we will not be vnmindfull thairof when any occasioun shall offer, whairby you may find the effects of oure princely favour. Wee bid yow fairweill; frome oure court at Whitehall, the nynt of Aprile 1638.

25 April 1638.
Missive from his Maistie.

16 May 1638.

The said day the provost, baillies, and counsell ordaines intimatioun to be maid be the drum throw the haill toune, that na taverne nor aill seller within this burghe sell any wyne, aill, or bier in tyme coming eftir ten houres at evin, under the paine of ten punds of unlaw, to be exactit of the contraveinar, *toties quoties*, efter convictioun, but fauour or mitigatioun, and employit on the tounes commoun effaires.

16 May 1638.
Anent the sale of wyne, aill, or bier.

23 May 1638.

The said day George Pyper, deacone, conveineir of the craftis of this burghe, Williame Nicolsone, deacone of the hammermen, Williame Ord, deacone of the wrights and cowperis, Johne Middiltoune, deacone of the baxtares, James Geddes, deacone of the tailyeouris, George Farquhar, deacone of the cordonares, James Clark, deacone of the wobstaris, and Thomas Dempster, deacone of the fleshoures, being convenit befoir the provest, baillies, and counsell of the said burghe, for the riott eftir specifeit, and compeiring personallie befoir thame, wer accusit for convocating the haill friemen of thair saidis craftis, with all thair servantis and prenteissis, vpon Mononday last, the tuentie ane day of Maii instant, be fyve houris in the morneing at the craftis hospitall, and thaireftir convening thame all at the mercat croce in armes be eight houris, and in the meintyme, when as a number of seckis of meill to the number of fourescoir seckis or thairby

23 May 1638.
Deacones of craftes conviet for convocating thair craftis in armes.

23 May
1638.

Deacones of craftes convict for convocating thair craftis in armes.

that wer brocht in that day frome Skeine, to hawe beine embarked in Martin Schankis schip, wes stayed and laid donne at the mercat place, the saids craftis with thair servantis and prentisses being convenit at the mercat croce in armes as said is, with swords, pistollis, and lang wapynnes, thay mellit and intromittit with the said wictuall, wiolentlie and at thair awin handis compellit the men that brocht in the same to carie it on thair awin horssis fra the mercat place to the said hospitall, and convoyit the same the haill way in armes as said is, notwithstanding that thay wer commandit and chairgit be the magistrattes, and particularly be Mr Thomas Gray and George Moresoun, baillies, in his maiesties name, to dissolue thair tumultuous and mutinous meiting, and to desist and cease from melling with the said wictuall or carricing the same away, bot depairt and go home in peace to thair houssis, quhilk thay most proudlie and contemptuouslie disobeyit, be going on insolentlie in caricing away of the said wictuall to thair said hospitall, whairby they keip, hauld, and detein the same as yit; quhilkis deacones being accensit of the said convocatioun, insolencie, contempt, and disobedience to thair lawfull magistrattis, thay confest thair mettinge at the said hospitall the tyme foirsaid, and that the said deacone, conveinar, gaine order and directioun for that meitting, and that the haill friemen of the saidis craftis, with thair haill servants and prenteissis, suld be in reddines to stay the transportatioun of any victuall out of the herbrie of this burghe, bot denyes that thay gawe command or wer anywayes accessorie, airt or pairt, of the melling or intromitting with the said victuall, or tacking away of the same, bot wes mellit with and cariet away be a confused multitude, wha wald not be stayed be thame as thay alledgit, and for quhome thay culd not answir: anent the quhilkis premissis, the saidis provest, baillies, and counsell hawing taikin in tryell and probatioun, they fynd the saidis haill deacones, and principallie the said George Pyper, deacone conveinar, giltie of the said convocatioun, and consequentlie of the said tumult, disorder, and commotioun that followit thairupoun, as lyikwayes of the said contempt and disobedience gewin to the command and chairge foirsaid of thair law-

full magistrattis, in sa far as the said craftismen, thair servandis and
prenteissis wer all convenit in armes the tyme forsaid, at command and
be warrand of thair saids deacones, and wald not be stayed frome thair
violent melling with the said wictuall, and caricing the same to thair
said hospitall, notwithstanding of the chairge forsaid, gewin to thame to
desist and cease thairfra, and to depairt and ga hame to thair houssis in
peace; and sielyik finds that the said Thomas Dempster, deacone of the
flesheris, was personallie present in armes, and assistit the away tacking
of the said wictuall, be convoying the same fra the mercat place to the
said hospitall; in respect wherof the saids pronest, baillies, and counsell
decernis and adjudges the said George Pyper, deacone conveinar, in ane
vnlaw of ffourescoir pundis, and ilk ane of the remanent deacones aboue
named in ane vnlaw of ffourtie pundis, to be payed to the deane of gild
of this burghe for the publict vse of the tonne, and ordaines the said
haill deacones to be presentlie committed to waird, and to remaine
thairin till thay pay the saidis vnlawes; and lykwayes ordaines thame
to satisfie and pay the awnares of the said wictuall the full pryces thairof,
sic as sould hawe beine payed to thame be the merchandis that bought
the same, and to restoir and delywer back againe to the tennentis
inbringeris of the said wictuall, thair awin seckis, or the just valour and
pryce thairof; and withall ordaines the saids haill deacones to compeir
within the tolbuith of this burghe, in ane fenceit court, and thair in presens of the magistrats and counsall, humblie to crawe God and thame
pardone for the said riott and dissobedience, and promeis opinlie newir to
commit the lyik in tyme coming.

23 May 1638.
Deacones of craftis convict for convocat- ing thair craftis in armes.

4 *July* 1638.

The said day, the pronest, baillies, and counsell ordaines Adame
Gordoun, maister of impost, to caus big and put wp ane heid of steine
wark at the end of the Trinitie freiris burne, forgainis the kirk of Futtie,
for livering and loadning of shippis and barqueis thairat, quhilk at all
occasiounes cannot convenientlie floitt with thair gudes.

4 July 1638.
A heid of steine wark for livering and load- ning ships.

16 July 1638.

16 *July* 1638.

The councellis refusall as of befoir to subscrywe the covenant.

The quhilk day the prowest, baillies, new and auld counsellis and deaconis of craftis, with dywers wther nighthonres of gude respect within the toune, who wer warnit to be present this day to giwe thair adwyse in the matter eftir following, being convenit in the tounes counselhous, it wes exponit to thame be Robert Johnstoun, prowest, that advertesiment is come frome South that some noblilmen, barrones, and ministeris ar to repair to this burghe on Friday nixt, the tuentie day of Julii instant, and to deall with the magistrattis and councell, as also with the bodie of the toune, for mowing thame to subscrywe the new covenant and oath obtrudit of late vpoun this kirk and kingdome, without warrand from his Maiestie, or Lordis of Privie Counsell; quhilk covenant being presented of befoir to the magistrattes and councell of this burghe vpoun the sexteine day of Marche last, be some barrones and commissionares fra some of the burrowes, to hawe beine subscrywit at that tyme, the magistrattes and councell then plainelie and absolutelie refuisit to subscrywe the same, for divers just reasones signifiet and imparted be thame to the saids barrones and commissionares: lyikas notice being gewin to his sacred Maiestie of oure refuissall to subscrywe the said covenant, his Maiestie wes thairwpoun gratiouslie pleased to direct his missive to the prouest, baillies, and councell of this burghe, acknowledging that thair refuissall to be gude service done to his Maiestie, which he declaired to be the more considerable in regaird of the neglect of otheris, willing ws to continew as we hawe begwn, and assuring ws that he shuld not be vnmyndfull thairof when any occasioun shuld offer whairby we might fynd the effectis of his princelie favour, as the said missive gewin frome his court at Whythall the nynt of Aprill last, at more length proportis. In consideratioun whairof, as lyikwayis be reasoun of his Maiesties proclamation this day, published at the mercat croce of this burgh, whairby his Maiestie not onlie makes ample declaratioun that his true meaning and intentioun is not to admitt of anie innovatiounes nther in religioun or lawes, bot cairfullie to mantein the true Protestant Christian religioune professit and established in this kingdome, and nowayes to suffer the lawes to be infringit, bot lyikwayes requyres and heartilie wishes all his gude people cairfullie to aduert to any suggestiones in the contrair, and not to permitt thameselflis blindlie, vnder pretext of religioun, to be led in disobedience, and draw on (infinitlie to his Maiesties greiff) thair awin rwine, as at mair length is contenit in the proclamatioun, and therefor the said Robert Johnston, prouest, most earnestlie desyred the said new and auld couneellis and deacones of the craftis, conveint as said is, to carie thameselflis wyislie and circumspectlie in the busienes, exhorting thame to continew in thair dutiefull obedience and service to his sacred Maiestie, and to refuise as of befoir to subscrywe any such covenant, vnder the paine of his Maiesties high displeasour, and as thay would eschew thair awin rwine and loss of oure toune liberties, for quhilk effect causit reid opinlie in couneell the said proclamatioun: eftir the reidinge quhairof, the saids prouest, baillies, new and auld couneellis, and deacones of craftis, and remanent nightboures present for the tyme, finding thairby such a reall testimonie not onlie of his Maiesties sinceritie for manteinance of the true religioun professit and established in this his Maiesties ancient kingdome, lawes, and liberties thairof, bot lyikwayes of his Maiesties speciall grace and favour in passing ower all bygaine misdemeanours of his subiectis, so long as his Maiestie sies not royall auctoritie shaiken aff be thame: Thairfoir the saids prouest, baillies, couneellis, deacones of craftis, and remanent nightboures conveint for the tyme, representing the bodie of the toune, declaired that thay were resolved, Godwilling, according to thair bund ductie and alledgance to thair sacred soveraigne, to continew in obedience and loyaltie to his Maiestie, and nowayes to do or attempt anything that may giwe his Maiestie just occasioun of offence, and for this effect votted and concluded that the magistrattes and counsall sall absolutlie refuis as of befoir to subscrywe the said covenant as magistrattes and counsallours, or in name and takand burdine wpoun thame for the bodie of the toune: bot if any particular persone of the toune or

16 July 1638.

The couneellis refusall as of befoir to subscrywe the covenant.

16 July 1638.
—
The councellis refusall as of befoir to subscrywe the covenant.

counsell, of thair awin acord as privat men will tak wpoun thame to subscrywe the same, notwithstanding of this his Maiesties gracious declaration foirsaid, published as said is, thay declair that what thay do in this kynd salbe wpoun thair awin perrill and hazard, as thay wilbe answerable to his Maiestie.

24 July 1638.
Anent the escaping of Alexr. Keyth out of waird.

24 *July* 1638.

The quhilk day in presens of Mr Thomas Gray and George Moresoun, baillies, Elizabeth Keith, relict of vmquhill, Willeame Leisk of that ilk, being accusit for being airt and pairt of the escaiping of Alexander Keith of Balmuir out of waird furth of the tolbuith of this burghe, the tuentie third day of July instant, in ane trunck whairin he wes secretlie inclosed be the said ladye of Leisk, and Marie Keith, daughter of the laird of Ludquhairne, be the assistance of   Hay, relict of vmquhill, Maister Gilbert Keith, minister at Skeine, wha wer lattin in to the wairdhous to visite the said Alexander Keith, declairit that quhat scho knew of that busines scho wald not tell it till scho wer convenit befoir Supreme Judges; bot it being declarit to her be the baillies, that the toune wes lyabill to great prejudice be the said Alexander his escaiping, she ansuerit that quhen the matter was in plotting, scho spak to her brother in thir termes, "God forbid that the toune of Aberdeine be wrangit;" and forder, scho declarit that there was none that helpit to put her brother in the trunk bot onlie herselff, Ludquhairne's daughter, and ane wther gentill woman callit   Hay: and the rest of the wardouris, to witt Johne Tillideff, Thomas Watsoun, his wyf, and Willeame Gordoun, being demandit quhat they knew of the busines, declairit that at Alexander Keith's intreatie they wer remowit to the heighe chamber of the said wairdhous, and knew nothing of his escaiping, neither did they sie any persone thair but onlie the wemen, Nathaniell Leysk, and George Panton.

Eodem die.

The said day in presens of Maister Thomas Gray and George Moresoun, baillies, Robert Sleike, ane of the tounes ordinar serjands of the said burghe, being accusit for suffering and permitting of Alexr. Keith of Balmuir to escaip furth of waird yeisterday be his sleuth and negligence, and for being airt and pairt thairof, he being keipar of the wairdhous, and hawinge the keyis thairof for the tyme, and not hawing his nichtboures with him at the opning of the doore according to the injunctiounes, and for suffering and permitting Elizabeth Keith, ladye of Leysk, Marie Keith, daughter to the laird of Ludquhairne, ___ Hay, Nathaniell Leysk, and George Pantoun, to hawe access to the wairdhous for accomplishing of the said work, denyit that he was anywayes airt or pairt of the committing of the fact, or that he knew anything thairof, but confest the escaiping of the said Alexander be his sleuth and negligence, in that he sufferit the foirnamed persones to go wp to the wairdhous and remaine thair till the turne wes done, and till the trunck whairin he wes inclosit wes brought out of the wairdhous and cariet to the pier, whairas he sould not hawe permittit any trunck, kist, or coffer to hawe beine transportit or cariet furth thairof, bot by the consent and warrant of the magistrattis or some of thame, for the quhilk the said Robert wes committit to waird, thairin to remaine till the magistrattis tak forder ordour in the busines.

Sleick officier committit to waird.

25 July 1638.

The quhilk day the provest, baillies, and councell ordaines a commissioun to be procured frome the lords of his Majiesties most honorable privie counsall for searching, seiking, and apprehending of Alexander Keith of Balmure, who escaped by a slight out of waird furth of the tolbuith of this burghe vpoun the twentie thrie day of July instant, and siclyik to send for letteris to inhibite all the lieges to intercommoun with him, as also to rais letteris againes the laird of Ludquhairne and his com-

25 July 1638. Commissioun to be procured for searching and apprehending of Alexr. Keyth.

25 July 1638.
Commissioun to be procured for searching and apprehending of Alexr. Keyth.

plices, to vnderly the law for tacking violentlie and perforce frome Robert Merser and Robert Irwing, messingeris, tuo captives, to witt Willeame Daniell and Willeame Fywie, in Conyach, whome thay had apprehendit vpoun captioun raised againes thame at the tounes instance, as being his maiesties rebells for the caussis mentioned in the saids letteris of captioun, and ordaines to send informatioun in thir particulares to Mr Robert Farquhar, baillie, who is presentlie at Edinburghe, and withall to desyre him to gett our tounes signature advysed and consulted with his maiesties advocat, and to gett the same docketed be his lordship, that the same thaireftir may be in all convenient diligence send to court to be past be his maiestie, and ordaines to wrett to the said Mr Robert to deburse sic sums as salbe requisite for all theise effaires, and what he sall deburse thairwpoun, ordaines to be refoundit to him be the thesaurar at his returne.

8 August 1638.
A wapinschaw indicted.

8 August 1638.

The quhilk day florsameikill as be act of parliament it is appointed that thair shall be publict wapinschawing keipit yeirlie, alsweill to burghe as land, throughout the whole kingdome, for obedience to the quhilk act, and according to the laudable custome observed in this burghe, hes appointed a wappinschaw of all the inhabitantis of this burghe, fensible persones, to be keiped, God willing, on Friday, the sewinteine day of this instant moneth of August, and for that effect ordaines ane chairge to be gewin be the drum, chairging all the inhabitantis within this burghe, both frie and vufrie, fensible persones, to prepare thameselflis and be in redines to giwe thair mustures and wapinschawing in the commone linkis of this burghe, the foirsaid seventin day of August instant, weill furnished and armed with pickes, corslettis, muskattis, bandelines, and swordis, vnder the paine of fourtie pundis, to be payed be ilk persone absent, or that comes not sufficientlie armed, and gines thair aith that the armour thay bring belongis properlie to thameselflis, to be payed to the dean of gild to the publict vse of the tonne.

15 *August* 1638.

The samen day the prouest, baillies, and counsall findis it expedient that thair shall be foure capitanes, foure lieutenentis, foure ensingzies, and twelff serjandis, for leading and commanding the inhabitantis of this burghe at the ensewing wapinschaw appoyntit to hauld the sewinteine day of August instant; and incaice any difference arryse amongst the commanderis anent thair places, the same to be decydit be lott, and appointis the baillies to mak chuise and nominatioun of suche as thay sall find to be most capable and fitting for commandement.

The baillies appoynted to mak chois of capitanes and commanders at the wapinschaw.

15 *August* 1638.

The prouest, baillies, and counsell having this morninge receaved a pacquett, wherein was inclosed a letter direct to thame frome his sacred maiestie, and ane other frome his maiesties commissionar, the Lord Marquis of Hammiltoune, quhilkis letteris being disclosed at the counsell-table and opinlie red thairat, the magistrattes and counsell ordaines the samen to be registrat in thair counsell register, thairin to remaine *ad futuram rei memoriam*, whairof the tenour followes:—

A missive frome his sacred Maiestie.

"To oure trusty and weilbeloued, the prouest, baillies, and counsell of Aberdeine,

"Charles R.,

"Trustie and welbeloued, we greet yow well, hauing vnderstood how dutiefullie yow carried your selflis at this tyme in what concerned the good of our service, and particularlie in hindering some stranger ministeris frome preaching in any of your churches, we hawe taken notice thairof, and do giue yow hartie thankis for the same, and doe expect, as your careage hitherto hath beine goode, so yow will continew, assuring yow that when any thing that may concerne your good shall occur, we will not be vnmyndfull of the same. Wee bid yow farewell, frome oure court at Oatlands, the last day of July 1638."

The Lord Marquis of Hammiltoun, his grace letter.

15 August 1638.

Missive frome the Marquis of Hammiltonne.

"For my very louing freinds, the prouest, baillies, and counsell of Aberdeine.

"Werie louing freinds, I hould it my ductie to accompanie this his maiesties letteres with theis few lynes, haning hard since my coming heare of the great zeale yow beare to his sacred maiesties service, and lyikwayes not onlie yow, but your tonne ar still pressed to subserywe a covenant nowayes acceptable to his maiestie, and thairfoir I, as his commissionar, doe earnestlie requyre yow cairfullie to avert, and so far as lyes within your power in a fair and peaceable way, to hinder the subscriptionne thairof by anie within your tonne, as you wald deserue thankis frome his maiestie, and receane favouris frome him as occasionn sall offer. Thus with my hartie wishes for your prosperities, I rest your verie louing and assured good freind, HAMILTON."

Halyruidhous, 10 Aug. 1638.

26 Sept. 1638.

26 September 1638.

A missive from his Majestie.

The quhilk day the prouest, baillies, and councell of the burghe of Aberdeine vnderwrittin, thay ar to say, Robert Johnston, prouest, Mr Thomas Gray, Mr Mathew Lumysdane, George Moresone, baillies, Mr Alex. Jaffray, Thomas Mortimer, Mr Willeam Moir, Alexr. Burnett, eldar, Robert Cruikschank, younger, Alexander Jaffray, Willeame Trup, Adame Gordoun, George Mengzies, Thomas Paip, Paull Mengzies, Robert Leslie, Johne Malice, cowper, and James Hall, cordoner, being convenit in the counsalhous of the said burghe as wpoun the ordinar day appointit for electionn of the new counsall, magistrattis, and officemen of the same burghe for the yeire to come, and after incalling of God, the said Robert Johnstonne, prouest, exhibite a letter direct to thame frome his sacred maiestie, quhilk wes sent to him be the Marquis of Huntlie, together with a particular letter of the said Lord Marquis direct to the said Robert himself, requyring him to delywer his maiesties letter to the counsall, quhilk was instantlie opinit and publictlie red in audience of the counsell, quhairof the tenour followes:—

26 Sept. 1638. A missive from his Majestie.

"To oure trustie and weilbeloued the pronest, baillies, and councell of oure citie of Aberdeine,

"Charles R.,

"Trustie and weilbeloned, wee greet yow well, whereas wee hawe at seuerall tymes vnderstood, and now particularlie by oure right trustie and wellbeloued cosen and counccllour, the Marqueis of Hammiltone, oure commissionar, how dutiefullie and cairfullie yow hawe caried your selflis at this tyme in what concerned the good of oure service, wee hawe thought fitt to tak notice of it vnto yow againe, and to give yow hartie thankis for the same. And as wee hawe now found your affection in a singular way, so wee do assure yow that we shall hawe a particular cair of what shall concerne yow, being confident that yow will still continew to carye your selflis as yow hawe done for the furthering of oure service, and in so far as yow can in a fair and peaceable way wee authorise yow heirby to hinder any other frome taking anie course that is derogatorie therevnto, and so we bid yow fairweill frome oure court at Bagshot, the 7 September 1638."

Efter reiding of the quhilk letter, in consideratioun of the contentis thairof, the said Robert Johnston, pronest, Mr Thomas Gray, and George Moresoun, baillie, for thameselflis and in name of sic otheris of the councell as will adhere vnto thame, protestit that nane within this burghe who hes subscryvit the covenant be puttt vpon litt, or be chosin a councellour or magistratt at this electioun inrespect of the present caice and estate of the toune whairin it standis, for feare of givinge offence to his Maiestie, and breiding alteratioun in the toune; to the quhilk protestatioun, George Moresoun, Thomas Paip, and Paull Meingzie, thrie of the councell, adherit, and thairwpoun asked instrumentes, &c.

5 Oct. 1638.

Exhibition be the Marquis of Huntly of his Maiesties declaration anent the annulling of the service book.

5 *October* 1638.

The said day the right noble Marqueis, George Marqueis of Huntlie, Erle of Engzie, Lord Gordoun, and Badgenocht, having schawin and exhibite to the prouest and baillies of this burghe his Maiesties declaratioun anent the annulling of the Service Book, Book of Cannons and High Commission, dischairging the pressing of the fywe articles of Perth Assemblie, macking all persones ecclesiasticall and civill, of what tittle or degrie soever, lyable to the tryell and censure of Parliament, Generall Assemblie, and other judicatories competent, anent the not giveing to ministeris at thair entrie any other oath than that which is contained in the act of parliament, anent the subscryweing and renewing the Confessioun of Faith subscrywit by his Maiesties father of blessed memorie, and his houshold in anno 1580, and generall band followeing thairwpoun, anent the indiction of a Generall Assemblie to be hauldin at Glasgow, the tuentie ane day of November, and a Parliament at Edinburghe, the fyfteine day of May, j^m sex hundrethe threttie nyne, and anent his gracious goodnes in forgetting and forgeving all bygaines and indiction of a fast for craveing of Gods blessing to this Assemblie: the said noble Marques signifiet to the saids prowest and baillies, that by warrant frome the Lord Marqueis of Hamiltoun, his Maiesties commissionar, and Lordis of Privie Counsall, he was to caus ane of his Maiesties herauldis proclaime this day at the mercat croce of this burghe his Maiesties declaratioun foirsaid, and thairfoir desyred the saids prouest and baillies, with thair tounes counsell and otheris most respective nichtbouris of the toune, to be present at the said proclamatioun, whairwnto the saids prouest and baillies most hartielie and willinglie condiscendit, promising to attend the said proclamation, and to applaud the same with most joyfull acclamatiounes, for suche reall expressions of his Maiesties most gracious favour and goodnes bestowed vpoun this his ancient kingdome for setling of the peace thairof, both in kirk and State.

8 October 1638.   8 Oct.
                                                         1638.

The quhilk day the provest, baillies, and counsell, wponn just and   Discharg-
knowin considerationnes mowing thame, and namelie be resone of some ing of the
disorderlie and vnpeaceable careage of the trayned band, have dis-   trayned
chairgit, and be thir presentis dischairges the cumpanie of the said band.
trained band, that hawe beine exercising thame selflis in armes in dreilling
sen the late wapinschaw, frome any forder dreilling, convocationn,
musturing, or lifting of armes within the toune, or in the feilds, till thay
procure a new warrant frome the magistratts and counsell for that effect,
vnder all hiest paine and danger that may incur for thair disobedience be
the lawes of this kingdome, and ordaines intimatioun heirof to be made
be the drum thron the haill streittis of the toune, commanding and
chairging in our soueraine Lordis name, and behalff of the Lord Provest
and baillies of this burghe, that no inhabitant within the same of whatsoeuir ranck, qualitie, or degrie, presume or tack vpoun hand to touch
drumme, lift cullouris or armes, or vse any suche publict exercise of
dreilling or convocatioun in tyme comeing, wntill thay be warranted be
the magistrattis and councell to that effect, vnder the paine aboue
specifeit, quhilk chairge was instantlie intimat be the drum to the effect
none should pretend ignorance thairoff.

8 October 1638.   8 October
                                                         1638.

The quhilk day the right nobill Marqueis, George Marqueis of Huntlie, The tounes
Erle of Engzie, Lord Gordoun and Badyenocht, accumpanied with the   consent to
                                                                      subscrywe
right worschipfull Sir Alexander Irwing of Drum, knight, schirreff of Aber- the Con-
deine, commissionares appointit be the Lord Marqueis of Hammiltoune, fession of
                                                                      Faith and
his maiesties commissioner, and by the Lords of his maiesties most honor- generall
able privie counsell, for requyreing all his maiesties lieges of whatsoeuir band ap-
                                                                      poynted
rank and qualitie within the schirrefdome of Aberdeine, to subscrywe the be his
                                                                      Maiestie to
Confession of Faith, dated the second day of Marche 1580, togidder with be sub-
                                                                      scrywed
                                                                      be all his
                                                                      lieges.

October 1638.

The tounes consent to subscrywe the Confession of Faith and generall band appoynted be his Maiestie to be subscryved be all his lieges.

the generall band for mantenance of the trew religion and the kingis person, dated in anno 1589, conforme to his maiesties royall commandement and warrand givin for that effect be his maiesties declaration and letteris patent, published at the mercat croce of this burghe wpoun the fyft day of October instant, hawing schawin and exhibit the said Confessioun of Faith and generall band, markit and subscryuit be the clerk of privie counsell, to the pronest and baillies of the said burghe, the said Lord Marqueis of Huntlie requyred the saids pronest and baillies to subscrywe the same, and to conveine thair counsell and whole bodie of thair towne, and to requyre thame also to subscrywe the said Confession of Faith and generall band, as thay will be answerable to his maiestie and to the saids Lords wpoun thair dutie and obedience: the saids pronest and baillies, in humble acknowledgment of his maiesties pious and gratious dispositioun and affectioun to the puritie of God's trueth, and thairby finding thameselffis band in ductie and conscience to obey his maiesties royall commandiments, causit conveine this day within thair tolbuith the whole bodie of thair toune be touk of drum, and being convenit, Mr Alexander Jaffray, pronest, causit reid publictlie in thair audience his maiesties declaratioun foirsaid, togidder with the said Confession of Faith and generall band, and requyred thame all to subscrywe the same conforme to his maiesties royall pleasour published to that effect, as thay will answer at the contrarie wpoun thair obedience; lykeas the said Mr Alexander Jaffray, pronest, for removeing all scrupill out of the mynds of the people, desyred Doctor Robert Barroun and Doctor James Sibbald, twa of the tounes ministeris, to subscrywe the said confession and band, who, befoir thay gave thair subscriptiones, declared and protested befoir God and all men that wer present, that thay wer to subscrywe the said confessioun as it condemneth and abjureth all popish erroris, idolatrie, and superstition, reallie and indeed repugnant to God's holy word, and that thay do not wnderstand Perth articles and Episcopall government, or any doctrine, rite, or ceremony not repugnant to scripture, or to the practice of the ancient or moderne reformed and sound churches, or to the confessioun

of the Church of Scotland registrat in the acts of parliament, to be con-
demned and abjured in it, and desyred that ane act sould be sett donne
and enacted heirwpoun, in perpetuall evidence and testimonie of this thair
conceptioun and vnderstanding of the foirsaid oath or confessioun; lykeas,
accordinglie thay did subscrywe the same in presens of the magistrattis
and of the toune convenit as said is, and the said Mr Alex. Jaffray,
proueest, Johne Hay, and Willeam Forbes, declaired that thay wer to subscrywe the said Confessioun of Faith rightlie wnderstood, and as it doth
condemne and abjure all popish erroris, idolatry, and superstitioun repugnant to God's holy word, and that thay wnderstand not Perth articles
nor Episcopall government to be abjured in it, and also without prejudice of sound and laudable discipline authorysed and approven by the kirk
and lawes of this kingdome, whairwpoun thay desyred ane act, *ad futurum
rei memoriam*, and immediatlie thaireftir thay did subscrywe the said
Confessioun of Faith and generall band, to the quhilk declarationn made
be the saids prouest, baillies, and ministeris, the most pairt of the bodie
of the toune, convenit as said is, adherit, and so went on and subscrywit
the samen confessioun and generall band accordinglie, with great harmonie
and applaus; lykeas Robert Crukschank, younger, adheres to the foirsaid
declarationn made be the saidis prouest and baillies, notwithstanding that
he subscrywit the said confessioun and band, eftir the assemblie.

8 October 1638.

The toune consent to subscrywe the Con- fession of Faith and generall band ap- poynted be his Maiestie to be sub- serywed be all his lieges.

10 October 1638.

In the first, the prouest, baillies, and counsell ratifies and approves
the act and statute maid be thair predicessoures anent the keiping of the
sermones on the Sabboth day, whilk they ordaine to hawe effect and to
be putt in executioun againes the contraveinares, vnder the paines thairin
contenit, towitt, wnder the paine of twentie schillingis to be payed be
ilk persone contraveinand, quha salbe fund absent from sermones ather
befoir or afternoone on the Sabboth, to the collectour of the kirk sessioun,
for the vse of the poore, *toties quoties*, and incais of inhabilitie or refuissall

10 Oct. 1638.

Statute anent the keiping of the ser- mones.

10 Oct. 1638. Statute anent the keping of the sermones.	of any offending in this kynd to pay the said penaltie presentlie eftir tryell and conviction, the offendares to be pwnished in thair bodies be imprisonment, or aftir sic wther maner as the magistrattis sall injoyne, conforme to the Actis of Parliament made againes the brakeris of the Lordis Sabboth.

31 October 1638.

31 Oct. 1638. The haill inhabitants of the toun, fensibill persones, to be trayned vp in militarie exercise.	The said day anent the supplicatioun giwen in and presented to the prouest, baillies, and counsell vpoun the sewinteine day of October instant, be the subscrynares of the militarie band, for thameselflis and representand all wtheris of this burghe who hes in mynd to follow militarie exercise of old in vse, bot now dishanted in this burghe, humblie intreating thair wisdomes of the counsall, that the said militarie exercises for thair educatioun and handling of armes and vse of militarie discipline be not interrupted nor hinderit, since the same wes undirtakin be warrant frome the late magistrattis and counsell, bot that thay may hawe culloris, drum, and vse of the said exercise and militarie discipline as formerlie thay had, promising, by God's assistance that thair salbe no disorder nor trubill be occasioun thairof as far as in thame lyes, as at more length was contenit in thair said supplicatioun, quhairenent the prouest, baillies, new and auld counsallis having deliberatlie advysit, howsoewir the said exercise vpoun just grounds and reasones was dischairget and interrupted, newirtheless, in hope of a more dutiefull and respectiue cariage heireftir, thay find the exercise in itself laudabill and profitabill, and necessarie for the common weill, and thairfoir thay hawe statute and ordanit, and be thir presentis statutes and ordaines that the haill nichtboures of the toune, alsweill brether of gild, as craftismen and other inhabitantis thairof, fensabill persones, sic as pleassis to learne to handle thair armes, salbe traynit and instructit in the said militarie exercise of dreilling, and for that effect maid instantlie choose and nominatioun of Johne Leslie, ane of the present baillies, to be capitane, Mr Thomas Merser, lieutenant,

Johne Mengzeis ensengyie, Walter Moresone, Alexander Alshinour, and Andro Knowis, serjandis, to whome the saids provest, baillies, and counsall committs the present chairge of the said militarie exercise of dreilling, and that during the counsellis pleasour, with power to the said capitane and remanent officiares to caus carrye cullouris, beat drummes, and lift armes for dreilling and trayning wp of the nichtbouris of the toune sic as pleassis, in militarie exercise and discipline weiklie ilk Monenday, begynnand wpown Monday nixt, the fyft of November, at aucht houres in the morning, and so further weiklie thaireftir during the counsallis pleasour as said is, prowyding allwayes that sic persones as sall frequent and vse the said exercise carrie thameselffis modestlie and calmelie, and that thay reteir to thair houssis at thair dissolving ilk day of thair meeting, without shooting or spending of pulder; and forder, the saids provest, baillies, and counsall hes dischairgit, and be thir presentes dischairges, the late militarie band and all bandis to be made of that kynd heireftir, except sic as salbe warrantit be the magistrattis and counsall of the burghe for the tyme.

31 Oct. 1638.
The haill inhabitants of the toun, fensible persones, to be trayned vp in militarie exercise.

5 November 1638.

The quhilk day anent the petitioun gewin in to the prowest, baillies, and councell be a great number of the nichtbouris of this burghe, concerning the directing of a commissioner to the Generall Assemblie, indicted to hauld at Glasgo, the twentie ane day of November instant; of the quhilk petition the tenour followes:—Please your w[orships] my Lord Provest, baillies, and counsall, we ane great number of your brethrene ar informit that ye intend to send ane commissioner to the Assemblie, and the materis to be handlit thairin being so weichtie and important, we desyre your worships seriouslie to consider with ws the inexpediencie of sending ane commissioner, for the reassones following, and if thair be ane chosen that we be callit and conveinit in the tounes hous, and consent to his instructiounes befoir his instructiounes be subscrywit be yow, sieing the gude or ewill thairof glaides or greives the haill bodie : The resones

5 Nov. 1638.
Petition anent the directing of ane commissioner to the General Assembly.

5 Nov. 1638.

Petition anent the directing of ane commissioner to the Generall Assembly.

ar, first to considder if it be fitting to send ane commissioner at all, sieing at this tyme ye hawe no warrant, direction, or command by missive or letter frome his Maiestie, or his hienes commissioner for that effect, as in former Assemblies ye was wont to hawe; and if it be objectit the proclamatioun to be ane sufficient warrant, it is ansuerit thairto, besyd the proclamatiounes, this burgh was ewir in vse abefoir to resawe his Maiesties missive, his Commissionares, or the Lordis of Privie Counsell; secondlie, the commissionares chairges (the Assemblie sitting long as is expectit) will be exceiding great, and your worships knowes sufficientlie quhow great the tounes burding is alreddie, quhilk we ar confident your worships will strywe rather to diminish (as your predecessoures did this last yeir) then to augment the samen; thirdlie, the commissioner that sal happin to be chosin (if any be), quhow weill affectit soewir, must neids ather displease his Maiestie (as God forbid), to quhome this toune stands so mutche obleist, or oure neighbour burrowes, or sall wrong the trust committit to him be this burghe, or wtherwayes wrong his awin conscience in assenting or dissassenting, protesting or not protesting; fourthlie, if any commissioner be chosin, that he be suche a persone quha hes subscrywit the Confessioun of Faith and generall band now warranted be his Maiestie and Lordis of Secret Counsell, and quha will be gracious to his Maiestie and his commissioner, as not subscrywer of the first covenant, nor in any caice ane assenter or conniver yairto; fyiftlie, that inregaird of the weightie materis in hand, the haill brethreine of gild and bodie of this toune (being abusieres concerning oure consciences) sould be convenit and be acquaint with the iniunctiounes and instructiounes to be gewin to the said commissioner to this Assemblie, and that his commissioun be so limitat that wpoun quhatsumewir respect he presume not to transgres the meanest poynt of his commissioun; sextlie, we earnestlie desyir that oure commissioner (if any be chosin) be expresslie by his commissioun directit and commandit not to voice againes the kingis prerogative, articles of Perth, nor Episcopall government; and if anything be concludit in the said Assemblie againes ather of these, in that caice the commissioner be obleist to disassent thairfra, and in name of this burghe and bodie thairof, protest in the contrair, sieing we hawe all for the maist pairt subscrywit the Confession of Faith and generall band warranted be his Maiestie and Lords of Secret Counsell, with these reservatiounes quhilkis ar enactit in your bookes: remitting the consideratioun of these particulares to your wisdiomes, we expect your answer. Quhilk petitioun being red, hard, and considderit in counsell, and thay therewith being advysit, in respect of the weight and importance of the busienes, thay ordaine the haill toune to be warnit be the hand bell to conveine the morne in the tolbuith at ten houres, to giwe thair advyse whether a commissionar sall be send or not to this ensewing assemblie; and if any salbe send, to resolue vpoun the tenour of his commissioun and instructiounes, whairwnto he sall be tyed and limited.

5 Nov. 1638. Petition anent the directing of ane commissioner to the Generall Assembly.

7 *November* 1638.

The samen day the prouest, baillies, and counsell, finding be the petitioun gewin in to thame be a great many of the nichtboures of this burghe, vpoun the fyft day of November instant, that thay ar desyrous that no commissioner be send at this tyme to the Generall Assemblie, indicted to hauld at Glasgo, the twentie ane day of November instant, for the caussis at length sett donne in the said petitioun, thay therefoir find it not expedient to conveine the toune for that purpose, since thay hawe alreadie declaired thair mynd and advyse thairin be thair said petitioun, and be resone thairof the counsell ar content that no commissionar be direct frome this burghe at this tyme to the said Assemblie, except thay gett a particular letter or warrant frome his Maiestie, or frome his hienes Commissioner, or Lords of Privie Counsell in his Maiesties name, for sending thair commissionar to the said Assemblie, as formerlie thay hawe beine in vse to receawe when thay directed commissionares to bygaine Assemblies.

7 Nov. 1638. Anent the Generall Assemblie.

2 January 1639.

Leslie chosin commissionar anent Alexr. Keyth.

2 *January* 1639.

The quhilk day Patrik Leslie, late prowest, wes chosin commissioner to Edinburghe, for attending the defence of the actiounes intentit at the instance of the creditoures of Alexander Keith of Balmuir, against the magistrattes of this burghe, the yeire immediatlie bygaine and this present yeire, be reason of the said Alexander his escaping out of ward furth of the tolbuith of this burghe in the moneth of July last, and the said Patrik is ordanit to keip the eight day of this instant in Edinburghe for that effect, and to employ Sir Thomas Hope, his Maiesties advocat, and alsc Sir Thomas Nicolsonn, Mr Roger Mowat, and Mr James Baird, advocattis, to compeire for the magistrattis in the saids actiounes.

5 January 1639.

Anent the actiones intentit againes the magistrats be the creditoris of Alexr. Keyth.

5 *January* 1639.

The quhilk day the haill toune, both brethrene of gild and craftismen, being warnit be the hand bell to conveine this day within the tolbuith, and conveining thairin for the most pairt, it wes exponit to thame be Maister Alexander Jaffray, prowest, that the prowest and baillies of this burghe, the yeire bygane, so lykwayes the present prowest and baillies for thair entres, ar summundit at the instance of the creditoris of Alexander Keith of Balmure, to compeir befoir the Lordis of Counsell and Sessionn to heire and sie thameselflis decernit to mak payment to the saidis creditoures of the sounes of money debtfull to thame be the said Alexander Keith, be resone of his escaping furth of ward out of the tolbuith of this burght, in the moneth of July last bypast, efter he was arrested thairin at thair instance for the said debtis; and inrespect the said Alexander Keith his escaipjing wes nowayes in default of the magistrattis for the tyme, bot onlie be a slight, he hawing causit inclose himsellf within a trunck, and convoy himsellf thairin furth of the said wairdhous to the peir and shoir of this burgh, quhair he had a bott attending him, in the quhilk he was transportit be sea to his awin hous at Boddum;

as lykwayes be reason the magistrattis hawe bene vsing thair best diligence for apprehending of the said Alexander Keith, be procuring a commissioun frome the Lordis of his Maiesties Privie Counsell for that effect; and that thairwpoun the late magistrattis, and a number of nichtboures with thame, hawe past to Stratherne and maid searche for the said Alexander Keith, bot culd not apprehend him, the said Maister Alexander Jaffray thairfoir inquired of the toune if thay wald contribute for releiff of thair magistratts of sic soumes of money as shall happen to be evicted againes thame for the escaping of the said Alexander Keith; and, in the meane tyme, if they wilbe content to contribute to send out men of new againe for searching and seiking of the said Alexander; and the toune being conveinit as said is, both brethreine of gild and craftismen, thay not onlie disassentit to contribute for releiff of thair magistrattis of sick soumes of money as salbe evietit againes thame for the escaiping of the said Alexander Keith furth of ward, bot lykwayes disassentit that any commissioner be direct to Edinburgh to attend on that proces, bot that the magistrattes wreitt to the tounes ordinar procuratouris and agentis for thair awin defence, and that nothing reflect againes the bodie of the toune to thair prejudice; and as for the searching and seiking of the said Alexander Keith, the toun for the most pairt condiscendit to contribute for defraying the chairges of thrie scoir men to be furneist and send frome this burghe for his searching and seiking, for the space of fyfteine dayes, and to be taxt for that effect, whairwpoun the said Mr Alex. Jaffray, prowest, askit act and instrumentis.

5 Jan. 1639.
Anent the actiones intentit againes the magistrats be the creditouris of Alex. Keyth.

16 *January* 1639.

The quhilk day, anent the ouertures proponit to the magistrattis be the brethreine of gild and haill deacones of craftis convenit in the tolbuith vpoun the ellevint day of Januar instant, for the better defence of the towne now in thir dangerous tymes, when trubill and warr is likelie to fall out throughout this haill kingdome, quhilkis owertures thay desyrit

16 Jan. 1639.
Ouertures proponit be the brethreine of gild and craftis for defence of the toun.

16 Jan.
1639.
Overtures proponit be the brethrene of gild and craftis for defence of the toun.

the magistrattis to represent to the tounes counsell that spedie order may be takin thairwith, whairof the tenour followes:—

In the first they desyre that the toune be provydit with pulder, and for that effect that no pulder be sauld be the merchantis of this burghe, that latelie arryvit frome Flanderis and Danskin, to no persone whatsumewir, nather to burghe nor land, but onlie to the deane of gild, whome thay desyre to by frome the nichtboures all thair pulder at a reasonable pryce, and then to distribute the same amongst the nichtboures of the toune; and whosoewir sellis anie pulder to any other except to the deane of gild, to incur the wnlaw of ane hundreth punds, and that this be intimat be the drum throw the haill streites of the towne.

Item, thay desyre that all the portis of the toune be closed and locked everie night.

Item, that thair be a nightlie watche of twentie foure persones out of the haill inhabitantis of the toune, both frie and vnfrie, and that ilk man watche in proper persone, vnder the paine of fywe punds, to be payed be the absent.

Item, that thair be catbands of irne provydit and put on at everie port, and other convenient places quhair formerlie thay hawe beine, and that thair be lockis provydit for the same.

That the great ordinance be brocht in within the towne, and putt in a sure place, that they get not wrong.

That no strangeris be ludgit within the toune till first the magistrattes be acquainted.

That the baillies pas throw the haill towne, ilk baillie throw his awin quarter, and sight and consider how everie fensible man is furneist with armour, that thay who wantis may be causit provyd thame selflis in all possible diligence.

That the back gettis and vennellis be all closed.

That victuall be restraned to go out of the cuntrie; and the brethrene of gild and deacones of craftis, in name of the haill craftis of this burgh, ar content to be taxt for sic sommes of money as salbe requyred for performance of the premisses.

Whairanent the provost, baillies, and counsall advysing, thay allow of the saids owertures as necessar and proffitable for the publict good of the toun in these dangerous and trubilsome tymes, and for the better performance thairof, thay ordaine Walter Cochrane, deane of gild, to enter craftismen in all convenient diligence to repair the haill portis of the toun, and in macking of catbands and all thingis neidfull thairwnto, and to lift moneyes on profitt for defraying of the chairges that salbe debursit thairwpoun, becaus the toune ar content to be taxt and stented for refounding of the said chairges.

16 Jan. 1639.
Overtures proponit be the brethrene of gild and craftis for defence of the toun.

26 *January* 1639.

The quhilk day anent the supplication gewin in to the prowost, baillies, and counsell, be the collective bodie of this burghe, mackand mention that it is too manifest that this whole kingdome, throw the present distractiones and divisiounes thairof, standis in feare of hostilitie and apparent warr (quhilk God avert), and that other cheiff burrowes who ar not in so great danger as this burghe, ar daylie (to thair great commendation) exerciseing thameselffis and thair haill inhabitantis in martiall discipline vnder thair capitanes, liewtenentis, and other officieris, and hes thair councell of warr appoynted for rewling, commanding, and directing of thair capitanes and cumpanies in thir apparent trubles; nevertheles this towne lyes still in securitie, without tacking any suche course or ordour for his Maiesties service, and thair awin saiftie, entreatting thairfoir thair wisdomes of the councell to tak the premisses to thair consideratioun, and to accept frome the supplicantes the twa littes giwen in with thair petition, and to nominatt and chuis out of the ane litt sa mony as thay shall think most fitt, to sitt conclude and determine as councell of warr within this burghe, and to appoynt and nominat out of the other litt four persones most fitting to be capitanes over the foure severall quarteris of this burghe, both for exerciseing all fensible persones in militarie discipline, and siclyk for leading thame wpoun all suche peices

26 Jan. 1639.
Chusing of councell of warr, capitanes, and vnder officieris.

26 Jan.
1639.
——
Chusing of
councell
of warr,
capitanes,
and vnder
ollicieris.

of service that shal happin to occur in these trubilsome tymes, als oft as
salbe fund expedient for his Maiesties service and defence of this burghe,
as at moir length was contenit in the said supplicatioun; quhilk being
red, hard, and considerit in councell, and thay thairwith being advysit,
thay find the desyre thairof to be werie expedient, and conforme thairto,
they instantlie nominat and chusit Mr Alex. Jaffray, prowest, Johne
Hay, Willeame Forbes, Thomas Mortimer, Johne Leslie, baillies; Lieu-
tenent-Colonell Willeame Johnstonne, Thomas Nicolsonn, Mr Thomas
Gray, George Johnstoun, George Moresoun, Mr Robert Farquhar, Thomas
Collisoun, Paull Collisoun, Mr Patrik Chalmer, Willeame Patrie, George
Bruce, saidler, and Hew Andersone, goldsmith, to be a councell of warr,
and siclyik nominat and chusit the said Thomas Nicolsone to be capitan
of Futtie quarter; George Johnstoun, capitan of the Greine quarter; Mr
Thomas Gray, capitane of the Cruiked quarter; and George Moreson,
capitane of the Evin quarter, during the pleasour of the councell of this
burghe allanerlie; and in lyik maner nominat and chuse Willeame Hay,
Alexander Robertsoun, Alexander Burnett, younger, and Willeam Cut-
berd, to be lievtents; Johne Mengzeis, Thomas Buck, James Collison, and
Walter Moreson, to be ensengzies beraris; Andrew Burnet, younger, James
Blakhall, Johne Ray, Alex. Ashenour, Mr Robert Innes, Henrie Dwn,
Andro Knowes, Charles Kelo, Thomas Gairdyne, tailzeour, Willeame
Andersone, couper, George Pyper, wricht, and Alex. Patersone, armorar,
to be serjands, towitt, thrie for ilk companie, quhilkis haill persones electit
to the generall offices aboue writtin, ar chosin during the councellis
plesure allanerlie, and with conditioun that thay ressawe thair ordour
frome the counsell, als oft as occasioun shall offer.

4 March
1639.
——
Councell
Gordoun.

4 *March* 1639.

The quhilk day, the prowest, baillies, and counsell, all in ane woice,
condiscendis and agries to accept of the band of warrandice giwen be the
Lord Marqueis of Huntlie to the toune anent the escaiping of Willeame

Gordoun, sometyme in Melingsyid, furth of the wairdhous of this burghe; and be resone of thair ressait of the said band, the counsall continewes the prosequnting of the commission raisit at the tounes instance for apprehending of the said Willeame Gordoun, during the spaice contenit in the said band.

4 March 1639.
——
Counsell Gordoun.

Eodem die.

The said day, the prowest, baillies, and counsall of warr, in consideratioun of the intelligence gewin to the towne that thair is ane great armie coming hither from the south for persute and invasion of the toun, ordaines the toune to be fortified in all convenient diligence after the best and surest maner that salbe thought meitt and expedient be the counsall of warr, and for that effect ordaines the haill inhabitantis within this burghe to prosequute the work as thay salbe appoynted, be casting of fousses and ditches according as thay ar lyable in taxatioun, till ane thousand elnes of ground be cutted, and the persone absent or deficient in working of his pairt of the wark foirsaid after directioun, to be deprywit of his fredome, by and attour the refounding of sic chairges as salbe bestowit in working of the work in absence of the persone deficient, and for wther penaltie as salbe imposit vpoun thame be the magistrattes; and neither magistrattes, officemen, ministeris, wedowes, nor na wther inhabitant within this burghe to be eximit frome working of thair awin pairtes of this wark, notwithstanding of any immunitie thay may challenge in wther of the tounes effaires.

Eodem die.
—
The toun to be fortifeit.

15 *March* 1639.

The quhilk day, the haill toune both burgessis of gild and craftismen being convenit in the tolbuith be the drum going throw the haill streites, Maister Alexander Jaffray, prouest, causit publictlie reid in thair audience the act and ordinance, of the dait the fourt of Marche instant, maid and

15 March 1639.
—
Consent brethrene of gild and craftismen to fortifie the toun, and to by muskats and pickis.

150   EXTRACTS FROM THE   [1639.

15 March 1639.
—
Consent brethrene of gild and craftismen to fortifie the toun, and to by muskatis and pickis.

sett doune be the counsall of warre anent the fortiflieing of this burghe, and casting of trinshes and fousies about the same, and craved thair consent thairto: eftir reiding of the quhilk ordinance, the haill towne declairit thameselffis content thairwith, and willinglie promeist ilk ane for thair awin pairtes, to wnderly, obey, and fulfill the said ordinance efter the forme and tenour thairof in all pointes: Lyikas the nichthoures of the toune convenit as said is, wer content, and condiscendit and agriet that the magistrattes sould by twa hundreth muskattes, with bandieliers, pulder, ball, and matche, and ane hundreth pikis frome the Lord Marqueis of Huntlie, for serving of sic thair inhabitantes as hes not armour to furnish thame selffis, and to give band for peyment of the saidis armes in the tounes name.

16 March 1639.
—
The deane of gild and thesaurar ordanit to giwe thair band to the Marquis of Huntly for the muskattis and pickis.

16 *March* 1639.

The quhilk day, fforsamickill as the toune being convenit in the tolbuith wpoun the fyfteine day of Marche instant, condiscendit and agriet that the magistrattes and counsell shuld by twa hundreth muskattes, with bandelieris, pulder, and leid affering thairto, with ane hundreth pickes, fra the Lord Marqueis of Huntly of his maiesties armour latelie send to his lordship from England: thairfoir the counsall ordaines Walter Cochraine, deane of gild, and Andro Burnet, thesaurar, to giwe thair band to the said Lord Marqueis for payment of the pryce of the said armes at Martimes nixt, with ane halff yeires annuall, viz., for ilk muskatt, bandelier, and reast, tuelff pundis Scottes money, for twa pund of pulder, Inglis weycht, to ilk muskat, threttie sex schillingis Scottes money, for ilk pik, fourtie aucht schillingis, for twa hundreth pund weicht of matche, threttie sex pundis four schillingis, extending in all to thrie thowsand thriescoir nynteine pundis four schillings, with ane hundreth twentie thrie pundis for the said halff yeires annuall thairof; and the prouest, baillies, counsall, and communitie become actit to releiwe the saidis deane of gild and thesaurar, of the premisses, and of all that may follow thairon.

20 March 1639.

The quhilk day, the councell giwes power and commission to the prouest, baillies, Patrik Leslie and Robert Johnstoun, to consult and advyse whair the tounes evidentis and registeris salbe putt in custodie and keiping in this dangerous time, and what they do thairanent the counsell promettis to hauld firme and stabill.

Anent the tounes evidentis and registeris.

Eodem die.

The said day, the prouest, baillies, and counsall, ordaines Willeame Blakburne, maister of kirkwark, to len fywe hundreth merkis of the kirk moneyes to Walter Cochraine, deane of gild, for the tounes vse; and the said Walter to giwe band thairfoir, payable at Witsonday nixt, quhairanent the counsall obleissis thame to releiwe him, and sic of the kirk moneyes as the said Willeame hes besyd him, attour the said fywe hundreth merkis, the counsall desyres him in this dangerous tyme to putt it in the best custodie he can, as if it wer his awin.

Kirk moneyes to be lent to the toun.

Eodem die.

The samen day, Doctor Willeame Johnstoune and George Moresoun ar chosin commissionares to pas to the nobilitie of the covenant convenit at Montrois, and to capitulat with thame vpoun sic articles as shalbe gewin in commissioun to the saids commissionares, anent the repairinge of thair armie to this burghe, as lyikwayes to confer be the way with the Erll Marshall wpoun the same busienes, that his lordship wald be pleased to contribute his assistance to the saids commissionares for the peace and quyet of this toune, and George Jamesoun is appoyntit to accumpanie and assist thame in the said commissioun, quhilk is gewine to the effect following, viz., to petition and desyre the nobilitie that they send in a peaceabill maner ane hundreth men at the most for holding of thair committie

Commissionares direct to the nobilitie of the covenant.

Eodem die.	in the auld college, and publicatioun of the actis of the generall assemblie
Commissionares direct to the nobilitie of the covenant.	in the cathredrall kirk of this diocie; and if the college and cathedrall kirk be not made patent to thame for that effect, to declare unto thame that thay sal have oure paroche kirk patent for the said intimatioun, the nobilitie alvayes keipand thameselffis and thair forces alse far distant frome this burghe as the Marqueis of Huntlie sall do with his forces.

Eodem die.

Thesaurar deane of gild.	The said day Andro Burnet, thesaurar, exhibit on the counsell tabill the wreittis and bands of the tounes mortifiet moneyes scalled within a codwair, and desyrit, in respect of the present imminent danger, that thay be put wp in sure custodie amongst the tounes evidentis; and Walter Cochraine, deane of gild, exhibit lyikwayes the bands and wreittes belonging to the deanrie of gild, scalled and bund togidder in a paper, and desyred the same in lyik maner tobe putt amongst the tounes evidentis, quhilk wes accordinglie done.

25 March 1639.

Commissionares direct of new agane to the nobilitie.	The quhilk day, in respect that Doctor Willeame Johnstoun and George Moresoun, who wer directed commissionares from this burghe to the Erle of Montrois wpoun the twentie day of Marche instant, with Mr Robert Gordoun of Straloch, and Doctor Willeame Gordoun, commissionares, lyikwayes to his lordship frome the Marquis of Huntly, did receawe a delaying answer at that tyme frome the said Erle of Montrois to suche propositiones as thay did remonstrat to his lordship: thairfoir the prowest, baillies, and counsall thinkis it expedient to direct the same commissionaris of new againe to the said Erll of Montrois, and to propone to his lordship and otheris of the nobilitie there present with him, the articles following, and to crawe thair answer thairwpoun, off the quhilkis articles the tenour followes :—

It is desyred be the toune of Aberdeine that thay may hawe assurance that no hostilitie be vsed againes thame, nor name of thair magistrattes, ministeris, nor otheris, thair inhabitantis, be forced in thair consciences, nor wronged in thair bodies nor gudes, and that thair toune be left in peace, as thay ar content to giwe a peaceable entrie to the nobilitie and thair armie.

25 March 1639. Commissionares direct of new agane to the nobilitie.

Item, if anie particular persones giwe any offence, that it be repared in privat, but reflecting vpoun the publict peace.

Item, that the toune be not urgit to receawe nor harbour mair people nor thay may conveuientlie ease.

And the toune promeissis a peaceable entrie, and issue, and sic accomodatioun as thay can affoord, during the abod of the nobilitie there. Subscrywed be the prowest and baillies, and be the Marquis of Huntly as consentar the 25 day of Marche 1639.

28 *March* 1639.

The quhilk day the haill toune, both frie and vnfrie, being convenit in the tolbuith be the drum, Mr Alex. Jaffray, prowest, schew and declaired to thame the articles mentioned in the act immediatlie befoir writtin, quhilk the magistrattes and counsall had send with thair commissionares to the Erle of Montrois and remanent nobilitie of the covenant approching towards this burghe with thair armie, and withall the prouest schew the answer quhilk oure commissionares had receawed in wreitt to the saids articles, of the quhilk answer the tenour followes:—The Erle of Montrois did expres that his intended voyage for Aberdeine is onlie for performing the appointment of the late generall assemblie according as it hath bene done in other places, and in no way to do the smallest wrong or injurie to any (as perhaps is supposed), nor vse the meanest violence, except in so farre as his lordship and his lordschipis followeris salbe be necessitat for thair awin saiftie and thair caus; inrespect of the quhilk diligence vsed by the magistrattes and counsell in directing com-

28 March 1639. The Erle of Montrois answer to oure commissionaris propositiones.

28 March 1639.

The Erle of Montrois answer to oure commissionaris propositiones.

missionares to the said Erll of Montroise, and of the said Erle, his answer forsaid gewin to the saidis commissionares, the toune declared that thay ar content to receawe the said nobillmen and thair followeris, and to harbour thame eftir the most commodious maner thay can, and desyres the magistrattes to giwe ordour ilk baillie throw his awin quarter for that effect, and for furneshing competent ludginges unto thame sic as the toune can affoord.

Eodem die.

The townes capitanes quyttted thair charge.

Eodem die.

The samen day Mr Thomas Gray, Thomas Nicolsone, George Johnstoun, and George Moresone, the foure capitanes latelie chosin be the counsell for trayning and exerceising the inhabitantis of this burghe fensible persones in militarie exercise and disciplin, laid doun and quyttit thair chairge, in presens of the toune convenit this day in the tolbuith, be resone of the cessationne of imployment for defence of the toune be armes, quhilk the toune publictlie acknowledged that thay wer not abile to doe nor to withstand the great power and armie approching to this burgh, a great many of the inhabitantis hawing alreddie deserted and left the toune, and thay hawing no help nor supplie of men frome the cuntrie to resist the invasioun of the said armie.

Memorandum on Saturday, the penult day of Marche 1639.

Entrie of the first armie.

The Erll of Montrois, Generall of the armie, accompanied with the Erll Marshall, the Erll of Kingorne, Generall Leslie, the Lord Coupar, the Lord Elcho, the Lord Fraser, the Maister of Forbes, and many barones of Angous, Mearnes, Mar, and Buchan, come to the toune of Aberdeine with thair armie of horsse and fute, whair thay entered and marched through the toune to the linkis, and there they pitched thair camp, being accompted, sex thowsand men, satt at thair counsell of warr, and thaireftir the Erles of Marshall and Montrois, Generall Leslie, and the greatest pairt of the armie marched that day frome the linkis to Inverurie, leaving behind thame the Erll of Kingorne with aughtene hundreth men to ly in the toune till thair bak cumming; and befoir thay marched out of the linkes, the nobillmen send for oure prouest and baillies, and chairgit thame to fill vp and cast in oure trinshes in all possible diligence, and to enter to wark for that effect on Mononday nixt, and to continew thairat till all the trinshes wer filled vp againe, vnder the paine of plundering and raising oure toune, quhilk wes accordinglie obeyit.

Eodem die.

Entrie of the first armie.

2 April 1639.

The quhilk day the haill toune being convenit be the drum in the Grayfreir Kirk, it was publictlie declaired and schawin to thame be Mr Alexander Jaffray, prouest, that the Erll of Kingorne for himselff, and in name of the Erle of Montrois, generall, and remanent nobilitie of the present armie within and about the toune, hes peremptorlie commandit and chairgit the toune to dismount thair cannones, and to delywer thame to be placed befoir the Erll Marshall his hous in the Castellgett, and thairwith to delywer oure haill pulder and bullett to be sequestrat for thair service and vse, as lyikwayes to tak donne and remowe oure haill catbands with all possible diligence; and siclyik shew and declared that the nichtboures of the toune are commandit to receawe within thair houssis the haill fute soiouris of the armie, and to giwe thame intertenement in bed and buird for sex schillings aught pennies ilk soiour in the day, for the spaice of eight dayes, for payment whairof the said Erll of Kingorne commandit the prowest and baillies to giwe thair word and assurance to the nichtboures of the toune that thay shuld be thame fullie payed; lyikas the said Erll of Kingorne promeist to relieve the saids prouest and baillies thairof, and to mak thankfull payment of the allowance foirsaid for everie soiour so long as thay wer intertenit in this burgh, and thairfoir inquyred of the toune convenit as said is what answer thay wald giwe, and what course thay wald tak in the premisses, quha answered that it behoved thame to obey what is injoyned since thay ar vnder bondage and thraldome for the

2 April 1639.

Charge gewin be the nobilitie to the toun.

2 April 1639.

present, and nowayes habill to resist, and thairfoir consentit to giwe obedience to the foirsaid injunctiones.

3 April 1639.

The toun chargit to subserywe the covenant.

3 April 1639.

The quhilk day the prouest intimat to the toune convenit be the drum in the Grayfreirs Kirk, that thay ar requyred be the nobilitie to subserywe thair covenant, and article following eiked thairunto, vnder the paine of disarming thame and confiscatioun of all thair goods, of the quhilk article the tenour followes:—The article of this covenant quhilk was at the first subscriptioun referred to the determinatioun of the Generall Assemblie, being now determined at Glasgow in December 1638, and thairby the fywe articles of Perth and the governament of the kirk by bishops being declared to be abjured and remowed, and the civill places and power of kirkmen declared to be unlawfull, we subseryue according to the determination of the said frie and lawfull Generall Assemblie hauldin at Glasgow; in witness whairoff we hawe subserywit the haill premisses with oure hands. Eftir the reiding of the quhilk article, the toune tuke to be advysed befoir thay wald giwe thair answer.

9 April 1639.

A new charge gewin be the nobilitie to the toun, with thair answer thairto.

9 April 1639.

The quhilk day the toune being convenit be the drum within the Grayfreir Kirk, it was declaired to thame be Mr Alex. Jaffray, prouest, that the nobilitie convenit heir in this present armie, had expreslie commandit and injoyned that the toune shuld in all diligence possible fortifie thair blockhous for the tounes defence aganes forane enemies, and lyikwayes that the toune shuld subserywe the covenant, and contribute with the rest of the kingdome in all thinges for defence of the common caus; and forder, seing as the nobilitie alledges the toune wes the caus of thair heir cumming with thair armie, the nobilitie thairfoir wald exact frome the toune a taxatioun of ane hundreth thowsand merkis, togidder with the haill chairges of the soiouris since thair coming to Aberdeine, off the quhilkis taxatiounes and chairges the nobilitie declaired that thay wald hawe the covenanteris in Aberdeine to be frie; whairunto it was answered be the toune convenit as said is, that thay wer content to fortifie thair blockhous, and the most pairt also wer content to subscrywe the covenant, and to contribute proportionablie in tyme coming in that buscues with the rest of the burrowes, bot refused and disasscented to pay the foirsaid taxatioun of ane hundreth thowsand merkis, since thair wes no just ground nor reasone to impose the same vpoun thame, nather wer thay habill to pay the same; and if the nobillmen, notwithstanding of the tounes refuisall, will insist to hawe the said taxatioun, thay desyre a competent tyme for the space of a moneth or thairby, to be granted to thame to remowe thameselffis, wyllis, and bairnes, with bag and baggage, out of the toune, and thaireftir lat the nobillmen dispose of the toune at thair pleasure.

9 April 1639.
A new charge gewin be the nobilitie to the toun, with thair answer thairto.

10 April 1639.

The quhilk day, eftir sermone made be Maister James Row, minister, the toune for the most pairt subscrywit the nobilities covenant.

10 April 1639.
The townes subscription of the covenant.

15 April 1639.

The quhilk day, the toune being convenit this day in the tolbuith be the drum, it wes exponit to thame be the prouest that the Erll of Montrois and remanent nobilitie convenit heir with thair armie, had appointed and nominat Johne Hay, baillie, Mr Robert Farquhar, Mr Thomas Gray, and George Moresoun, to go commissionares frome this burghe to the nobillitie and commissionares of the tables in Edinburgh, to joyne and concur with thame in all things tending to the glorie of God, the king's honor, the mantenance of the true religione, lawes and liberties

15 April 1639.
Hay, Farquhar, Moreson, appoynted be the nobilitie to go commissionares to Edinburgh.

15 April 1639.

Hay Farquhar Moresoun appoynted be the nobilitie to go commissionares to Edinburgh.

of the kingdome, and thairfor inquyred of the tounne convenit as said is, gif thay will consent to the directing of the saids commissionares to the effect foirsaid, and mak thair chairges during thair employment in the said commissioun, wha answered, that since thay hawe subscryvit the covenant, thay must neidis concur and contribute in all thingis concerning the same, and thairfoir consentis that the saids commissionares be directit south, and that thair expenssis be made at the common chairge of the tounne, and that a commissioun be gewin to thame, subscryvit be the magistrattes and counsall to the effect aboue specifeit.

Eodem die.

Eodem die.

Protestatioun Willeame Erskyne for him self, and in name of the auld covenanters.

The said day the inhabitantis of the burghe of Aberdeine, being convenit in thair Tolbuith be the drum, anent the directing of commissionares to Edinburgh in the matter of the covenant, Willeame Erskine, burges of Aberdeine, for himself, and in name and behalff of the remanent nichtbouires and inhabitantis of the said burghe, quha wer first subscryveris of the covenant, protestit that thay and everie ane of thame be frie and liberat fra payment of any taxatioun or impositioun to be sett or imposit vpoun the tounne, for intertenement of the souldiouris of the armie during thair abode in Aberdeine, and for quhatsumewir wther caus bygane concerning the covenant, preceiding the date heirof, in respect it was the directioun of the nobilitie that were heire present with the armie, that these who first subscrywit the covenant in Aberdeine should be frie of all bygane burdines and taxationes to be imposit vpoun the tounne concerning the said covenant, be resone thay wer not the occasioun of the saidis burdings, as thay alledgit, and thairwpoun the said Willeame Erskine askit act and instrumentes.

17 April 1639.

The said day in presens of the provest, baillies, and counsall, compeirit Andro Burnet, thesaurar, and gawe in and produceit befoir thame ane compt of the soumes of money debursed be him at command and be warrand of the magistrattis to the persones eftir named, for intertenement of thameselffis, thair sojouris, and followeris, at the late heir being of the southland armie, viz., to Capitane M'Gill ane hundreth twentie foure pundis, to Capitane Hay foure scoir fyftene pundis sevintene schillingis foure penneis; to the Laird of Lawers, leader of aucht hundredth Argyle men thrie hundreth threttie thrie pundis sex schillings aucht pennies; to Capitane Cambell twantie pundis; to Harie Lindsay ten pundis foure schillingis twa penneis; and in respect the said thesaurar debursit the saids soumes be warrand of the magistrattes, as said is, and for preveining a forder prejudice to the toune incais the moneyes had not bene delywered, he desyrit the counsallis allowance and approbatioun thairunto; eftir consideratioun quhairof, and of the knowin gude done to the toune by the debursing of these moneyes, whilk hinderit the sojowris frome plundering, the saidis provest, baillies, and counsall, in ane voice ratifiet and approveit the compt abonewrittin, and ordaines the saids soumes to be allowit to the said thesaurar in his comptis, but preyudice alwayes of the protestatioun made be Willeame Erskyn in fauouris of the auld covenanters.

Compt of Andro Burnet, thesaurar, his debursementis to capitanes and others of the armie.

20 April 1639.

The quhilk day, both the counccellis being convenit, concludes all in ane voice that supplie be sent frome this burghe to concur with the nobilitie and gentrie for defence of the cuntrie againes the Laird of Banff and his confedarattis, opposeris of the covenant and disturbares of the peace, and that ane commissioner be send for this effect frome this burghe to the nobillmen and brrones wha ar to meitt at Monymusk on Monday

Moir chosin commissionar to meitt at Monymusk.

20 April 1639.	nixt at aucht houres; lyikas instantlie Mr Willeame Moir wes chosin com-
Moir chosin commissionar to meitt at Monymusk.	missioner for keiping of the said meitting, and to be acquantit with the noblemenis myndis what course thay will tak in the busines, and the toune ar ordanit to be presentlie convenit that order may be gewin for sending out a supplie of men to the effect foirsaid.

Eodem die.   Eodem die.

The townes consent to send fourscoir men to Monymusk.
The said day, the haill toune, both frie and unfrie, being convenit in the tolbuith be the drum, condiscendis all in ane voice that fourscoir men be sent to meit the nobilitie and gentrie at Monymusk, on Monday nixt, at aucht houres in the morning, togidder with commanderis fitt for a companye, and that ilk persone be in redynes in his best armour, as he salbe warnit, vnder the paine of ane hundreth pundis, and warding of the persones vnwilling to go in that service.

A watche appoynted.
Item, it is ordanit that a nightle watche be sett of fourtie persones, and ilk man to watche in propper persone, vnder the paine of ten pundis, to be exacted of ilk persone absent, *toties quoties.*

6 May 1639.   6 May 1639.

Thesaurar Farquhar.
The quhilk day the counsall ordaines Andro Burnet, thesaurar, to refound to Maister Robert Farquhar, ane hundreth dolouris advanceit be him in Edinburghe for defraying of his awin and the rest of the commissionares charges, wha wer direct to attend the tables, attour the fourtie dolouris debursit be the said Andro to the saids commissionares at thair south going, whilk salbe allowit to the said thesaurar in his comptis.

Eodem die.   Eodem die.

The said day, the toune being convenit be the drum in the tolbuith,   A letter
Mr Alexander Jaffray, provest, causit reid and intimat vnto thame the froine the
letter direct frome the nobilitie of the taibles to the provest and baillies taibles to
of this burghe for sending the fourt man to the bound rod, off the quhilk fourt man
letter the tenour followes :—" To oure worthie freindis the provest and Bound rod.
baillies of Aberdeine. Right Honorabill the approaching of his Maiesties
shipes to the number alredie of tuentie nyne, within the firth aboue North
Bervick, where thay hawe bene since yesterday in the efternoone, giues
ws iust reason to feare that the land armies on the borderis will mak ane
suddane assault; these ar therefoir earnestlie to intreatt you to vse all
possible diligence to haist to Edinburghe (which is the place appointed for
the first randevous to these in your boundis), the fourth man in your
schirefflome, alsweill within burghe as to landward, sufficientlie armed,
and with ten dayes provisioun of victuall; we expect that with your fute
companies yow will send a competent number of horsemen with carabines,
pistollis, gunes, or jack and lances. We know not how soone the charge
may be gewin be the enemie, and therefoir we most yet againe entreat
a speedie dispatche, as we salbe your affectioned freindis and servandis.
Sic subscribitur Dalhousie, Balmerino, Naper, Forrester. Edinburghe, first
May 1639." Eftir the reiding of the quhilk letter, the provest inquyred of
the toune, both brethreine of gild and craftismen, convenit as said is, what
course they will tak in the buisienes, quha tuke to be advyisit, and to giwe
thair answer thairanent on Fridday nixt, the tent of May instant.

10 May 1639.   10 May
                                                                      1639.
The quhilk day, the toune being convenit be the drum in the tol-   The tounes
buith, it was declared to thame be Maister Alexander Jaffray, provest, answer to
that ane letter was direct to him and to the baillies from the Lord Fraser, ties letter.
the Maister of Forbes, and some barones, schawing that certaine persones,

I   X

10 May 1639.

The tounes answer to the nobilities letter.

enemies to the peace of the churche and state, wer to assault the toun, and to captivat the same to thair behowe, and thairfor willit the toun to advert thair awin skaith, promeising thair assistance vpoun adverteisment, and withall desyring the toun to giwe notice thairof to the Erll Marschall, who wilbe redie to giwe his aid as neid requyres; quhilk letter being red, the prouest demandit of the nightboures convenit if thay thought it expedient to acquaint the Erll Marschall with the busienes, and to crawe his lordshipes help and assistance, whairunto thay willinglie condiscendit, prouyding alvayes if any cuntrie man salbe send hither to the effect foirsaid, that thay be interteneit wpoun thair awin chairges and expenssis, as is done be the gentrie and otheris that repaires to the toune of Montrois for thair help and defence againes the forane enimie; and forder, the toune being desyred be the prouest to giwe thair answer anent the sending of the fourt man of thair towne to the bound rod, conforme to the letter direct to thame for that effect frome the nobilitie of the tables, quhilk letter being intimat to thame wpoun the sext of this instant, thay tuke this day to be advysit anent the gewing of thair answer thairwnto, and thair answer being craved, as said is, thay declared that, in respect of the present danger whairin the toune standis of invasioun both be brockin hielandmen and cuntrie gentilhmen, as lyikwayes be resone the greatest pairt of the nichtboures of the toune ar gone out of the cuntrie, and that the halff of the toune ar ilk nicht vpoun watche, they wer not habill in these respectis to send any men to the bound rod, quhilk thay desyred the magistrattes to remonstrat to the taibles, and to schaw thame the tounes just excuse be reasone of thair paucitie and weaknes, and that the toun are threatned to be invaded both be foran and intestine enimies, for quhilk caus thay ar seikand help frome the nobellmen and gentrie to defend thair toune, and so ar made altogidder vnhabill to send any men to the bound rod.

13 *May* 1639.

The quhilk day the tonne being convenit in the tolbuith be the drum for gewing aniswer to the Erle of Marschall, his letter direct to the prowest and baillies of this burghe on Satterday last, the allevint of this instant, whairby his lordship desyres the len of sex peice of cannon for the vse of the tonne of Montrois; quhilk letter being publictlie red in audience of the tonne, and thay being asked be the prowest if thay will consent to len sex peice of thair cannon to the said Erll Marschall for the vse foirsaid, thay all in ane voice, refuisit to len any of thair mmnitioun out of the tonne now in this dangerous tyme, becaus sex of thame belongs to the Kings Maiestie, whairin his Maiestie hes the tonnes bond for redelywerie thairof, when thay shalbe requyred, so that without his Maiesties speciall command and warrand in wreitt thay cannot tak vpoun thame to len any of his Maiesties cannon, and as for the vther sex belonging to the tonne thay stand in als great neid thairof thameselffis, and are lyabill to the same danger that the tonne of Montrois ar, and so cannot, without thair awin great prejudice, len any of thair cannon at this tyme, and thairfoir desyirit thair magistrattes to remonstrat thair just and lauchfull excuse heiranent to the Erle Marischall, not doubting but his lordship will tak the same in gude pairt; and siclyik, anent the letter direct the day foirsaid to the magistrattes and councell of this burghe frome the Lord Fraser, the Maister of Forbes, the Laird of Frendraucht, and some other of the barrones and gentrie, schawing that the Laird of Banff and his associatis had brockin the peace of the cuntrie, plunderit dyveris of the Laird of Towies tenentis, and come to the Barnezardis of Towie, and thair in opin hostilitie persewit the said noblemen and otheris that were with thame, and not getting thair intent but some of thair awin companie hurt, went away to mak thameselffes stronger, for quhilk caus the said nobillmen, with thair confederatis, hawe resolued to follow thame, desyring ws thairfoir to send suche a supplie of men out of oure tonne as we may spair to meitt the Erle Marishallis, and thair companies at Kintoir this Mononday

The townes refusall to len thair cannon.

13 May
1639.
———
The townes
refusall to
len thair
cannon.

The tonnes
answer to
the letter
direct to
thame
from the
Lord
Fraser and
Master of
Forbes.

at night, as at moir length wes contenit in the said letter, quhilk being also opinlie red in audience of the toune convenit as said is, the prowest inquired of thame what answer thay wald giwe thairwnto, who declared be reson of the danger of invasioun whairwnto oure toune is presentlie lyable now in this trubilsome tyme both be forane and intestine enemies, oure towne being continewall watched, and a quarter of the towne being ilk night on watche, so that ilk fourth night euerie man most neidis watche, as lyikwayes inrespect a great many of oure nightboures and inhabitants are gone out of the cuntrie, and sindrie and dyveris of thame are daylie going furth thairof and leawing the toune, thay thairfore, all in ane voice, answered that thay culd not possiblie, for the present, send any supplie of men since they stand in neid of help of men to guard and defend thair towne, quhilk thay in the lyikmaner willed thair magistrattes to represent to the said nobillmen and barrones, and to mak thair lauchfull excuse at thair hands, lyikas the said nobillmen and barones, be thair former letter direct to the toune, willit thame to seik supplie of men from the Erle Marshall, for guarding oure toune frome the persute and invasioun of the said Laird of Banff and his adherentis, and so they culd not at the present send furth any supplie of men.

16 May
1639.

The townes
answer to
the Laird
of Banff
and his
associattis
anent thair
demand of
frie quarteris to
thair
soiouris.

16 May 1639.

The quhilk day the haill toune, both frie and wnfrie, being warnit to this day be the drum passand throw the haill streittes of the toune, and convening for the most pairt within the Tolbuith, it wes exponit to thame be Mr Alexander Jaffray, prowest, that the Lairds of Banff, Haddo, Gight elder and younger, Foverane, and dyweris wtheris of the gentrie, who come in this toune yeisternicht, declaired be thair commissionares to the magistrattes that thay wold hawe frie quarteris to thair soiouris during the tyme of thair abod in this burghe, as the nobillmen who wer laitlie heir had frie quarteris also for thair soiouris, and that thay wald hawe this quartering imposed and laid oulie wpoun the auld covenanteris within this burghe, seing thay hawe beine exonered frome quartering in tymes bygoane, whairwith the nightboures being advysit, answerit all in ane voce that thay wold not separat nor divyde thameselffis frome the auld covenanteris, since they ar all memberis of on bodie and incorporatioun with thame, bot wald willinglie contribute and bear burding with the saids auld covenanteris for thair greater ease of suche ane heavie burding, and for eschewing the plundering of thair houssis and gudes whairwith they wer threatned; lyikas for that effect thay wer content to harbour and quarter the soiouris of this present armie, and to bear equall burding *pro rata* with the saids auld covenanteris, prowyding that thay contribute lyikwayes with the rest of the bodie of the toune for defraying of the chairges debursit wpoun the first and second quartering of the soiouris of the tuo bygaine armies, as also for these debursementis that sallhappin now to be bestowed on this third armie, and all other debursementis that sall heireftir occur for quartering of soiouris, proportionablie according to the estate and meanes of everie nightbour in the toune, and with conditioun lyikwayes that all protestationes made heirtofoir be auld covenanteris for thair exemptioune frome suche contributiounes be now rescinded, and that the haill inhabitantis of the toune, but exception of persones, be lyable as on bodie to contribute for quartering all soiouris, both for bygaines and to come. As for the wther desyre maid be the saidis barones and gentrie for sending furth some inhabitantes of this burghe with thame in his Maiesties service as thay alledgit, it wes answerit be the toune that thay wer not abill to send furth any of thair tounes men, be resone a great many of thame wer removed to foraine cuntries, whairof some ar alreddie employed in his Maiesties service with his navie lying in the firth, and the remanent who are remaining in the toune ar ower few to guard and watche the same in thir dangerous tymes, the toune having rather neid of supplie of men, nor to grant any of thair few number to go frome thance.

16 May 1639.

The townes answer to the Laird of Banff and his associattis anent thair demand of frie quarteris to thair soiouris.

27 May 1639.

Ten thousand merkis imposit vpoun the toun for the Generall and remanent nobilitie of the present armie.

27 *May* 1639.

The quhilk day the haill toune, both frie and unfrie, being warnit to this day, be the drum passand throw the haill streittes of the toune, and conveninge for the most pairt in the laich counselhous of the tolbuith, it wes exponit to thame be Mr Alexander Jaffray, provest, that the Erle of Montrois, Generall of the present armie, the Erles of Marshall, Atholl, Kingorne, the Lords Fraser, Cowper, Drummond, Maister of Forbes, Maister of Gray, and other nobillmen and barrones heir present with thame, hawe imposit vpoun the inhabitantis of this burghe the soume of ten thousand merkis Scottes money, to help to defray thair soiouris wages in this present expeditioun againes the Laird of Banff and his associattes, and declaired that thay wald hawe the same to be preceislie payed to thame this day, or the morne befoir ellevin houres at farrest, whairin, if the toune failziet, the soioris wald be permittit to spoill and plunder the toune, to the owerthrow and ruine thairof, and thairfoir the prowest inquired of the toune convenit as said is, what course thay wald take thairanent, quha all in ane voice but oppositioun or contradictioun, for eschewing of the danger threatned, wer content to contribute proportionablie, and *pro rata*, and to be stentit be taxatioun with all convenient diligence for payment of the said soume of ten thousand merkis, ilk persone according to thair generall rankis and estates, but exceptioun of any inhabitant whatsumewir that may pretend immunitie frome payment of taxatiounes, and as for suche nightboures of the toune that ar absent out of the cuntrie, some nightboures that wer present tuke burdeine for thame and promeist to pay thair pairt of the said taxatioun ; and becaus the said ten thowsand merkis cannot be sett and wpliftted in sic haist, as the sume most be payed to the nobilitie, the toune desyres the magistrattes and wther nichtboures of the toune of best moyen and habilitie, to lift the said soume vpoun the bank, and to giwe thair band for repayment thairof, with ane halff yeires annuall of the same, of the quhilk band and soumes of money foirsaid, both principall and annuelrent, the toune convenit as said is, obleissis thame ilk ane for thair awin pairts to warrand, frie, releiwe, and skaithles keip the saidis prowest, baillies, and wtheres that salbe lund for the same, and that be payment of the said taxatioun, ilk ane for thair awin pairtes, as thay salbe taxit and stentit conforme to the stent roll to be gewin out thairwpoun, within tuentie foure houres nixt thaireftir, vnder the paine of poynding of thair reddiest gudes and geare, and wairding of thair persones, the ane but preuidice of the wther; whairwpoun the said Mr Alexander Jaffray, prowest, for himselff, and in name of those that salbe bund for the said soume, askit act and instrumentis.

27 May 1639.
Ten thousand merkis imposit vpoun the toun for the Generall and remanent nobilitie of the present armie.

28 May 1639.

The quhilk day, the toun being convenit in the tolbuith be the drum, it was intimat to thame be Mr Alexander Jaffray, prowest, that the Erle of Montrois, Generall of this present armie, and the remanent nobillmen and barrones heir present in this toune, hawe concludit and expreslie declaired be warrant from the taibles, that thay will hawe oure tounes tuelff peice of cannon transportit heirfra to the tounes of Montrois and Dundie for thair defence againes the invasioun of Inglishmen, and that lyikwayes thay wall hawe the haill inhabitantis of this burghe disarmed, and thair haill wapynnis and armour, both offensive and defensive, to be exhibite and delywered in the tolbuith of this burghe, to suche as salbe appoynted to receawe thame, for arming of all persones in the armie who ar not sufficientlie armed; lyikas publict proclamatioun is made throw the haill streittis of the toune, be sound of trumpett in name of the said Lord Generall, chairging all the inhabitantis of this burghe to exhibit thair whole armour, both offensive and defensive, in the tolbuith, within tuo houres efter the chairge, vnder the paine of confiscatioun of all the goods and geare of suche persones as wold not delywer thair armour within the spaice foirsaid, by and attour the punishing of thair persones; and thairfoir the prowest inquyred of the nichtboures of the toune, convenit as said

28 May 1639.
The toun disarmed.

28 May 1639.
The toun disarmed.

is, what thay will do, and how thay shall carie thameselffis in this busienes, since he and his colligis, the baillies, culd not gett the same hinderit nor stayed, notwithstanding of all the reasones thay culd bring or alledge againes the wnlauchfullness of suche chairges, and albeit thay had offerit that the toune shuld marche in armes, and goe forward with thame to any service thay hawe adoe for the king and cuntrie, so being thay wold not doe suche indignitie to oure toune as to disarme thame, bot wold permitt thame to bruike thair awin armour; anent the quhilkis particulares the nichtboures advysing, declared that, since thay wer not habill to resist, it behowed thame to suffer and give obedience; lyikas accordinglie thay went furth to thair awin houssis and causit bring thair armour to the tolbuithe, and delywered the same to Sir Robert Grahame of Morphie knight, commissioner appoynted for receawing thairof.

29 May 1639.

A note vpon the payment be the toun of ten thowsand merkis imposed vpon thame be the nobilitie.

29 *May* 1639.

The quhilk day James Guthrie of Petforthie, and Johne Grahame, baillie of Montrois, decleired to the Erlis of Marishall and Montrois, and other nobillmen present with thame, within thair ludging in skipper Andersoun his hous on the north syid of the Castellgett, and in presence of Mr Alexander Jaffray, prowest of Aberdeine, that, according to the ordour gewin to thame frome the said nobillmen for receawing frome the prowest and baillies of Aberdeine of the somme of money efter specifiet, thay had receaved in reallie doun tauld moneyes frome Andro Burnet, thesaurar of the said burghe of Aberdeine, in name of the haill bodie of the toune the somme of ten thowsand merkis vsuall Scottes money, imposed wpoun the said towne of Aberdeine be the said nobillmen, for paying the wages of thair soiouris of this present armie; quhairwpoun the said Mr Alex. Jaffray, prowest, asked instrumentis.

29 *May* 1639.

Item this day the Erll of Montrois, Generall of the armie, causit mell and intromett with tuelff peice of demiculvering, whairof sex belonges to the king, and other sex to oure toune, and causit carie and ship thame in a barq of Dundie, the master callit Willeame Coull, to be transeportit some of thame to Montrois, and some to Dundie, and lyikwayes tuke with thame oure pulder and ball.

The townes tuelff peice of cannon, with pulder and ball mellit with be the Erle of Montrois.

7 *June* 1639.

The quhilk day the haill toune, both frie and unfrie, being warnit be the hand bell passand throw the haill streittes of the toune to conveine presentlie within the Tolbuith, and a verie few convening, the greatest pairt of the nightboures hawing removed thameselflis out of the toune, and daylie ma of thame yit removing, Willeame Forbes, baillie, causit reid publictlie in presens of these quha wer convenit, the remonstrance presentit in wreitt to the said baillie and his colliggis, be the tounes foure commissionares, to witt Johne Hay, baillie, Mr Robert Farquhar, Mr Thomas Gray, and George Moresoun, who wer latelie send to Edinburghe in the moneth of Aprill last, be ordour frome the Erle of Montrois and sic otheris of the nobilitie as wes then present heir in Aberdeine, bearand that the saids commissionares after thair coming to Edinburghe, wer deteinit thair be the spaice of sex weikis, and at thair coming having presented thameselflis to the Lordis tables, thay and some wther few nichtboures of this burghe wer fyned in the soume of fourtie thowsand merkis, and confyned for the spaice of fywe weikis till thay sould either pay or report the tounes answer anent the said fyne; and eftir report of the townes refuissall to pay the samen for the resone showin to the saidis Lordis, the said commissionares wer committit to waird within the Tolbuith of Edinburghe, be a warrand subscrywit be the nobilhnen and commissionares for the shyres and burrowes whairin thay remanit be the spaice

The townes answer to the remonstrance made to thame be thair foure commissionares that wer send to Edinburgh be appoyntment of the nobillmen.

7 June 1639.

The townes answer to the remonstrance made to thame be thair foure commissionares that wer send to Edinburgh be appoyntment of the nobillmen.

of tuentie foure houres, till be the mediatioun of the prowest and baillies of Edinburghe, and of Willeame Gray of Pettindrum, thay obtenit libertie to returne home to this burghe to deall with the toun for thair relieff wpoun band gevin be the saidis commissionares as principallis, and the said Willeame Gray as cationer for thame; as lyikwayes wpoun thair great oath, solemnelie sworn, for thair returne bak againe to Edinburghe, and to obey thair directiounes, or then to reentir thair persones in ward within the said tolbuith of Edinburghe betwixt and the first day of July nixt, wnder the paine of fourtie thowsand pundis; and seing the tyme approaches of the saids commissionares thair reentrie, thay desyrit the toune to frie and liberat thame of the said fourtie thowsand merkis, that thairby thay may be free of thair reentrie and incarceratioun in waird. Eftir reiding quhilk remonstrance, sic nightbours of the toune as wer convenit, not exceiding the number of twentie persones, answerit that the toune was nowayes habill to pay any suche fyne as wes imposit, inrespect that sin thair subscryving of thair covenant, thay ar so wrakit and wndone in thair estates, that thay ar skairce abill to interteine thameselflis and thair families, far les to pay any fyne, be the occasiounes followeing, first, be frie quartering of the whole fute soiouris, and mony gentlemen and horssis of the first armie, to the number of sex thowsand men, some of thame the space of aught dayes, and the most pairt for the space of fyften dayes; secondlie, be the frie quartering of the Earle Marshallis armie, consisting of the number of aught hundreth men or thairby, the space of four dayes; thirdlie, be frie quartering of the Laird of Banflis cumpanie of ane thowsand men, horssis, and fute, or thairby, the spaice of aught dayes; fourthlie, be frie quartering of the Earle Marshall and Mernes companye, to the number of ane thowsand men, horse, and fute, or thairby, the space of thrie dayes befoir the coming of the Earles of Montrois, Atholl, Kingorne, Lords Cowpar, Drummond, Fraser, Maister of Forbes, with thair forces, and thaireftir for interteining both the armies, consisting of sex thowsand men, horse, and fute, the space of four dayes, besyids the exacting frome the toune the soume of ten thowsand merkis, the taking of thair tuelff peice of cannon, with pulder, ball, and thair haill furniture, the disarming of thair nichtboures; and lastlie, be leaving the toune so disarmit and disabled, whairby thay ar exposit to the mercie and danger of all enimies that pleassis to invade thame, for which respectis, and many wther considerationnes, the nightboures convenit as said is, humblie desyrit that thair magistrattes wald represent and putt wp this thair just grewances to the noblemen, gentrie, burrowes, and wtheres havand vote and power at the tables in Edinburghe, and be resone thairof to petitionn thame that thay and thair commissionares may be fred and liberat of suche ane heavye and intollerable burdine laid wpoun thame without any just ground or reasone, and that thair commissionares may hawe thair band delywered bak againe to thame to be cancelled and distroyed.

7 June 1639.

The townes answer to the remonstrance maide to thame be thair foure commissionares that wer send to Edinburgh be appoyntment of the nobillmen.

10 *June* 1639.

The quhilk day, the haill inhabitantis of this burghe, both frie and wnfrie, being warnit be the drum to convene this day in the tolbuith, and convening thairin for the most pairt representand the bodie of the toune, thay wer demandit be Robert Johnstoun, late prowest, gif all or any of thame had any accusatioun, challenge, or grevance to giwe in againes Mr Alexander Jaffray, thair present prowest, of any disloyaltie or miscariage committit be him in his said office of prouestrie, to the hinderance of his Maiesties service, or to the prejudice and hurt of the toune, thay all in ane voice, but any oppositioun or contradictioun, answered that thay had no point of disloyaltie or miscariage to say againes him, nor any brak of duetie in his office to lay to his chairge, but be the contriar thay giwe him thair approbatioun and applause that he has dischairgit and acquytted himselff in his said office most dutifullie and honestlie as ane loyall and gude subject to his Maiestie, and as a most cairfull and painefull magistratt for the weill and gude of the toune; lyikas the haill inhabitantis convenit as said is, declared in ane voice that thay do adhear trulie and sincerelie to his Maiesties proclamatioun gewin at York, the twentie fyft

10 June 1639.

The townes testimonie and approbation gewin to Mr Alex. Jaffray, thair prowest, of his dutifull and gude careage in his office.

10 June
1639.
—
The townes
testimonie
and appro-
bation
gewin to
Mr Alex.
Jaffray,
thair pro-
west, of his
dutifull
and gude
careage in
his office.

of Aprill last, and published at the mercatt croce of this burghe vpon the sext day of Junij instant; and to his Maiesties gracious and frie pardon thairin contanit, and offeris thameselffis most willing and redie to expres thair realitie and sinceritie heirin, and in approving thameselffis loyall and true subjectis to his Maiestie, be going on in his Maiesties service at thair vttermost endevouris, and particularlie as thay salbe injoyned at this tyme be the Lord Vicount of Aboyn, his Maiesties lievtenent in the north, and for this effect desyred the said proclamatioun to be registrat in the tounes buikes *ad futuram rei memoriam*, vpoun the quhilkis premissis the said Robert Johnstoune, in name of the said Mr Alexander Jaffray, prowest, and also in name of the baillies, counsall, and communitie of this burghe, asked act and instrumentis.

11 June
1639.
—
The townes
disassent-
ing that
thair
commis-
sionares
re-enter in
waird, or
that the
fynes im-
posed vpon
thame and
some other
nichtbouris
be payed.

11 *June* 1639.

The quhilk day, the toune being convenit be the drum in the tol-buith, and being callit be the sute roll and the absentis noted, thay that wer present disassented that oure townes late commissionares, towitt, Johne Hay, baillie, Mr Robert Farquhar, Mr Thomas Gray, and George More-soun, shuld returne back to Edinburghe to reenter thair persones in waird within the tolbuith of Edinburgh, notwithstanding of the band gewin be thame as principallis, and Willeame Gray of Pettindrum, cationer for thair reentrie in the said waird, under the paine of fourtie thowsand punds, betwixt and the first day of July nixt to come, and disassentis that the fyne of fourtie thowsand merkis imposed wpoun the saidis com-missionares and some few wther nichtboures of the toune be the nobilitie and wtheris of the Tables, should be payed, or any pairt thairof, inrespect the Lord Vicount of Aboyn, his Maiesties lieutenent in the north, hes this day gewin a peremptorie chairge in wreitt vnder his lordships hand, to the prowest, baillies, counsall, and communitie of this burghe, to the con-trarie, commanding that the saids commissionares shuld not in any caice go south, or pay the said fyne, or any pairt of the same; and farder, in caice any inconvenient fall legallie wpoun the saids commissionares or thair eationer for thair not reentrie in waird, the brethreine of gild sic as wer present ar content to contribute for thair releiff pairt and pairt lyik, according to thair meanes, with the whole bodie of the toune, and the deacones of craftis desyred a tyme to be gewin thame to advyse for gewing thair answer in the premisse, and the saidis commissionares protestis for costis, skaithes, and dammage againes the toune incaice thay suffer any prejudice or damage be this delay; and the prowest protestit in the contrair, alledging he shuld vse no delay but sic as he was necessitat to, be his Maiesties service in the dispatche of the nichtbouris and inhabitantis of this burghe that ar to marche furth this day with the Lord Aboynes armie towardes the Mearnis.

11 June 1639.

The townes disassenting that thair commissionares re-enter in waird, or that the fynes imposed vpon thame and some other nichtbouris be payed.

Eodem die.

The said day, the prowest intimat to the toune convenit this day be the drum, that all fencible persones, both frie and wnfrie in this burghe, conveine at the mereat croce in thair best armour at the first touk of the drum, to marche fordward with the present armie led be the Lord Vicount of Aboyn in his Maiesties service againes the covenanteris, conforme to the warrant and ordour gewin for that effect be the said Lord Vicount of Aboyn, his Maiesties lievtenent in the north, and that nane who enteris in service and tackes armes desert thair service and returne back fra the armie, without licience, vnder the paine of death and confiscatioun of all thair goods moveable.

Eodem die. The toune chargeit to marche in armes with the Lord Aboyne.

Eodem die.

The toune being convenit, as said is, ar content and consentis that all the inhabitantis of this burghe, both frie and vnfrie, fensible persones, betwixt sextie and sexteine, keip the watche in propper persones be course as thay salbe warnit, vnder the paine of ten punds, to be payed be

Eodem die. A watche appoynted.

Eodem die. ilk persone absent, *toties quoties*, wnforgewin, and that sic nichtboures as
A watche ar abowe the aige of sextie yeires, being able in meanes, furnish a fensible
appoynted. man sufficientlie armed for keiping watche for thame, vnder the paine
abowespecifeit.

17 June 1639.

17 *June* 1639.

The Lord   The quhilk day, the toune being convenit in the tolbuith be the drum,
Aboyn, his it wes exponit to thame be Mr Alexander Jaffray, prowest, that the Lord
demand of Vicount of Aboyn, his Maiesties lieutenant in the north, and Colonell Wil-
the toun   leame Gun, who hes the chairge and conducting of the present armie
for inter- lyand in this burghe for his Maiesties service, hes commandit the magis-
tenement   trattis to conveine the toune, and to signifie to thame that the said lieu-
of his   tenent, for the furtherance and advancement of his Maiesties service, must
armie, and neids hawe frie quarteris wpoun the inhabitantis of this burghe for inter-
the townes tenement of foure hundreth futemen and twa hundrethe horsmen of the
answer.   said armie for the space of fyfteine dayes, or then the toune must furnishe
moneyes for thair intertenement during the spaice foirsaid, at the proportioun following, towitt, sex schillingis daylie for ilk fute soiour, and
fyfteine shillings daylie for ilk horsman, and the toune furnishing the
moneyes, the said Lord Aboyn and Colonell Gun promeissis to giwe securitie to the towne for refounding back againe to thame of sic moneyes as
thay shall presentlie advance and furnishe to the vse foirsaid, and
thairfoir inquired of the toune convenit as said is, what answer thay will
giwe to the saids propositiones, quha eftir advysement and consideratioun
of the busienes, answerit all in ane voice, that thay ar content that ane
thowsand dolouris be lifted in banck and gewin to the said Lord Vicount
Aboyn for intertenement of the foirsaid number of horsmen and soiouris
for the spaice of fywe dayes, rather or the toune shuld be burdinit with
the frie quartering of thame, and desyrit the magistrattis to try whair
moneyes may be had, and to lift the same wpoun band, to be subscrywit

be the prowest, baillies, deane of gild, thesaurar, and certaine otheris of the most speciall men of the toune, thay getting alvayes securitie frome the said Lord Aboyn and Colonell Gwn, for refounding of the same bak againe to the tounes thesaurar, with ane half yeires annuelrent thairof at Martimes nixt, and the toune convenit as said is, all in ane voice, but oppositioun or contradictioun obleissis thame to frie and reliewe thair magistrattis and sic as salbe bund with thame for the said soume of ane thowsand dolouris, of the haill contentis of the band to be gewin be thame for the same, incaice the said soume be not refondit bak againe to thame be the said Lord Aboyn, and to contribute *pro rata* be taxatioun with the haill bodie of the toune for thair releiff.

Memorandum.—Albeit the toun condiscendit to len ane thowsand dolouris to the Lord Aboyne and Colonell Gwn for the caussis contenit in the act immediatlie befoirvrittin; nevirtheles, becaus the Erlis of Marshall, Montrois, and Kingorne, come with ane armie of four thowsand men or thairby to the Brig of Dee in the morne thaireftir, the eighteine day of Junij, and tuke in the said brig the nynteine day of the said moneth, at the intacking whairof the said Lord Aboyne and Colonell Gwn with thair whole companie, both horse and futt, left the feildis and fled; thairfoir the moneyes wer not delyvered to thame.

17 June 1639.

The Lord Aboyn, his demand of the toun for intertenement of his armie, and the townes answer.

26 *June* 1639.

The quhilk day, the prowest, baillies, and counsell, ordaines the toune to be convenit the tuentie aught of Junij instant, and the Kings Maiesties letter direct to the magistrattis and counsell of this burghe to be intimat to the nichtbouris of the toune, and thair consent to be craved for releiff of the prowest, baillies, deane of gild, and thesaurar, of the soume of sewin thowsand merkis borrowit be thame and gewin to the noblemen eftir manifestatioun of the peace, for saifling the toune vnplundered and

26 June 1639.

The toune to be convenit, and his Maiesties letter to be intimat to thame.

EXTRACTS FROM THE   [1639.

26 June 1639.
The toune to be convenit, and his Maiesties letter to be intimat to thame.

spoilled be the soiouris of thair armie, quhilk was absolutelie concluded to hawe beine done, if the foirsaid soume had not beine presentlie furnished and delywered to thame for compensatioun to thair soiouris of the spoill of the toune.

Eodem die.

Eodem die.
Charge for restoring of plundered goods.

The said day, the prowest, baillies, and counsell ordaines a chairge tobe gewin be the drum to all inhabitantis in this burghe byares and havares of any goodes plundered frome thair nichtboures or otheris quhatsumewir, that thay restoir the same to the righteous ownares within thrie dayes eftir the chairge, with certificatioun to all these in whose possessioun any plundered goods salbe fund thaireftir, that thay salbe conveined and punished as actores and plunderares thameselflis.

Eodem die.

Eodem die.

Ordinance to the Thesaurar.

The samen day the councell ordaines Andro Burnet, thesaurar, to borrow sex hundreth merkis to helpe to pay the poore peopill, inhabitantis of this burghe, of a pairt of thair chairges debursit and susteaned be thame in quartering of soiouris the tyme of the herbering of the late armies, quhilk soume thay ordaine tobe allowit to the said thesaurar in his comptis.

28 June 1639.
The Kings Maiesties letter manifesting the peace.

28 *June* 1639.

The quhilk day, the haill toune, both frie and vnfrie, being warnit be the drum passand throw the haill streittes of the toune, to conveine this day within the tolbuith, and conveining thairin, for the most pairt representand the bodie of the toune, Maiester Alexander Jaffray, prowest, intimat to thame the missive direct to the prowest, baillies, and counsall of this burghe frome oure dread soueraine the kingis sacred maiestie, manifesting the peace betwixt his maiestie and the nobilitie of the covenant, and causit reid publictlie the said missive in audience of the toune, whairof the tenour followes:—"To oure trustie and weillbelouned the prowest, baillies, and councell of Aberdeine. Charles R. Trustie and welbeloued, wee greet yow well, hawing fullie vnderstood of your constant affectioun to oure service and sufferingis, for the same we giwe yow heartie thankis, and as heirtofore wee hawe written, we will not be vnmyndfull thairof: but oure subjectis who had offended ws, hawing at this tyme given ws satisfactioun, accepting of that which we propounded vnto thame, we hawe thought it fitt to acquaint yow therewith, to the end yow do not proceed in any thing touching hostilitie, but that yow setle your toune in a peaceable way, and so we bid yow heartilie fareweill. Frome oure camp at the Birkes the 18 June 1639." After the reiding of the quhilk missive, the said Mr Alexander Jaffray, prowest, shew and declaired to the toune, convenit as said is, that it is notourlie knawin to thame, notwithstanding of the manifestatioun of the peace betwixt the king and the nobilitie, that the magistrattis of this burghe wer forced to furnishe and borow the soume of sewin thowsand merkis money, and giwe the same to the Erlis of Marshall, Montrois, and Kingorne, to be distribute amongst the soiouris of thair late armie at the intaking of the brig of Die, for saiffing the toune vnplunderit and spoilled be the soiouris, and that the prowest, baillies, deane of gild, and thesaurar, hes gewin thair band for payment thairof bak againe at Martimes nixt, with ane halff yeires annuall to the persones eftirnamed, fra whome the same wes borrowed, ilk ane for thair awin pairtes, as is vnderwrittin, viz.: borrowit

28 June 1639.
The Kings Maiesties letter manifesting the peace.

Fra Gilbert Hervie, elder, .	Thrie thowsand merkis.
Fra Thomas Robertson, .	Tuelff hundred merkis.
Fra Johne Fraser in Watterton,	One thowsand merkis.
Fra Mr Thomas Gray,	Foure hundreth merkis.
Fra George Richard,	Thrie hundreth merkis.
Fra Richard Cruikshank, .	Thrie hundreth merkis.
Fra Willeame Forbes, eldar,	Twa hundreth merkis.
Fra Alexander Howyesone,	Twa hundreth merkis.

28 June 1639.

The Kingis Maiesties letter manifesting the peace.

The tounes consent to contribute for friing of thair magistrattis of the sewin thowsand merkis gewin to the nobillmen at the intacking of the Brig of Dee.

Fra Johne Raitt,	.	.	Ane hundreth merkis.
Fra Patrik Fergussonne,	.		Ane hundreth merkis.
Fra Androw Howyesone,	.		Ane hundreth merkis.
Fra Dauid Lindsay,		.	Ane hundreth merkis.

And thairfoir inquired of the toune, convenit as said is, if thay will frie and warrand thair magistrattis of the soumes of money particularlie aboue writtine, and annualrent thairof, at the hands of the particular personnes befoir named fra whome the same wes borowed, wha all in ane voice, but any oppositioun or contradictioun, consented and become bund, actit, and obleist to frie and liberat the said prowest, baillies, deane of gild and thesaurar, of the foirsaid soume of sewin thowsand merkis and annualrent thairof, till the same be payed, at the handis of everie ane of the particular persones befoir named, fra whome the same wes borrowit, and for that effect ar content to be taxt and stentit for the same, howsone the magistrattis and counsall for the tyme sall think expedient, and that taxtares and stentares be chosin thairof on the haill inhabitantis of this burghe ; lyikas thay become obleist to pay ilk ane thair awin pairtis of the said stent, conforme to the taxt roll to be sett doune, and gewin furth thairament within thrie dayes miet eftir the chairge, vnder the paine of poynding and horning and wairding of thair persones, and ar content that letteris be direct to that effect be the Lordis of Counsall and Sessioun at the instance of the prowest, baillies, deane of gild, and thesaurar of this burghe for the tyme.

Eodem die.

Gray and Chalmer chosin commissionares to go to his Maiestie at Bervick.

Eodem die.

The samen day, the toune being convenit be the drum within the tolbuith, thay all in ane voce electit, nominat and chused Mr Thomas Gray and Mr Patrik Chalmer, thair commissionares, to pas to the toun of Bervick in England, to oure dread soveraine the kingis sacred Maiestie who is there for the present, and to mak remonstrance to his Maiestie of

oure townes sufferingis, and of thair great loss and skaith both of men
and gudes, sustenit be thame be occasioun of the repairing of the severall
armies to this burghe in the monethis of Marche, Aprill, Maij last, and
June instant, and most humble to petitioun his Maiestie in the tounes
behalff, to repair and sett wp thair losses efter sic forme as his Maiestie,
out of his princelie wisdome, shall find most convenient, and ordaines ane
commissioun to be gewin to the saids commissionares to the effect foirsaid, and ane letter to be drawin wp in most humble and submissive
maner, and direct from the prowest, baillies, and counsall of this burghe,
to his Maiestie to the same effect, and for making of the saids commissionares expenssis in the said commission, thay appoint the soume of fywe
hundreth merkis to be gewin to thame be Andrew Burnett, thesaurar, to
ane compt, quhilk salbe allowit to him in his comptis.

Eodem die.
*Gray and Chalmer chosin commis-
sionares to go to his Maiestie at Bervick.*

2 *July* 1639.

The quhilk day, it was intimat be the prouest to the haill toune
convenit in the tolbuith be the drum, that the Erle Marshall had written
a letter to the magistrattis and counsall, shawing that he had taken
exceptiounes againes the toune, in that some of his soiouris that followit
him at the Brig wer committit in waird, and that his Lordship wes informed that the nichtbouris of this toune wald not suffer James Geddes,
Andro Rob, and some otheris, inhabitantis of this burghe, who wer at the
Brig Road with the said Erle Marshall, to returne to the toune; quhilk
letter being red publictlie, the nichtboures for keiping of the publict peace
declaired that thay wer content that the foirnamed persones be receaved
and admittit within the toune, and promeist to do no harme, nor to vse
any deid of violence againes thame or any of thame heirafter; and as for
Georg Keith and Alexander Kempt, who ar in the tolbuith for convoying
some soiouris of the armie for plundering of some nichtboures houssis, the
toune wer content that the magistrattis should tak ordour with thame
and after thair tryall and censure, to dismiss thame furth of waird.

2 July 1639.
A letter of the Erll Marshallis intimat to the toun.

11 July 1639.

11 July 1639.

The townes answer to the demand made to thame for imposing a taxatioun for payment of a pairt of the quartering moneyes.

The quhilk day, the haill toune being convenit be the drum passing throw the haill streittes, it wes exponit to thame be the prowest, that some inhabitantis of this burghe of the meaner sort, be quartering of the soioris dyvers tymes of sindrie armies, wer brought to extreme povertie, for quhoes help and support in some measour the prowest declaired that it wer expedient, if so be the toune wald consent, that to the former taxatioun granted for the ministers stipend and the poore, thair be addet some foure or fyve thowsand merkis, that be that meines the poore nichtbouris may gett some help and payment for thair quartering, according to thar mein estates, some of thame halff payment, some les, some moir, according to the discretioun of the magistrattes; quhairwnto it wes answerit be the toune in ane voice that thay wald giwe no support nor grant, nor stent thameselflis for any sowme of money quhatsumewir for quartering of soioris, vntill suche tyme as the commissionares returned bak frome his Maiestie with thair report, and answer to the greivances gewin in to his Maiestie be this burghe, as lyikwayes till the ending of the Generall Assemblie and Parliament, indicted to hauld in August nixt, eftir the ending quhairoff thay will then advyse wpoun the busienes.

17 July 1639.

17 July 1639.

Aneut the entrie of tenentis to tempill landis and abbottis landis.

The quhilk day the new and auld counsallis votes and concludes that quhair any persone sall enter be dispositioun to any of the temple landis within this burghe, and to the landis holdin of old of the abbacie of Aberbrothock within the same, whairof the superioritie belongis now to the towne be vertew of his Majesties late gift and donation, sall pay a yeires dewtie of the land wherwnto they enter for the vse and benefitt of the tounes communn gude, and ane air to pay onlie the double of the feu dutie contenit in thair auld infeftmentis; lyikas it is also declairit that albeit the sone or dochtour of the heretour of these landis

1639.]   RECORDS OF THE BURGH OF ABERDEEN.   181

enter thairto be dispositioun of thair parentis, thay sall onlie pay for thair entrie as ane air, and no forder to be exactit of thame thairfoir, and Mr Robert Farquhar dissassentit to the exacting of any forder entres silver frome any assignay, or to other persone whatsumewir entering to any of these tenementis, bot as is done be the magistrattis to intrantis to any other burgage tenement within this burghe, be resone that the saids tempill tenementis and lands hauldin of old of the abbacie of Aberbrothok, ar now disponit be his Majestie to the toune to be hauldin in frie burgage, and thairfoir being now of the lyik nature of haulding with the remanent burgage tenementis within this burghe, alledgit that the entrie of tenentis sould be all after ane forme, and thairwpoun askit instrumentis.

17 July 1639. Anent the entrie of tenentis to tempill landis and abbottis landis.

24 July 1639.

The quhilk day the prowest, baillies, and counsall dischairges Mr Daniel Wedderburne of foure pund ten schillingis restand be him for his pairt of the calsey be quytting his haill quartering moneyes debtfull to him be the toune, quhairwith the said Mr Daniel wes content, and accordinglie dischairgit the same, and siclyik dischairges Robert Paull of twentie merkis for his luith maill of the Martimes and Witsonday termes last bypast, be quytting for the same the haill moneyes debtfull to him for quartering of soiouris, extending to fiftie ane pundis ten schillingis, whairwith also the said Robert Paull wes content and dischairgit the same *simpliciter*.

24 July 1639. Discharge be Wedderburne and Paull, of thair quartering moneyis.

31 July 1639.

The said day the counsell appointis Andro Burnet, thesaurar, to deburse the somme of thriescoir eighteine schillingis foure penneis to Mr Robert Farquhar, whairin he was super expendit for the foure commissionares chairges that wer sent to Edinburgh in Aprill last to the Taibles, and some debursement to Nathaniell Leysk, quhilk somme salbe allowit to the said thesaurar in his comptis.

31 July 1639. Thesaurar Farquhar.

Eodem die.

Eodem die.

The counsellis obleisment of thame and thair successouris to releive the present prowest, baillies, deane of gild, and thesaurar, of the moneyis gewin to the nobillmen.

The same day, forsameikill as wpoun the tuentie aught of Junij, the haill toune, both brethreine of gild and craftismen being convenit in the tolbuith, consentit and agreit for the soume of sewin thousand merkis money, quhilk wes borrowit vpoun the twentie day of the said moneth of June, to be gewin to the Erlis of Montrois, Marishall, and Kingorne, eftir the intaiking of the brig for saiffing the toune wnplundered, and that the prowest, baillies, deane of gild, and thesaurar, has borowed and gewin thair band for the said sewin thowsand merkis to the particular personis fra whome the same wes borrowit, to be all payed at the feast of Martimes nixt, with ane halff yeires annuall thairof to that terme; thairfoir the prowest, baillies, and councell binds and obleissis thame and thair successoris, prowest, baillies, and councell of this burghe *successive*, ane after another, to be lyable in payment of the said soume of sewin thousand merkis to the said particular personis fra whome the same is borowed with the annualrent thairof, ay and quhill the same be payed, togidder also with the soume of ten thousand merkis borowit of befoir be the magistrattis and gewin to the said nobillmen, for defraying of thair soiouris wages at thair second coming with thair armie to this burghe, the 27th May last, and for that effect obleissis thame and thair successoris, *successive* ane after another as said is, to releiwe the present prowest, baillies, deane of gild, and thesaurar thairof, be resone the toune ar content to be taxt and stentit for the saids soumes, howsone the magistrattis for the tyme shall think expedient.

Eodem die.

A missive to be direct to the toun of Edinburgh for excusing our absence from the Generall Assemblie.

Eodem die.

The same day the counsell, inrespect that the missive direct to thame be the toune of Edinburgh for sending a commissioner to the Generall Assemblie, requyres that the commissioun be direct frome the prowest, baillies, councell, ministrie, and kirk sessioun of this burghe joyntlie, and

be resone our ministeris ar out of the cuntrie, thairfoir finds it expedient *Eodem die.*
that no commissioner be direct to the Assemblie, bot that a missive be
direct to the prowest, baillies, and counsell of the burghe of Edinburgh,
berand oure excuse that we culd not at this tyme send a commissioner to
the Assemblie, be occasioun of the absence of oure ministeris, and that we
hawe not a kirk sessioun throw thair absence.

A missive to be direct to the toun of Edinburgh for excusing our absence from the Generall Assemblie.

Eodem die.

Eodem die.

The samen day Mr Thomas Blakhall confessis in presens of the
prowest, baillies, and counsell, that he past to New Castell in England,
and there sauld his shippis laidning of bear and malt, notwithstanding of
his band gewin to the towne that he should not transport the said shippis
laidning of victuall out of the kingdome, wnder the paine of two thowsand merkis to be payed to the deane of gild, alledging he hes licience and
warrand from his Maiestie to do the same; inrespect quhairoff, the counsell ordaines the said Mr Thomas to be persewit be the dean of gild befoir
the prowest and baillies for the twa thousand merkis, to heir and sie himselff decernit to pay the same be resone of his contraventioun of the said
band.

Blakhall to be persewit for selling of bear and malt at Newcastle.

7 *August* 1639.

7 August 1639.

The quhilk day the prowest, baillies, and counsall, notwithstanding
at the last counsell day it wes thought expedient, for the resones contenit
in ane act made at that tyme that no commissioner shuld be direct frome
this burghe to the Generall Assemblie now approaching, yet inrespect
thay ar informed that exceptioun wilbe takin againes this burghe incaice
no commissioner be send to the said Assemblie, thairfoir thay nominat
and chuisit Willeame Forbes, baillie, commissioner for this burghe, for
keiping of the said Generall Assemblie at Edinburghe, the   day of
August instant, with continewatioun of dayes, and ordaines ane commissioun to be gewin to him for that effect, and the thesaurar to furnishe
moneyes for macking of his expenssis.

Forbes chosin commissionar to the Generall Assemblie.

Eodem die.

Eodem die.

Discharge be Gray and Chalmer of thair commissioun to his Maiestie.

The said day, in presens of the prowest, baillies, and counceell compeirit Mr Thomas Gray and Mr Patrik Chalmer commissionares direct frome this burghe to Bervick, for making remonstrance to his Maiestie of oure tounes sufferingis, and of thair great lossis both of men and goodis sustenit be thame, be occasioun of the repairing of the senerall armies to this burghe in the monethis of Marche, Aprill, May, and June last, and eftir thay had at length declaired thair proceedingis in the said commissioun, and how thay wer graciouslie acceptit of his Maiestie, and had delywered to him oure tounes letter, thay producit the copie of the petitioun putt wp be thame to his Maiestie in the behalff of the toune, whairof the tennour followes:—"To the kingis most excellent Maiestie, the humble petitioun of the citizens and wther inhabitantis of the citie of Aberdeine, most humblie showing vnto your dread and sacred Maiestie that thes poore petitionares your Maiesties loyall subjectis, in these trubilsome tymes, and especiallie since February last, hawe susteaned many and great losses by being inforced to giwe frie quarteris to fywe senerall armies brought thither, some consisting of thrie, some foure, and some sex thowsand men, horse and fute, sometymes by the spaice of thrie, sometymes of eight, and sometyme of fyfteine dayes, and by being compelled to cast downe thair trinshes, removwe thair catbands, taking away tuelff peice of cannon, pulder, ball, and all wther furniture perteining thairto, by disarming thame of all thair muskattes, pickes, corslettis, swords, and pistollis, exacting frome thame sexteine thowsand merkis in moneyes, whereoff sex thowsand merkis was exacted efter your Maiesties letteris touching the peace were manifested, cutting and wholly destroying there corne with horses, restrayning the taking of salmonds in there fishings, and taking away fishe befoir slaine by plundering many houssis in the said citie, battering the bridge of Dee, and demolishing the porche and other pairtes thairof, by all which the poore petitionares ar dampnified, the sowme of tuelff thousand pundis sterling, and mairower and

besyids the killing of foure of the saids citizens in defence of the said *Eodem die.*
bridge, and the wounding of many more, and the fyning by the tables of *Discharge*
threttie twa persones of the said cittie in the somme of fortie two thou- *be Gray and Chalmer of*
sand merkis Scottes money, and confyning and wairding within the tol- *thair commissioun*
buith of Edinburghe of foure of thame, vntill thay shuld mak payment of *to his*
the said 42,000 merkis; lyikas these foure ar obligit to reentir there per- *Maiestie.*
sones in prison the last of August nixt, or otherwayes pay fortie thowsand
punds Scottes, all which tend to the vtter vndoing of the poore petitionares and the said cittie: thay most humblie pray your Maiesties
gracious and tender consideratioun of the premisses, and that your
Maiestie wilbe graciouslie pleasit to grant wnto thame (as a way for
helping to restoire thair losses) a tack of thair customes, great and
small, and impost of wynes betwixt North Esk and Spey, frielie for
ten yeires, at leist ane assignatioun to the tack dewtie thairof; and
if any taxatioune happines to be granted for the spaice of ten yeires,
to be frie thairof within thair cittie; and if your Maiestie sall think
that the granting of these thingis may be of greater value than there
saidis losses susteanit in your Maiesties service, in that caice they onlie
desyre to hawe the benefitt of thame ay and quhill it sall be made
knowin vpoun just accompt that thay ar satisfied for thair saids losses,
extending to the said somme of tuelff thousand punds sterling, and
no longer; and that your Maiestie wald caus redelywer the band
gewin be Johne Hay, Mr Robert Farquhar, Mr Thomas Gray, George
Moreson, and Willeame Gray, burges of Edinburghe, thair cationer for
re-entrie of thair persones in waird, vnder the paine of fourtie thousand
punds Scottes; and lastlie, that your Maiestie wilbe lyikwayes graciouslie
pleased to provyd for thair indempnitie in tyme coming, and (as in
humble duetie bund) thay sall daylie pray for your Maiesties long and
prosperous reigne in health, honour, and happines; and farder, the saids
commissionares declared that some few dayes efter the giving vp of
the said petitioun, thay gatt presence againe of his Maiestie, and after a
short repetitioun made be thame of the effect and contentis of the said

Eodemdie.
Discharge be Gray and Chalmer of thair commissioun to his Maiestie.

petitioun, thay humblie supplicatt his Maiesties gracious answer thairwnto, who shew thame in regaird of the absence of the Erle of Traquair, his thesaurar, he culd not for the present giwe a determined answer to thair petitioun, bot promeist and gawe thame assurance that he shuld not be vnmyndfull thairof, and of oure tounes sufferingis and losses for thair loyaltie in his service, and suld giwe thame satisfactioun howsone he fand convenient occasioun; quhilk report abowe writttin being made be the saidis commissionares of thair proceidingis in thair said commissioun, the prowest, baillies, and counsell findis that thay hawe done ane sufficient and honest diligence therin, and hes acquyttit thameselflis sufficientlie in what wes intrusted to thame, and thairfoir exoneris and dischairges thame of thair said commissioun.

14 Aug. 1639.

Jaffray chosin commissionar to the Parliament.

11 August 1639.

The quhilk day, the counsall nominattis and electis Maister Alexander Jaffray, prowest, commissionar for this burghe for keiping his Maiesties Parliament appointed to hauld at Edinburghe, the twentie sext day of August instant, and ordaines ane commissioun to be gewin to him for that effect vnder the townes secret seall, and the subscriptiounes of the baillies and clerk, with particular instructiounes in suche materis as salbe gewin to him in commissioun; and for macking his expenssis and suche as accompanies him, and also for paying oure tounes dues in his Maiesties Exchequer, as lyikwayes oure dewes quhilkis wer payable at the late conventioun of Burrowes hauldin at Dumfermlin in July last, ordaines the somme of twa thousand merkis to be gewin to the said commissionar to ane compt, to be payed to him be Andro Burnet, thesaurar, quhilk salbe allowit to him in his comptis.

4 September 1639.

The said day, the counsall ordaines Walter Cochraine, deane of gild, to compt with the baxteris, and Willeam Scott, for the breid and bier coft for the armies, and the thesaurar to pay thairfoir according to the deane of gilds subscryvit compt, quhilk salbe allowit to the said thesaurar in his comptis.

Ordinance to the deane of gild and thesaurar.

11 September 1639.

The qubilk day, the baillies and counsell ordaines Walter Cochraine, deane of gild, to take ane exact accompt of the deallcs, timber, and yron work that wes furnishit be Willeame Rolland, George Johnstoun, Willeame Scott, Johne Scott, and sic wther nightboures of the toune wha prowydit for the scousses and fortificatiounes and fenceing of the munitioun within and about the toune, befoir the heir coming of the late armies from the south, and ordaines the said deane of gild to pay to the saidis persones sic [soumes] as shalbe justlie restand to thame, quhilk salbe allowit to him in his comptis.

Ordinance to the deane of gild.

Eodem die.

Followis ane nott of the dettis and soumes of money contracted by the toune of Aberdene, the yeire immediatlie bygaine, be occasioun of the late trubles that fell out in the kingdome during that tyme, and of the seuerall armies that come to this burghe in the monethis of Marche, Aprill, May, and Junij last bypast, 1639, as the comptis of Androw Burnet, thesaurar, and Walter Cochraine, deane of gild, the said yeire, does testifie:—

Debts contracted be the toune in the late trubles.

Imprimis at Martimes 1638, borrowit be Andro Burnet, thesaurar, of Doctor Cargillis mortifeit moneyes, j^m iij^c lib.
Off Mr Patrik Coplands moneyes, j^m iij^c xxxiii lib., vj ss., viij d.

11 Sept.
1639.
—
Ordinance
to the
deane of
gild.

Off Secretarie Reids moneyes, j^m lib.
Off the Ladye Drummes moneyes, ix^c lib.
All payable at Martimes 1639, with ane yeires bygaine annuelrent thairof at that terme.
Item at Witsonday 1639, borrowit be the said Andro Burnet, thesaurar, of Futtie kirk moneyes, j^m iij^c xxxiij lib., vj ss., viij d.
Item borrowit frome Mr Johne Gellie, minister at Monymusk, sex thowsand pundis.
Frome Patrik Davye, vj^c lxvj lib., xiij ss., iiij d.
Frome Gilbert Hervye, eldar, ij^m lib.
Frome Johne Fraser in Wattertoune, vj^c lxvj lib., xiij ss., iiij d.
Frome Thomas Robertsoun, viij^c lib.
Frome George Rickard, ij^c lib.
Frome Patrik Fergusson, lxvij lib., x ss.
Frome Androw Howyesoun, lxvj lib., xiij ss., iiij d.
Frome Willeame Forbes, eldar, j^c xxxiij lib., vj ss., viij d.
Frome Mr Thomas Gray, ij^c lxvj lib., xiij ss., iiij d.
Frome Richard Cruikschank, ij^c lib.
Frome Alexander Howyesoun, j^c xxxiij lib., vi ss., viij d.
Frome Dauid Lindsay, lxvj lib., xiij ss., iiij d.
Frome Johne Raitt, lxvij lib,, x ss.
All payable at Martimes 1639, with ane halff yeirs bygaine annuall thairof.
Summa of the principall sommes befoir writtin, borowit be the said Andro Burnet, extendis to the soume of sevinteine thowsand, thrie hundreth ane lib., xiij ss., iiij d.
Item restand to the said Andro Burnett, whairin he is fund super expendit at the fute of his thesaurar compt, sevin hundreth sevin pundis, eightene ss., ellevin d.
Nota, payed be the said Andro Burnett, a pairt of the dettis abouewrittin, viz.:—
To Mr Thomas Gray, ij^c lxvj lib., xiij ss., iiij d.
To Richard Cruikschank, ij^c lib.

To Alexander Howyesone, jc xxxiij lib., vj ss., viij d.
To Dauid Lindsay, lxvj lib., xiij ss., iiij d.
Summa payed be the said Andro Burnet of the foirsaid borrowit moneyes, extendis to sex hundreth thrie scoir sex pundis, threttene ss., foure d.
Item at Witsonday 1639, borowit be Walter Cochrane, dean of gild, frome Patrik Duvye, Mr of the gild brethreinis hospitall, of the said hospitall moneyes, viijc lib.
Frome Willeame Blakburne, Mr of the kirkwark of the Bridge of Dee moneyes, iijc xxxiij lib., vi. ss., viij d.
Frome George Gordoun, collectour of the kirk sessioun of the poores moneyes, iiijc lib.
Item of the Gildwyne silver, iijc lxxviij lib., xvj. ss., iiij d.
All payable at Martimes 1639, with ane halff yeires bygaine annuall at that terme.
Summa of the principall soumes borowit be the said Walter Cochrane, extendis to the soume of tua thousand tuelff pundis thrie shillings.

11 Sept. 1639.
Ordinance to the deane of gild.

11 October 1639.

The said day, the prowest, baillies, and counsall discharges holding of any kynd of mercat, or selling keall, fruict, or any wther sort of wair on the Sabboth day in tyme coming within this burghe, vnder the paine of confiscatioun of all goodes offerit to be sauld, and ordaines intimatioun to be maid be the drum on Setterday nixt, and on Sonday out of pulpett, that nane pretend ignorance heirof.

11 October 1639. Act discharging the holding of any kynd of mercat on the Sabbath day.

23 October 1639.

The said day the prowest, baillies, and counceell ordaines that no mercat be maid of tymber brocht frome the Hielands to this burghe befoir ten houres ilk Fridday and Setterday, vnder the paine of ten punds of wnlaw, to be exactit of ilk persone contraveininge, *toties quoties*, for the vse

23 October 1639. Anent the timber mercat.

23 October 1639.
Anent the timber mercat.

and benefitt of the tounes commoun warkis, and that nane by bark nor tymber to sel againe till the mercat be endit, and the toune and cuntrie people serveit, vnder the lyik paine, and ordaines intimatioun heirof to be maid be the drum passand throw the haill streittis of the toune on Setterday nixt, that nane pretend ignorance.

23 October 1639.

A bell to be rung for convening and dissolving of the schoolles at thair ordinarie houres.

23 October 1639.

The quhilk day the prowest, baillies, and counsall considdering that the schollares in all the schoolles within this burghe does not tymouslie keip the houres of thair convening and dissolving as is prescrywit vnto thame, thairfoir and for observing of better conformitie and gude ordour in tyme coming; thay hawe statute and ordanit that the bell of Gilbert Leslies schooll salbe preceislie rung ilk day for both convening and dissolving of the whole schoolles at the severall houres following—viz., at sex houres in the morning, thaireftir a little befoir sewin till the hour strick; at ten houres befoir noone and twa houres eftirnoone, for convening of the haill schollares; and siclyik at nyne houres, twelff houres, and sex houres at nicht, for dissolving of the haill schoole, and that na maister direct thair bairnes hame at nyne, twelff, or sex at ewin till the said Gilbertis bell first ring; and ordaines intimatioun heirof to be maid to all the maisteris and schollares within thair schoolles, that nane pretend ignorance, and that gude ordour may be keiped accordinglie in all tyme heireftir.

20 Nov. 1639.
Anent keiping of sermones.

20 November 1639.

In the first the prowest, baillies, and counsell ratifies and approves the act and statute maid be thair prediecessoris anent the keiping of the sermones on the Sabboth day, whilk thay ordaine to hawe effect, and to be putt to executioune againes the contraveinares wnder the paines thairin conteinit, towitt wnder the paine of twentie schillingis, to be payed be ilk persone contraveinand, quha salbe fund absent frome sermones ather befoir or efter noone on the Sabboth, to the collector of the kirk sessioun for the vse of the poore *toties quoties*, and incaice of inhabilitie or refuisall of any offending in this kynd to pay the said penaltie, presentlie eftir tryall and convictioun the offendares to be punished in thair bodies be imprisonment, or after sic wther maner as the magistrattis sall injoyne, conforme to the Actis of Parliament made aganes the brakeris of the Lordis Sabboth.

Anent keiping of sermones. [20 Nov. 1639.]

20 November 1639.

Item, it is statute and ordanit that everie man keip cleine the streetis befoir his awin hous, and if any privie be castin donne on the streitis or wnder staires, the indwellar in the houssis nixt adjacent thairto salbe obleist to remove the same befoir aught houres in the morning, wnder the paine of foure merkis, to be exactit of the contraveinar but favour, and the hous being tryit out of the whilk the privie is brocht, the awnar thairof sall pay ten merkis thairof, the halff to the maister of the hous wha salbe wrongit, and the wther halff to the deane of gild, and the servand fund giltie of casting out suche privies to be joggit for the space of twa houres; and siclyik, it salbe lesome to any persone wha pleassis at thair awin hand to take away ilk morninge quhatsumewir fulzie thay find uther on the streittis or wnder staires to thair awin vse but controlment, and if any makis impediment to pay fourtie shillingis of vnlawes *toties quoties*.

Anent keiping of the streittis clene. [20 Nov. 1639.]

Item, it is statute and ordanit that na hyrer of horsses within this burghe tak any more hyre for his horse fra any of his Maiesties lieges bot onlie eighteine penneis for the myill, and that nane that hes horse to hyre refuis to serve of that pryce vnder the paine of ten pundis, to be payed be the contraveinar *toties quoties*, but prejudice to the magistratt to compell thame to serve his Maiesties lieges of the pryce foirsaid, wnder the paine of wairding of thair persones.

Hyrers of horses.

20 Nov.
1639.
Ratification of sundry acts.

Item, the prowest, bailles, and counsell ratifies and approves the statutes and ordinances made and sett doune be thair predicessouris, magistrattes and counsall of this burghe, against blasphemares of God's Holie Name, prophanares and brakeris of the Lordis Sabboth, with the statutes made against cowpares, wobsteris, cordoneris, and purchessoures of suspensionnes and advocationnes againes the magistrattis and counsall of this burghe, ressettares of strangeris, and settares of houssis to thame without licence of the magistratts, againes superfluous banquetting at baptismes, wachting and scoulling, anent the selling and distributing of coll, lyme, and sklaitt, anent the keiping of the loche cleine frome filth and corruptioun, againes keipares and gadderares of middingis on the hie streittis, againes abstracteris of cornis from the tounes commoun mylnes, anent officiares for careing daylie thair swordis and halbertis, and all and sindrie wther ordinances, actis, and constitutiones whatsumewir maid be thair predicessoris for observing gude rule and ordour within this burghe, to be keiped and observeit be the nichtboures and inhabitantis of the samen efter the forme and tenour thairof in all pointes, wnder the paines contenit in the said actis, to be wpliftit of the contraveinares but favour.

27 Nov. 1639.
Moresoun appoynted to tak ane accompt off muskattis and pickis.

27 *November* 1639.

The said day, the prouest, baillies, and counsell appoints George Moresoun to tak ane accompt of the muskattes and pickes sauld and disposit to the toune be the Marquis of Huntlie, and gewin out to the nichtboures of this burghe in the monethis of Marche and Junij last, and ordaines the said George to report his diligence thairanent this day aught dayes.

19 *December* 1639.

The quhilk day, the haill toune, both frie and vnfrie, being warnit be the drum passand throw the haill streittes of the toune to conveine this day within the tolbuith, and conveining thairin for the most pairt, representand the whole bodie of the toune, it wes exponit to thame be Patrik Leslie, prowest, that he had received a letter from the Erll Marshall, whairin was inclosed a commoun letter direct frome ye nobillmen at south to the said Erle Marshall, and to the nobillmen, barrones, and heretouris of the shirrefdome of Aberdeine, and to the magistrattis of this burghe, with a list of the names of the commanderis and officiares that ar appointed to be intertenit at the commoun chairges of this whole schirrefdome till the spring of the yeire, beiring a nott of the pay allotted monethlie to everie ane of thame, the first moneths pay begynning the first of December instant, as the said commoun letter at moir length beires, whairof the tennour followes:—" To the right honorable the Erle Marishall and to the remanent nobillmen, barrones, and heritoures of the schirrefdome of Aberdeine, and to the magistrattes of the burghe of Aberdeine. Honorable and lowing freynds, whairas diverse caviliers and souldieris, out of thair affectioun to religioun and thair native cuntrie, haue come hame frome thair imployment abroad to mak offer of thair service heir, whose expenssis, paynes, and gude will deserves kynd vsage, and most be payed wpoun the commoun chairges of the kingdome, and becaus all nationes in Christendome hath warres and exercise of armes, and we know not how long it sall please God to continew oure peace, it is necessar that the officiares and souldiares that ar come home, both for militarie discipline and exercise of armes, and as the most convenient and easie way of the officiares intertainment may be keipit till the spring of the yeire, and distribute throw the haill shyres; and thairfoir we have sent yow ane list of suche officiares with thair severall chairges and quantitie of pay, as we conceive to be most necessar for thair vse, recommending to your care to conveine with diligence and sett doune a course for thair pay and intertene-

Letter from the nobillmen at south for interteneing of some commanderis till the spring.

19 Dec. 1639.

Letter from the nobillmen at south for intertencing of some commanderis till the spring.

ment, and dispone so of thame as thay may be most vsefull to yow, and may best instruct your men in all your seuerall parochines (being contryved in companyes and regimentis) to exercise thair armes, and what salbe bestowit for thair pay, salbe allowit in the first end of the commoune taxatioun and contributionne of the schyires: for the performance quhairof, your cair of preservatioun of religioun, and saiftie of the cuntrie, we trust wilbe sufficient motives, whiche is the ernest desyre of your affectionat and faithfull freindis. *Sic subscribitur* Marshall, Montroise, Mar, Seafort, Kinghorne, Loudone, Dalhousie, Lowthean, Sinclair, Balmerino, Forrester, A. Forbes, Yester, Arthure Erskyne:" quhilk letter being publictlie red in audience of the toune, convenit as said is, the prowest inquyred of thame what thay wald do thairanent, and what obedience thay wald giwe to the desyre thairof, to the effect answere may be accordinglie returned to the said Erll Marshall, wha all in ane voice, without any oppositioun or contradictioun, willinglie consentit and agriet for thair pairtes to contribute with the nobillmen, barrones, and heretoures within this schirrefdome for the intertenement of the saidis commanderis fra the first of December instant till the spring of the yeire, proportionablie, conforme to the generall stent roll of the whole schirrefdome in former taxationne.

Followes the list of the officiares for the shyre of Aberdeine, to be payed out of the commoun contributioun be the toune and shyre of Aberdeine, frome the beginning of December 1639.

Lieutenent Colonell George Forbes, monethlie, to be payed 133 lib. 6ss. 8d.

Capitaine George Mackengzie, 66 lib. 13ss. 4d.
Capitaine George Forbes, 66 lib. 13ss. 4d.
Lieutenent Robert Lumsdane, 30 lib.
Lieutenent Willeame Forbes, 30 lib.
Ensengzie James Cruikshank, 24 lib.
Ensengzie Frances Forbes, 24 lib.
Sergeant Johne Mathie, 12 lib.
Sergeant James Lithgow, 12 lib.

Sergeant Johne Cowper, 12 lib.
Sergeant Johne Minister, 12 lib.
Sergeant Alexander Lovell, 12 lib.
    Summa, 501 lib. 6ss. 8d.

19 Dec. 1639.
Letter from the nobillmen at south for inter- tewing of some com- manderis till the spring.

Eodem die.

Eodem die. Suspension to be raised of the charge gewin to the toun for pay- ment of the armes receaved be thame frome the Marquis of Huntly.

The said day Patrik Leslie, proueist, signifiet to the toune convent as said is, that James Smith, merchant, burges of this burghe, as assignay to the Marquis of Huntly, is vrging payment frome the magistrattis and counsell for the muskattis and pickes bocht for the toune fra the said Lord Marquis in the monthe of Marche lastbypast, and thairfoir inquired of the nichtbouires what thay will doe in the busienes, quha answered in ane voice that thay wald not pay for that armour, except thay be com- pellit be law to do the same, be resone not onlie that the armour gottin frome the said Lord Marquis, bot lykwayes the most pairt of all the armour within the toune wer plundered and takin frome thame be armies that come to this burghe in the moneth of May and Junij last bypast, and sic as wer preserved wnplundered, wer tackin frome thame at the intaking of the Bridge of Dee, and thairfoir desyred the magistrattes and councell to raise suspensioun of the chairge that salbe gewin at the instance of the said James Smith, for the pryce of the said armour for the resone aboue specifeit, and als becaus they wer a pairt of the armes send heir be his Maiestie to the said Lord Marquis for his Maiesties service, and that sic armes as the toune receaved wer all lost in that service; and Wil- leame Blakburne, Alex. Alshoner, and Thomas Cushnie, for thameselflis and in name of sic nichtbouires of the toune as had not receaved any pairt of the said armes, protestit that thay be frie frome payment of the same or any pairt thairof, and thairwpoun asked instrumentis.

1 January 1640.

The said day, the prouest, baillies, and conncell, for satisfieing the desyre of ane missive direct to thame frome the commissionares of Edinburghe, tuitching the particular eftir specifeit, of the date the tuentie fyft day of December last bypast, electit, nominat, and chuisit Mr Alex. Jaffray the prouest of the said burghe commissionir for thame, to meit and conveine with the remanent commissionares of burrowes to be assemblit at Edinburghe wpoun the sewint day of Januar instant, for heiring of the report of Mr Williame Cunynghame, his diligence in his commissioun laitlie to Court, and for advysing wpoun what is most incumbent to be done for the gude of religioun and the cuntrie, and ordaines ane commissioun to be given to the said Mr Alexander for that effect, subscryvet be the magistrattis in dew forme as effeires.

8 January 1640.

The quhilk day, the prowest, baillies, and counsell ordaines ane act anent ressetting of strangeris, of quhat qualitie soewir thay be, without leiwe of the magistrattes, to be intimat be the drum throw the haill toune, to be observed vnder the paines thairin contenit, with this farder additioun, that none sett houssis to excommunicat papistis, wnder the paine of confiscatioun of the maill of the hous to be sett in this kynd, for the publict vse and benefitt of the toun and punishment of the persones setteris of sick houssis, at the arbitriment of the magistrattis, whilk act wes accordinglie intimat be the drum passand throw the haill toune, that nane sould pretend ignorance.

10 January 1640.

The quhilk day, fforsameckle as Walter Cochraine, laite deane of gild, and Andro Burnet, late thesaurar of the said burghe ar chairgit

1640.]   RECORDS OF THE BURGH OF ABERDEEN.   197

be vertew of letteris of horning rasit at the instance of Robert and   10 Jan.
James Smythes, merchandis, burgessis of Aberdeine, as assignayas   1640.
lauchfullie constitute be ane noble and potent Marquis George Marquis of   Suspension
Huntlie to the soumes of money wnderwrittin, to mak payment to the   to be raised
                                                                      of the
saidis Robert and James Smythes or uther of thame, of the soume of thrie   charges
                                                                      for the
thowsand thrie scoir nyntein pundis foure shillingis money as principall,   Marquis of
                                                                      Huntlyes
with ane hundreth and thrie punds money for ane halff yeires annuall armour.
thairof, togidder with the soume of ane thowsand punds of liquidat expenssis, togidder also with the ordinar annualrent of the said principall
soume till the soume be payed, conforme to the band gewin be the saidis
Walter Cochrane and Andro Burnet to the said Lord Marquis thairwpoun,
of the dait the sexteine day of Marche j^m sex hundreth threttie nyne
yeires, registrat in the bookes of councell and sessioun wpoun the tuentie
aucht day of December in the said yeire; and becaus the band foirsaid
was gewin to the said Lord Marquis for twa hundrethe muskattis, with
thair furniture, and ane hundrethe pickes delyverit be his lordship to the
toune of Aberdeine, of his Maiesties armour that wer send laitlie to the
said Lord Marquis for his Maiesties service, whilkis pickes and muskattes
with thair furniture being all plunderit and tackin frome the nichtboures
of this burghe be the late armies that come to this toune, in the monethis
of May and Junij last, quairthrow the nichtboures of this burghe that
resawed the saidis muskattis and pickes refuissis to pay the same, bot hes
desyrit to raise suspensioun of the chairge foirsaid gevin be vertew of the
saidis letteris of horning; thairfoir the proust, baillies, and councell of
the said burghe eftirnamed, thay ar to say Patrik Leslie, proust, Mr
Thomas Gray, Mr Matho Lumysdane, Mr Robert Farquhar, Mr Willeame
Moir, baillies, George Moresone, George Mengzies, Alexander Burnet,
Adame Gordoun, Willeame Andersone, cowper, and James Hall, cordoner,
ordaines Alexander Jaffray, present deane of gild, and Thomas Buck, present thesaurar, to give thair band as cationeris for the saids Walter
Cochrane and Andro Burnet for raising of the said suspensioun, and for
payment to the pairtie chairger, of the saids soumes, principall, expenssis

10 Jan.
1640.
—
Suspension to be raised of the charges for the Marquis of Huntlyes armour.

and annualrentis, incais it salbe fund be decreit of the Lordis of Counsell and Sessioune, that thay aucht so to do eftir the discussing of the suspensioun to be raisit thairanent; lyikas the provest, baillies, and counsell abouenamed, binds and obleissis thame and thair successoris, provest, baillies, and counsell of the said burghe present and to come, to warrand frie releiwe and skaithles keip the saidis Alexander Jaffray and Thomas Buck, thair aires, executoris, and successoris of thair said catiourie and haill sommes of money, principall, expenssis, and annualrentis abone specifeit, and of all that may follow thairon at all hands and againes all deadlie.

15 Jan.
1640.
—
Psalms to be sung daily at evening as well as morning service.

15 *January* 1640.

The quhilk day, the provest, baillies, and counsell, considering that praising of God be singing of psalms, is in itselff most laudable at all tymes and occasiounes, and especiallie eftir publict prayeris both evening and morning everie day as befoir and eftir sermones, and that hitherto the practise of that exerceis hes not beine wsit within the kirk of this burghe at the evening prayeris as in the morning, and thay being most willing and cairfull that equall respect be had to Goddis publict worship amongst thame, hes appointit, and be thir presentis appoyntis the maister of the musick schoolle with his scholares to attend the evening prayeris to be red nichtlie, bothe sommer and winter, within the paroche kirk of this burghe; and eftir reiding of the prayeris, to praise the Lord be singing of psalmes with the congregatioun in all tyme comeing.

29 Jan.
1640.
—
Jaffray, his discharge of his commissioun.

29 *January* 1640.

The quhilk day, in presens of the prowest, baillies, and counsell, compired Mr Alexander Jaffray, late provest, commissioner chosine for this burghe to ane meitting with the remanent burrowes at Edinburghe, wpoun the sewint day of Januar instant, with continewatioune of dayes, for heiring of the report of Mr Willeam Cunninghame his diligence in his commissioun latelie to court, and for advysing wpoun quhat is most incumbent to be done for the gude of religioun and the cuntrie, and made declaratioun at length of suche materis as wer treatted at the said meitting—namelie, that thair is ane subsidie granted be the nobilitie, gentrie, and burrowes present thairat of ten merkis Scotts money, to be wplifted of everie hundrethe merkis of yeirlie rent dew and payable to whatsumewir persone within this kingdome, alsweill to burghe as landwart, for defraying of the chairges bestowed on the late trubles, and releiff of theise that hes wndergone the burdine, and deburst out moneyes, wictuall, or other prowisioun in that commoun business, and thairwith declared that he insisted, also earnestlie as possiblie he culd, that oure tounes debursments and losses in these trubles shuld be satisfied and refoundit be the said subsidie, quhilk was refuisit, as lyikwayes dyvers wther petitions of that kynd made be some of the gentrie for refounding of thair losses was also refuisit; and forder, the said Mr Alexander Jaffray, commissioner foirsaid, producit the copie of the latter will and testament of wmquhill Mr Robert Johnstoun, Esquire, resident at Londoun, quhairin he has left the somme of sex hundreth punds stirling money to this burghe to be imployed in forme and maner, and wpoun the conditioun mentioned in his said testament, quhilk is of the date at Londone, the threttie day of September, j^m sex hundreth threttie nyne yeires, the coppie whairof sa far as concernis the said legacie heireftir followes—viz., also I giwe and bequeath wnto the prowest and baillies of Aberdeine, in the said realme of Scotland, sex hundreth punds stirling, wpoun thair putting in sufficient surities wnto my saidis executores and owersier, to imploy the said somme in a stock to remaine in perpetuitie forewir, that the poore people of the said citie of Aberdeine may be sett at wark in lauchfull treddis and manufactories for the benefite of the commounwealth, quhairby the aged, blind, leame, and impotent people of the said citie of Aberdeine may be releiwed yeirlie out of the profite and incres of the said stock.

29 Jan. 1640.

Jaffray, his discharge of his commissioun.

Legacie, Mr Robert Johnstoun to the toun of Aberdeine.

5 Feb. 1640.
Anent the Generall Band of Releiff.

5 *February* 1640.

The quhilk day the prowest and baillies hawing resawed instructiones frome the nobilitie at southe wnder thair handis, and some of the gentrie and burrowes, anent the forme of payment of the subsidie appointed to be wplifted of all persones within this kingdome, alseweill to burghe as landwart, for defraying of the commoun chairges bestowit on the late trubles, togidder with ane copie of the generall band appointit to be subscrywit for payment of the same subsidie, as lyikwayes a letter sensyne frome the noblemen, whairby thay recommend Mr David Dalgleish, minister at Cowper, to be ane of the ministeris of this burghe, and withall bering thair advyse to this burghe to keip vnion as other burghes with the rest of the nation for mantening the puritie of religioun and liberties of the kingdome, and the saids instructiounes, generall band, and missive being all red and considderit in counceill, and thay finding that no answer culd be returnit thairanent till first the busienes be emparted to the bodie of the toune, and that thay expres thameselflis how thay ar affected in all these particulares, thairfoir thay ordaine the haill toune to be warnit to Twysday nixt, the ellevint of this instant, to the effect the premisses may be intimat to thame, and thay required to giwe thair answer and advyse thairanent.

Followis the tenour of the saids Instructiones, Generall Band, and Missive.

The Instructiones.

Instructiones anent the Band of Releiff.

Forsamekill as manie and dyvers nobillmen, gentilmen, burgesssis, and vtheris, out of thair gude affectiones to religione and liberties of this kingdome, haue debursed moneyes, gevin out wictuall, or ingadged thameselflis for soumes of money, and vther provisioune necessar and vrgent for the publict vse of this kingdome, the releiff quhairof wes ex-

petit to haue beine made by Act of Parliament, and now seing the
determinatioune of the Parliament is delayed, and the tyme thairof as
yit wncertane, quhairby these who have ingadged thameselffis, or debursed
the saidis moneyes or wther provisiounes, lyes out of payment, alsweill of
principall as annualrent, to the hazard of thair credite and danger of thair
fortunes, quhilk is contrarie to equitie and resone, seing the benefite
arrysing to ws, alsweill in removeing of our evilles as in the secureing
and reforming of religione ar equallie communicate to ws all, according
to oure seuerall estates and degries we aucht thairfoir in equities to
beare ane proportionall burding of the saidis chairges, according to oure
estates and fortunes: for effectuating quhairof, necessar it is that the rule
of proportioune be keiped, and everie man, alsweill to burghe as landwart, pay ane equall and proportionall pairt, according to his estate and
yeirlie rent of lands, money, traid, or wtheris, quhairby yeirlie profite and
commoditie arryses: and to the effect the samen may be performed in the
most equitable and fairest way, it is necessar first, that the generall
band be subscryvit be all the noblemen, gentlemen, heritouris, and wtheris
within the shirefdome, quha salbe convened for that effect be the persone
intrusted efter specifeit, and quhilk persone sall make ane accompt thairof
betwixt and the sevint day of Marche nixt to come, with a particular
note of the names and designatiounes of these who hawe subscrywit the
same, and of these quho refuise or delayes to subscrywe the samen,
alsweill burghes as landwertmen.

Next, that the noblemen, gentilmen, and wtheris heritouris within
ilk presbitrie, at leist so manie of thame, as eftir intimatioune to be made
to thame, may conveine and mak choyse of foure or mae suorne landit
men or vtheris of gude fame and credite, who sall tak exact tryell in like
maner as thay sall think fitt of the yeirlie worthe of everie man's rent,
estate in wictuall, money, or wther rent, quhairby yeirlie proffeit and commoditie arryses without burghe, and to distinguish the particular rentis
of everie seuerall paroche.

Secondlie, thay must keip the particulares of everie particular man's

5 Feb.
1640.

Instruc-
tiones
anent the
Band of
Releiff.

5 Feb.
1640.
———
Instructiounes
anent the
Band of
Releiff.

rent besyd thameselflis, that the samen be not divulgat but to thair awin nichtboures among thameselflis; thirdlie, the saids persones sall take vp and esteime the saids rentis, all as frie rent, without deductioun of any burding except ministeris stipendis and few-dueties, and wtheris dew to his Maiestie, or wtheris superiouris, with clauses irritant; the rent of buyares and sellares of wictuall, and wtheris handleris and trafficqueris without burghe, most be estimat according to thair stock.

Lyfrentares must pas as heritouris, and thair rent gevin wp in lyk kynd as heritouris; consideratioune most be had, quhat grassmes ar payed at the entrie and small dewtie thairefter, that thair rent may be esteimed conforme; so soone as the saids persones hes takine ane exact tryall of ilk man's particular rent within ilk parochin of that said presbitrie, thay must set donne ane roll of the parochinares within that presbytrie, togidder with the total soume *in cumulo* of the rent of the said parochine, alsweill in wictuall as money, quhilk roll most be subscrywit be thame, testifeing the samen to be trew, wpoun thair honour and credite, according to thair knowledge. Thair is ane appointed in ewerie presbitrie within this kingdome for agenting of this busienes, and sic it putt to ane speidie and finall conclusionne, quho most be answerable to giue ane accompt thairof, and to report the same to these at Edinburghe, quho salbe instrusted in the commoune bussines, and that betwixt and the said sewint day of Marche nixt to cum; and for the knowing of the proportioun dew be the burghes, it is condiscendit that the magistrattis within burghe sall mak choyse of thair ordiner number and quantitie of persones vsit in lyke caises, who salbe sworne to mak ane just and trew estimatioun of everie manis rent within the burghe, of burgage, land, and trade, thair dwelling houssis onlie exceptit, and give wpe the same in particular to the saidis magistrattes, who salbe obleist to report the same *in cumulo* to these who shall resyde at Edinburghe, vnder the saids magistrattes hands on thair credite and honour; and for eschewing of the discowerie of ewerie manis estate, within or without burghe, quhairby thair credite may be indangered, it is to be remembred that everie man

must pay for his rent except the ministeris stipends, few-ducties, and
wtheris foirsaids as frie rent, without anie burding or debt, walued bollis,
or wther dewties quhatsomewir; for recompence quhairof, ewerie debtor
sall have retentioune frome his creditour of anie proportionale pairt,
according as the impositioune salbe layed on, and the annuelrent salbe
frie of anie wther payment for that somme quhairout the said proportionall
pairt salbe deducit, and sall not be stentit for the same, whether he dwell
within burghe or without burghe, prowyding alwayes that incaice the
said annuelrent be not payed yeirlie, at least within thrie moneth thaireftir, thair salbe no retentione of the said proportionall.

The lyik proportionall retentione is to be had for walued bollis, or
wtheris burdingis or dewties payed out of the lands or rentis, and least
the said commoun releiff sould be hindred or delayed in anie sort, it is
condiscendit that gif the said report sall not come frome the saidis
parochines, or presbitries, or burghes *respective*, at the day to be prefixed,
in that caice, it is determined that these who sallhave trust in the com-
monne affaires sall have power to impose vpoun the saidis presbytries,
parochines, or burghes sick a proportionall pairt as thay sall think expedient; so we intreat yow to sie all thir things done, as we salbe youre
assured freinds. *Sic subscribitur*, Argyll, Rothes, Montrose, Eglintoun,
Wauchope, J. Burghly, J. Smyth for Edinburgh; James Fletchir, Dundie;
Tho. Bruce for Stirling; T. Semple, M. Campbell. Edinburgh, 18 Jan.
1640.

5 Feb. 1640.

Instruc-
tiones
anent the
Band of
Releiff.

The Generall Band.

The Generall Band.

We, the prowest, baillies, counsall, and deacones of craftes and
wtheris of the burghe of Aberdeine, onder subscryvand, considering how
just and neidfull a thing it is to hawe the commoune charges bestowit in
the lait trubles of this cuntrey payit, and these quho have ather wndergone the burding or hawe debursit out money, victuall, or vther prowisioune, be payed and releiwit of the same alse speidilie and tymouslie as

5 Feb.
1640.

The Generall Band.

may be, doe heirby heartilie, frielie, and willinglie offer and promeis for ws and oure successouris, to pay and delywer to   , or thair deputtes appointed for the samen, the somme of ten merkis money Scottes of everie hundreth merkis of yeirlie rent dew and payable to ws and the remanent burgessis, inhabitantis, and wtheris lyable in extentis within oure said burghe for burgage and trade, or wther commoditie within burghe and liberties thairof, and that conforme to the estimatioune to be made be ane competent number of the ablest, most judicious, and wnderstanding honest men to be chosine be the magistrattes and counsall of the said burghe, for setting donne ane estimatioun and valuation of all the saidis inhabitantis, burgessis, and wtheris forsaids within the said burghe, or lyable thairto of thair estates and meanes dew to thame be burgage, land, trade, or wther commoditie within burghe and liberties thairof (thair dwelling houssis, hospitallis, college, or schooll rentis being exceptit), and quhilk estimatioune so to be made, we obleis ws with all diligence to expeid and report the samen *in cumulo* vnder the magistrattes hands to the saidis collectouris and thair foirsaids, and sall pay the said somme of ten merkis of everie hundreth merkis of rent foirsaid betwixt and the first day of April nixt to cum, togidder with ten merkis money foirsaid for everie hundreth merkis failzie, and annualrent thaireftir incaice of retentioune eftir the said day of payment, termelie, but prejudice to sute executioune heirwpoun; and becaus that everie man alsweill to burghe as landward payes for his rent as frie rent, and not burdined with any dett or wther burding, except as in the generall bandis exceptit, thairfoir it is heirby declairit that the debtour shall have retentioune frome the creditour of the lyik somme payit be him out of everie hundreth merkis of annualrent or wther burding, provyding the said annualrent or wther dewties be alvayis payed within the yeire, at the least within thrie monethis thaireftir, otherwayes he sall hawe no retentioune of the samen, and for the more securitie, we ar content and consentis that thir presentis be insert and registrat in the bookis of counsall and sessioun, to have the strengthe of ane decreit of the lordis thairof, that lettres of horning on sex dayes and wthres as effeires may pas heirwpoun, and thairto we constitute oure procuratoris. In witnes quhairof we hawe subscryvit thir presentis with oure handis written be Robert Neill, servitour to Willeam Inglish, wreitter.

5 Feb. 1640.
The Generall Band.

THE MISSIVE.

"To oure affectionat and worthie freinds the prouest, baillies, and counsall of Aberdeine, These. Worthie freinds being remembered of the great want youre cittie hath of some minister, and beinge cairfull that ye might be provydit with on of the best in thir pairtes, we hawe writtin earnestlie to Mr Daniel Dalglesh, minister at Cowper, a man of great learninge and abilities, both for preaching and sustaning disputes againes papistes, wishing God his paines may be effectuall amonges yow, and that ye may be all cairfull to keip vnion as wther burghes with the rest of this natioun, for mentening the puritie of religioun and the priviledges of the kingdome, and that ye wold lay asyde all prejudices, and labour to hold out those evillis intendit for both; doe not as many who think themselfis tyed to mentein thair former practise ; remember how ye hawe beine mislead against the whole kingdome with some particular persones who desserted yow, and seing by oure cariage we hawe vindicatt oureselfis frome these aspersiounes which thay suggested to yow, and without any by respect hawe onlie sought the publict good, we doe most earnestlie beseach yow to joyne with us heartilie heirin, and latt the euidence heirof be suche as to remove frome oure adversaries all hopes of your concurrance, that so thay may be divertit frome landing amongst yow, and making your toun the principall seatt of war and divisioun; and if any among yow hearteneth enemies to come, ather convert thame by richt informatioun, or els remowe thame, and joyning with us by all your best meanes to preserve the bodie of this kingdome frome ruine, we sall acknowledge yow as fellow feiling memberis thairof, and be in everie

5 Feb.
1640.

thing youre most affectionnat freinds to serve yow. *Sic subscribitur* Argyll, Rothes, Montrose, Dalhousie, Lowthian, Yester, Lindsay, Balmerino. Edinburgh, 25 January 1640.

11 Feb.
1640.

The toun convenit.

11 *February* 1640.

The quhilk day, the toune being convenit in the tolbuith be the hand bell, Patrik Leslie, prowest, shew and exponit to thame that the nobilitie at south, with some of the gentrie and burrowes had send thair instructiounes vnder thair hands anent the forme of payment of the subsidie appointed to be wplifted of all persones within this burghe, alsweill to burghe as landwart, for defraying of the commoune chairges bestowit on the late trubles, togidder with a copie of the generall band appointed to be subscrywit for payment of the same subsidie, togidder also with a letter sen syne frome the nobillmen, whairby thay hawe recommendit Mr Daniel Dalgleish, minister at Couper, to be ane of the ministeris of this burghe, and withall bering thair advyse to this burghe to keip vnion as other burghes with the rest of the natioun for mantening of the puritie of religioun and liberties of the kingdome; quhilk instructiones, generall band, and missive being oppinlie red in audience of the toune, convenit as said is, the prowest inquired of thame what answer shuld be returnit to the nobilitie concerning the same, quha tuke to be advysit for geving thair answer thairanent till Friday nixt, the fourtene of this instant.

14 Feb.
1640.

The townes answer anent the subscryving of the Generall Band of Releiff, and other particulares demandit of thame.

14 *February* 1640.

The quhilk day, the toune being convenit within the tolbuith be the hand bell for gewing thair answer anent thair subscriptioun of the generall band, and contributiones accordinglie for defraying of the commoun chairges bestowit in the late trubles, as lyikwayes for gewing thair answer anent Mr Daniel Dalgleishe, minister at Cowpar, who is recommendit be the nobilitie to be one of the ministeris of this burghe, and withall anent thair vnion and joyning with the rest of the natioun for mantening the puritie of religioun and liberties of the kingdome, and being demandit vpone everie ane of the same particulares, answered as followes: And first, anent the subscryving of the generall band, thay ar content for thair pairtes, according to the weaknes of thair meanes, to go on subscrywe and contribute proportionablie with the remanent burrowes and bodie of the kingdome, and be resone thairof desyres thair magistrattes to entreatt the nobilitie that thay wald be pleased so to respect oure toune in that contributioun, that thay may be satisfiet amongst the rest of what thay hawe reallie deburst and spent on the armies during the tyme of the same trubles. Nixt, anent the keiping of vnion with other burghes, and joyning with the bodie of the kingdome as fellow feilling memberis thairof againes forane invasioun, in that particular also thay promeist to contribute thair best helpis for the publict good of the kingdome; and last, anent the planting of the said Mr Daniel Dalgleish in the vacant roume of oure ministrie, thay answered, becaus the provisioun and stipend of that minister must be payed be a voluntarie contributioun of the inhabitantis of oure toune, thay wold not contribute to any but to those whome they knew and vnderstude both of his giftis, lyff, and conversatioun, and declaired that thair ar sindrie worthie men within this province whois giftis and lyff is weill knowin to thame, off whome they desyred thair magistrattes and counsell to mak chois who sall give content both to the nobilitie and whole kirk of Scotland, and thairfoir desyred thair magistrattis to writt to the nobillmen for macking a charitable constructioun of thair proceidingis heirin, and not to suffer any forder harme or violence to be vsed vnto thame, bot to esteime thame as fellow feilling memberis of the bodie of this kingdome.

14 Feb. 1640.
The townes answer anent the subscryving of the Generall Band of Releiff, and other particulares demandit of thame.

18 *February* 1640.

The samen day, in presens of Patrik Leslie, prowest, and Mr Willeame Moir, baillie, Issobell Davidsone, servant to Johne Smith, fleshour, wes convict and put in amerciament of court for vsing imprecationis aganis

18 Feb. 1640.
Imprecationis against the covenanters.

18 Feb. 1640. Imprecations against the covenanters.	the covenanteris be saying. Let newer the covenanteris hawe any pairt in the kingdome of heavine, nor no pairt moir nor schoe had gude of thame ane number of traitoris, and being forbidden to curse, for saying shoe should neither ban thame nor blood thame, bot bursen be thow within; Johne Smith foirsaid become cautioner for the said Issobell Davidsoun for payment of sic vnlaw as the counsell sall modifie for hir transgressioun to forbeare, ffor the quhilk the said Issobell is ordanit to be putt in the joigs, thairin to remaine fra nyne houris to twelff; farder, the said Issobell ordanit to pay ane dolour to the deane of gild, and to be frie of her personall punishment.

19 *February* 1640.

19 Feb. 1640. Act anent Rob, Calsey-macker.	The said day, the prowest, baillies, and conncell ordaines Andro Rob, calsiemaker, personallie present to tak doune the tuo long jeastis infixit be him in the midst of the kingis calsie forgaines the tenement of Daniel Aidye in the Greine for holding wp the foirwall of his house whairin he dwellis, and to sett the saids trees within the gutter alsueir to the said wall as possible may be, and that withall convenient diligence, to the effect his maiesties liedges may have frie passage that way at all occasiones, but trubill or impediment, whilk the said Andro Rob promeist sa to doe.

11 *March* 1640.

11 Marche 1640. Deane of Gild appoynted to advance ye merkis to Lieutenant Colonell Forbes.	The said day, the prowest, baillies, and counsall ordaines Alexander Jaffray, deane of gild, to advance and deburse the somme of sex hundreth merkis money to Lieutenant Colonell George Forbes for himselff, and to help to pay the rest of the commanderis wha ar recommendit to the toune be the Earle Marshall his missive letter, direct to the counsell for that effect, whilk somm salbe allowit to the said deane of gild in his comptis.

8 April 1640.

8 April 1640.

Jaffray chosin commissionar to a meitting of the nobilitie and estates at Edinburgh.

The quhilk day, the prowest, baillies, and conncell of the burghe of Aberdeine being convenit in the tounes counselhous, electit, nominat, and chusit Mr Alexander Jaffray, thair lait prowest and commissioner of parliament, to be commissionar for this burghe, for keiping of a meiting of the nobilitie, barrones, and burrowes of this kingdome, appointed to hauld at Edinburgh the sevinteine day of Apryll instant, conforme to the missive direct for that effect to the prowest, baillies, and conncell of this burghe be the commissionares of the burghe of Edinburghe, dated the twentie fyft day of Marche last bypast, with power to the said Maister Alexander Jaffray, to treatt, resone, vote, conclude and determine with the estates there to be convenit vponn such materis as salbe treatted at the said meitting tending to the glorie of God, and mantenance of religion, lawes, and liberties of this kingdome, promitting to hauld firme and stabill whatsumewir thair said commissioner shall doe in the premisses, and ordaines Thomas Buck, thesaurar, to deburse the somme of thrie hundreth merkis money to the said commissionar for macking his expenssis to ane compt, quhilk salbe allowit to the said thesaurer in his comptis.

9 April 1640.

9 April 1640.

Chusing of taxstares for stenting the toun for payment of thair tent partis conforme to the Generall Band.

The quhilk day, the toune being convenit in the tolbuith be the handbell for electing and choosing of taxstares to stent the nightboures and inhabitantis of this burghe, who hes subscrywit the generall band of releiff, for payment of the somme of ten merkis money of everie hundreth merkis of yeirlie rent, dew and payable to thame for burgage, land, trade, or wther commoditie within burghe and liberties thairof (thair dwellinghoussis, hospitallis, college and school rentis being exceptit), and that for defraying of the commoun chairges bestowit in the late trubles of this kingdome, and whairas sindrie of the nichtboures makis scrupule to subscrywe the said band becaus it is not set doune thairin for what spaice of

9 April 1640.

Chusing of taxtares for stenting the toun for payment of thair tent partis conforme to the Generall Band.

tyme the said contributioune sould endure; thairfoir, and for satisfeing the haill inhabitantis of that surupule, Mr Thomas Gray, baillie, caused reid publictlie in thair audience a letter direct frome the nobilitie and otheris of the committie at Edinburghe to the prowest, baillies, and counsall of this burghe heirand that the said contributioun sall indure for the yeire of God 1639 allanerlie, off the quhilk missive letter the tenour followes:—" To our worthie freindis the prowest, baillies, and counsall of Aberdeine. Worthie freinds, we hawe hard of some doubtis yow mak anent the subscription of the band for the tenth pairt; and first in the durance thereof; for answere wherewnto yow may mend it in the margine (for the yeire of God 1639 allenerlie.) Secundlie, yow say that some will pay money and not subscrywe the band. This will not be receivèd frome any, seeing it is of ane ill example, and will open a doore to many inconveniences, we hope ye will goe on hartilie as other burghes in the kingdome, and giwe no occasioun of suspitioun, but rather to be a guide example to the rest of that shyre, we have thought it fitt to levie a regiment to be vnder Colonell Monrois command, which is appointed for the north, as weill to keip off foraine invasion as to redres intestine jarris, whome we intreatt yow further and assist in all things tending to the weill of the cuntrie; and becaus we have no tyme in this present to wreitt moir largelie to yow, yow shall know that we ar to send on to yow and the rest of that shyre with such instructiounes and informatiounes as ar fitting to be represented to yow and thame for the weill of the cuntrie in generall and yourselflis in particular, to which tyme we rest your affectionat friends. *Sic subscribitur* Montrose, Lowthian, Balmerino, Burghly, Forrester, Patrik Hepburn of Wachtoun, F. Hepburne, Richard Maxwell. Edinburghe, 20 Marche 1640." Eftir the reiding of the quhilk letter, the toune convenit as said is, electit, nominat, and chusit George Richard, Mr Patrik Chalmer, Robert Smith, Alexander Farquhar, James Smith, Thomas Gray, Thomas Burnet, Robert Forbes, Walter Cochrane, Willeame Forbes, elder, Dauid Aidy, Johne Leslie, George Pyper, Willeame Ord, wricht, James Christie, tailyeour, and James Hall, cordoner, to be taxtares and stentares for setting donne ane estimatioun and valuatioun of all the inhabitantis of this burghe subscryvares of the said band, of thair estates and meanes due to thame be burgage, land, trad, or wther commoditie within burghe and liberties thairof (except befoir exceptit), and for setting donne and giving furth a stent roll thairwpoun subscry wit with thair handis beirand the particular soume of money whairwnto ilk persone is stentit, quhilkis taxtares being all personallie present except the said George Ricard, acceptit the said chairge in and wpoun thame, and gave thair solemone oathes for stenting thair nichtbouris wprichtlie according to thair knowlege, without partialitie or respect of persones, conforme to the order preseryveit be the said generall band, to the quhilkis taxtares abonenamed, Mr Thomas Gray, Mr Wm. Moir, baillies, wpoun considerable respectis, wer conjoynit to sitt as taxtares with thame as being abill, judicious, and vnderstanding men for setting of the said stent, and was sworne to that effect.

9 April 1640.

Chusing of taxtares for stenting the toun for payment of thair tent partis conforme to the Generall Band.

15 April 1640.

The quhilk day, the prowest, baillies, and counsell, for satisfactioun of the desyre of a letter direct to thame frome the Erll Marischall, dated at Dunnotter the tuelff of Aprill instant, ordaines the soume of ane thowsand merkis money to be advanceit and delyvered to Levetenant Colonell George Forbes be the deane of gild, thesaurar, and Mr of the Impost, proportionablie amongst thame as followes, viz., be Alexander Jaffray, deane of gild, twa hundreth merkis, be Thomas Buck, thesaurar, foure hundreth merkis, and be Patrik Moir, Mr of Impost, foure hundreth merkis, quhilkis soumes, with the soume of sex hundred merkis formerlie advanceit be the deane of gild to the said levetenant colonell Forbes, is ordanit to be refoundit bak agane to the advanceris thairof in the first end of this burghes taxatioun, payable to the nobilitie be vertew of the generall band of releiff.

15 April 1640.

1000 merkis advancit to Leutenant Colonell Forbes.

15 April 1640.

15 April 1640.

Isobel Blak to be joggit.

The said day, Issobell Blak, spous to William Baxter, convict, be the depositioun of witnessis, for injuring and slandering of George Boyes, laxfisher, in saying he had stolen a kow from Petfoddellis, and sould have bein hangit thairfoir, ffor the quhilk the said Issobell is ordanit to be joggit or then to redeime herselff be payment of ane dolour, and to crave the pairtie offendit pardon in a fenceit court on Friday nixt, otherwayes no redemptioun frome the joggis.

22 April 1640.

22 April 1640.

Licence gewin to Rob anent the bigging of the steppis of his stair.

The quhilk day, anent the supplicatioun gewin in to the prowest, baillies, and counsell be Andro Rob, calsiemaker, mackand mentioun that quhair out of ignorance he did latelie put wp ane stair for entring to his foir hous biggit be him in the south syid of the Greine, hoping the same sould nather give offence to any, nor yit be preiudiciall to the kingis hie streit; and becaus the said stair is so necessar for a passage to his said hous whilk he hes biggit wpoun his great expenssis for decoratioun of that pairt of the toune sa far as in him lay, thairfoir he humblie desyrit thair wisdomes that thay wald be pleasit to suffer the said stair to stand wndimolished, ffor the quhilk he sould obleis himselff to repair and help any defect in the calsies of this burghe whilk he laitlie repairit, and that wpoun his awin expenssis during his lyftyme, as in the said supplicatioun at lenth was contenit, whilk being at length considderit be the saidis prowest, baillies, and counsell, and eftir ocular inspectioun had be thame being convenit wpoun the ground abefoir for that effect, thay fand that the said hous cannot be convenientlie servit wanting a stair to enter thairwnto, and that the holding wp of the said stane steppis does not hinder the passage in the kingis hie streit, thairfoir thay hawe giwen and grantit, and be thir presentis giwes and grantis licence and tolerance to the said Andro Rob to hold and keip wp the stane steppis biggit be him to the foirsaid wall of the said hous for cutring to the owerhous thairof wpoun the conditiounes eftir following, ffor the qubilk licence abouewrittin the said Andro Rob bindis and oblessis him, his aires and successoures, heretabill proprietares of the said ffoirhous, to pay and delywer to the thesaurer of the said burghe tuentie sex schillingis aucht penneis Scottis money of yeirlie dewtie in all tyme coming, efter the said Andro his deceas whom the same salhappin, and in the meane tyme to wphold, manteane, and repair the new calsies of this burghe, biggit and to be biggit thairin in all the defects and ruynes thairof on his awin proper charges and expenssis duringe his lyftyme, whilk the counsall ar content to accept in satisfactioun of the said yeirlie dewtie during the said space, and thaireftir the said foirhous to be onlie affectit with the payment of the samen yeirlie dewtie of tuentie sex schillings aucht penneis in all tyme thaireftir, to be payed at Witsonday and Martimes in winter be equall portiounes to the thesaurar of this burgh for the tyme; provyding alwayes if the charges to be made be the said Andro in furneshing sand and steanes for repairing the defectis of the saidis calseyis exceid in a yeir the foirsaid yeirlie ductie of tuentie sex ss., eight d.; in that caice the toun to be lyable in payment to him of the super plus of his debursementis for sand and stanes, nor the said yeirlie ductie extendis to.

22 April 1640.
Licence gewin to Rob anent the bigging of the steppis of his stair.

5 *May* 1640.

In presence of Mr Robert Farquhar, baillie, Helen Mearnes, spous to Willeame Wilsoun, watterman, convict of her awin confessioun, and be the depositioun of witnessis, for injuring of Janet Walker in rugging her be the hair, and casting a cap at her [ordered] to forbeare, &c., . . . her vnlaw modefeit to fourtie shillings.

5 May 1640.

6 *May* 1640.

Jaffrayes discharge of his commissioun.

The said day, in presens of the prowest, baillies, and counsell, compeirit Mr Alexander Jaffray, lait prowest, commissionar chosin for this burghe to the Parliament and Generall Assemblie laitlie hauldin at Edinburghe, and to twa wther meitingis of the estates sensyne, twitching the effaires of this kingdome, and made ane ample declaratioun of suche materis as wer treatit at the saids twa last meittingis, as he had done abefoir of the proceidingis in Parliament and Assemblie; inrespect quhairoff the saidis prowest, baillies, and counsall findis that the said Mr Alexander hes dewlie and faithfullie acquytit himselff in his saids commissiounes, and thairfoir dischairges him of the samen.

Followes the particular instructiounes and ordour sett donne be the estates of this kingdome for mantenance of commanderis and soiouris of the regimentis appointit to be levied for the publict service of the cuntrie, quhilkis instructiounes the said Mr Alex. Jaffray producit, and the prowest, baillies, and counsall ordaines the samen to be registrat in the counsall register *ad futurom rei memoriam*.

Instructiones for commanderis and soiouris.

Efter dew consideratioun and long debait be the nobilitie, barones, and burgessis convenit for the tyme at Edinburghe, the sevinteine day of Aprill instant, anent the most expedient and easiest way for defence of oure religioun, lyves, and liberties in this vrgent extremitie, efter consideratioun had of oure present estate and conditioun, togidder with all objectiounes and inconvenientis might follow, being confident that all who loves religioun or the liberties of this kingdome, will rather adventure what they have than run the hazard of being perpetnallie miserable, hawe thoght it necessar that the tent pairt of the rentis alreddie appoyntit be with all possible diligence ingathered and sent to Edinburghe to the collectoris generall appoyntit for that effect, togidder with the valuationnes and bands which ar not yet come in, for effectuating quhairof, the collonellis in euerie shirefdome or presbiteries, togidder with the nobillmen and gentillmen there, ar appointit to haist in the saids valuatiounes, lands and money betwixt and the tuelff day of May next to come at fardest; lyikas the said chairge is imposit vponne thame, with certificatioun if thay doe not send in the said money or diligence betwixt and the said day thay salbe lyable thameselffis thairto—viz., the Earle of Marschall, the Lord Fraser, and the Maister of Forbes for your schyre, who sall hawe power to seik acompt of the collectoris, and put everie man to it according to the last instructiounes; lyikas the haill commissionares of burrowes presentlie convenit wer appointed to giwe either reall moneyes or securitie for payment of thair severall pairtes, with thair valuationes betwixt and the said tuelff day of Maij nixt to come; and becaus efter exact tryell be commoun calculatioun of the said tent pairt, it is found that the present necessar imployment will neid a stock of money alsweill for payment of the twa standing regimentis for the south and north, and of the commoun magazines and officiares of artiliaries, as of the third pairt of the wther soiouris pay, to be levied out of the schyres conforme to the proportioun of everie schyre; therefoir all in ane voice efter long reasoning and disput, thought most fitt that when we shalbe necessitat to bring ane armie to the feildis, or to defend anie pairt of the cuntrie which salbe invaded, that all the men who sall be sent out or made vse of within any schyre or schyres sall be intertained according to the proportioun of men and quantitie of wictuellis where out of they come, or to whome they sall belong, for the spaice of fourtie dayes efter thair outcoming, conforme to the proportioun of the saids schyres, and that by and attour the said tent pairt—viz., for your proportioun tua thousand ane hundreth foote, twa hundreth horse, twa hundreth cariage horse, twa hundreth gnardis haglbutteris, tua hundreth pyners. A commone soiour hes for meat and drink munethlie ane firlott twa peckis meall, ane firlott malt, with twa schillingis in the day of money. All wther officers vnder the ensignes to have pay payit the twa pairt thairof in meall and malt, and the rest in money.

The capitane of foot not being a soiour of fortunes, twa furlots wheat, ane boll twa furlotts meall, ane boll malt, twa bollis aites, and

6 May 1640.
———
Instructiounes for commanderis and soiouris.

> 6 May 1640.
> Instructiones for commanderis and soiouris.

aughteine punds money. The lievtennent of foot the lyk kynd—twa furlots quheat, ane boll meill, twa furlots malt, ane boll aitts, twelff punds money.

The ensignes of fute of the lyk kynd—ane furlot quheat, thrie furlotts meill, twa furlotts malt, ane boll aites, and aught punds money.

The soiouris of fortune of the lyk qualitie to hawe the lyk proportion of victuell, and all the rest of thair pay in money.

A capitane of horsse to have thrie furlotts wheat, twa bollis meill, ane boll twa furlottes malt, foure bollis twa furlottes aites, and twentie-foure punds monethlie.

A lievtennent of horsse, twa furlotts wheat, ane boll twa furlotts meill, ane boll malt, thrie bolls aittes, and sexteine pund money.

The cornet of horsse is to have twa furlotts wheat, ane boll meill, thrie firlotts malt, thrie bolles aittes, and twelf punds money.

The trumpetar, thrie furlotts meall, ane furlott twa peckis malt, ane furlott twa peckes aittes, and aughteine pundis money.

The corporall the lyck victuell, and twelf pundis money.

The horsman the lyck victuell, and sex pundis money.

The carriage horsse, for boy and horsse, ane firlott twa peckis meill, ane furlet malt, ane boll aites, and threttie ss. money.

The guard and pyiners to have the lyck pay as the common soiouris.

As also it is thocht fitt that the Committie of Warre in ilk schirrefdomes cast the proportioun of men out of everie paroche, and cause thame be enrolled and commanders appointed to bring thame out upoun advertissement.

And siclyik that the provisioun of armes be maid with all diligence be the tennent who is able to buy, or be the heritouris quhair the tennent is not able.

And siclyik it is appointit that the heritouris within everie schyre or committie of warre therein appointit commissaris, ane or ma, within ewerie presbiterie, to tak wp alse mucke victuell by and attour the said tent pairt as will intertaine the proportioun of men forrsaid to come out of the seuerall schyres, for fourtie dayes at least; quhilk proportionne is to be taken wp conforme to the rentis of the said presbyterie or shyre.

And becaus the men must come out of euerie schirrefdome according to thair number, and thair interteinement must be according to thair rentis, thairfoir it is appointit, first, that if anie schyre be found efter dew calculationn, to be stentit in the divisioun foirsaid to moir than thair dew proportioun, it is declaired tharefter exact tryell, vpon remonstrance it salbe remedied: Secundlie, it is declaired that thir men, or anie necessar pairt thairof, salbe imployed according to the most vrgent necessitie for defence of any pairt of the kingdome which salbe in danger for the time.

Thirdlie, if any schirrefdome or burghe sall give out moir provisioun in victuell or money than thair dew proportionn, efter valuatioun of the haill kingdomes, it is hereby declaired that, efter compt and rekning, the same salbe repaid; and if thay have payit out les, the same most be payed into the common collectour, to mak wp wther mens losses.

It is earnestlie recommendit to all the shyres in the kingdome, that colonellis be chosin where thay ar not as yet, and that the haill schyres be maid wp in companies, everie man as thay lye in thair paroches, betwixt sextie and sexteine, to be in readines wpoun all necessar occasiounes to defend thameselllis from any suddane invasioun, or to assist thair nightbouring shyres, as thay sall gett ordour, and necessitie requyre.

Where the valuationes ar not trewlie done, it is appointed that what is concealled shalbe confiscat for the publique vse.

It is also appointed, that those of the committie of warr shall hawe power to designe the men, and cause put thame out when thay get orderis.

6 May 1640.

The said day, the prowest, baillies, and counsall, considering that Johne Leith of Harthill does continew in his disorderis and miscariage be shooting of gunes and pistolls out of the wyndoes of the wairdhous,

Margin: 6 May 1640. Instructiones for commanderis and soiouris.

Margin: 6 May 1640. Ordinance anent Johne Leith of Harthill.

6 May 1640.
Ordinance anent Johne Leith of Hartbill.

whairin he is detenit prisoner, and daylie caries wapones wpoun him as if he wer at libertie, quhilkis ar secretlie convoyit to him at the saids wyndoes, notwithstanding of many admonitiounes and chairges gevin to him in the contrair; thairfoir thay all in ane voice ordaines the wyndoes of that chamber in the wairdhous whairin he remaines to be securit in all convenient diligence ather be plet stansheonnes and tirleiss of yron, or some wther suir devyce that he may be debarrit frome the lyk insolencie heireftir.

12 May 1640.
Straquhyn convict of dinging Beith.

12 May 1640.

The said day, in presence of Patrik Leslie, prowest, and Mr Willeame Moir, baillie, James Straquhyn, servant to Mr Robert Farquhar, baillie, convict of his awin confessioun for the dinging and stricking of Willeame Beith wpon the mouth and face with his hand, to the effusion of his blood; for the quhilk the Councell ordanes the said James to be wardit for aucht dayes, or then to redeme him selff be peyment of four merkis.

Eodem die.
Patersones convict.

Eodem die.

The same day, in presence of Mr Wm. Moir, baillie, Jeane Patersoun, spous to Johne Wilsoun, convict of her awin confessioun for saying that shoe hard it said that John Lindsay, tinclar, had stollen a siluer quarter mease out of the Earle Marshellis place; and Jeane and Elspet Patersones, dauchters to Alexr. Patersone, horner, convict be the depositiounes of sindrie famous witnessis for casting ower of Agnes Ribbens, spous to Johne Lindsay, tincklar, and ryving of her cursh off her heid [ordered] to forbear &c.; and the said Alexr. Patersone, horner, become actit and obligit not to trubile nor molest the said Johne Lindsay, his wyf, bairnes, and servantis be way of dead under the paine of fourtie pundis; and the said John become actit and obleigit not to trubile the said Alexr. vnder the lyik

paine of ffourtie pundis, for the quhilk the counsall ordaines the said *Eodem die.*
Jeane Patersone to be joggit, or then to redeme hirselff thairfra be pay- *Patersones*
ment of ane dolour to the deane of gild, and to crave the pairtie offendit *convict.*
pardone in a fenced court, under the payne of jogging.

27 May 1640.

27 May 1640.

The quhilk day, anent the missive direct to the prowest, baillies, and *Commis-*
counsell of this burghe frome the commissionaris of burrowes on the com- *sionar*
mittie of estate, desyiring that our commissioner of parliament may keip *the Parlia-*
the second day of Junij next at Edinburghe as the dyett whairwnto the *ment.*
parliament wes prorogat, off the quhilk missive the tenour followes:—

"To our loving freindis and nichtboures the prowest, baillies, and counsell of Aberdeine. Loving freinds and nichtboures, whairas the parliament wes prorogat to the second of June nixt ensewing by his maiesties warrand, in consideratioun quhairof, and inrespect of the eminent danger we now stand in, we thocht gude first to lett yow know that the English (whether freebuters or kingis schippis we know not) hawe takin sindrie of oure Scottis men coming frome Holland and France, and hawe confiscat thair gudes and schippis, striped thair men naked, and wsed thame with all kynd of hostilitie, quhairof we admire, no injurie being done to thame. We sent to the deputie Governour of Berwick (who hath two of our shippis) to demand a reason of thair taking, who returnes answer that he can give no answer untill he acquaint the councell of England with oure letter. We wer in hops that the parliament of England now sitting sould take matteris to heart, and not suffer the busines come to ane nationall quarrell, bot be all appearance, oure long suffering is likelie to turne to oure ruine if the same be not prevented; and nixt, inrespect of the manie prejudices may aryse incaice we neglect what is propper to us for preservatioun of oure liberties, we entreat that thair commissioneris of parliament may keip the said dyet, and to be heir a day or two befoir the tyme, that, by Godis meanes, to preserve this land frome miserie and

27 May
1640.
—
Commissionar chosin to the Parliament.

threatned slaverie. The dyet is peremptour, whiche, if once slipped, cannot be regained, and makis ws the moir earnest to hawe everie thing done incumbent to ws, leist oure posteritie suld blame ws for neglect of what may conduce for preservationne of oure religioun, lywes, and liberties, which sould be oure cheifest cair, and is the earnest desyirs of your loving freinds and nightbouris. *Sic subscribitur*, J. Smith, Richard Maxvell, Tho. Bruce for Stirling. Edinburgh, the 9 of May 1640." For obedience and satisfactioun of the desyre of the quhilk missive, the prowest, baillies, and councell nominatis and appointis Mr Alexander Jaffray, late prowest and commissionar of parliament, to keip the forsaid dyett, whairwnto the said parliament is prorogat, with power to him to treatt, reasone, vote, conclude, and determine with the estates of this kingdome, to be convenit wpoun all materis to be treated in parliament tending to the glorie of God, the maintenance of the true religioun, lawes, and liberties of this kingdome, conforme to the commissioun givin to him at the first doune sitting of the said parliament; and becaus Mr Alexander Jaffray gawe in his compt this day in presens of the counsall, of the soume of two thowsand merkis receawed be him at the first going to the parliament in the moneth of August last, 1639, frome Andro Burnet, then thesaurer, as lyikwayes of the soume of sex hundreth merkis receaved be him sensyne from Thomas Buck, present thesaurar, being employed sen Michaelmes last twa seuerall tymes commissionar for this burghe to Edinburghe, first in October, and thaireftir in Aprill last, at the fute of the quhilk compt the said Mr Alexander is fund super expendit in the soume of ane hundreth threttie nyne pundis; thairfoir, and for payment to him of his said super expenssis, and for macking of his chairges in his present commissioun to the parliament, the prowest, baillies, and counsall ordaines the said Thomas Buck, thesaurar, to deburse to him the soume of fywe hundreth merkis money to ane compt, quhilk salbe allowit to the said Thomes Buck in his thesaurar comptis.

Eodem die.

The said day, the haill toune being warnit be the drum, and conveining for the most pairt in the tolbuith, Patrik Leslie, prowest, causit reid and intimat publictlie vnto thame the precept direct to him and to the baillies be the Erle Marshall and remanent of the committie of the schirefdome of Aberdeine anent the silver wark, goldsmith wark, and cunzeit moneyes belonging to the inhabitantis of this burghe, off the quhilk precept the tenour followes, "Ws. Willeame, Earle Marshall, and remanent of the committie of the schirefdome of Aberdeine undersubscryvares, conforme to the warrand direct to ws be the estates of this kingdome, be thir presentis commandis and ordaines yow the prowest, ballies, and magistrattis of the burghe of Aberdeine to tak wp a trew and exact inventar of all the inhabitantis within the citie of Aberdeine, and liberties thairof wpoun thair great aith of veritie of all silver wark, goldsmith wark, and cunzeit money perteining to thame, and that wpoun consideratioun that the same may be imployed and cunziet for the publict vse of the cuntrie vpoun sufficient securitie to be gevin to thame thairfoir, at thrie pundis for ilk vnce silver, and   for ilk vnce gold, to be payed within yeire and day thaireftir, with certificatioun to all concealleris, that not onlie the said silver and gold, bot all thair movable gudes sall be confiscat to the publick vse for thair disobedience and contempt, quhairof we will yow to mak intimatioun to your people, as ye will be answerable; subscryveit be ws at Aberdeine, the aucht day of May 1640, and this to be done both to covenanteris, and not covenanteris, and that ye report your diligence heiranent betwixt and the xv day of May instant. *Sic subscribitur* Marschall A. Forbes, Alex. Fraser, S^r Wm. Forbes, J. Forbes, Leslie, George Baird, M. J. Baird;" and siclyik the said Patrik Leslie, prowest, intimat to the toune, convenit as said is, the Erll Marshallis letter direct to the prowest and baillies of this burghe, desyiring the haill toune to meitt his lordship in armes at the Brig of Die the morne, in the eftir noone, off the quhilk letter the tenour followes :—

Eodem die.

Precept from the committe anent silver and goldsmith wark.

Eodem die.	"To my loving freinds the prowest, and baillies of Aberdeine. My
Precept from the committe anent silver and goldsmith wark.	very loveing freinds, these ar to show yow that I intend (God willing) on Thursday nixt in the eftirnoone to be at Aberdeine, quhair I will bring with me Generall Maior Munro and his regiment, for quhome I pray yow cause prowyd victuallis, for the payment, for nothing sall be takin without reddie moneyes, ye alwayes approving yourselfflis gude cuntrie men, and withall ye sall be in armes and meitt ws at the brig of Dee, that we may joyne for defence of your toune, and of so many honest men as sall be fund thairin, and for the peace of the cuntrie about, but I wish ye be better conveened, nor ye wer at your last wappingshawing. So not doubting of your cair and diligence heirin, I rest youris lowing freind, *Sic subscribitur,*
Charge to the toune to meitt the Erle Marshall at the Brig of Dee in armes.	Marshall. Dunoter, 26 May 1640." Conforme to the quhilk letter and for obedience thairwnto, the toune wer chargit be the said Patrik Leslie, prowest, to be in reddines the morne be tuellff houres in armes at the mercat croce, and to marche thairfra with thair magistrattis to the Brig of Dee for meitting of the said Erle Marishall and Generall Maior Munro thairat, and convoying thame thairfra to the toune.

29 May 1640.

29 May 1640. The toun convenit for subscryving the articles presented to thame be the Earle Marshall and Generall Maior Minro.	The quhilk day, Patrik Leslie, prowest, causit red publictlie in audience of the haill toune, convenit this day in the tolbuith be the drum, the articles underwrittin proponit and gewin in yisternicht to the magistratts of this burghe be the Erle Marshall and Generall Major Munro, immediatlie after thair incoming to the toune with thair armie, and declaired that the magistratts of this burghe wer chairgit to subscrywe presentlie the saidis articles, befoir the souldiouris laid doune thair armes or removed off the streets; lyikas than instantlie the prowest and baillies and sic of the nichtbouris as wer present with thame, for obedience to the chairge subscryvit the saidis articles, and wer commandit to convene the haill toune this day, to the effect thay might lyikwayes subscrywe the same, wha being

convenit in the tolbuith, as said is, the Erll Marshall and Generall Maior Munro being both present for the tyme, requyred and commandit the nightboures and inhabitantis to subscrywe the saidis articles, as thay wald be answerable wpoun thair perrill; for obedience to the quhilk chairge, the inhabitantis suche as wer present, subscrywit the saids articles, whairof the tennour followes:—

29 May 1640.

The toun convenit for subscryving the articles presented to thame be the Earle Marshall and Generall Maior Munro.

"The tuentie eight day of Maiy 1640. Articles of Bonaccord, to be condiscendit wnto be the magistrattis of Aberdeine for thameselflis, and taking the burdinge wpoun thame for all the inhabitantis, to be presentlie sealed, subscrywit, and delywerit to Generall Maior Munro, as hawing warrand frome the Earle Marischall in the estates name of this kingdome, and Generall Leslie.

1. First desyres the magistrates to giwe in a roll or list of thoise inhabitantis, absent or present, that hath not subscrywed the Covenant and Generall Band, that thay may be disarmed as bad and evill patriottis.

2. Desyires the prowest, magistratts, and all the inhabitants to gieue thair great oath of fidelitie not to correspond or keip interchange of intelligence with any that hes not subscrywed the Covenant and Generall Band, under paine of lossing thair lyffs and confiscatioun of their goods.

3. Desyres thay condiscend willinglie to contribute to the intertainment of the regiment, according as thay salbe stentit in paying of thair tent pairt; and the soldatesta being quartered in thair toune, that they be obleiged, for thameselflis and thair inhabitantis, not to harme or injure thame indirectlie, vnder the paine of death.

4. Desyires thay be obleiged, for thameselffis and inhabitantis, not to heare any minister preache within the toune who hath not subscryed the Covenant, under the paine of being banished the toune, both preacheris and heareris.

5. Desyires the regiment, being quartered and billated within the toune, may be intertained during thair residence thair in meat, drink, and ludging, according to the generall ordour subscryved be the Committie of Estate for the twa pairt of meanes allowed to inferiour officiares and

29 May 1640.

The toun convenit for subscryving the articles presented to thame be the Earle Marshall and Generall Major Minro.

souldiouris a day, according to the list of pay to be givin in to the touneschip be the Generall Major under his hand, in name of the Committie of Estate, the Generall, and the Earle Marishall.

6. Desyires the magistrattis to delywer to the Generall Major, befoir his entrie, in name of the Committie of Estate, Generall Leslie, and the Earle Marishall, the keyes of thair portis and entries, of thair magassines and storehousses, tolbuith or meiting hous of the toune, togidder with the keyes of thair joylhous and prison, to be wsed at his pleasour during his abod thair for the good of the kingdome, and saifftie of the toune and regiment against intestine or forrane enemies, in name foirsaid.

7. Desyires that all the cornes in store within the toune be put wnder inventar for interteining of the regiment, in pairt of payment of thair tent pairtis; and that magistratis and inhabitantis be obleiged to pay the rest in moneyes once in the fourthnicht, according to the ordour of paying the third pairt of the soldatista thair pay in money, till thay be super expendit of their tent pairt.

8. Desyires thay be obleiged to delywer all the cannon, spair armes, ammunitioun, spaids, shoolis, or mattockis thay hawe or can command, on thair great oath, to be vsit at his pleasure, in name foirsaid, for the good of the kingdome against intestine or forane enimies for both thair saifftities; and that thay be obleiged, be thair great oath, to joyne with him and his regiment or associatis in fechting or working againes the enemie to thair power, in qulatsoewir the Erle Marshall and he commands thame for the good of the kingdome and their awin saifftities.

9. Desyires thay be obleiged to sett all thair baxteris and browsteris to work, and caus prowyd, and hawe in redines against the secund of Junij, twelff thowsand pund wecht of biscott bread, togidder with a thowsand gallones of aill and beir, to be putt in small barrellis, for the intendit expeditioun, for which thay salbe payed, or at least allowed, in the first end of the tent pairts.

10. Desyires that, in testimonie of thair Bonaccord with the soldatista that hes come so farre a marche for thair saifftities from the invasioun

of forrane enimies, and the slaverie thay and thair posteritie micht be brocht under, thay may be pleased, out of thair generositie accustomed, and present thankfulnes to the soldatista for keiping of good ordour and eschewing of plundering, provyd for thame twelff hunder pair of schoes, togidder with thrie thowsand elnes of hardin tyiking or saill canves for making thair tentis, to ease and frie the soldatista fra the great invudatioun of raines accustomed to fall out in the northren climat.

11. Desyires against the secund of Junij, to provyd for the intendit expeditioun for setling good order in the countrey, and for suppressing oure intestine enimies and evill patriotts, that fiftie horses may be in readines for transporting of oure cannon, ammunitioun, spair armes, and prouisioun whithersoewir the Earle Marischall leadis the armie; which being accordit to, sealed, and subscrywed by the magistrattes and ministrie for thameselffis, and taking the burdine, as said is, for all the inhabitantis of the toune, we will entir the cittie freindlie, and be answerable for oure selffis and soldatista for any disordour beis committit be any of oure number or vnder oure command; and encaice of not obeying and fulfilling of thir oure resonable demands, so far as concernis the militarie pairt alanerlie, we doe heirby signifie unto yow, in name of the Estate and Generall of the armie, that we will tak suche ordour and speidie course with yow and all the inhabitantis refractorie, as may strick terror in the hearts of all vther oure opposites following your example in disobedience, as evill and wicked patriotts; for eschewing whairof we heartilie desyre your subscriptiounes and seall to thir reasonable demandis, or a peremptorie present answer of Bon-accord or Mal-accord.

29 May 1640.
The toun convenit for subserving the articles presented to thame be the Earle Marshall and Generall Major Monro.

10 *June* 1640.

The said day, the warrands direct be Generall Major Monro for interteining his soldiouires, and lykwayes for thair shoes and thrie thowsand elne of hardin, and otheris thairin contenit, ar ordanit to be registrat in the Counsall book *ad futuram rei memoriam*, quhairof the tenour followes:

10 June 1640.
Warrandis from Generall Major Monro anent the souldiouris of his regiment.

10 June 1640.

Warrandis from Generall Major Monro anent the souldiouris of his regiment.

"Prowest, you shall be pleasit to caus delywer to the beirer heirof, my secretarrie, called Niniane Johnstoune, these moneyes appointed to be payed for the showes, extending to the somme of sevin hundreth and twentie pundis, togidder with thrie thowsand elne of hardin for the soldatista thair vse, for whiche these shalbe your warrand; taking a not of ressaitt frome the secretarrie vnder his hand. As also desyires by thir presentis yow to caus delywer unto him fywe thowsand pund Scottis, for cleiring the rest dew to the officeris and souldieris of the regiment preceiding thair entrie in this toune the twentie-aught of May, and that according to my instructiounes subseryved by the Committie and Generall for that effect; and this warrand, with the secretarie's not of ressaitt in my behalf of the same, wilbe allowed to yow as payment in the first end of your tent pairts. In verificatioun quhairof I have subscrywit thir presentis with my hand, at Aberdeine, the sext of Junij 1640. *Sic subscribitur*, ROBERT MONRO."—"Worthie freindis, ye sall be pleasit to resaue heir according to my promise vnder my hand, the allowance of enterteinement allowed, conforme to the order sett doune by the Committie of Estate, for interteining of inferiour officiaires and souldioures quartered in your toune, according to the two pairt and third eache day, viz., To everie commoun souldiour, foure schillings a day; to everie serjant, aucht schillings a day; to every Scriver, capitane of armes, furier, and furer, everie on sex schillings aucht penneis a day; to everie corporell, fyve schillingis foure penneis a day; to everie drummer, fyve schillingis foure penneis a day: and according to this allowance yow shall caus these thay ar quartered with keip what they gett in accompt, quhairof the officiares must hawe a duble, and thair double most be subscrywit by the officiares, and thair double by yow or your clerk; and quhat salbe deburst for the said interteinement salbe allowed after compt in the first end of your contributioun: and so I rest your freind to power, *sic subscribitur*, ROBERT MONRO."—The accompt goeth on frome the 28th of May at night, and this warrand is to be keiped by the magistrattis of the toune.

17 June 1640.

The said day, Mr Mathew Lumisdane, baillie, wes chosin commissioner for this burghe to the Generall Convention of Burrowes, appointit to begin and howld at the burghe of Irving the sewint day of July nixt to come, with continewatioun of dayes; and ordaines ane commissioune to be gevin to him for that effect, vnder the tounes secrett seall, and subscriptioun of the magistrattes and clerk; and sielyik ordaines Thomas Buck, thesaurer, to deburse sex hundreth merkis to the said commissioner for payment of the tounes dewes at the said conventioun, and making his awin expenssis thairat, quhilk salbe allowit to the said thesaurar in his comptis.

Lumisdane chosin commissionar to the Generall Conventioun of Burrowes.

17 June 1640.

The quhilk day, the prowest, baillies, and counsall appointes measones and wrightis to be enterit presentlie to the wark of the Greyfrier kirk for prepairing convenient seattis within the same to the memberis of the Generall Assemblie indicted to hauld and begin at this burghe the twentie eight day of Julij nixt to come, and appointis George Anderson to attend the warkmen, and to assist George Mengzies, maister of wark till the perfyting thairof, and the expensses and chairges to be debursit be the said maister of wark thairupon, is ordanit to be allowit to him in his comptis.

The Grayfreir Kirk to be repared for the Generall Assemblie.

8 July 1640.

The quhilk day, in presens of the prowest, baillies, and Counsell of the burghe of Aberdeine, compeirit Mr Daniel Wedderburne, maister of the grammer schoole of the said burghe, who, eftir due consideratioun of his weaknes and inhabilitie of bodie to discharge the said functioune in suche exact and painfull maner as the exigence of that place requires, he being now past the age of thriescoir yeires, and having continewit fourtie yeires in the said service, with the applaus and acceptatioun of the

Dimissioun Wedderburne of his office of maister of the grammer schoole.

8 July 1640.

Dimissioun Wedderburne of his office of maister of the grammer schoole.

Counsell and toune, thairfoir the said Mr Dauid, voluntarlie of his awin consent, unsoacht or compellit, friclie dimittit, dischairged, renunced, and *simpliciter* owergawe, and be thir presentis willinglie, hartelie, and friclie dimittis, dischairges, renunces, and *simpliciter* owergiwes his said office and functioun of the maister of the grammer schoole of this burghe, with his yeirlie stipend due and payable to him for the same; and all benefitt he may ask or crawe be his said office in any tyme heirefter, in the hands of the prowest, baillies, and Councall of this burghe, as in the hands of his superioures, of whom he hauldis the said office, to the effect thay may dispose thairwpoun, and may chuis and admitt any other they think fitting to exercise the said functioun and chairge of maister of thair grammer schoole in tyme coming. Quhilk dimissioun the saids prowest, baillies, and Councell accepted and receaved; and thairon Patrik Leslie, prowest, for himselff, and in name of the prowest, baillies, and Councell, asked act and instrumentis. Lyikas the said Mr Dauid, in token of this his dimissioun, hes subscryvit the same with his hand.

M. DAVID WEDDERBURNE,
Sexagenarius et ultra.

15 July 1640.

Chalmer admittit maister of the grammer schoole.

15 *July* 1640.

The said day, the prowest, baillies, and Councell elected, nominat, and chused Mr Thomas Chalmer, sone lauchfull to umquhill Mr Thomas Chalmer, advocat in Aberdeine, to be maister of the grammer schooll of this burghe in place of Mr Dauid Wedderburne, last maister of the said schoole, who, in respect of his old age and debilitie of bodie, hes dimittit his place in the Councellis hands, to the effect thay might mak chuis of any thay thocht most fitting to fill the said vacant rowme. To the quhilk place the said Mr Thomas is admittit wpoun the conditionnes condiscendit on betwixt the Councell and him, specifeit and conteinit in the contract past betwixt thame thairanent, of the date of thir presentes, whairof the tenor followes:—

At Aberdeine, the fyfteine day of July, the yeire of God j^m sex hundreth and fourtie yeires,—It is appointed, contracted, and agriet betwixt Patrik Leslie, prowest of the burghe of Aberdeine, Maister Thomas Gray, Mr Mathew Lumisdane, Mr Robert Farquhar, and Mr Williame Moir, baillies of the said burghe, Alexander Jaffray, dean of gild, and Thomas Buck, thesaurar of the same burghe, for thame selffis and in name and behalff of the Councell and communitie of the said burghe, on the ane part, and Mr Thomas Chalmer, sone lauchfull to vmquhill Mr Thomas Chalmer, advocat in Aberdeine, on the other pairt, in substance and effect efter following,—That is to say, fforsameikill as Maister Dauid Wedderburne, late maister of the grammer schoole of the said burghe, he reasone of his great aige and inhabilitie of bodie, hes voluntarlie and frielie dimittit his said office in the handis of the saids prowest, baillies, and Councell, to the effect thay might mak chuse and nominatioun of any thay thoght most fitting to fill the said vacant rowme: and the saids prowest, baillies, and Councell having certaine knowledge and experience of the literature qualificatioun and gude conversatioun of the said Mr Thomas Chalmer, and of his habilitie and sufficiencie to dischairge and occupie the said plaice, and to performe all duetie incumbent thairto,—he having served as doctor in the said grammer schoole dyveris and sindrie yeires heirtofoir, have thairfore elected, nominat, and admitted, and by thir presentis electis, nominatis, and admittis the said Maister Thomas Chalmer to be maister of the grammer schoole of the said burghe of Aberdeine *ad vitam vel ad culpam*; quhilk fault, gif any shalbe committit be him worthie of deprivatioun, shalbe tryed and judged be the prowest, baillies, and Councell of the said burghe for the tyme, as onlie judges thairto. Lyik as the said Maister Thomas hes accepted, and be thir presents accepts, the said chairge and functioun in and wpoun him, and faithfullie promittis, bindis, and obleissis him to teache and instruct his schollares in the airt of grammer, gude letteris, and maneris, and to exercise doctrine and discipline as apperteins, conforme to the lawes of the said schoole alreddie sett doune and to be sett doune at any tyme heirefter, be the prowest, baillies, and Councell of the

15 July 1640.
Chalmer admittit maister of the grammer schoole.

Contract betwixt the toun and Mr Thomas Chalmer, maister of thair grammer schoole.

15 July 1640.
—
Contract betwixt the toun and Mr Thomas Chalmer, maister of thair grammer schoole.

said burghe for the tyme, and to observe and keip the saids lawes and injunctiounes strictlie and preceislie as thay ar sett doune, or salbe set doune heirefter, efter the forme and tenour thairof in all poyntes, and to find sufficient and qualifiet doctoures, ane or ma, vnder him to teache and examine his schollares, and to assist him both in doctrine and discipline, as the exigence of that service sall require: for the quhilkis caussis and dew performance thairof the saids prowest, baillies, and Counceell obleissis thame and thair successoures, prowest, baillies, and Counceell of the said burghe for the tyme, to content and pay to the said Mr Thomas Chalmer yeirelie, and ilk yeire during his continewance in the said office, the somme of two hundreth merkis vsuall Scottis money, to be payed to him be the tounes thesaurar at two vsuall termes of the yeire, Witsunday, and Martimes in wynter, be equall portiounes,—the first termes payment thairof begynnand at the feast of Martimes nixt to come of this instant yeire, j^m sex hundreth and fourtie yeires, and that by and attour his sallarie and schollage, to be payed to him quarterlie be his schollares eftir sic proportioun as wes in vse to be payed to the said Mr Daniel Wedderburne, viz., be ilk tounes bairne quarterlie, threttene shillingis foure penneis; be ilk landvart barne quarterlie, twentie sex schillingis aught penneis; be ilk tounes barne to the doctour sex schillings aught penneis, and be landvart barnes to the doctour, thretteine schillings foure penneis quarterlie. Quhilk stipend and salarie aboue writtin is heirby declaired to be in full contentatioun and satisfactioun of all farder stipend or salarie he may ask or craue at any tyme heirefter, except in so far as he may wponne just grounds procuire by his supplicatioune to the prowest, baillies, and Counsall of the said burghe for the tyme, renunceand be thir presentes all other judicatorie for craving any augmentatioun of stipend, or decyding in any questioun or controversie whatsoewer betwixt the toune and him, except allanerlie the said prowest, baillies, and Counceell for the tyme, all fraud and gyill seeludit. And for the more securitie, the saids pairties ar content and consentis that thir presentis be registrat in the buikes of Counceell or Burrow Court buikes of the said burghe, thairin to remaine *ad futuram rei memoriam*, and to have the strength of ane confessit act and judiciall decreit, that letteris and executoriellis of horning may be direct heirin vpoun a single chairge of ten dayes, and all other executoriellis necessar may be direct heirin in forme as effeiris, and to that effect constitutes . . . . thair lauchfull procuratores, *promittentes de rato* be thir presentis, written be Walter Robertson, clerk of the said burghe, and subscryvit be the saids pairties, day, moneth, yeire, and place foirsaidis, befoir thir witnesses,— Maister Alexander Jaffray, late prowest of Aberdeine; the said Walter Robertsoun, Mr George Robertsone, and Walter Guthrie, notaris publict. *Sic subscribitur*, Patrik Leslie, prowest; Mr T. Gray, baillie; Mr Robert Farquhar, baillie; Mr Willeame Moir, baillie; Al. Jaffray, dean of gild; Thomas Buck, thesaurer; Mr Tho. Chalmers. Mr Al. Jaffray, witnes; W. Robertsone, witnes; Mr George Robertson, witnes; Walter Guthrie, witnes.

Marginal: 15 July 1640. Contract betwixt the toun and Mr Thomas Chalmer, maister of thair grammer schoole.

15 *July* 1640.

The quhilk day the prowest, baillies, and councell tacking to thair consideratioun that Maister Dauid Wedderburne, late maister of the grammer schoole of this burghe, in regaird of his old aige and inhabilitie of bodie to serve in that functioun efter suche a laborious and toilsome maner as the exigence of that place doeth requyre, voluntarlie vpon the eight day of July instant, dimittet his said office in the councellis hands, to the effect they might make chuse and nominatioun of any other thay thocht most fitting to vndergo the chairge, and with all havand respect that he had served fourtie yeires in that statioun with commoun applaus both of the councell and communitie of this burghe, and lyikwayes be reasone he hes the burdine of a wyff and childreine; in these consideratiounes, the saids prowest, baillies, and councell gevis and grantis to the said Mr David ane pensioun of twa hundrethe merkis money yeirlie during all the dayes of his lyftyme, to be payed to him be the tounes thesaurer

Marginal: 15 July 1640. Pension to Wedderburne.

15 July 1640.
Pension to Wedderburne.

out of the tounes commoun gude at Martimes and Witsonday be equall portiounes, begynnand the first termes payment thairof at Martimes nixt to come in this instant yeire of God, j^m sex hundreth and fourtie yeires, and so furth termelie thaireftir duringe his lyftyme; with this alvayes conditioun, that when the conncell of this burghe for the tyme, sall find out ony vther meanes equivalent or more nor the pensioun abouewrittin, that the said Mr Dauid salbe lyable to dimitt the foirsaid pensioun, and to accept of the secund provisioun, and to undergo sic chairge thairfoir as the conncell of this burghe for the tyme shall injoyne him and that he is able to dischairge.

22 July 1640.
Leslie and Jaffray chosin commissionares to the Generall Assemblie.

22 July 1640.

The quhilk day Patrik Leslie, prowest, and Mr Alexander Jaffray, late prowest, wer chosine commissionares for this burghe to the Generall Assemblie, indicted to begine and hauld at this burghe the twentie aught day of July instant, with continewatioun of dayes, and ordaines ane commissioun to be gewin to thame for that effect, vnder the tounes secreitt seall and subscriptiones of the baillies and clerk.

Eodem die.
A guard at the Assemblie.

Eodem die.

The said day Patrik Moir wes appoynted to be keiper and distribnter of the partizeances to the nichtbonres of the toune quha ar appointed to be ane guard for attending the Generall Assemblie, for eschewing of disordour and confusionne thairin, throw throng and multitude of people that wald trubill and disquyet the commissionares and memberis of the Assemblie, if thay wer not hauldin out be a guard.

Eodem die.

22 July 1640.

Lumisdanes discharge of his commission at the Convention of Burrowes.

The samen day, in presens of the prowest, baillies, and counsell, compeirit Mr Mathow Lumisdane, baillie, commissioner chosin for this burghe to the Generall Conventioun of Burrowes of this kingdome, whilk began and held at the burghe of Iruing, wpoun the secund day of July instant, and made ample declarationn of the whole proceidingis at the said conventioun, and thairwith producit the agent of burrowes his discharge and acquittance gewin to this burghe wpoun the payment of thair whole dues quhilkis wer payable at the said conventioun—namelie, on the somme of twa hundreth thrie scoir thrie pundis money, as the said acquittance does testifie; inrespect quhairof the prowest, baillies, and counsell fund that the said Mr Mathew had acquytted himsellf duelie in his said commissioun, and exoneris him thairof.

Eodem die.   *Eodem die.*

Charge that nane of the inhabitantis remowe out of the toune.

The quhilk day, forsameikill as the Erle Marschall, who is appoynted by the Committie of Estate to wplift a regiment of men within the schirrefdome of Aberdeine for the publict service of the kingdome, hes chairgit the magistrattis of this burghe to furnishe out of oure toune ane of the companyes of the said regiment, and to hawe thame in redines to marche in all convenient diligence wpoun the nixt aduerteisment, with fourtie dayes lone: thairfoir the prowest, baillies, and counceill ordaines intimatioun to be made be oppin proclamatioun at the mercat croce of this burghe, as also throw the haill streittes of the toune be the drum, chairging all and sindrie inhabitantis of this burghe, alsweill frie as unfrie, maisteris, servantis, and prenteissis, that nane of thame remowe furth of this burghe without licience of the magistrattis, till the said companye of men be lifted for serving in the said Erll Marischallis regiment, vnder the paine of tinsell and loss of all friedome and libertie, thay or any of thame who salbe fugitive hawe, or may hawe, heireftir in this burghe; and

22 July
1640.

Charge that nane of the inhabitantis removve out of the toune.

siclyik chairgeing suche inhabitantis of this burghe, maisteris, servantis, and prenteissis as hawe alredie removed thamesellfis, and hawe beine fugitive out of the toune in prejudice of the publict service of the cuntrie, that thay returne bak againe within this burghe within fyfteine dayes nixt efter the chairge, vnder the paine aboue specifeit, quhilkis premisses wer accordinglie published and intimat both at the mercat croce, as lyikwayes be the drum throw the haill streittis of the toune.

Eodem die.

Eodem die.

Letteris to be direct to the moderatoris of Presbyteries for sending in vivares for the Generall Assemblie.

The samen day the prowest, baillies, and councell findis it expedient that letteris be writtin to the moderatores of Presbytries within this diocie, desyring thame to requyre thair brethreine of the ministrie to adverteis, and desyre thair parochineris to prouyd and send to this toune all kynd of vivares, sic as beiff, muttoun, lambis, foullis, eggis, butter, cheis, fishes, wyld meat, venisone, and sic wther prowisioun as the cuntrie can affoord, with grasse, corne, and stray for horsses, for serving of the nobillmen, gentrie, commissionares of burrowes, and ministeris that ar to be heir at the Generall Assemblie, to be hauldin in this burgh the twentie aucht day of July instant; and, forder, that thay desyir thair brethreine of the ministrie to intimat to thair parochineris, if any of the inhabitantis of this toune, maisteris, servantis, or prenteissis, be fugitive within thair boundis, that thay chairge thame to returne hither vnder the paine of tinsell of all friedome, and benefitt, and libertie thay hawe, or may hawe, heireftir in this burghe, and vnder all hyest paynes to be incurrit be thair ressettares and keipares preseryit be the Committee of Estate, and siclyik ordaines proclamatioun to be made of the premisses at the mercat croce of this burghe, and throw the haill streittis of the toune be the drum, quhilk wes accordinglie done.

3 *August* 1640.

The quhilk day the prowest, baillies, and counsell ordaines the Act made anent the reiding of the morning and evening prayeris in the Gray-freir Kirk of this burghe to be putt in executioun immediatlie eftir the dissolving of the present Generall Assemblie, in respect that the seattis buildit in the said kirk for accommodatioun of the Assemblie will serve convenientlie for the people resorting to the prayeris; and ordaines this present Act to be intimat out of pulpitt on Sonday nixt in both the kirkis of this burghe, and to begine and receawe executioun and be put in practise wponn the morne immediatelie thaireftir, conforme to the mynd and tenour of the said former Act of counsall, of the date the 14 of August 1633 yeires.

The prayers to be red in the Gray-frier Kirk.

3 *August* 1640.

Eodem die.

The said day, the prowest, baillies, and counsell being convenit in the tounes councel hous, for making nominatioun and electioun of ane minister to serve in this burghe in the vacant roume of doctor James Sibbald, ane of thair ministeris, who is deposed from his ministrie be this present generall assemblie now sitting in this burghe, for not subscryving the covenant, and for other causses mentioned in the proces of his deprivatioun; and efter mature advysement and deliberatioun taken be the saids prowest, baillies, and councell thairanent, thay in end condiscendit wponn a list of actuall ministeris for making of the said electioun, out of the quhilk list thay elected, nominat, and chuised Maister Androw Cant, minister at New-battle, to be ane of the ministeris of this burghe, actuallie to supplie and fill the vacant roume of the said doctour James Sibbald, the toune alvayes giveing thair consent and allowance thairwnto, ffor quhilk effect thay ar ordanit to be convenit this day be the drum in the new kirk immediatlie eftir the sermone, and the said electioun to be intimat to thame, and thay to be inquyred if any of thame hes ought to say againes the said Mr

Mr Andro Cant chosin ane of the Townes Ministers.

3 Aug.
1640.
———
Mr Andro
Cant
chosin ane
of the
Tounes
Ministers.

Andro, his doctrine, lyff, or conversatioun, or any other reasone to allege why he aucht not to be admittit and receaved in the said vacant roume of thair ministrie, that thaireftir the magistratts and councell may go on and proceid in the busienes as the exigence thairoff sall requyre . . . and the said toun being convenit, as said is, thay all in ane voice allowed of the said electioun of the said Mr Andro Cant to be thair minister . . .

12 Aug.
1640.
———
Jaffray
chosin
commis-
sionar to
the Com-
mittie of
Estate.

12 August 1640.

The quhilk day Mr Alexander Jaffray, late prowest, wes chosin commissioner for this burghe for keiping of the Committie of Estate at Edinburghe, conforme to the missive direct to this burghe for that effect fronne the Lordis of Committie, and instructiones ordanit to be gewin to the said commissionar for representing this burghes greivances to the said Committie of Estate, and the somme of twa hundreth merkis appointit to be gevin to him for making of his expenssis to ane compt, to be deburst be Thomas Buck thesaurar, quhilk salbe allowit to him in his comptis.

Eodem die.
———
A com-
pany of
soiouris to
be levied
to the Erll
Marishall
for the pub-
lict service
of the
cuntrie.

Eodem die.

The samen day, in presens of the prowest and baillies, the brethreine of gild being convenit in the Grayfreir Kirk be the drum, Patrik Leslie causit reid publictlie in thair audience ane peremptorie letter direct to the magistrattis and Councell of this burghe from the Erle Marishall, quhairof the tenour followes:—" To my lowing freinds the prowest, baillies, and toune counsell of Aberdeine.—Verie loving freinds, I thocht thair had beine no necessitie in putting yow in mynd to vplift that companye that comes frome your toune; bot since my brother schawes me that ye intend nothing bot delayes, I againe putt yow in mynd to hawe that companye compleit against Tuysday nixt at nicht at the farrest, for he most marche alonges with the rest on Thursday. And gif this be not done, ye will force me tak ane course with these oure tounes people as thay hawe not as yet fund the lyik. Bot hoiping ye will not putt me to that paines, I rest your loving freind, *sic subscribitur*, MARISCHALL. Dunoter, the 9 of August 1640."—Quhilk letter being opinlie red, the prowest schew to the brethreine of gild, convenit as said is, that as he had in July last impairted this busienes to the whole bodie of the toune, so now, in respect of this last and peremptorie chairge, he desyres that thay will tak the same to thair serious consideratioun, and resolve wpoun some solid course for leveing of the said companye tymouslie to the said Erll Marischall, lest throw longer delay his lordship tak a harder course with the toune thair-anent. And withall the prowest declairit that such of the inhabitantis as wold offer thameselffis frielie and willinglie to this service, that the toune sould defray thair chairges, and thay sould be frie of the taxatioun to be impoisit for recking turth of the companye. The brethreine of gild, so many as wer present, offered thameselffis willing for thair pairtis to contribute for leveing of the said companye of soiouris, according to thair awin proportioun, the craftis contributing lyikwayes for thair pairt what is due to thame in the lyik caise,—since everie ane of thame hes prenteissis or servantis who ar feucible persones and habile for service, and so may furnishe many ma men nor the brethreine of gild may do. After the quhilk answer, the magistratts went to the craftis hospitall, quhair thay wer convenit to the effect foirsaid be ordour and warrand from the magis-tratts, who having demandit what the craftis wold doe for obedience to the chairge foirsaid in furnishing ane companye of men to the said Erll Marischall, conforme to the warrand gewin to his Lordship from the Com-mittie of Estate, the craftis, in tokin of thair obedience and willingnes to the publict service of the countrie, gawe wp to the magistrattis a list of the names both of frie craftismen and prenteissis, sick as thay could spair or furnishe, quhilhis wer inrollit be the magistrattis, and assurance gewin be the decones of craftis that nane of thame sould be fugitive nor remowe out of the toune in prejudice of the said service.

12 Aug. 1640.

A company of soiouris to be levied to the Erll Marischall for the pub-lict service of the cuntrie.

19 August 1640.

19 Aug. 1640.

Thes that removed out of the Toun when the Tounes Company wes lacking wp to be depryvit of thair fredome.

The quhilk day the prowest, baillies, and Counceell ordaines sick burgessis of gild, frie craftismen, and prenteissis within this burghe as desertit and left the toune, and absentit thameselffis the tyme of the wptacking of the tounes companye for the bound rod, to be depryvit of thair fredome, conforme to the certificatioun gewin to thame be oppin proclamatioun at the mercat croce of this burghe, and be the drum throwe the haill streittis of the toune, that nane should hawe remowed out of the toune vnder the paine of deprivatioun and forfaiture of thair friedome and libertie: and the deane of gild is ordainit to cause execute the summoundis to the effect foirsaid againes the particular persones that absentit thameselffis, and to caus summond thame be oppin proclamatioun at the mercat croce of this burghe, wpoun fyfteine dayes warning.

Eodem die.

Eodem die.

Warrant to Mr Robert Farquhar for the moneyes advanceit be him for shoes and hardin to Monrees soiouris and for fourtie dayes Lone to the Townes Company.

The said day in presens of the prowest, baillies, and conneell, Mr Robert Farquhar, baillie, declaired that, conforme to thair ordour and directioun, he had deburst to Generall Maior Monro in the beginning of Junij last, for tuelff hundreth pair of shoes to his soiouris, sewin hundreth and twentie pundis. Item, for hardin to his soiouris sex hundrethe thriescoir sex pundis, thretteine schillingis, foure d. Item, for fourtie dayes lone to the sex scoir soiouris furneist out of this toune to the bound rod, vnder the conduct of Capitane Robert Keith, brother to the Erll Marishall, and delyvered all to the said capitane wpoun the aughteine day of August instant, as ane of the companyes of the said Erlis regiment, eight hundreth thriescoir nyne pundis: quhilkis debursementis the counsall acknowleges to be gewin be thair order, and thairfoir ordanes the same to be allowit to the said Mr Robert in the first end of the moneyes debtfull be him to the toune, whairanent thir presentis shalbe warrant, and dischairge to him *pro tanto*.

Eodem die.   19 Aug. 1640.

Memorandum.—Deburst be Alexander Jaffray, deane of gild, at command of the magistrattis and councell to Generall Maior Monro, for harden to his soiouris, tuentie foure pundis, nyne ss., by and attour the soume of ane thowsand merkis money, quhilk was deburst be Mr Robert Farquhar, baillie, to that vse, conforme to the act immediatlie preceiding.

9 September 1640.   9 Sept. 1640.

The quhilk day, forsameikill as wpoun petitioun putt wp be the burghe of Innernes to the burrowes in thair late Generall Convention, hauldin at the burghe of Irving, in the moneth of July last bypast, the burrowes wer pleased to appoint twa commissionares for Edinburghe, twa for Perth, twa for Dundie, twa for Aberdeine, and twa for Elgine, to meitt at Innernes the twentie twa day of September instant, for trying of the grounds and occasionne of the divisioun and distractioun that is fallin out amongst the inhabitantis of the said burghe of Invernes, concerning the electioun of thair magistrattis and councell, and suche wther particulares as ar mentioned in thair petitioun, and for setleing and pacefieing of the said distractiones, and making of ane perfyit reconciliatioun and agriement amongst thame; thairfoir the prowest, baillies, and councell for satisfactioun of the burghes pairt of the act and ordinance of burrowes sett doune anent the premisses, electit, nominat, and chuisit Johne Hay, late baillie, and Danid Aedye, commissionares for this burghe of Aberdeine, to keip the said meitting at Invernes, the foirsaid twentie twa day of Septr instant, with continewatioun of dayes, and thair to advyse, consult, resone, vote, conclude, and determine with the remanent Commissionares of the burrowes there to be convenit, wpoun suche materis as ar gevin thame in commissionum frome the said generall conventioun of Burrowes at Irving, for setling of the divisioun and distractioun that is fallen out within the said burghe of Invernes, and

Hay, Aidy chossin commissionares to Invernes.

9 Sept. 1640.
Hay, Aidy chossin commissionares to Invernes.

for setting doune a solid order and forme anent the electioun of thair magistrattes in all tyme coming for intertening of peace and vnitie amongst thame.

11 *September* 1640.

11 Sept. 1640.
Christen Brow convict.

The said day Christen Brow, in Sklaittie, convict and putt in amerciament of court for injuring Elspet Donaldsoun, spous to Andro Burnet, calling hir a lier in her throt, in the publict mercat, to forbear, and James Mathosoun become cationer for the said Elspet for payment of sic vnlaw as the counsell sall modefie. The vnlaw of the said Christen modefiet to ten merkis, provyding if sho satisfie the pairtie be craveing hir pardone in a fenceit court, the said Christen Brow to be free for payment of fyve merkis of the said vnlaw.

23 Sept. 1640.
Names of the provost, baillies, and counceell.

23 *September* 1640.

Folowes the names of the Provest, Baillies, and Counceell of the burgh of Aberdene, chosin vpon the tuentie third day of September 1640, for the yeir to come:—
Patrick Leslie, Provest.
Williame Forbes
Thomas Mortimer
Johne Leslie
Alexander Jaffray, Baillies.
Maister Alexander Jaffray, late Provest.
Doctor Patrick Dwn.
Robert Crukshank, Deane of Gild.
James Robertsoun, Thesaurar.
Williame Blakburne, Maister of the Kirk and brig warkis.
David Aidy. Patrick Duvie.
Walter Cochrane.
Thomas Gray, Maister of the Gild Brethrenes hospitale.
Alexander Ramsay, Maister of Impost.

Thomas Burnett, Maister of the Mortifeit moneyis.
Maister Alexander Gordon.
George Pyper, Wright
Thomas Clerk, Wobster.

23 *September* 1640.

The samen day the prowest, baillies, new and auld conncellis, with consent of the deacones of craftis, all personallie present at the electioun, appointis a watche of twelf persones to be keiped everie night, beginning at eight houres at evin till fywe houres in the morning, for keiping and watching of the wairdhous of this burghe, in respect of the insolence and miscareage of Johne Leithe of Harthill, and some other of the persones that ar presentlie lyand within the same. And the said watche to continew vnto the tyme a solid order be sett doune for the sure keiping of the said wairdhouse in tyme coming, and the haill inhabitantis of this burghe, both frie and vnfrie, ar ordanit to keip watche as thay salbe warnit to that effect be thameselffis in thair owin propper persones, or be a sufficient habill persone for thame, under the paine of ane vnlaw of twentie sex schillingis eight penneis, to be payed be ilk persone absent to the deane of gild for the publict use of the toun, and furnishing candill and other necessaris to the watche, by and attour the refounding of suche losses as the toune shall happin to incurr, in default of any that sall be absent fra the watche, being warnit thairto as said is.

3 *October* 1640.

The said day the Councell ordaines searche to be maid be the Baillies for sic rwnawayes as hes fled frome Capitane Robert Keythe's company, and thair maisteris and putteris out of these rwnawayes wha hes recept thame since thair away coming, to be made lyable to present thame befoir the magistrattis, and thay to tak notice of suche as may be convenientlie had within the toune for the publict service, with diligence.

7 October 1640.

Dr Wm. Guild chosen to be Principal of the King's College.

7 *October* 1640.

The samen day, in presens of the provest, baillies, and counceill, compeirit, Mr James Sandelandis, civilist; Mr Johne Lundy, humanist; Mr Robert Ogilvy, sub-principall; and Mr Alexander Gairdyne, ane of the regentis of the kingis college of Aberdeine: and declaired that doctour Willeame Guild, ane of our tounes ministeris, is chosin principall of thair college, and thairfoir desyired the magistrattis and counceill to give way to his transplantatioun, for the reasones following gevin in be thame in wreitt under thair hands, whairof the tenour followes—"Certaine resones represented be the memberis of the Universitie of Aberdeine to the provest baillies, and counsell of Aberdeine, quhairby the present necessitie of hawing Doctour Guild transplanted to the office of principalitie is declared.

"1. Becaus without ane present principall the whole estate and rentis of the college ar lyklie to be shaken louse; for the principall representing the dean, and the takes being sett for his lyftyme, quhairin the cheiff rent of the college consistis, neither the said takes nor anie other evidentis can be formallie passed without the said principall presentlie in office.

"2. The principall be oure fundatioun is admitter both of Bursares and regentis of philosophie; and now presentlie there are thrie bursares and on regent to be admitted, quhilk cannot be done without ane principall.

"3. The Kirk of Machar is destitute of ane minister, quhilk cannot be planted without the principall, he representing the deane, quho was both persone and minister of Machar. For these present necessities and many other urgent and grawe caussess, we intreat the provest, baillies, and counsall shall tak to heart the case of our universitie, and shall not shaw thameselffis opposeris or hinderares of the foirsaid transplantatioun, as we, the memberis of the Universitie shall evir be willing to assist and serve your wisdomes according to our strenth and power. Subscribit the sewint October 1640. *Sic subscribitur,* J. Sandilands, Civilist; M. Jo.

Lunde, humanist; M. Ro. Ogilvie, sub-principall; M. A. Gairdyne, regent." Quhilkis resones being red, hard, and considderit be the saidis provest, baillies, and counsell, and thay thairwith being at lenth advysit, and being unwilling for the causses aboue writtin, and for sindrie other respectis moving thame, to enter in contestatioun with the said Universitie or yit with the said doctour Guild, ther pastor, for opposing his transplantatioun; and finding him inclyned to remowe, they thairfoir gave way to his transplantatioun, and consentis thairwnto, with this alvays conditioun, that the said doctour Guild remane in this burghe, and exercise his functioun of the ministrie within the same till Witsonday nixt, quhilk he promeist to do, als cairfullie and painfullie as possiblie he culd. Lyikas the Counsall ordaines to intimat to the toune the said doctour Guild his transplantatioun, to the effect be thair advyse ane other minister may be chosin to supplie his roume.

7 October 1640.

Dr Wm. Guild chosen to be Principall of the King's College.

14 October 1640.

The quhilk day the Prowest, Ballies, and Counsall, at the desyre of Doctour Willeame Guild, now primar of the Kingis College of Aberdeine, condescendis and agries to len him the bell of the grammer schuill of this burghe, for the vse of the said college wpoun his tiequett, to be givin for redelywerie of the same back againe, betuixt and Lambes nixt to come, to be thane puttt wp againe in its awin houssing, wpon the said Doctour Guild his chairges.

14 October 1640.

The bell of the grammer schoole lent to Doctour Guild.

22 October 1640.

The quhilk day it wes exponit be Patrick Leslie, provest, to the nightboures of the toune, convenit in the tolbuith be the drum, that the Lord Sincler come yesterday to this burghe, who shew that his regiment of souldieris wer approching to this toune, quhairof fywe hundreth wer to come in this day, and thairfoir desyired that thay might hawe quarteris within oure towne for thair awin payment; and for oure townes better

22 October 1640.

The toun and the Lord Sinclare anent the quartering of his soiours.

22 October 1640.	
The toun and the Lord Sinclare anent the quartering of his soiours.	

assurance thairanent, Mr Robert Farquhar, commissar, wold take vpoun him to pay the nichtboures of thair quartering moneyes, anes ilk week. Lyikas the said Mr Robert being personallie present, declaired opinlie in face of court that he had resawed from the said noble Lord thrie thowsand merkis money, to be debust be him, for intertinement of his soiouris so long as the said somme might last, quhilk he accordingly promeist to pay ilk fridday, to the inhabitantis of this burghe vpoun quhome the saids soiouris sould be quartered, conforme to the ordinarie allowance formerlie bestowed wpon soiouris be Generale Maior Monro, at his late being in this burghe, and quhan the said thrie thowsand merkis salbe spent, the said Mr Robert Furquhar promeist to do his best to prowyd for thame thairefter, as he sould resawe ordar and warrand for that effect. And thairfoir the said Patrik Leslie, pronest, inquyrit of the nightboures, convenit as said is, quhat answer thay wald giwe to the said Lord Sineler, to his desyre aboue specifeit: quha all in ane voice, be resone of the said Mr Robert Farquhar his promise of payment to thame of thair quartering moneyes, so far as the said thrie thowsand merkis might extend to, and of his promeise lyikwayes to wse his moyan and diligence for thair payment thairefter, were content and consentit to accept and resawe the said regiment of soiouris and thair commanderis, and to giwe thame quarteris within thair houssis, wpoune the conditiounes aboue mentioned, payed be the said Generall Maior Monro for his soiouris.

23 October 1640.	
George Ross convict.	

23 October 1640.

The same day, in presence of Mr Alexander Jaffray, baillie; George Ross, hors-hyrer, convict for drawing a durk and persewing Johne Dempster, fleshour, this day, and stricking at him thairwith, throw the juip; James Forbes, fleshour, become cautioner for the said George to pay sic vulaw for the said riot as the counsall sall modefie, and the said George became actit to releiwe his said cationer, and Alexander Clerk, webster, became actit cationer and law-burrowes for the saidis Johne Dempster

and George Ross, that ather of them sall be frie of the vther be way of
dead, in tyme cuming, vnder the paine of ane hundredth pundis, and they
become actit to relieve their said cationer. The vnlaw of the said George
Ross modefeit to aucht merkis, to be payed to the deane of gild, and to
be committit to waird till the same be payit, and thaireftir to crave the
pairtie pardon in fenced court.

23 October 1640.

George Ross convict.

28 October 1640.

The said day Mr Willeame Moir, late baillie, was chosin commissionar
to the Committie of Estate at Edinburghe, as he that was nominate
Commissioner for this burghe be the said Committie, with Mr Alexander Jaffray, late prowest, quho is latelie returnit frome Edinburghe,
and whose absence is to be supplict be the said Mr Willeame Moir, whome
they appoint to represent oure Tounes greivances to the said Committe,
by the lying of tuo Regimentis of souldiouris in this Toune, towitt the
Lord Sinclair and Maister of Forbes regimentis, and to petitioun that the
Toune may be fred of thame both, at the least of ane of thame, for the
reasones to be sett donne in the Instructiounes to be giwin to the said
Commissioner: and sielyik giwes him commissioun to deall with Mr Andro
Cant, minister at Newbotle, for his repairing hither with all convenient
diligence, for accepting wpoun him the functioun of ane of the ministeris
of this toune, conforme to the act of the late generall assemblie, and
ordaines the soume of ane hundreth merkis to be gewin to the said Mr
Willeame for macking his expenssis, to ane compt to be payed be Robert
Cruickshank, deane of gild, quhilk sall be allowit to him in his comptis.

28 October 1640.

Moir chosin commissioner to the Committie of Estate.

11 *November* 1610.

11 Nov. 1610.

Patrick Leslie chosin commissionar to the Parliament and to a meitting of the burrowis.

The quhilk day, anent the missive direct frome the Prowest, Baillies, and Conncell of the Burghe of Edinburghe to the Prowest, Baillies, and Conncell of this burghe, for keiping of the parliament appointed to sitt donne the nyntene day of November instant, and also for keiping a meitting of the burrowes, the sexteine day of the said moneth, immediatlie befoir the donnsitting of the parliament; off the quhilk missive the tennour followes:—"Richt honorable and loving freinds and nichtbouris, Whairas the commissioneris of the burrowis of this kingdome, laitlie convenit at Irwing, hes appointed ane meitting of the whole burrowes, to be at this our burgh of Edinburghe, the sexteine of November nixt, with continewatioun of dayes, immediatlie befoir the donnesitting of the parliament; theise ar thairfor according to thair directioun to requyre yow to send your commissioneris sufficientlie instructed, not onlie for keiping of the said conventioun, appointed to be wpoun the said sexteine of November nixt, bot also for keiping the dyet of parliament, and that suche as yow shall send to the said parliament be men favouring and practised in the effaires of their estate, and of thair degrie, and rank, and merchand trafficquer, beiring burdine, and indwellar within your burghe, and who may tyne and win in the caus of the burrowes, and in the particular of youre burghe, for whome youre burghe will be answerable, and who will abyid consteintlie at all suche conclusiones as sall be maid be the most pairt of the burrowes, and that you conteine bot on persoun in your commissioun to the parliament, without prejudice to you to direct moe if you pleas, as assessouris, of the qualitie abowewrittin, to hawe voice in absence of your commissioner. The whiche particular aboue writtin, we requyre yow to keip and observe vnder the generall paines contenit in the actis of borrowes maid thairanent. As also that yow send your commissioneris sufficientlie instructed for staying of friemen from being pertineris with vnfriemen and vnfrie skipperis. Item, for stopping of casting out of ballast abowe the Queensferrie. Item, anent the explaining and enlairging of the jurisdictioun gewin to the conventioune of burrowes. Item, anent the procuring of letteris for causinge of vnfriemen to find catioun not to vsurp the liberties of the borrowes vnder ane liquidat pecuniall penaltie. Item, for dischairging the lait augmentatioune of the customes and lait impost wpoun the tune of wyne, or rectificing the present book of raittes, conforme to the 17 act of the said last generall conventioune. Item, that yow send with your commissioneres ane perfyt compt of the impost layed wpoun all goodes transported or imported to or frome your port to or frome the provinces of Pichardie and Normandie, with payment thairof frome the first of July 1638 to the first of July last, to the effect the saidis compts may be fitted be the commissionares, thair to be convenit, conforme to the 32 act of the said late generall conventioune. Anent all and whiche particulares aboue writtin we expect your commissionares sufficientlie instructed, as you tender the weilfair of the burrowes, and vnder the paine of tuentie pundis, and thus committing you to the protectione of Almightie God, we take our leive, and restis youre loving freindis and nichtbouris. The prowest, baillies, and councell of Edinburgh, subseryving be Mr Alexander Guthrie, our common clerk, at our command. *Sic subscribitur*, A. Guthrie, Edinburghe, this 2 of September 1640. Item, to send with your commissioner your pairt of the somme of ane thowsand pundis, grantit to the burghe of Kirkendbricht, to be payed to the agent, conforme to the 31 act of the said last generall conventioun." Quhilk letteris direct wpoun the back—"To the richt honorabill our loving freindis and nichtbouris, the prowest baillies and counsall of the burghe of Aberdeine, these." Efter reiding of the quhilk missive, and for satisfactioun of the desyre thairof, the magistrattes and counsall nominat and chuisit Patrick Leslie, prowest, commissioner for this burghe, for keiping the dyett, foirsaid, of the parliament, as lyikwayes the said meitting of the burrowes, and siclyik nominattis and appointis Mr Willeame Moir, who is presentlie at Edinburghe, commissioner for this burghe at the committie of estate, to be assessour to the said Patrick Leslie, prowest, both at the parliament and meitting of the

11 Nov. 1640.

Patrick Leslie chosin commissionar to the Parliament and to a meitting of the burrowis.

11 Nov.
1640.
—
Patrick
Leslie
chosin
commis-
sionar to
the Parlia-
ment and
to a meit-
ing of the
burrowis.

burrowes, and to voice for him in his absense, and instructiounes appointit to be gevin to thame anent the tounes greivances, be the lying heir of two regimentis of souldioures, and anent suche wther particulares as salbe thought convenient to giwe tham in commissioun concerning this burghe; and ordaines commissiounes to be giwin to tham under the tounes seerettes seall; and the subscriptiounes of the magistrattis and clerk, both for the parliament and meitting of the burrowes, and appointis the soume of thrie hundreth merkis to be gewin to the said Patrik Leslie, proveist, to ane compt for macking of his expenssis in the saids commissiounes, to be payit to him as followes: towitt, twa hundreth merkis be James Robertsoun, thesaurer, and ane hundreth merkis be Robert Cruikshank, dean of gild, quhilk salbe allowit to thame in thair comptis.

18 Nov.
1640.
Act of the
committie
of estates
of Parlia-
ment anent
the pryces
of shoues,
bootes,
hyddis, and
tanning of
leather.

18 November 1640.

The act of the committee of the estates of parliament set doune anent the pryces of shoes, boots, hydis, and tanning of leather, quhilk is ordanit to be proclaimit at the mercat croce of this burghe, and to be registrat in the tounes counsell booke, thairin to remaine *ad futuram rei memoriam*, and to the effect the samen may be put in executioune within this burghe friedome and jurisdictioun thairof eftir the forme and tennour of the samen in all pointes vnder the peines thairincontenit: of the whilk act the tennour followes:—

"At Edinburghe the tvantie sex day of November, j^m vi^c fourtie yeares, the committee of the estates of parliament with advyse of the nobilitie, commissionares of the sheyres and burrowes convenit for the tyme, haveing appointit ane number of eache estait to setle the pryces of the shoes, bootis, hydis, and tanning of leather, whilkis personis, after full deliberatioun thairanent, resoluit and concludit wpoun thais articles wnderwrittin, whiche thay presentit and producit in presence of the said committee of estaites, nobilitie, and commissionares foirsaid, and after the samen articles war red and considerit in thair whole presence, and they all in one woice ratifiet and approveit the samen as they ar heireftir set donne; of the whilkis articles the tennour followis:—

18 Nov. 1640.

Act of the committee of estate of Parliament anent the pryces of schoone, bootes, hydis, an tanning of leather.

Thais on the committee appointit for setling some course to the cordineris, hes, efter deliberatioun, considderit that, inrespect of the pryceis of the roughe hydis ar almost at the samen rate sold for the present that they war sold this tyme tuelff month, hath thairfoir thocht expedient that the pryceis of the roughe hydis may be ordanit to be sold in maner following, viz.:—

That the best ox hyid be sold for eight merkis, and inferiour sortis of oxen hydis for fyve pund, seven merkis, and four pund, and so furthe according to thair worthe, being rouche hydis.

Item, the best kyne hydis being rouche, be sauld for four lib., and the inferiour sortis for fyve merkis, thrie pund, and four merkis, and so furthe according to thair worthe.

Item, that thair be allowit for tanning of the best ox hyid for materiallis, paines, and gaines, fiftie shilingis, and for the second sortis of ox hyidis and kyne hydis, ane heid, fourtie s.; and for sur performance heirof, it is ordanit that the magistrattis of each burghe and justices of peace in landward, sall have power to caus mak oppin the bark pottis for wisiting the leather, and for urging the tanneris to sell the samen at the pryceis foirsaids, at the discretioun of the magistratis and justices of peace, conforme to the ordour befoir preseryvit of the rouche hydidis: and the contraveiner, in refusing to sell the rouche hyds at the pryces foirsaidis, to pay fourtie shilingis for ilk hyd, and the tanner whae refuissis, to pay thrie pund for ilk hyd, by and attour the fulfiling of the act, and the penaltie to be devydit as followeth, the ane halff to the delaiter, and the wther halff to the magistratis or justices of peace, for the vse of the publict.

And siclyik ordaines that the cordineris sell the shoes and bootis as follows, viz.:—

The inshe of thrie soillit shoes of the best leather, to be sold at twa shilingis twa penneis the inshe.

18 Nov.
1640.

Act of the committie of estates of Parliament anent the pryces of schooes, boottes, hyddis, and tanning of leather.

Item, the secund sort of thrie soillit shoes to be sold at tuantie penneis the inshe.

Item, the inshe of singill soillit shoes of the best sort, at sexteine penneis the inshe.

Item, the secund sort of single solit shoes at fourtein penneis the inshe.

Item, the inshe of bairnis shoes double sollit, of the best sort, at sextenne penneis.

Item, the secund of slichter leather, double sollit, at fourteine penneis.

Item of singill soillit of aucht inshis and wndir, at twelff penneis the inshe.

Item, that wemens shoes, timber heilit, of the best sort, be sold at tuantie sex penneis the inshe.

Item, the secund sort timber heilit shoes, at tuantie penneis the inshe.

And anent the prycis of bootis, it is ordanit that thair be allowit of the best leather for each insh of the length of the foote of bootis, the quadruple of the prycis of the inshes of the best sort of shoes, being tuantie sex penneis for eache inshe thairof, the topis being large, and of the best leather.

Item, that the secund sort of leather maid in bootis, that the inshe of the length of the foote thairof, be sold at the quadruple pryce of the shoes maid of the secund leather as is befoir preseryvit, extending the pryces of the said shoes of that sort to tuantie penneis the inshe, the topis thairof being also lairge.

And the said committee of estates, with consent foirsaid for sindrie canssis and consideratiounes, hane thought fit for the bruche of Edinburghe, that the cordonaris within the said burghe sall have for eache inshe of shoes of the best sort of leather thritie penneis, and for the secund sort of leather, tua shilingis for the inshe, and so furthe according to the lyik proportioun in singill solit and wemenis shoes; as also thay sall have the quadruple of the pryce of the inshe of the best leather of shoone for the inshe of the best leather of bootis, and siclyik of the second sort, according to the samen proportioun of the second sort of shoes. And the penalties againes refuisaris to sell at the pryceis foirsaidis, and the fynis of not sufficient gear, to be confiscat, the ane halff to appertaine to the delaiter, and the wther half to the Judge for the wse of the publict, and who refuissis to work and leaveth of, to pay fourtie pundis, by and attour punishement to be inflictit on thair personis, *toties quoties*, as thay salbe chalengit and fund guiltie, and thair penalties to be imployit in maner befoir preseryvit, and thaise of the poorer sort to be punishit at the discretioun of the Judge.

margin: 1st Nov. 1640. Act of the committe of estates of Parliament anent the pryces, houttes, byddis, and taming of leather.

2 December 1640.

The said day the magistratis and counsell, inrespect of the lewd vitious and scandalus lyf and conversatioun of Patrik Stewart, ane of the beddellis in the gild bretherenes hospitall, quho hes fallin in the sin of adultrie with Margaret Shirres, spous to Williame Scott, mariner, confest be thame both in the presence of the kirk session, have thairfoir depryvit and be thir presentis depryvis the said Patrik Stewart of his place in the said hospitall, and of all benefitt thairof in tyme coming, and declairis him to be incapable of the said place in any tyme heirafter; and farder, ordaines him to be presentlie tackin furth of ward out of the Tolbuith of this burghe, and had to the mercat croce, and thair be oppin proclamatioun the caus of his deprivatioun to be publictlie intimat, and his goune to be instantlie takin from him and pullit ower his heid at the mercat croce, and to be banc[i]st the toune as ane vnvorthie member to abyd in the samen; lyikas publict intimatioun was maid at the said mercat croce, that whosoeuir sould resave him in thair hous, or giue him any ludging frome this day furthe, they sould pay the unlaw of ten pundis to the deane of gild unforgivin, to the tounes wse, and be lyable to farder censur as the magistratis and counsell sall find the circumstances of thair fault to deserve.

margin: 2 Dec. 1640. Patrick Stewart depryved of his place in the Gild Bretherenes Hospitall.

16 December 1640.

16 Dec. 1640.
Yoole vacance dischairgit.

The qubilk day, the magistratis and counsall, all in ane woice, dischargis the masteris of all the scollis within this burghe frome keiping of anie yule wacance, or giving thair scollaris any tyme to play, except wpoun the ordinar play dayis; and for reformeing of the bygaine abuses, ordaines the saidis masteris to attend thair charge, both in teacheing and examining of thair scollaris as at wther ordinar tymis in the yeir, inrespect of the act of parliament dischargeing all suche waccance; and in place of the said yule wacance, the counsall grantis to the scolleris thrie dayis play at the begining of ewerie quarter, whilk was intimat to the masteris personnallie present.

23 December 1640.

23 Dec. 1640.
Leslye his discharge of his commission at the Parliament and meitting of the burrowis.

The said day, Patrick Leslie, prowest, compeir and in presens of the counsall, whae, being commissioner direct frome the burghe to the late meiting of parliament and conventioun of burrowes, hauldin at Edinburghe in November last, maid ane ample declarationn of suche matteris as wer treatit of and handlit, both at the parliament and burrowis. Lyikas the said Patrick produceit ane letter frome the Committie of Estates to the counsell of this burghe, with ane act of the said committie, and the actis of burrowis anent the soume of ane hundrethe and feftie thowsand gilderis, appointit to be lent and advanceit be the whole burrowis of this kingdome, for the wse of the publict. In respect of the whilk report, the counsell findis that the said Patrick hes dewlie acquytit himselff in his commissionn, and thairfoir discharges him of the samen for ewer.

6 *January* 1641.

6 Jan. 1641. Iniunctions to the kirk sacristar.

Followis the iniunctionis maid and set donne be the provest, bailyies, and counsell of this burghe, to be keipit and observeit be the Sacrister or kirk warden tharof, in all tyme cuming.

Imprimis, it is ordanit that the Sacrister be present himselff at all sermonis and commone prayeris, evening and morning, and sall wear his goune, with ane staff in the kirk for choping of sleiperis, as also for removeing of meane men and boyis whae occupeis honest men's daskis, and will nather remove nor mak rowme to men of better qualitie and strangeris, and for that effect to goe frome kirk to kirk in tyme of sermone.

Item, for preserveing the windowis unbrokin, aither himselff or his servandis, ane of thame at least salbe continowallie present in the kirk frome the oppening of the duris in the morning till they be shut at nicht; and if it sould happin that any of the windowis sal be brok in the nicht, in that cais, whane they come to oppin the duris in the morning thay sall weire all the windowis, and if they find any brokin, they sall intimat the samen to the master of kirk wark, for cleiring thameselffis thairof, wtherwayes they sall mak report of the brakeris thairof, or else pay the skaith thameselffis. They sall keip preceislie the magistratis dask fast shut, till the magistratis come thameselffis, and not oppin the samen to any of what qualitie soever they be, till the magistratis come to the kirk; and incais any sould tak exceptioun againes the sacraster thairfoir, in that cais he sall declair he hes no key, bot that officiaris whae attendis the saidis magistratis hes that key. He sall command his servandis everie Saterday at night to watter and sneap the flooris of the kirkis, and dicht ewerie dask, least honest men sould spoyle thair clothis and hattis thairon.

In respect that the steippill getis great skaith throwe slouth in leaveing oppin the doris and windowis thairof night and day, the great windis blowing throw within the steippill, and the raine roting the timber thairof, thairfoir it is ordainit that all the doris and windowis, heighe and lauche, be ewer fast, bot whane the bellis ar in ringing, and thairafter

6 Jan. 1641.
Injunctions to the kirk sacristar.

the laiche windowis to be fastenit everie night, and especiallie in winter, for eschewing the great skaithe that may occur thairthrow. For observeing the preceis tyme of ringing on the bellis of the Sabbothe day, it is ordanit that the kirk bellis be rung as followis—viz., the first bell at halffayne, the secund at nyne, and the third at halff ten houris; and on the weik dayis—the first bell to ring at halff sevin preceislie, the secund at sevin, and the third bell at halff hour to aucht in the morning, and the bellis to ring ane quarter of ane hour at ilk tyme, and for the prayeris the bell to begin at halff hour to sevin in the morning, and to ring to sevin houris; and at nicht to begin at halff hour to fyve, and to ring till fyve houris compleit; and in the winter seasone, the candlis to be all lichtit and set in order befoir the bell be halff endit; and for observeing dew tyme in oppening of the kirk doris, it is statut and ordanit that the kirk doris betwixt the first of November and the last of February salbe oppenit no sooner nor fyve houris in the morning. Twa candlis thane to be lichtit, and shut at halff sevin at night, twa candlis still burning; and all the rest of the yeir, the doris to be oppenit preceislie at four houris in the morning, and shut at nyne houris at nicht; the sacrister himselff, or ane of his servandis, being ewer present, as also that thay hawe ane cair of keiping the kirk yeardis frome horssis and wther bestiall cuming thairin, and frome drying any kynd of clothis thairin, or webis; and that they suffer not the scollaris nor wtheris thairin at any pastim, nor to cast stanes on the kirk, whilk hes bein oftymis sufferit in thair default, they not being present. Item, that the sacrister, nor neane of his servandis lay tapestrie befoir none, except suche as thair qualitie deservis the samen, and that to be done be advyse of some of the magistratis or master of kirk wark.

Item, that he suffer none to goe or walk in the croce kirk in tyme of sermone heirafter.

Whilkis injunctionis aboue writin war instantlie intimat to Thomas Cowie, present sacrister, wha was chargit to performe and obey the samen in all pointis.

17 *February* 1641.

The samen day, it is ordainit be the provest, bailzeis, and Counsell, that if any nighboure or inhabitant within this brughe salbe fund to grind any of thair cornis at outlandis milnis, whilk tholis fyre and watter within the toune, the persoun contraveining in this kynd sall not only be lyable in payment of double multur to the taikisman of the tounes milnis for thair abstractit cornis, bot also salbe unlawit in thretein shilingis foure penneis, to be payit to the deane of gild, for ilk boll of thair cornis abstractit be thame, *toties quoties*, for the publict wse and benefit of the toune; whilk act was intimat to the whole toune, conveinit in the tolbuith wpoun the fyft day of Marche 1641, to the effect nane sould pretend ignorance.

Act aganes abstracteris of thair cornes from the tounes mylnes.

17 *March* 1641.

The said day, Peter Hay, James Morgan, his servand, and Andro Mowat, pickiemen at the townes commone milnes, in presens of the provest, baillzeis, and Counsell, was convict and put in amerciement of court for exacting of ane goupin out of ewerie seckfull of malt grund at the saidis mylnes mor nor the dew multur and knauship allotit to the tackisman and his servandis for thair service, and in particular for deteaning within the saidis milnes of the malt belonging to James Crystie, tailzeoir, and Wm. Patirsoun, maltman, till they sould be answerit of the said exactioun mor nor the dew multur and knauship.

Hay and his servantis pickiemen at the tounes mylnes convict.

Eodem die.

17 March 1641.

Ordinance of counsell aganes servandis gewares of any more na or the dew multur and knaveschip for grinding of thair masteris malt and aganes pickmen exacteris of more nor thair due.

The samen day, fforsameikile as the proues, bailzeis, and Counsall, considering the great abuss cropin in of lait within this brughe betwixt honest menis servandis within the samen and the pickiemen at the tounes commone milnis, in the giveing and exacting of more nor the dew multur and knaueship for the malt grund at the saidis milnis, be thair masteris knoweledge or allowance, to thair great prejudice: Thairfoir, and for eschewing of the lyik deceait and fraudfull dealling in tyme coming, the saidis prouest, bailzeis, and counsall ordaines intimatioun to be maid be the drume throw the haill streites of the toune, That nae servand grinding malt at any of the tounes milnis sall pay moir nor the dew multur and knaneship for thair masteris or mestressis malt, conforme to the measure appointit be the Counsell for that effect; and if any servand contravein and transgres this present ordinance, be giveing of ane gowpin or any wther quantitie of malt mor nor the dew multur according to the measure foirsaid, or if any pickiemen or thair servandis at the saidis milnis sallbe fund guiltie of resaveing or exacting of any farder nor thair just dew, the servandis haveand the chairge of the malt sallbe accomptit as stealleris of thair masteris guidis, and the pickiemen or wther servandis about the milne as receptaris of stollen malt, and sallbe punishit accordinglie be scurging and banishment, or vthervayis at the arbitriement of the magistratis.

19 *March* 1641.

19 March 1641.

Vulgine and Bellie convict.

The said day, Helene Vulgine and Margaret Bellie was conviet and put in amerciement of court for injuring and stricking mutuallie ilkane of thame the wther, and serating and ryveing of wtheris faces to the effusioun of other of thair blodis. Alexander Findlater. litster, cautionar for the said Helene Vilgine, and Wm. Gray, wricht, cautioun for the said Margaret Bellie, for payment of sic vnlaw as the Counsell sall modifie for thair saidis convictionis.

25 *March* 1641.

The quhilk day the provest, bailzies, and Counsell, considdering that the commissionaris whae wer appointit be the late Generall Assemblie to meit at this brughe the twantie fourt day of Marche instant for planting of the wacand placis of the ministrie within the samen, hes refusit to grant warrand for transplanting to the ministrie within this brughe of Master Johne Annand, minister at Inuerness, of whome the Counsell, with consent of the haill toune maid electioun, and that in respect the said Master Johne was bot laitlie transplantit be the said Assemblie frome the kirk of Kynnoir to the said toune of Inuerness, whair he is scarcelie weill setlit as yit: Thairfoir the saidis provest, bailzies, and Counsell, being carefull to have the wacancie of thair pulpittis supplied be ane wther qualifeit and habill persone, hes electit, nominat, and choisin, and . . . . . with consent of the whole toune convenit in the tolbuithe electis, nominatis, and chuisses Mr George Gilespie, minister at the kirk of Weymes, to be ane of the actuall ministeris of the said brughe, as ane man fit and habill for the place. Whilk being remonstrat to the saids commissionaris, they ordainit the said Mr George Gilespie to be transplantit frome his present charge at the kirk of Weymes to the ministrie of this brughe. . . .

25 March 1641.

Electioun of Mr George Gilespie minister.

31 *March* 1641.

The quhilk day, efter sermone made be Doctor Williame Guild in the auld kirk of this brughe, Master Andro Cant, whae by the Act of the late Generall Assemblie was ordainit to be transplantit frome Newbottell to Aberdein, was publictlie and solemnlie resaveit ane of the actuall ministeris of this brughe, with commone applaus of the haill congregatioun conveinit for the tyme, and in presence of the bretherene of the presbitrie of Aberdein, whae instantlie gave him the hand of fellowship.

31 March 1641.

Mr Andro Cant resavit as ane of the ministers.

7 April 1641.

Deane of Gild, calsie-macker.

7 *April* 1641.

The said day, the provest, bailzeis, and Counsell ordaines Robert Cruikshank, deane of gild, to enter Andro Rob, calsie maker, to wark with all convenient dilligence for calsaying of that pairt of the kingis streit forgaines the mid milne in the Greine, and the calsay passand frome the Braidget by Patrik Walkaris hous to the tolbuith, and the gutter to be laid with flag stanes.

28 April 1641.

Ratification of the Act maid anent the entrie of tenentis to Tempill Landis and Abbottis Landis.

28 *April* 1641.

The said day, the provest, bailzeis, and Counsell ratifies and approvis the act of Counsell of the dait the tuantie sevint day of July j^m vi^c thretie nyne yeiris, maid be thair predecessoris anent the entrie of tenentis to temple landis and abbottis landis within this brughe, whairby it is ordanit that ilk intrant tenent, as assigney, sall pay ane yeares dewtie of the land whairwnto thay entir to the tounes thesaurer for the benefit of the commoun guid, and ane air to pay onlie the double of the fewdewtie conteanit in the predicessoris infeftment; and that the sone or dochter of the heretour of any of thaise landis entering thairto be dispositioun of thair parentis, sall pay onlie for thair entrie as ane air, and no farder to be exactit of thame, for the samen; and ane clause to be insert in ewerie infeftment and saising to be givin of the saidis landis of the tenour above writin. Lyikas instantlie the saidis provest, bailzeis, and counsell ordaines saisiu to be givin to Patrik Gordon, litster, of the foirland and warkhous of the tenement in the Netherkirkget, conforme to the dispositioun thairof maid to him be Johne Forbes, sone to umquhile Johne Forbes, for the compositioun of fourtie merkis, to be payit to the tounes thesaurer; and ane wther saising of the inland and yeard of the said tennement, to be givin to Michaell Findlater merchand, for the compositioun of wther fourtie merkis of entres siluer, in consideratioun that the said haill tenement is become ruinous and likelie to decay.

4 *May* 1641.

Helen Sherar, conviet of her awin confessioun for casting a cvp and ane trien muskkin stoup at Margrat Burnett, and hitting of hir thairwith, to the effusion of hir blood, to firbear; and the said Margrat wes conviet for putting hands on the said Helene, and for preassing to tak the said Helenes bairne from hir, for the quhilkis injuries they both were ordanit to be jogget, or than to redeim thameselffes thairfra as followes, viz.—the said Helene be payment of fourtie ss. of wnlaw to the deane of gild, and the said Margrat be peyment of twa merkis money.

7 *May* 1641.

The whilk day, the whole toune being warnit to this day be the hand bell, and conveinand for the maist pairt within the tolbuith, it was exponit to thame be Patrick Leslie prowest, that the magistratis and counsell, considdering the great abuse committit be dyuerse inhabitantis of this brughe in persewing maliciouslie thair nighbours befoir the commissar and schirreff in actiouns whairunto the prouest and baillies ar competent judgis, and thairby not onlie draveing thameselffis and thair pairties to extraordinarie paines and charges, bot also disclameing their ordinar judicatorie and neglecting their dew respect to the toune and liberties thairof, had inactit and ordanit, conforme to dyverse auld statutis and ordinances maid be thair predicessoris, magistratis and counsell, of this brughe abefoir, that it sall naewayis be lesume to any nighbour nor inhabitant within the samen to persew ane wther befoir the schirreff or commissar, in actiouns whairwnto the prouest and baillies of the said brughe ar judgis competent, bot that all sick actions sallbe persewit befoir the saidis magistratis in tyme comeing, under the paine of ten pundis of unlaw, to be exactit of ilk persone contraveineand, be the dean

7 May 1641.
The touns ratificatioun of the act of counsell maid aganes persewers of actions befoir inferiour judges.

of gild *toties quoties*, for the weill and benefit of the toune, as in the ordinance of counsell maid thairanent of the dait the fyft day of May instant at lenthe is conteanit: And thairfoir the said Patrick Leslie, prowest, inquyrit of the toune convenit as said is if they wer content to adhear to the said act, and giue thair approbatioun thairwnto; quhae finding the samen to be deliberatlie set donne for the weill of the inhabitantis of this brughe, gave thair consent thairto, and ratifiet and approveit the samen in all pointis, bot any oppositioun or objectioun in the contrair.

19 May 1641.
Act for dimolishing the fauld biggit in the Linkis.

19 *May* 1641.

The said day the prouest, bailyeis, and counsell ordainis the fauld bigit vpoun the linkis benorth brabneris goat to be dimolishit and cast down and the faill to be cuttit and laid in the lair whair thay wer castin be the directioun of the deane of gild, whilk wes accordinglie done.

Eodem die.

Eodem die.

The samen day the prouest, bailyeis, and counsell ordaines that na sand be taken heirafter frome the hill besyd the castell hill, callit the heiding hill, as in tymes past, under the paine of fourtie shilingis, to be exactit of the contraveiner but fauour, and the master of impost to hawe ane cair to see that abuse reformit, and to report his diligence thairanent to the counsell.

Restraint of carcing sand from Hedinishill.

26 May 1641.
Statute anent the woll mercat.

26 *May* 1641.

The said day the prouest, bailyeis, and counsell statutis and ordainis that nae man nor woman whatsomener, nether stranger nor inhabitant, presume nor tak vpoun hand to sell or buy any wooll in tyme coming, or to arle any wooll, till the samen present the commone mercat of this brughe wpoun the mercat day, and remaine thairin till aucht houris in the morning, and neane to be sold, coft, nor arlit befoir that hour, and if any sall controwein in buying, seling, or arleing any wooll befoir the samen present the mercat, and remaine thairin till the hour foirsaid, the contraveinar alsweill sellar as buyar sall incur the vnlaw of ten pundis *toties quoties* efter convictioun, and the samen to be tryit alsweill be aith of pairtie as be witnessis, and ordaines intimation heirof to be maid be touk of drum throw the haile toun, quhilk was done.

26 May 1641.
Statute anent the wooll mereat.

14 June 1641.

The said day, in presence of the prouest, compeirit, John Straquhan, merchand, and Peter Moir, skipper, whae ar presentlie bound to Dantzick, and become actit bund and obleist to transport nae persone nor persons whatsumener, nor passingeris, in the said ship this present voyage, unles the said merchand and skipper acquaint the magistratis thairwith, and thair warrand had and obtainit thairunto, under the paine of fyue hundreth merkis money to be payit be them to the dean of gild for the publict vse and benefit of the toune incais of failyie.

14 June 1641.
Act anent transporting of passengeris out of the cuntrie.

15 June 1641.

The said day Mariorie Jack, spous to Thomas Marshell, was convict and put in amerciement of court for injureing of Elspet Gray, and callit hir whoore, wpoun Friday last. The vnlaw of the said Mariorie modifeit to twa merkis, to be payet to the deane of gild.

15 June 1641.
Mariorie Jack, convict.

[1641.

15 June 1641.

Andersone and Makie convict of usurping the rights of gild burgessis.

Eodem die.

The said day, in presence of the provost, baillies, and counsell, William Andersone and Johne Makie, coupers, friemen of this burgh, wer convict of thair awne confessioun for franchting of William Walker, skiper, his ship laitlie to Norrovay, contrair to the priniledgis and liberties of craftismen, and bringing of the said ship to this brughe, loadenit with timber and daillis, contrair to the privileges and liberties of the said burghe as said is, and thairby wsurping the libertie of gild burgessis, whairanent they referrit thameseltlis in the counsullis will, be thair supplicatioun subscriuit with thair hand. For the qubilk, the said Wm. Andersone and Johne Makie wer unlawit in the somme of ane hundrethe poundis, to be payit equallie betwixt thame to the deane of gild; and ordains the said deane of gild to buy the said loadening frae the saidis comparis for the vse of the toun, as he buyes the lyk commodities frome strangeris and unfriemen, be resone they haue no richt to traid with ouersea wairis.

16 June 1641.

Moresone admittet ane of the doctouris of the grammer schoole.

16 *June* 1641.

The said day anent the edict serveit to this day for filing up of the place of Master James Boyd ane of the doctoris of the grammer scoolle of this burghe, now waccand in the tounes handes be his dimissioun, compeirit within the kirk sessioun hous, Master Robert Morisone, lauchfull sone to vmquhill Johne Moriesone, burges of the said burghe, and offerit himselff reddie and willing to underly tryall and examinatioun for the said plaice, whae, being examinat and tryit in his literature, guid lyf and conversatioun, was fund meit and qualifeit for the place, and thairfoir the saids provest, baillies, and counsell hes admittit, and, be thir presentis, admittis the said Mr Robert Moriesone to be doctour of the said grammer scoole during thair plesour, in place of the said Master James Boyd, and grantis to the said Master Robert yeirlie dureing the space foirsaid for his service, the stipend qubilk the said Mr James had obefoir, viz., the somme of ane hundrethe merkis, to be payit to him yeirlie at the feast of Witsunday, be the deane of gild, togidder with the profit and annuelrent of the somme of fyve hundrethe merkis, mortifiet for that wse be ane neighbour of the toune, whae obscuirit his name, to be lyikwayes payit to the said Mr Robert at the term foirsaid, be the master of the mortificatiounes; and the said Master Robert being personallie present, acceptit the said charge in and wpoun him, and promeisit to acquyitt himsellf faithfullie thairintill.

16 June 1641. Moresoun admittet ane of the doctouris of the grammer schoole.

23 *June* 1641.

The quhilk day, in presence of Patrick Leslie, prouest, and Alexander Jaffray, bailyie, James Peir, borne in Nisbit, besyid Haddingtoun, as he alledgit, being accusit for cruell hurting, wounding, and blouddraveing of Johne Crombie, chapmane trader to England, vpon the tuantie nynt day of May last bypast, on the mercat streit of the said brughe, by giveing the said Johne vyn diverse wounds with ane durk. Confest the samen. As lykewayis being accusit on his behauiour and affairis in thir northe pairtis, and whether or not Jonet Stark, whome he brocht with him in thir quarteris, be his lawfull wyf, confest that he had no wairis for seall, neither any trad or calling heir, but pretendit he was goeing north to wisit freindis; confest the said Janet was not his lawfull wyf, but ane concubin; quhairfoir the said James haveing remanit within the wardhous of the said brughe be the space of tuantie dayis and aboue, and not haueing meanes neither to intertain himsellf nor to pay the chirurgian for cureing the said John, the saidis magistratis decernis and ordanes the said James his best plaid, with his pistole, and ane pair of blewshankis, to be presentlie apprysit for paying the officiaris of suche money as is restand to thame, and the superplus to be delyverit to the chirurgiane. Whilk guidis wer instantlie delyverit and apprysit, the plaid at aucht pundis, the pistoll at tuantie sevin shilingis, and the shankis at saxtein shilingis, and wer delyverit be himsellf to Thomas Urquhart, chirurgian, for the wse foirsaid. And as for his ryot, the saidis magistratis ordaines the said

23 June 1641. James Peir convict of assaulting Crombie.

23 June 1641.
—
James Peir convict of assaulting Crombie.

James Peir to be presentlie [sent] to Morpeth as ane sojour for this brughe to the companie of Capitane Robert Keith, vnder the conduct of John Scot, sergand, in the most commodious way, for preventing of his flicht; whae instantlie, be his great oathe solemnelie suorne, promeist not to desert nor leaue the said John Scot, nor to withdraw him from his companie, vnder the paine of hanging.

6 July 1641.

Fraser convict of injuring Bessie Forbes.

6 *July* 1641.

The said day Elspet Fraser, spous of Duncane Philip, fermorar, was convict for injuring of Bessie Forbes, spous to Johne Dempster, publictlie vpoun the hie streit, be vttering syndrie and dyverse injurious and scolding speeches aganies hir. The vnlaw of the said Elspet modifiet to four merkis, to be payit to the deane of gild. As lykwayis, shae wes ordanit to mak ane publict mendis to the pairtie offendit in presens of the magistratis, be craveing hir pardoun, and promeising not to dae the lyk in tyme cuming.

Eodem die.

Watsone convict of dinging over Margaret Andro.

Eodem die.

The samen day Christane Watsone, spous to Johne Touch, warkman, was convict of hir awin confessioun, for striking and dinging over ane poor woman callit Margrat Andro, wpoun the calsay, and thairby braking of hir arme. James Rany, cordiner, cautioner for payment to the deane of gild of sic vnlaw as the councell shall modefie; for the quhilk the councell ordaines the said Christian to pey four merkis to the pairtie wrongit, and to satisfie the chirurgeon.

Eodem die.

Robert Massie convict for putting hands on Wm. Gordon.

Eodem die.

The same day, in presence of John Leslie, baillie, Robert Massie, glasir wricht wes convict for putting violent handis on Wm. Gordon, tailzeour, vpone Sunday last, at nicht, be taking from him his bannet and joyp, and stricking him with his hand in the face, and appealling him to the combat, whilk combat the said William refuset. For the quhilk, the counsell ordanit the said Robert to pey four merkes to the deane of gild, and wther four merkes to the pairtie wrongit, and to crave him pardone in presence of the magistrates, and ordanes the said Robert to be wardit till he mak satisfaction accordinglie.

7 *July* 1641.

The quhilk day the magistratis and counsell for just respectis moweing thame, dischargis any ringing or tolling of bellis in the tyme of buriallis; as lyikwayes discharges the setting of the bier and mortclothe on the gravis of any defunct persones whosoever, in any tyme heiraftir, as smelling of superstition; whilk was instantlie intimat to Thomas Cowie, kirk sacristir, personallie present.

9 *July* 1641.

The quhilk day, the haill toune being warnit be the drume, to conveine in the Tolbuithe, and being convenit thairin for the most pairt representand the bodie of the toune, it was exponit to thame be Thomas Mortimer, bailzie, in respect the Lord Sinclair cannot haue moneyes for the present for intertainement of his regiment of soiours lyand in this toune, that the toune wald thairfoir be pleasit to advance to his lordschip fyve thousand pundis for intertaining of thame, or thane that thay wald accept the soioris in thair houssis, as they should be billettit wpoun thame, and giwe to ewerie soiour intertainement till the samen should amount to ten pundis, at quhilk time they sould be disburdenit of any farder advancement to thame; besyidis, that the said Lord Sinclair, and Maister Robert Farquhair, commissair, sould giew thame band for repayment to the toune of what they sould furnish and advance ather in present moneyis or be intertaineing of the soiouris in maner foirsaid; whilk desyre the toune convenit as said is taking to thair consideratioun, answerit that thay ocht not to be furder burdenit for advancement of money for intertaining

9 July
1641.

Lord Sinclare and the toun anent the billeting of his soiouris.

of soioris, but proportionablie with the rest of the borrowis and whole kingdome, and what the committie of estates shall injoyne to be done in this kynd be the whole kingdom and borrowis, thay ar content for thair pairt to contribut accordinglie and no farder, and that becaus they have alreadie payit thair tent and twantie pairtis to the full extent with thair woluntar contributionn, and had furnished and send soioris to the airmie; and withall, they had latelie advancit for the wse of the publict in Flanderis tuantie thousand merkis money, quhairof as yit they haue receivit no payment, and thairby ar so disablit and weakened in thair meanis as thay may not advance any moir in this kynd.

10 July 1641.

Intimationn anent the soiours.

10 *July* 1641.

The quhilk day the magistratis and counsell, all in ane woice, ordaines intimationn to be maid be the drum that the soioris whae ar quarterit in any houssis within this burgh sall remaine in thair avne quarteris till Wednesday nixt at night, at the ordinarie allowance of four shilingis for ilk soior in the day; and in the meane tyme to certifie the nighboris with whome they ar quarterit, that they salbe satisfiet be the commissar, Mr Robert Farquhar, as he hes promesit to the consell for this present weikis quartering, and till Wednesday nixt, but longer delay.

12 July 1641.

The tounes consent to quarter the Lord Sinclares soiouris for twentie dayes.

12 *July* 1641.

The said day the toune being convenit in the Tolbuith be the drume, it wes exponit to thame be Thomas Mortimer, bailzie, that Master Robert Farquhair, commissar, is willing and readie, conforme to his promeis, to satisfie and mak payment to the nighbouris of the toune of all bygane quartering muneyis restand to thame for quartering of the soioris of the Lord Sinclaris regiment till Wednesday nixt; and that the said Lord Sinclair is desyrous that the toune wilbe pleasit to quarter his soioris, be the sicht and directioun of thair magistratis, for the space of tuenetie dayis to come, beginning on Wedinsday nixt, the fourtene of July instant, for four shilingis in the day for ilk soiour, according to wse and wont, for the quhilk tuantie dayis quarteris, the said Master Robert Farquhair, commissar, is content to act himselff in the tounes buikis, for payment thairof to the nighbouris at the tuantie dayis end, ilk ane for thair avne pairtis, according to the number of soioris quarterit wpoun thame; and thairfoir the bailzie foirsaid, desyirit the toune convenit as said is, in respect that the said Master Robert Farquhair is content to act himselff for payment to thame of thair quartering money dureing the said space, that they will condiscend to accept of the saidis soioris to be quarterit with thame, as the magistratis sall appoint, dureing the said tuantie dayis; to the whilk the toune willinglie condiscendit, in testimonie of thair affectioun to the service of the publict, and wer content to accept of thame for payment, to be maid be the said Mr Robert Farquhair to thame, as said is.

12 July 1641.
The tounes consent to quarter the Lord Sinclares soioris for tuentie dayes.

3 August 1641.

3 August 1641.

The quhilk day in presence of William Forbes, baillie, William Walker, lax fisher, wes convict and put in amerciament of court be the depositiones of sindrie famous witnesses, admittit, suorne, and examined, for injureing of James Andersone, his maister, be provocking the said James, and saying he should work aganes his maister's will, and for misspersoning his said maister, be calling him theiffes geit, and for shooteing his said maister in the watter, and for hitting him with a stone in the breist.

Walker convict of injuring his maister.

Eodem die.

Eodem die.

The quhilk day, in presence of Thomas Mortimer, baillie, James Alexander being accuset be Alexander Davie, litster, for comeing to Patrick Jack, younger, litster, his hous in the Gallowget, and injureing the said Alexander be saying to him quhat lies had he spockin on him, avoweing he sould beat the said Alexanders skin, and for stricking the said

James Alexander convict.

Alexander with his hand; quhilk being referrit to the said James his aith of veritie, refuisit to swear: Quhairfor the said baillie held the said accusatioun as confest, for the quhilk, the councell adjudges the said James in four merkis of vnlaw, and to crave the pairtie offendit pardone.

11 *August* 1641.

The quhilk day, in presens of the prowest, bailzeis, and counsell of the burghe of Aberdein, compeirit Master Robert Farquhar, burges of the said burghe and commissar in the northe, and declairit that vpon remonstrance maid be him to the inhabitantis of the toune, convenit in the Tolbuith, the twelff day of July last, that he was exhaustit in moneyis, and thairby maid vnhabile to advance any farder for furnisheing of the sojers of the Lord Sinclair his regiment, lyand in this burghe, the toune at that tyme, out of thair respect for the publict service of the kingdome, and to plesour the said Lord Sinclair, tuik vpoun thame and condescendit to quarter the soiors of his regiment for the space of tuantie dayis thaireftir, till moneyes wer provydit, vpon the said Master Robert his promeis thame maid to the toune, that he sould satislie thame for the said tuantie dayis quarteris, towit four shilingis ilk day for ewerie sojoris intertainement at the expyreing of the samen tuantie dayis; and becaus the said regiment of sojors ar yet lyand in the said burghe, and intertainit be the nichtbouris of the toune, whae formerlie had thame in quartering the tuantie dayis bygane, the said Master Robert became actit and obleist to pay to the nighbouris and inhabitantis of this burghe, on whome the saidis sojoris ar or salbe quarterit, wther tuantie dayis quarteris, at the proportioun aboue writin, beginning on Wednesday the fourth of August, and sicklyik continowallie thairafter, sae lang as the saidis soioris remainis in this burghe (he alwayis continowing in the said office and charge of commissar), and that of the first and rediest of the money he happenes to resave aither of his avne proper money, or of the money belonging to the publict.

25 August 1641.

The quhilk day, the balzeis and counsell finds it expedient that commissioun be givin and send to Patrik Leslie, provest, the tounes commissionar at Parliament, and to Master Wm. Moir thair present with him, to petitioun his Maiestie for ane gift of the tack dewtie of oure tounes customes, and for the great and small impost of the wynes arryveing and wentit in oure toune, and that oure toune be fred and liberat of all taxationes and subsidies whatsumeuer to be impoisit wpoun the kingdome and burrowis dureing the space of ten yeires, or for sick space of tyme as the samen with the foirsaidis giftis may be procured, in regaird of oure tounes extraordinarie losses be the troublis that hes continowit in this kingdome thir thrie yearis bygane; bot findis it not fitting to seik ane tak of the customes to the tounes behove, for respectis moveing the consell, but onlie the tak dewtie thairof; and siclyik ordaines oure patent of admiralitie to be send to the saidis commissionaris for procureing of the Duk of Lenox his subscriptioun thairwnto.

6 September 1641.

Elspet Smith, servant to Alexr. Cuming, maltman, wes convict this day be the depositiones of sindrie famous witnessis, admitted sworne and examined, for putting violent handis on Elspet Craig, spous to Johne Milne, tailzeour, be ryveing doun the said Elspet Craig hir hair about her eyne, and for abciseing hir face, and making the same bla, and for trailling hir in be the curtch to hir sellar, and thairby almost wirreing the said Elspet Craig: Quhairfoir the said Elspet Smith wes instantlie adjudget in ane unlaw of four merkis, to be payit to the deane of gild, and wes ordanit to compeir befoir the baillies in ane fencet court, and crave God and the pairtie wrongit pardon, and the said Elspet Smith become actit not to trubill nor molest the said Elspet Craig heirefter be deid of wrong, vnder the pain of banishment.

17 Sept.
1641.

Anent two
boothis in
the Round
Table.

17 *September* 1641.

The quhilk day, in presence of Johne Leslie, ane of the baillies of the burghe of Aberdene, compeired Johne Stewinsoun, mercheant burges of the said burgh, heretabill proprietar of the mercheant booth, presentlie occupeit be him, lyand in the Round tabill, on the north syd of the Huckster wyn, quhilk sumtyn pertenit to wmquhill Duncan Donaldson, and thaireftir to wmquhill Robert Ramsay ; and in respect that the two boothes on ilk syd of the said mercheant booth and dwelling houssses abone the same belonges heretablie to Gilbert Hervie, eldar, who hes gewin consent to the said John Stewinson to strick out a window in his said booth, whair newir any windo wes abefoir, thairfoir the said John Stewinsoun become actit and obleist, and be thir presentes bindis and oblessis him, his aires, assigneyes, and successores whatsumenr, heretabill proprietares of the said booth, to warrand frie and skaithles keip the said Gilbert Hervie, his aires, assigneyes, and successores, heretabill proprietares, possessouris, and occupeares of his two mercheant boothes, nixt and contigue adjacent to the said John Stewinsones booth, on ilk syd thairof, as lykwayes the heretouris possessoris and occupeares of the duelling houssis aboue the saids mercheant boothes, of all danger, hurt, detriment, skaith, and inconvenient that the said Gilbert or his forsaids may susteane and incur in his saidis boothes and vpper houssis aboue the same, be the present stopping and breaking of the forsaid wall of the said John, his mercheant booth, and siclyke perpetuallie in all tyme comeing : And wheras ther is ane bolt of yron infixt in the foirsyd wall on ilk syd of the said John Stevinsones booth doore to denotat and signifie in all tyme comeing, the space of bounds appoynted on the said foirwall, for haveing of standis or buirdis to hauld cloth and other merchandries thairwpon ; quhilk boundis is designet to be ane elne and ane halff quarter of ane elne, outwith the foir wall of the said Johnes mercheant booth, on the east syd thairof, betwixt it and the eastmest booth laitlie occupiet be wmquhill Andro Howesone, and now be Alexander Middeltoun, and on the west syd there is designet thrie quarteres of ane elne, outwith the foirwall towardis the booth now occupeit be Robert Smith, be the brecking and stopping of the quhilk wall there is ane of the said yron boltes takin furth therof: Thairfoir the said John Stewinson obleissis him and his forsaids, not onlie to infrie the said bolt of yron in the pairt quhair it wes infixt abefoir, bot also to keip thair merchandice to be put out at the booth door, within the boundis aboue designet on the foirwall, and nowayes to transgres the saidis boundis in any tyme heirefter; and the said John bindis and obleissis him, with all diligence to put up on his awin charges, betwixt his awin booth door and the cistmest booth door ane louse mouieing pres or taffell for easment of himselff and the possessor of the said cistmost buith, to be occupeit be ilk ane of thame, proportionablie, according to the saids designet merches; and the steins taken out of the said John Steuinsones booth for stricking out of the said window, ar declairid heirby to pertein to the said Gilbert: Quhilkes premisses the said Johne Stewinson obleisses him and his foirsaidis to keipe, obserue, and performe to the said Gilbert Hervie and his foirsaids in all thinges as is aboue wreiten vnder the pain of fyve hundreth merkis vsuall Scots money, to be payit be the said John and his forsaids in caice of failzie, and that but prejudice of performance of the premisses, and of sic action and execution as may be competent to the said Gilbert and his forsaidis to that effect.

17 Sept. 1611.
Anent two booths in the Round Table.

Eodem die.

In presence of William Forbes, baillie, Peter Cromlie, merchant, was convict and put in amerciament of court be the depositioun of sindrie famous witnessis, admitted, suorne, and examinet, for comeing at nyne houris at ewin to John Scott, tailzeour, his hous, and injuring Marie Crystie, spous to the said John, be stricking the said Marie with his hand in the breist, and thairby dinging her over,—to forbear, his vnlaw modicfeit to ancht merkis, to be payet to the deane of gild.

Eodem die.
Peter Cromlie convict.

6 October 1641.

The samen day it is statut and ordanit be the prouest, bailzeis, and counsell, that the gravis for the buriallis in the kirkyeard of the brughe salbe decentlie and ordourlie maid in tyme coming, begining at the south east styill of the said kirkyeard, and so goeing along in ordour round about the haill kirkyeard as salbe enjoynit be the master of kirkwark, and the kirk officiar to haue ane cair to see this act preceislie observeit, that no ordour be givin for braking of the earthe and making of gravis in the kirkyeard, but as is aboue speecfiet.

25 October 1641.

The whilk day the old barrowis and pheasses of the pack hous ar ordanit to be presentlie comprysit be Mr Wm. Moir, bailzie, Johne Jaffray, the thesaurar, Williame Ord, wricht, and James Smith, hammerman, and being comprysit, the consell grantis the len of thame to the masteris of the Correctioun hous, till Candlemes nixt, to be delyuerit back againe to thesaurer at that tyme in alse guid caise as they are resaueit, or thame the masteris of the said correctioun hous to keip the saidis barrowis and pheasses at the pryce for whilk they shalbe apprysit, to be payet be thame to the present thesaurar.

20 November 1641.

The said day James Smith, wobster, and Alexander Kempt, wricht, wer conuict for comeing in the monethe of August last to the hous of Alexander Sangster, wobster, vnder clovd and silence of night, and braking wp the dore of the said Alexanderis hous with ane foir hamer, and entering the samen with draven suordis in thair handis; for the whilk, the counsell ordaines the said James Smith and Alexander Kempt to be wardit till this day aucht dayis, and thairefter to be bancist the toun.

RECORDS OF THE BURGH OF ABERDEEN.

Eodem die.

The samen day, Williame Duncane, servitur to Thomas Walker, cordoner, was convict for comeing to the buithe of James Hall, cordonar, vpon Saterday last, at night, and draweing of ane qubinger, and thairwith etleing to haue presewit the said James, and for injuriouslie speiking to the said James *dirt in his cheick* becaus he wald not suffer his servand to goe out of the chop with him to eat ane lambis leg as he desyrit, for the qubilk, the counsell ordanes the said Williame Duncane till remain in ward till Frydday come aucht dayis, and that day, in tyme of court, to compeir in presence of the magistratis, and crave the said James Hall pardone for his offence, and act himselff for his behauiour in tyme comeing, vnder the pain of

Eodem die.

Robert Gordon, tailzeowr, convict and put in amerciement for drawing of a qubinger to William Walker, skipper, and etling to haue strickin him thairwith, thay being both efter drink; for the qubilk the said Robert Gordon wes ordanit to be wardit in the wardhous of this burgh till he releive himselff out of ward be payment of a dolour to the deane of gild.

11 *December* 1641.

Sara Fowler this day wes convict and put in amerciement be the depositiones of sindrie famous witnesses, admitted, sworne, and examined for scolding and mispersoning of Andro Birnye, merchant, in the calling of him *Cankerit Carle*, and for saying thair wes no carle that threw about a key of a booth door in Aberdeen bot micht haue gewin hir waill, and for vaiging and exclameing on the streites, and giueing a lye to the said Andro his wyff, and saycing shoe wes als gentill a woman as shoe wes her selff; for the qubilk the councell ordanes the said Sara to be committed to ward

274 EXTRACTS FROM THE [1641.

11 Dec. 1641.
Sara Fowler convict.

in the tolbuith, thairin to remain aucht dayes, and to crave the pairtie pardone in a fenect court, with certificatioun if shoe be convict heirefter to be joggit

15 Dec. 1641.
Thrie dayes play grantit to the scholares at the beginning of ilk quarter.

15 *December* 1641.

The quhilk day the prouest, bailzeis, and counsell condiscended and agried that the haill scolleris within the scoollis of this burgh have thrie dayes play at the begining of ilk quarter, and that in recompence of the yule waccance whilk is now dischargit be actis of the generall assemblie and parliament, begining thair first thrie dayis play at Candlemes nixt, 1642.

22 Dec. 1641.
Patent Robert, Duke of Lennox, to the toun of the office of admiralitie within thair boundis.

22 *December* 1641.

The prouest, bailzeis, and counsell ordaines the patent grantit be the Duk of Lennox, his grace to the prouest and bailzeis of this burghe, wpoun the office of admiralitie within the boundis mentionat in the said patent, to be registrat in the tounes buikis, thairin to remaine *ad futuram rei memoriam*, whairof the tennour followis:—"Be it kend till all men be thir present letteris Ws James, Duck of Lennox, and Richmond, Earle of Darnley, Lord Torboltoun, Methvein Obignie, and Sanctandrois, great admirall and chalmerlane of the kingdome of Scotland, that for sae meikle as we understanding perfytlie the guid, trew, and thankfull service done to vmquhill Lodvock duck of Lennox, our vncle of vorthie memorie, be our trustie and welbelowit the prowest and bailzeis of the brughe of Aberdeine, thairfoir and for the lyk service to be done and performit be thame to ws and our successouris, as occasioun sall offer, to haue maid, constitut, and ordanit lykas we, be thir presentis, mak, constitute, and ordaine the saidis prouest and bailzeis of the said burghe of Aberdein, and thair successoris, prouestis, and bailzeis thairof, present and to come, coniunctlie and generallie, our werie lawfull undoubtit and irrevocable admirall deputtis within the said brughe of Aberdein port and herberie thairof, and betwixt the watteris of Die and Don, including bothe

the saidis watteris and riveris on bothe the syidis thairof, and that dureing our will and pleasour allanerlie, and ay and quhill they be dischargit be ws; and givis and grantis to thame the said office of Admiralitie within the boundis and dureing the space aboue exprest, with all full casualities, priviledges, and immunities pertening and belonging thairto, with full power to the saidis prouest and bailzies of the said burghe of Aberdein and thair successoris foirsaidis, present and to come, coniunctlie and seuerallie to substitut under thame clerkis, serjandis, dempsteris, and all wther memberis and officiaris of court neidfull, to elect, creat, and caus be suorne, and to tak thair aithis, with cautioun for dew administratioun, for whome our sadis deputis salbe hauldin to answer, courtis ane or mae of the said admiralitie alse oftin as neid beis, within any boundis of the pairtis aboue exprest, to hauld, affix, affirme, and continow, preceptis and all wther executoriallis necessar, in whatsomewer actiones and caussis, alsweill criminall as civill, concerning the said admiralitie within the saidis boundis, againes and in favouris of all pairties haveand entres, to direct and caus be execut decreitis, arreastmentis, poindingis, and all wther executoriallis give pronunce and caus be put to dew executioun in all pointis, wnlawis, bloodwytis, and amerciamentis of the saidis courtis to wplift and resaue, and generallie all and sindrie wther thingis, to doe wse and exerce anent the premisses, sicklyik and alse frielie in all respectis and conditiones as the saidis prouest and bailyeis or thair predecessoris wseit or exerceisit the said office of admiralitie within the saidis boundis, or as any wther deputis of the said admiralitie wsit and exerceit the samen at any tyme by gane, or as we micht doe our selffis if we wer personallie present, dischargeand be thaise presentis lyik as we be thir presentis, expreslie discharge all and whatsomewer deputis and substitutis in the said office if any be, within the boundis aboue written, of all farder wseing and exerceising of the samen, and of all stoping, debaring, or impeding of the saidis prouest and bailyeis or thair successoris foirsaidis, in the lawfull bruiking and joyseing of the said office within the saidis boundis, and dureing the space aboue exprest. And farder, we be thir

22 Dec.
1641.

Patent Robert Duke of Lennox to the town of the office of admiralitie within thair boundis.

presentis ratifie and approve the saidis prouest and bailyeis of the said brughe of Aberdeine and thair predicessoris thair possessing, vseing, and exerceising of the said office of admiralitie within the boundis aboue specificit, at any tyme bygane preceiding the dait heirof, with thair haill laufull and legall procedouris thairintill. Prowyding alwayis as it is heirby speciallie prowydit that thir presentis be naevayis extendit to matteris of prysse nor pyrecies, whilk we alvayis reserve to be judgit in our principall court of the said Admiralitie, and also that the saidis prouest and bailyeis of the said brughe of Aberdein and thair successoris foirsaidis, mak just compt rekoning and payment to ws or any wtheris in our name, haveing our power, of the haill casualities to be intromettet with be thame be vertew of thir presentis, whanesoewer they salbe requyrit for that effect, the trew and necessar expenssis to be deburst be thame in the discharge of the said office, being alwayis allowit to thame in the first end thairof, and for the mair seenritie we ar content and consentis that thir presentis be insert and registrat in our principall court buikis of the said admiralitie, thairin to remaine *ad futuram rei memoriam*. And to that effect constitutis our irrevocable procuratoris, coniunctle, and senerallie *promitten, de rato, &c.* In witnes whairof, written be Robert Hay, servitour to Thomas Forrest, writer to the signet, and principall clerk of the said admiralitie, we hawe suvseryvit thir presentis with our hand, and commandit our seall of office of the said admiralitie to be affixit thairto, at Halyrud hous, the allevint day of November, the yeir of God j^m, sex hundreth fourtie ane yearis.—*Et sic subscribitur.* J. Lennox and Richmond."

5 Jan. 1642.

Act anent the tounes mort-clothes.

5 January 1642.

The quhilk day the prowest, baillies, and councell vnderstanding that the ducties payable for the tounes mortcloathes ar not dewlie nor tymeouslie payed by theise who seikis the wse thairof at buriall, be reason the said mortclothes ar given furth befoir payment be reccavit for the same, whairthrow delayis is maid of payment, and petitiones given in to the counsall for dischargis, for remeid whairof it is ordanit that the thesaurar shall not giue furth any of the saids mort cloathis to any whatsoeuer within or without burgh, till he receave present payment in hand, at the least ane sufficient pledge for the same, conforme to the former ordinance maid thairanent.

5 Jan. 1642.
Act anent the tounes mort-clothes.

11 *February* 1642.

The said day, the councell considering, that the Lord Sinclairs regiment is removed from this burgh southward vpon thair march for Ireland, ordanis the court de guard quhilk was bigit be Generall Major Monro, vpon the mercat place, to be takin doun and the streete maid free thairof, and Jannet Touch, spous to Willeame Scott now in his absence furth of this realme, to be requirit be George Cullen and George Menzies to tak doun the same, in respect the timber whairwith the said hous wes bigit, belongit to the said Willeame Scott, and if she refuise, ordanes the samen hous to be instantlie demolishit, and the timber and daillis thairof to be carried to that place on the shoir quhairfra they wer takin, and thair laid doun and steplit to the behove of the said Willeame Scott. Conform quhairvnto the said George Cullen and George Mengzeis past immediatlie to the dwelling hous of the said Willeame Scott, and being debarred frome acces to the said Jannet Touch, in absence of her said husband, requirit hir at hir said dwelling hous to red the streete and calsey of the said timber and daillis, and to tak thame to hirselff, certifieing hir if she refuisit, the toun wald caus carry thame to the place whairfra thay wer takin. And siclyke the said George Cullen and George Menzeis past to the dwelling hous of John Scott, son to the said Willeame, and requirit him alse at his said dualling to the effect foirsaid. And seing thay could not haue acces to the said John Scott nor yit to the said Jannet Touch, his mother, they tuik instruments on thair reqwsitioun in the handis of Johne Ingrahame notar publict, and protestit that the tonne be free of all action, skaith, and damage thairanent in all tyme coming, in presens of Mr Alex. Menzeis, of Kinmundie, and Wm. Murear, burgessis of Aberdeine, witnessis present and requirit.

11 Feb. 1642.
Act for removing of the court de guard.

16 Feb. 1642.
Commission to Farquhar.

16 *February* 1642.

The samen day the councell ordaines the provest and baillies to subscryve ane commission to Mr Robert Farquhar of Mowny, to tak course and agree with James and Robert Smithes assignayis constitute be the Marques of Huntlie to the tounes band, for the pryce of the armour bocht be the magistrats fra the said Lord Marques for the tounes vse, in Marche 1639, and that for releife of Walter Cochrane, late deane of gild, wha is bund to the said Lord Marques for the pryce of the said armes, quhairanent thir presentis sall be a warrand to the saids provest and baillies, and the council and thair successors ar herby obleist to releive thame thairanent.

Eodem die.
Lumisdane his discharge of his commission.

Eodem die.

The samen day, in presens of the provest, baillies, and councell, compeirit Mr Matthew Lumisdane, baillie, commissionar chosen frome this burgh vpon the twentie nynt day of December last, for attending at Edinburgh the discuss of the tounes twa suspensions, the ane raisit against the maisteris of the correction hous, and the other against the Lord Marques of Huntlie, James and Robert Smithis, his lordships assignayis, for the armes receavit be the toune from his lordship, as also for attending the matter of tounes customes set to thame be the Earle Marshall, and other the tounes effaires committed to his chairge, and maid report of his haill proceidingis in the saids particulars, quhairanent the provest, baillies, and councell findis that the said Mr Mathew Lumisdane hes deuly acquytit himselff in the said commission: lykeas the said Mr Mathew gave back to John Jaffray, thesaurar, fourscoir merkis money of the four hundreth merkis quhilk he receavit for making of his expenssis and payment of his debursements in his said commission.

16 *February* 1642.

The quhilk day the provest, baillies, and councell inrespect the ministeris of this burghe hane appointit and agreit among thamselflis to keep ane ordinar lector thrise euerie week in place of the evening prayers; thairfoir finds it expedient that the saids lectors, as lykewayis the morning prayers, be maid and keipit in the aulk kirk of this burghe till Hallow mess nixt, as the most convenient place for the same, notwithstanding that be ane former act the morneing and evening prayeris have bene said in the Gray frier kirk.

[margin: The lectures and morning prayeris to be in the auld kirk.*]*

16 *March* 1642.

The said day the provest, baillies, and councell considering that thair ar diverse Actis of Parliament maid against blasphemaris of Godis holie name, conteining alsweill pecuniale as bodily punishments to be inflicted vpon these that shall be noted and hard banning and swearing, conforme whairunto sindrie actis have bene set doun be the magistratis and councell of this burgh from tyme to tyme for restraining of that hainous sinne within this citie; quhilkis actis, throw the not punishing of delinquentis, have not receavit due executioun, quharby the sinne multiplies and increasses to the high dishonour of God, and scandall of the gospell. For remeid quhairof, and for curbing and punishing all offendars in this kynd within this burgh, the saids provest, baillies, and councell ratifies and approves all actis and statutes maid be thair predecessouris thairanent in any tyme bygane, and particularlie ane act of the sewint day of December 1605, and of new statutis, and ordainis that ilk master and mistres of ane familie within this burgh sa oft as any of thame happins to be found banning or swearing any sort of oath, sall pay aucht d. to the vse of the poore, and ilk servant four penneis, quhilk salbe presentlie payit or exactit of thame be the Mr of the familie, or wtherwayis allowit

[margin: Act aganes bannares and swearares.*]*

16 March 1642.

Act aganes bannares and swearares.

in thair lie be thair maisteris, and this to be extendit alsweill to women servandis as to men servants, and ane box to be in euerie familie for this effect ; and for restraining of bairnes frome swearing, that thair be palmers in euerie familie, and the bairnes to be punished thairwith in the hand so aft as they be found swearing, and thay of the poorest sort that offends in this kynd, sic as beggars, scoldis, and vagabonds not haveing meanes to pay the penalties, to be put in the joggis be the captors efter mentionat, and to stand thairin for the space of three hours or longer, according to the gravitie of thair fault. And becaus swearing and curseing is most frequentlie vsit vpon the common streetes of this burghe at the burne heid, flesh, fishe, malt, and meill marcats, and at the mercat croce, quhair coall, fruit, and sic sort of commodities ar sold, thairfoir the magistratis and councell hes nominat and chosin thir persones efter following captors and searchars to note all such persones, both landwart and tounes persones as shall be found banning and swearing at any pairtes befoir specifeit ; Towit for the flesh marcat, fruit and keall sellaris about the croce, David Melvell, Gilbert Hervie, eldar, Alexander Williamson, baxter, Alexander George and George Ross for the timber mercat ; Thomas Clerk, William Lumisdane for the malt, meall, and fishe mercats ; Johne Maleis, Alex. Burnet, John Galloway, Alexander Henrie, for the the shoir ; Alexander Burnet yonger, John Duncome : for the Grein, James Blackhall, Alex. Blak, younger, Alex Findlater ; for the burne heid, Leonard Leslie, Charles Dune ; for the flour milne, and boundis thairabout, Andro Meldrum, Patrik Annand ; for the Overkerkget and Scoolehill, Andro Ingrahame, George Pyper, and Thomas Cushnie ; for the Gallowget, on both the syds thairof, Charles Robertson, William Forbes, elder, Patrik Jack, younger, Hector Smithe, and Henrie Dune ; for the Bredget, on both the syds thairof, James Christie, William Innes, Andro Rait, and Alex. Hoviesom ; for the Gaistraw, David Lindsay, William Nicolson ; to whome powar and commission is hereby given to exact the paines and mulcte aboue specifeit of this statut, and incais any resist and refuis to give obedience, that the said captors note and give in thair names to the magistratis, that thay may giue ordour for punishing and consureing thame conform to the mynd of this act. And forder, the saids captors ar heirby appointit to vesit families ance at least a month, to sie what ordour is in the families, if thair be boxes and exactiones, if thair be palmers and censures, if thair be amendiment and reformatioun, and if the pecuniall mulcte doe not redress and mak thame amend, then these delinquentis, whither thay be maisteris or servantis, parentis or children, to be delated to the Session, and publict repentance ordanit for thame in such maner as the Session shall think fitt; and if thair be any children scoollars, to sie thame condignelie punished by thair masteris; if thay be no scollars and young ones condignelie punisht by thair parentis, if parentis neglect, the magistrats to correct thame; and if they be ydle, wickit rogues liveing without all ordour, and be found to continew in this wickit sin, than to be brought to the correctioun hous, and thair to be exemplarlie punished at the sicht of the foirsaid captors, and by any other that shall apprehend thame on the streets or else where. And thir captors to continew till Michaelmes nixt to come.

16 March 1642.

Act against lammares and swearares.

30 *March* 1642.

The said day John Jaffray, thesaurar, is chosen collectour and receaver of the pryeis of muskatis and pickis bought be the toun frome the Marques of Huntlie in March 1639, and gif neid be with power to the said John Jaffray to call and persew the nightbors and inhabitantis within this burgh that receavit any of the saids muskatis and pickis befoir the baillies, and to obtaine decreits thairwpoun, and to caus put the same to dew executioun, and to report and give accompt of his diligence to the magistratis and counsell quhan he shall be requyrit to that effect.

30 March 1642.

Thesaurar appoyntit collector of the pryeis of muskattis and pickis.

30 March 1642.

The pheissis lent to the masters of the correctioun hous.

Eodem die.

The quhilk day the provest, baillies and councell ar content to len the pheissis to the maisteris of the correctioun hous till the first day of June nixt to come, and in caise they keepe thame any longer, that they pay twa hundreth feftie sevin pund ten shillingis for the same conforme to the compt of the buying of thame, produceit and red in presens of the councell.

6 April 1642.

Act againes prenteissis and wtheris sitting in daskis within the kirkis of this burghe.

6 *April* 1642.

The quhilk day the provest, baillies, and councell considering the great abuse committed be dyvers and sindrie commoun people, prenteissis, young boyis, and other persones of meane qualitie within this burghe, who presumptuouslie takis upon thame to sitt in eminent roumes and honest mens daskis at preaching and prayers within the kirkis of this burghe, no such places being due to people of thair qualitie, and notwithstanding of divers actis formerlie sett doun and intimat in the contrair, whirby sindrie of the councell and wther persones of gude note ar oftymes debarred frome thair awne daskis and disappointed of seatts convenient for thame; for remeid whairof, and for repressing the lyke abuse in tyme comeing, the saids provest, baillies, and councell statutis and ordanes that whatsumeuer person or inhabitant of the burgh, of inferior sort, and of the meine qualitie foirsaid, whether they be maried or vnmaried, sall be fund guiltie of the said disorder, in tacking presumptuouslie vpon thame to sitt in any eminent roume or honest mens daskis within any of the kirkis heirefter, shall be raised and taken furth of the saids daskis be the kirk officiar, and shall be vnlawed ilk ane of thame in tuentie schilling for the vse of the kirk work, and ordanes intimatioun to be maid thairof out of pulpit in both kirkis of this burgh on sonday next, to the effect nane pretend ignorance.

Eodem die.

The said day the provost, baillies, and counsell ordanis Georg̔e
Menzeis, maister of the kirk work, to caus mak ane greene cloth with ane
silk frengzie, for covering the foir pairt of the loft in the auld kirk whair
noblemen vsed to sitt, and that for the vse of the said noblemen whane
occasion shall offer of thair sitting there. And the expenssis to be
debursit thairin, the counsell ordanes to be allowit to the said maister of
kirk work in his comptis.

Eodem die.

The samen day the counsell gevis and grantis thair bonaccord siluer
cup double overgilt to the maister of kirk work, for the wse and serwice
of ye kirk in all tyme comeing. Quhilk cowpe vpone the last day of
May 1643 yeiris, wes delyverit be Walter Cochrain, deane of gild, to Wm.
Blakburne, maister of kirk wark, to be exchangit be him for wther coupes
for the vse forsaid, according to the weicht quhilk it weyis.

13 April 1642.

The samen day the sumonds raisit at the tounes instance against
the two colledgis of auld and new Aberden, concerning the patronage of
the kirk of Sanct Nicolas is appointit to be led on and execute aganis
tham to the first day of Junii nixt to come. And siclyke the tounes
lettres of lawborrowis raisit aganis those who caste up the tounes moss
and incroache vpon the tounes freedome at the heid of the den of Murthill,
and vpon the tounes marchis betwixt thame and Gilcomstoun, to be laid
on and execute with all convenient diligence, an to be prosecute thairefter as necessitie sall require.

13 April 1642.

Act for ane taxatioun.

Eodem die.

The quhilk day the provest, baillies, and councell taking to thair consideration the great burden of dett whairin the toun is involved be reason of the lait troubles that hes bene in this kingdome these four yeiris bygane; quhilk dett being aboue fourtie thousand pundis money, the tounes whole commoun gude will not amount to so much as will pay the annelrent and profite thairof, besyde that the commoun guid hes its awin ordinarie burdins, which dois exhaust the same, and seing the dett increases throw not paying the annelrent, the councell thairfoir thinkis it fitting for staying the forder growth of the said dett, that the toun be stentit for twa thousand fyve hundreth merkis for defraying ane half yeiris anuell thairof fra Mertimes last 1641, to Witsonday nixt to come 1642; and withall, that they be taxt and stentet for payment of thair ministers stipends, and defraying the chairge deburst vpon thair transportation to this burghe frome the places of their former residence, in the sommes of money following—viz., in the soume of ane thousand pundis deburst vpon the transportation of our three ministers; towit fyve hundreth merkis to ilk ane of thame. Item for two yeirs superplus of Mr Andro Cant's stipend is payit to him yeirlie out of the teyndis of the parochin of Sanct Nicolas, four hundreth and twentie pundis. Item for ane yeirs stipend, hous maills, and coalls to Mr John Oswald and Mr John Row, ministers, fra Mertimes 1641 to Mertimes 1642, twa thousand three hundreth merkis; extending in all to the somme of four thousand six hundreth and twentie pundis. And for the better effectuating heirof, ordanes this thair resolution and conclusion to be remonstrat to the haill toune, to be convenit in the tolbuith on Tuysday nixt at their heid court, and thair consents to be then cravit to the same, and to be taxt and stentit for the saids sommes for this present yeir allanerlie, for staying the farder increas and gronth of the tounes dett, till it please God that some meanes or way be found out heirefter to help and releive the same; and if the toun condiscendis, to go on accordinglie with all convenient diligence in setting and lifting of the said taxation for the generall vses, befoir specifeit.

22 April 1642.

The said day, in presens of Mr Alex. Jaffray, provest, and Mr Wm. Moir, baillie, Elspet Meldrume, spous to Archibald Meldrume, wes convict for resetting of prophane people within hir hous, and for scolding, waging, and blaspheming Godis name, and thairfoir wes ordanit to be committit to ward within the tolbuith, thairin to remain fourtie aucht houris, and to pay to the deane of gild aucht merkis of wnlaw befoir shoe be sett at libertie.

4 May 1642.

The quhilk day Patrik Leslie, lait provest of Aberdene, in face of the councell of the said burghe, exponit and declairit that seing his majestie hade mortified and gifted to this burghe furthe of the bishoprick of Aberdene and Ross, a competent yeirlie rent for paying thair ministers stipendis, that it was not expedient to taxt the toun for thair stipends except for so much thairof as his majesties said mortificationnes doth not extend vnto; and for himselff and in name of the most pairt of the inhabitantis of the said burghe as he alledgit, protested aganis the taxation now stenting and imposeing vpon the said burgh for the ministers stipends, and that they now, and in all tyme heirafter, should be free of any pairt thairof, notwithstanding of the conncells ordinance of taxting of the burghe for thair ministeris stipends foirsaid, since it was never the custome of this burghe to taxt for thair whole stipend, and the preparative is dangerous. As lykewayis protestit that he and such others who hade first subscrived the covenant, and haue given no offence neither to kirk nor cuntrie, should be free of any pairt of the foirsaid impoisit taxation presentlie appointit to be raisit in this burghe, or shall be impoisit or stentit heirefter for paying of the principall sommes or annuellis, or any pairt thairof which was exacted frome this burghe in tyme of the late

13 April 1642.
Act for ane taxatioun.

22 April 1642.
Elspet Meldrume convict.

4 May 1642.
Protestation Leslie.

4 May 1642.

Protestation Leslie.

troubles, and for himselff and the foirsaids adherentis to the protestation formerlie maid in a publict court in this burgh be umquhill Williame Erskin, then burges of this burghe, in his awin name, and in the name of his adherentis for the effect foirsaid, which was of the date at Aberden the fyfteine day of Aprile 1639; and on the premisses the said Patrik requirit act and tuik instrumentis; and Mr Alex. Jaffray, present provest, protestit in the contrair, inrespect of the councells ordinance, and the tounes consent to the granting of the said taxation for the ministers stipends for this present yeir allanerlie, in ane heid court, na opposition being maid against the same; as lykewayis in regaird of the tounes consent formerlie grantit to be taxt for releif of the soumes of money exacted of thame durceing the tyme of the lait troubles, and lying heir of the armies, and thairon askit instrumentis; and the said Patrik Leslie adhered to his former protestation made in name and behalf of the first Couenanters, as he alledgit, quha consentit not.

11 May 1642.

11 May 1642.

Licence to Dickson to vse his tred of macking gouff ballis.

The said day grants licence and tollerance to John Dickson of making gouff balls within this burgh durcing the councells plesure, and his gude careage and behaviour allanerlie, inrespect thair is not such ane tradisman in this burgh, and that he hes produceit ane testificat frome the toun of Leith of his bygane guid life and conversatioun amongst thame.

27 May 1642.

27 May 1642.

David Philp convict.

In presens of Mr Thomas Gray, baillie, Dauid Philp was conviet for taking ane helter out of Wm. Anderson hors heid, and for striking his servant thairwith sindrie straikis, efter that the said Wm. Andersones horse hade rin throw the said Dauids corne land.

1642.]   RECORDS OF THE BURGH OF ABERDEEN   287

30 May 1642.

May 1642.

The said day Margrat Bellie, spous to Robert Dewny, and Christen Wilson, relict of umquhill Patrik Cheine, for injureing each of thame the other, for sindrie scandalous and scolding speiches, thairfoir wer ordanit both to be put in the joggis, or thane to redeime thameselfflis thairfra be payment ilkane of thame of fourtie schillings to the dean of gild, and not the les they both ar ordanit to compeir befoir the pulpit the nixt Lords day in the auld kirk efter the ending of the sermon befoir noone, and craive God and the congregation pardon.

Bellie and Wilson convict.

Eodem die.

Eodem die.

The said day, in presens of the provest and Mr Thomas Gray, baillie, George Aidye, wricht, convict be the deposition of sindrie famous witnesses admitit sworne and examined, for drawing a whinger to Dauid Cramond, sklaiter, and striking of him thairwith on the breist to the effusion of his bloode, to forbear; for the quhilk the councell ordanes the said George to stand in waird aught dayis, or to redeime himselff thairfra be payment of twa dollours, the ane to the deane of gild, and the wther to the pairtie, and to mak a publict amends in the tounes court, in presens of the magistrats.

Aidye convict.

8 June 1642.

8 June 1642.

The said day Christan Mure, spous to James Forbes, flesher, was convict for injureing and sclandering Thomas Dempster, flesher, his wyff, and bairnis, in saying that the said Thomas father was hangit, and calling his bairnis theeffis and theeffis geits, and vttering many execrable oathes aganis thame; for the quhilk the said Christan is ordanit to be committit presentlie in waird, and to remaine thairin till Freddy nixt, and to pay aucht pundis of vnlaw to the deane of gild befoir she be takin furthe of waird, and the said vnlaw being payit, ordanes the said Christan to

Mure convict.

8 June
1642.

Mure convict.

compeir befoir the magistratis within the tolbuith in ane feneit court, and thair confes and acknowledge her wrong, craw the pairties injured pardon and forgivenes, and promis never to doe the lyke heirefter, and in caise the said Christan refuis to do the same, ordanes hir to be put up again in waird, thairin to remaine ay and quhill she amend publictlie as said is.

15 June
1642.

Lady Rothiemay hir mortification of ane thousand pundis for maintenance of ane maistres of schoole to bring vp young wemen.

15 June 1642.

The quhilk day fforsamekle as ane noble Lady Kathrene Forbes, Lady Rothimay hes freelie given and mortified to the provest, bailies, councell, and communitie of the burghe of Aberden the soume of ane thousand pundis vswall money of Scotland, to be employed or laid on annuelrent for the pious vse contenit in the letteris of mortificatioune vnderwretin, quhilk somme the said noble lady hes alreddie delyverit in gude and reall moneyis to the provest, baillies, and thesaurar of the said burgh, vpon the tent day of Junii instant, as thair acquittance given on the receipt thairof proportis; lykeas the saids provest, baillies, and thesaurar hes delyvered the same soume of ane thousand pundis to Patrik Moir, present master of the tounes mortified moneyis who grantis the recept thairof, to be employit be him be advyse of the councell to the proper vse quhairwnto the same is destinat. Inrespect whairof the councell of the said burgh in testimonie of thair thankfullnes to the said noble lady, and for hir ladyships assurance that the said soume of ane thousand pundis salbe employit perpetuallie in tyme comeing to the wse appointed be the said mortification, they ordaine the samen mortification to be registrat in thair councell register, to remaine *ad futuram rei memoriam,* whairof the tenour followes:—" Be it kend to all men be thir presents, me, Katherin Forbes, relict of the right honorable vmquhill Willeam Gordoun of Rothimay of guid memorie, for the honor of God, and for the love I heave to vertew in woman, and to all women vertuouslie disposed, and to testifie my love for the burgh of Aberdein whairin I was educat and bred the most pairt of my youth, to have freelie given, mortified, and destinat, and be thir presentis freelie gives, mortifies, and destinates to the provest, baillies, councell, and communitie of the said burghe of Aberdeine and to thair successors, provest, baillies, councell, and communitie of the said burghe in tyme comeing, the somme of ane thousand pundis vsuall current money of Scotland, which I have alreadie caused to delyver to the present provest and baillies of the said burghe, to be waired and employit vpon land or annualrent whair they find most convenient imployment, and the yeirlie annualrent thairof, sic as the same shall affoord and render for the tyme, to be givin and bestowed be the said provest, baillies, and counsell of the said burgh, present and to come, towards the help and mantenance of ane woman, to be ane mistress for keepeing ane schoole in the burghe of Aberden, and teacheing young women and lases to reid, wreit, and sew, and any other airt or science whairof they can be capable, of the qualitie and with the conditiones efter specifeit—viz., This woman and mistres of schoole to be a widow of honest report, grave and modest cariage and behaviour, and who haue lived both in the tyme of hir widowheid and in hir cariage and cohabitatioun with hir husband of gude lyfe and conversatioun, free of publict scandall, and that shall be religiouslie disposed, fearing God, or to be ane virgin or maid of aige and discretioun, grave and modest, fit for suche a chairge, and if it shall happin the said widow or maid to marie or to prove scandalous in thair cariage lyfe or conversation efter they be admited to the said place, vpon just tryall and notice to be takin be the said provest, baillies, and counsell for the tyme, in that caice, she to be depryved of the said benefite and put frome the place, and ane other woman of the qualitie and conditiones aboue specifeit to be chosin and put in hir place, lykeas, be thir presentis, I giue and grantis to the said provest, baillies, and counsell, and to thair successoris provest, baillies, and counsell of the said burghe, perpetuallie in all tyme comeing, the full and absolute right of patronage, presentation, and admission of the said widow or virgin who shall injoy the said place and benefite belonging thairto in all tyme heirefter. Reserveing alwayis to me, the said Kathrene Forbes, Lady widow

15 June 1642.

Lady Rothiemay hir mortification of ane thousand pundis for the intertainement of ane maistres of schoole to bring vp young women.

15 June 1642.
Lady Rothiemay hir mortification of ane thousand punds for maintenance of ane maistres of schoole to bring vp young wemen.

of Rothiemay, dureing my own lyfetyme, the presentation of the said woman, widow, or virgin, and admission to the said place be advyse of the said provest, baillies, and councell for the tyme. And lykwayis with this speciall provision and condition, that if it shall happin any of my kindred or freinds of the name of Forbes or Setoun to present thameselffis, efter just examination, and tryall to be maid be the said provest, baillies, and councell of the qualitication and conditions, to demand and sute the said place and benefite belonging thairto, she to be preferrit befoir all other whosoever, *ceteris paribus*. And farther, it is my speciall will and appointment, becaus the said schoole cannot be presentlie erectit, nor ane woman of the qualitie and condition foirsaid presentlie found out, that the annelrent and profite of the said soume sall accress and be added to the principall soume, and the profite of the whole soume, alsweill principall and byrane annelrentis, to be bestowit and given to the said mistres of schoole, in all tyme comeing; and this mortificatioun and schoole to be erected and set vp be the said provest, baillies, and councell with all possible convenient diligence. And since I haue committed the charge to them, to be managed and governed in all tyme comeing, as they will answer befoir the tribunall of our Lord Jesus Christ, whan He shall appear to judge the quick and the dead, that they shall faithfullie performe the conditions aboue specifeit in all pointis. And for the mair securitie, we ordane thir presentis to be registrat in the buikis of counsell or burrow court buikis of Aberdeine, thair to remaine, *ad futuram rei memoriam*, &c.

26 July 1642.
Donaldson convict.

26 *July* 1642.

The samen day Duncane Donaldsone wes adjudget in ane vnlaw of twantie merkis for striking of Johne Inglis, sone to wmquhill Paull Inglis, to the effusion of his blood. Lykeas Paull Colinsone wes adjudget in the lyik soume of tuantie merkis for injuring the said Duncan, both the saidis vnlawis to be payit to the deane of gild.

12 August 1642.

In presens of Mr Wm. Moir, baillie, Andro Mowat wes convict of his awin confession for striking and dinging of Alex. Melvill, his servant, with the bits of ane brydle, and giveing him ane bloodie strak thairwith in his thigh, and sindrie blae strakis on his back, and Alex. Mitchell became cationer for the said Andro to present him befoir the counsell on Wedinsday nixt, for sic vnlaw as the counsall sall modifie.

Andro Mowat convict.

16 August 1642.

The samen day James Smith, laxfisher, and Elspet Hoode, his spous, wer convict for injureing of James Rany, laxfisher, vpon the elevint day of August instant, lykeas the said James Rany was convict for injureing of the said James Smith the day foirsaid, conforme to the depositiones of diuerse famous witnessis verified and known to the counsell, and thairfoir the said James Smith was adjudget in ane vnlaw of ten merkis to be payit to the dean of gild, and the said Elspet Hoode to pay four merkis to the dean of gild, as lykewayis the said Elspet is ordanit to crawe the said James Rany pardon for hir offence committit aganes him vpon freday nixt in ane fencit court within the Tolbuith vnder the pain of jogging. Lykeas the said James Rany was ordanit to pay four merkis to the said deane of gild for his offence committit aganes the said James Smith. *Tandem* the said James vnlaw remodifiet to fyve merkis be the counsall, and the said Elspetis vnlaw dischargit inrespect she wes joggit.

Smith, Hoode, and Rany convict.

19 September 1642.

The said day, in presence of Maister Alex. Jaffray, provest, and Mr Wm. Moir, baillie, David Philp and Elspet Fraser, his spous, both convict and put in amerciament be the depositiones of sindrie famous witnesses admited sworne and examined, the said David for dinging and striking

Philp and Fraser convict.

19 Sept. 1642.

Philp and Fraser conuict.

Issobell Thomson, spous to Nicolas Bustoun, maister of the corection hous in the armes and heid, thairby geweing hir many bla strakis in both the armes, and dinging hir violentlie to the earth, quhairthrow she lay deid, and wes tane vp be George Gordon, officiar, and sindrie other persones, and caried to the hous of Patrik Ker, officiar, whair she lay ane long space litle better nor deid. As lykewayes the said Elspet wes conuict for saying *tow weill jrome yow, she is not sibb to me body heir*, to forbear, ffor the quhilk wrong the said Dauid wes committit in waird, and gave satisfaction conforme to the ordinance of counsell.

30 Sept. 1642.

Wm. Walker skipper oblist not to transport persons to forane countrie.

30 *September* 1642.

The quhilk day, in presence of Patrik Leslie, provest, compeired Wm. Walker, skipper and maister of the gud ship of Aberdeen, callit the John, and voluntarlie become actit and oblist that he sall not transport any persone or persones furth of this kingdome to Zeland, nor to no foran countrie, or any pairt quhatsumeuer without speciall licence, consent, and advyse of the said Patrik Leslie. Lykas the said William oblist him to give vp ane just roll to the said Patrick of the haill names of the persons that he sall receave within his ship, vnder the pain of fyve hundreth merkis money to be payit be said William to the said Patrik for the publict vse of the countrie, and this for ilk persone the said William happins to transport furth of this herbrie to any other pairt without licence asket and gewin.

5 October 1642.

Thesaurar collector of the muskat money

5 *October* 1642.

The said day the provest, baillies, and counsell nominatis and appointis Thomas Burnet, thesaurar, collector of the moneyes restand be the nichtbouris and inhabitantis of this burghe for the guns, muskatis, and pickis, coft and resauit be thame, and ordanes the said thesaurar to caus put the letteris of horneing alreadie raisit in the said matter to dew execution aganis sic as refuissis or delayis to pay, and the said thesaurar to give ane accompt of his diligence to the counsell efter Martimes nixt.

5 October 1642.
Thesaurar collector of the muskat money.

19 October 1642.
19 Oct. 1642.

The quhilk day, the provest, baillies, and counsell ordaines the whole bursars alreadie admitit, or to be admitit, within the colledge of this burghe, diligentlie to attend and be ordinar hearars of all publict lessons and lecturs to be teached be the professors of divinitie, mathamatiques, or other publict lessons whatsumewer, within the said colledge, dureing the tyme that they resaue the benefite of the saids burses, and on nawayis to absent themselues thairfra, without ane lauchfull excuse, notified and knowin to the saids professours; and that they wear daylie ane blak goun and blak hatt or blak bonnet, both upon the streits of the toun and within the colledge and kirk during thair courses in philosophie; whairin if it shall happin thame to faillie, or if (as God forbid) it shall happin any of tham to mak apostacie and defection frome the true protestant religion profest within this kingdome, at any tyme heirefter, in that cais the bursar or bursars, contraveinars of this present ordinance, to be depryvit of thair burses for that yeir. . .

Ordinance to bursars in the colledge.

23 November 1642.
23 Nov. 1642.

The said day, the provest, baillies, and counsell gives and grants the soume of four hundreth merkis money, for supplie of the work of the colledge of this burgh, and to help to repair the same. . .

An aid for repair of the colledge.

Eodem die.
Eodem die.

The same day, the provest, baillies, and counsell thinks it meit and expedient that ane Ebro lesson be teachit weiklie in the colledge of this

A weeklie lesson in Hebrew to be in the colledge.

burgh till Lambmes nixt, and ordaines Patrik Leslie, provest, and Doctor Patrik Dune, principall of the said colledge, to deall with Mr Johne Row, ane of the tounes ministers, for that effect.

23 Nov. 1642.
A weeklie lesson in Hebrew to be in the college.

14 Dec. 1642.
Swan admittet doctor of grammar scole.

14 December 1642.

The said day the provest, baillies, and counsell vnderstanding of the literatur and qualification of Mr David Swan, and of his habilitie to dischairge the place of ane doctor in the grammer scoole, hes receauit and admitit, and be thir presents receaues and admits the said Mr David as ane of the doctors in the said grammer scoole, *ad bene placitum consilii tantum*, with the casualities and pension belonging thairto, payable at tua termes in the yeir Witsinday and Martimes be equall portions, the first termes payment beginnand at Witsinday nixt, for the half yeir fra Martimes last.

21 Dec. 1642.
Act contra yoole day.

21 December 1642.

The same day the provest, baillies, and counsell ordane the haill inhabitants of this town thair bairnes, repair and keip the scoole preceislie vpon Sunday nixt and the weik therefter, vnder the pain of ten punds; quhairof intimation ordanit to be maid be the drum passing throw the haill streits of the toun for that effect.

Eiusdem die.
Moreson to set caution

21 December 1642.

The said day, the counsell ordanes Mr Robert Moreson to set caution for his continuance with his charge in teaching the principalls of arithmetik, within the colledge of this burgh, till Michaelmes nixt; and that he shall be ane ordinar hearer of all publict lessons, and shall not mak defection frome the religion presentlie profest.

INDEX.

INDEX.

ABERDEEN, provost and magistrates of, 210.
Aboyne, The Viscount, 172, 173, 175.
Adam, Bishop of Dunblane, 77; of Aberdeen, 89.
Adye, David, 17.
Alexander, Robert, dean of guild, 31.
Anderson, George, master of kirkwark, 25.
Annand, Mr Johne, minister at Inverness, 257.
Arbuthnott, Laird of, 53.
Athol, Earl of, 166, 170.

Baird, Mr James, advocate, 77.
Baird, Mr James, advocate, 111.
Balmerino, Lord, 194.
Banff, Laird of, 159, 161.
Baron, Robert, D.D., 60, 138.
Barron, Rev. Robert, 11.
Blakhall, Mr Thomas, 183.
Bonaccord, articles of, 223.
Boyd, Mr James, a doctor of the grammar school, 262.
Bowbrig, 49, 115.
Brastonne, Nicholas, Englishman, 100.
Brastonne, Robert, Englishman, 100.
Brynmond, Hill of, 17, 18.
Burnet, Sir Thos., of Leys, 15.

Caithness and Orkney, bishops of, and people of, 67.
Cant, Mr Andrew, minister at Newbattle, 235, 245, 257.
Chalmer, Mr Thomas, doctor of the grammar school, 63, 98.
Chalmer, Mr Thomas, master of the grammar school, 228, 229.
Chalmer, Mr Thos., 30.
Chalmer, Mr Patrick, sheriff-clerk, 70.

Chapel on the Castle Hill, 18.
Clatt, Mr John, canon of Aberdeen, 33.
College Library, 40.
Colinsone, Thomas, baillie, 26.
Correction House, 100, 106.
Coupar, Lord, 151, 170.
Cowye, Thomas, sacristar, 45.
Crombie, Thomas, of Kemnay, 27, 70.
Cullan, Mr Gilbert, baillie, 15.

Dalgleish, Mr David, minister at Cupar, 200, 207.
Dalhousie, Earl of, 194.
Davidson, Patrick, master of the grammar school, 35.
Douglas, Lady Marion, 61.
Dounye, Mr Robert, bibliothecar, 10.
Dun, Doctor, 11, 69.
Dun, Dr Patrick, 15, 63, 66.
Drum, Laird of, 26, 27, 53.
Drummond, Lord, 166, 170.

Edinburgh, Bishop of, 63, 64, 69.
Elcho, Lord, 151, 170.
Elsick, Laird of, 53.
English School, 14.

Farquhar, Mr Robert, dean of guild, 26, 27; baillie, 106, 160.
Farquhar, Mr Robert, commissary, 211, 266, of Mowny, 278.
Forbes, Capt. Arthur, 4, 10.
Forbes, Lieut.-Col. George, 191, 208, 211.
Forbes, Lady Katherine, 288.
Forbes, Master of, 151, 161, 166, 170, 215, 245.
Forbes, Patrick, Bishop of Aberdeen, 71.
Forbes, Professor John, D.D., 69.

INDEX.

Forbes, William, doctor in divinity, 11, 14, 60, 63.
Forrester, Lord, 194.
Foverane, Laird of, 164.
Fraser, Adam of Finzeauch, 20
Fraser, Alex., doctor of the grammar school, 30.
Fraser, Lord, 154, 161, 166, 170, 245.
Fraser, Mr Alex., 20.
Frendraught, Laird of, 70.

Gallowgate Port, 49, 115.
Gellie, Mr John, minister at Monymusk, 188.
Gight, Laird of, 164.
Gillespie, Mr George, minister at Weymes, 257.
Gordons, broken men of the name, 118.
Gordon, Dr William, 152.
Gordon, John, in Rothiemay, 70.
Gordon, John, of Park, 70.
Gordon, Mr Alex., a regent at King's College, 242.
Gordon, Mr Robert, of Straloch, 152.
Gordon of Ardlogie, 70.
Gordon of Auchanachie, 70.
Gordon of Gollachie, 70.
Gordon of Gight, 70.
Gordon of Invermarkie, 70.
Gordon, William, in Melingsyde, 149.
Gordon, William, of Rothiemay, 288.
Graham, John, baillie of Montrose, 168.
Gray, Alex., reader, 45.
Gray, Master of, 166.
Gray, Thomas, master of kirkwark, 67.
Gray, William, of Pettindrum, 170.
Guild, Rev. Wm., D.D., 22, 52, 66, 114, 242, 243.
Gun, Colonel William, 174, 175.
Guthrie, James, of Petforthie, 168.

Haddo, Laird of, 164.
Hallow mess, term of, 279.
Hamilton, Marquis of, 134, 137.
Harthill, Godeman of, 70.
Hay, Captain, 159.
Hay, John, baillie, 15.
Hervie, Gilbert, 6, 37, 270.
Hope, Sir Thomas, 114.
Howat, Mr Andrew, 19.
Hume, Mr Alex., 30.

Huntly, Marquis of, 134, 136, 137, 148, 150, 192, 195, 197, 278, 281.

Inglis, Paull, merchant burgess, 24, 34, 37.
Irvine, Robert, of Fedderat, 64.
Irving, Sir Alexander, of Drum, 26, 64, 137.

Jaffray, Mr Alex., 17, 26, 27, 41, 66, 116, 138, 144, 161, 168, 171, 186, 196, 199, 209, 214, 232, 236, 241, 285, 291.
Jamesone, George, painter, 55, 75.
Johnston, Dr Wm., 55, 102, 124, 151.
Johnston, Mr Thomas, baillie, 15.
Johnston, Robert, provost, 134.
Justice, Port, 115.

Keith, Alex., of Balmuir, 130, 131, 144.
Keith, Lord William, 64.
Keith, Mary, daughter of the Laird of Ludquharne, 130.
Keith, Mr Gilbert, minister at Skene, 130.
Keith, Mr Robert, brother of the Earl Marischal, 238, 241.
Keith, Sir Robert, of Benholm, 64.
Kennedy, John, baillie of Ayr, 120.
Kinghorn, Earl of, 154, 170, 177, 182, 194.
Kinnoul, Earl of, 77.
Kings College, Aberdeen, 69.

Laurence, a bell of St Nicholas church, 73.
Lawers, Laird of, 159.
Leisk, William, of that ilk, 130.
Leith, John, of Harthill, 217, 244.
Lennox, Duke of, 274.
Leslie, General, 154.
Leslie, Patrick, provost, 25, 193, 206, 218, 221, 232, 242, 244, 247, 252, 285, 292.
Leys, Laird of, 55.
Liddell, Dr Duncan, 43.
Lothian, Earl of, 194.
Loudon, Earl of, 194.
Lowsone, Mr Vedast, baillie, 36, 39, 40, 46.
Lumysden, Mr Mathew, 5.
Lundie, Mr John, humanist, King's College, 242.

Mackye, Colonel, 10.
M'Gill, Captain, 159.
Mar, Earl of, 194.
Marischal, Earl, 151, 154, 162, 166, 170, 177, 182, 193, 194, 208, 211, 221, 233, 237.

INDEX.

Melville, Andrew, master of the music school, 96, 97.
Meldrum, Andrew, baillie, 26.
Menzies, Gilbert, of Pitfoddels, 27, 66.
Menzies, Sir Paul, provost, 15, 25, 27, 41, 66, 72.
Merser, William, musician, 59.
Moir, Mr William, master of kirk work, 102.
Moir, Mr Wm., baillie, 218.
Monro, Major-General, 222, 226, 238, 241.
Month Cowie, 53.
Montrose, Earl of, 152, 154, 166, 167, 177, 182, 191.
Moreson, Mr George, dean of guild, 39.
Morison, Mr Robert, doctor of the grammer school, 262.
Mortimer, Mr John, baillie, 15.
Mowat, Mr Roger, advocate, 111.
Muchall, Laird of, 53.
Musick School, 11.

Nicolson, Sir Thomas, 141.
Nicolson, Mr Thomas, baillie, 26.

Ogilvy, Mr Robert, sub-principal, King's College, 212.

Patrick, Bishop of Aberdeen, 23.
Pitmedden, lands of, 102.

Raban, Edward, printer, 60.
Raitt, Mr James, minister at Marykirk, 39.
Reed, Mr Adam, 11.
Reid, Mr Robert, minister at Banchory, 41, 45.

Reid, Thomas, Latin secretary to James VI, 41.
Robertson, George, ...
Robertson, Mr Wm ... 111.
Rolland, Alex., ...
Ross, Mr Alex., ... 111.
Ross, William, in Ba..., 70.
Rothiemay, Lady, 28..
Rutherford, Mr David, ...

Sandelands, Mr Jac... 242.
Seaforth, the Earl ...
Sibbald, James, D.D., ...
Sinclair, Lord, 194, ...
Stewart, Patrick, ... Gil- Brethren Hospital, ...
St Catherine's H..., 7.
St Clement's Chapel, 1...
St Thomas Hospital, ...
Swan, Mr David, doctor of ... grammer school, 2...

Table, The Round, in Aberdeen, ...

Urquhart, Thomas, of ...
Urrie, John, ...

Wedderburne, Mr David ... grammar school, 19, 20...
Wollmanhill, 19, 115.

Yester, Lord, 194.

Zetland, 16.

www.ingramcontent.com/pod-product-compliance
Lightning Source LLC
Chambersburg PA
CBHW030745230426
43667CB00007B/853